A BEAUTIFUL PAGEANT

ALSO BY DAVID KRASNER

African American Performance and Theatre History: A Critical Reader
(co-editor, 2001)

Method Acting Reconsidered (2000)

*Resistance, Parody, and Double Consciousness in
African American Theatre, 1895–1910* (1997)

A BEAUTIFUL PAGEANT

African American Theatre, Drama, and
Performance in the Harlem Renaissance, 1910-1927

DAVID KRASNER

First published 2002 by
PALGRAVE MACMILLAN™
175 Fifth Avenue, New York, N.Y. 10010 and
Houndmills, Basingstoke, Hampshire, England RG21 6XS.
Companies and representatives throughout the world.

PALGRAVE MACMILLAN is the global academic imprint of the PALGRAVE
MACMILLAN division of St. Martin's Press, LLC and of Palgrave Macmillan Ltd.
Macmillan® is a registered trademark in the United States, United Kingdom and
other countries. Palgrave is a registered trademark in the European Union and other
countries.

ISBN 0–312–29590–1 hardback

Library of Congress Cataloging-in-Publication Data
Krasner, David, 1952-
A beautiful pageant : African American theatre, drama, and performance in the
Harlem Renaissance, 1910–1927 / David Krasner.
    p.   cm.
  Includes bibliographical references (p.) and index.
  ISBN 0–312–29590–1
    1. American drama—African American authors—History and criticism.   2.
African Americans in the performing arts—New York (State)—New York—
History—20th century.   3. African American theater—New York (State)—
New York—History—20th century.   4. Performing arts—New York (State)—
New York—History—20th century.   5. American drama—New York (State)—New
York—History and criticism.   6. African Americans—New York (State)—New
York—Intellectual life.   7. Theater—New York (State)—New York—History—
20th century.   8. American drama—20th century—History and criticism.
9. Harlem (New York, N.Y.)—Intellectual life.   10. African Americans in literature.
11. Harlem Renaissance.   I. Title.

PS338.N4 K73   2002
812'.5209896073—dc21

                                                                                    2002025109

A catalogue record for this book is available from the British Library.

Design by Letra Libre, Inc.

First edition: August 2002
10 9 8 7 6 5 4 3 2 1

Printed in the United States of America.

Now the colored people in this country form what may be called the "submerged tenth." From morning until night, week in week out, year in year out, until death ends us all, they never know what it means to draw one clean, deep breath free from the contamination of the poison of that enveloping force which we call race prejudice. Of necessity they react to it. Some are embittered, made resentful, belligerent, even dangerous; some again go to any extreme in a search for temporary pleasures to drown their memory and thought.

—Angelina Weld Grimké (1916)

The past seeks to damn him with its heritage and the present casts about him an environment which aims to restrict him much more than any other race is restricted. . . . Negroes are given inferior schools to meet equal tests; they are given inferior wages to pay equal prices; they are expected to work out their economic salvation with no political power, without even the ballot. . . . The Negro is constantly trying to manage the white man as "Br'er Rabbit" managed "Br'er Fox," by his superior wits: by indirection, circumvention, and cunning.

—William Pickens (1916)

Don't you see? We were colored! Therefore, we must not be permitted to act. . . . Apparently, colored folks were not supposed to be regular human beings, with knowledge of life. They were just human eccentricities, that did certain old tricks, wore certain kinds of queer clothes, and were funny, the way monkeys in a zoo are funny. . . . Well, you can't blame me if I wanted to be something more than a monkey.

—Charles Gilpin (1921)

IN MEMORY OF
BERNARD L. PETERSON, JR.
1927-2000

CONTENTS

16 pages of illustrations appear between pages 164 and 165.

ACKNOWLEDGEMENTS

My appreciation first and foremost to librarians and archivists for their invaluable support: James Huffman, of the Schomburg Center for Research in Black Culture; James V. Hatch, Hatch-Billops Collection in New York; Jo Ellen El Bashir, Moorland-Spingarn Research Center at Howard University; Annette Fern, Harvard Theatre Collection; Geraldine Duclow, Free Library of Philadelphia; Jennifer E. Bradshaw, George Mason University's Special Collection and Archives; Wayne Shirley, Library of Congress; and the librarians at the Billy Rose Theatre Collection, Library of Congress, Schomburg, Moorland-Spingarn, and University of Massachusetts, Amherst. My gratitude to friends and colleagues: Steven R. Bayne; my assistant Jan Foery; my co-editor for *African American Performance and Theatre History*, Harry J. Elam; and my Yale colleagues Joseph Roach, Murray Biggs, Toni Dorfman, Nadine George, James Luse, Deb Margolin, and Marc Robinson. Michael Flamini, Alan Bradshaw, Amanda Johnson, Bruce Murphy, and Erin Chan at Palgrave have been a pillar of support. Scholars Randy Roberts and Judith Stein were extremely helpful. My thanks to Anthea Kraut and Barbara Webb, two outstanding graduate students from Northwestern University, for providing not only documents and scripts, but for inspiring ideas as well. I owe my deepest gratitude to my family, my mother Anne Krasner, my late father Milton, and most especially my wife Lynda, her children Sam, Katie, and Bryan, and Lynda's parents, Tom and Lucy.

Finally, this book is dedicated to Bernard L. Peterson, Jr. He was one of the most important and least recognized scholars of African American theatre history. His books are valuable resources to everyone working in theatre history and performance studies. He rescued actors, directors, playwrights, and dancers from disappearing without a trace. Bernard was humble and genuinely modest, having little interest in conventions, networking, or career advancement. He labored quietly and alone, undertaking the monumental task of documenting the history of virtually every African American involved in theatre. His dedication to the task of keeping alive the history of African American performance and theatre history was one of the highest achievements in our field. I hope someday he will be recognized for this work.

Portions of chapters have appeared in previous works. Chapter 3 appeared in "Black Salome: Exoticism, Dance, and Racial Myths," *African American Performance and Theatre History: A Critical Reader,* edited by Harry J. Elam and David Krasner (New York: Oxford University Press, 2001; used by permission of Oxford University Press, Inc.), 192–211. Chapter 4 appeared in *Performing America: Cultural Nationalism in American Theater,* edited by J. Ellen Gainor and Jeffrey D. Mason (Ann Arbor: University of Michigan Press, 1999), 106–122. Chapter 6 appeared in *Theatre Journal* 53:4 (December 2001), 533–550; and chapter 9 appeared in *African American Review* 29:3 (Fall 1995), 483–496. I offer my gratitude to Elissa Morris (Oxford), Leann Fields (Michigan), Susan Bennett (*Theatre Journal*), and Joe Weixlmann (*African American Review*) for their invaluable editorial guidance. This book was published with the assistance of the Frederick W. Hilles Publication Fund of Yale University.

CHAPTER ONE

AFRICAN AMERICAN PERFORMANCE IN THE HARLEM RENAISSANCE

If in connection with it [art] we study the Negro we shall find that two things are observable. One is that any distinction so far won by a member of the race in America has been almost always in some one of the arts; and the other is that any influence so far exerted by the Negro on American civilization has been primarily in the field of aesthetics.

—Benjamin Brawley (1918)[1]

INTRODUCTION: THE PARADOX OF THE HARLEM RENAISSANCE

In the very process of being transplanted, the Negro is becoming transformed.
—Alain Locke (1925)[2]

This work brings together themes underlying black theatre, performance, and drama from 1910 to 1927. I pick up where my previous work, *Resistance, Parody, and Double Consciousness in African American Theatre, 1895–1910*, leaves off, with theatre and performance during what I term "the first half of the Harlem Renaissance–New Negro era."[3] The Harlem Renaissance was a watershed in American cultural history, and drama and performance were at the forefront of it. Regrettably, few studies acknowledge this fact. Yet drama and performance consistently played a pivotal role in the evolution of Black Nationalism, which in turn led to an indigenous black theatre; the development of black dramatic theory, which bolstered black literature as a whole; and the rise of black performance, which added significantly to black cultural expression. The era's musical and literary content have received significant attention, which has led to an emphasis on selected areas of aesthetic development at the expense of others. I hope to correct the imbalance by bringing theatre, performance, and drama into focus.

This book, however, is not a history of African American theatre and performance *per se*. Rather, it attempts to introduce *a way of thinking about that history*, in order that we may better understand the goals of the artists, the effects they produced, and the cultural conditions under which they worked. To this end, I concentrate on specific events in order to sketch a larger picture. The book is divided into three sections. The first three chapters following this introduction investigate sport, dance, and pageantry. Chapter 2 considers Jack Johnson's victory over Jim Jeffries for the heavyweight title in 1910 as exemplifying sports as performance. The dance performances of Aida Overton Walker and Ethel Waters are analyzed in chapter 3, in view of what might be called "highbrow and lowbrow" dance during the 1910s. In chapter 4, pageantry is examined. W. E. B. Du Bois's *The Star of Ethiopia*, produced in 1913, 1915, 1916, and 1925, was the first mass assembly of black people for the purpose of self-determination and cultural pride. Part II is devoted to dramas and the values they express; representative playwrights and plays are scrutinized. Angelina Weld Grimké's *Rachel* (1916) and Zora Neale Hurston's *Color Struck* (1925) are taken as paradigms in chapters 5 and 6, respectively. Chapter 7 considers the influence of Alain Locke on the dramas of Georgia Douglas Johnson and Willis Richardson.[4]

In Part III, I analyze events of the late 1910s to 1927. Chapter 8 examines the rise of Marcus Garvey's 1920 Universal Negro Improvement Association and its parade. In chapter 9, Charles Gilpin's performance of Brutus Jones in Eugene O'Neill's *Emperor Jones* from 1920 to 1926 is used to exhibit the tension that existed between black and white cultures. Gilpin viewed the role of Brutus Jones differently than the playwright, causing the actor to use language for his own ends. The rise of the Black Little Theatre Movement occupies chapter 10. The Broadway production of *Shuffle Along* (1921), black musicals in general, and the emergence of the touring circuits in African American communities constitute the subject matter of chapter 11. Here I will focus on librettos, performers, and audiences rather than music *per se*. Music obviously played an important role in the development of African American theatre; any examination of music during the period, however, requires lengthy discussion and musical expertise. I will therefore leave the analysis of Harlem Renaissance music to those better qualified.[5] Chapter 12 will summarize and attempt to explain why, by 1927, the Harlem Renaissance had moved into a new phase of aesthetic productivity.

The emphasis here will be on the core ideas of black performance and theatre of the Harlem Renaissance, ideas that determined black social awareness circa 1910 to 1927. Black theatre and performance at the time was a struggle for self-determination and the right to gain acceptance in commercial venues as well as bolster intellectual contributions to the arts. Black art arose from tensions existing between separatism and integrationism, folk art and propaganda, high art and popular culture, improvisation and text, and autonomy and solidarity.[6] These tensions surfaced within the performance style itself, yielding a new emphasis on improvisation as well as a formal approach to theatre and drama that eschewed improvisation as a relic of minstrelsy. Expressed in performances, plays, dance, sports, and politics, the "New Negro" identity would reveal itself as a break from the past: from rural to urban, from ex-slave to modern. At the same time it would show itself as an embodiment of the past, in as much as its folk roots were evident even among the most progressively minded.

The theories of Alain Locke, a key figure during the era, exemplified this twin emphasis on modernization and folk. In his 1926 essay "The Negro and the Stage," he said that black drama must "have the courage to develop its own idiom, to pour itself into new moulds," and "to be experimental."[7] Yet Locke also maintained in *The New Negro* (1925) that African American artists must look to the past and their African heritage—ancestral roots—for spiritual sustenance. He urged "the sensitive artistic mind of the American Negro, stimulated by a cultural pride and interest," to receive "from African art a profound and galvanizing influence."[8] From its inception, writes historian Gregory Holmes Singleton, the Renaissance period "looked to the future."[9] However, it simultaneously looked to the past in an effort to recoup what literary critic Bernard Bell calls "black ancestralism," because African Americans felt that "the soul was under siege by destructive forces," and as a consequence they experienced "a romantic longing for a freer, more innocent time and place,"[10] one situated in cultural roots.

Competing influences within African American performance took on the aura of a paradox. By paradox I mean a set of goals or ideals that, when enacted concurrently, are contradictory. "Paradox" derives from the Greek *para* (beyond) and *doxa* (opinion or belief), meaning literally an assertion "beyond belief." It is a contention that on the surface seems absurd or incredible, though upon examination it may prove reliable and accurate. A paradox is fundamentally an idea or concept involving two opposing thoughts, which, however contradictory, are equally necessary to convey a more insightful illumination into truth than either can secure alone.[11] For African Americans living at the time, cultural reality consisted in paradox, and this paradox informed black theatre and performance.

The desire to look forward and the desire to draw from the past thus created a contradictory state of affairs, yet this inconsistency revealed one of the most important facets of African American culture at the time: two opposing goals contributing simultaneously to form cultural and aesthetic ideas. In looking to the future as a condition of the present, African American "modern" culture was at first a coping strategy opposed to prior symbols and stereotypes; it was also the product of black intellectuals and performers who sought an end to racism and new standards of black art. At the same time, African Americans created their art and drama from African roots and southern traditions. The tensions between spirituals and jazz, dramatic literature and cabarets, parades and prize-fights, pageantry and melodrama, church and nightlife, underlie the paradox of the period. The period was a complex interplay of forces in which black artists were influenced by the search for new forms and values in American culture, and at the same time were also committed to a unique search of their own culture and artistic expression. Because of the rising interest in "primitivism" (the so-called link between black people and subconscious nature), black artists and performers had to walk the tightrope bridging the mainstream and the "exotic." Popularity in mainstream entertainment followed, bringing increased attention. Yet this attention was not always welcomed, resulting in what musicologist Samuel A. Floyd, Jr., called "new tensions for African Americans who were seeking new roots and comforts."[12] The conflict resulting from attempts to accommodate the mainstream and resisting it was one of several cultural paradoxes that complicated the decisions of black performers and playwrights.[13]

The force of this paradox was captured most succinctly by W. E. B. Du Bois's term "double consciousness." The feeling of twoness, wrote Du Bois, of being an American and black, in which "two souls, two thoughts, two unreconciled strivings" existed in "one dark body," was never far from the minds of many African Americans.[14] Yet paradox in this instance describes something more complex than double consciousness. It also incorporates living with contradiction and inconsistency. Historian Thomas C. Holt appears to take Du Bois's concept as a working hypothesis when he claims that black people "*live* a kind of paradox embodied in their lives, which are shaped profoundly by conflicts of identity and purpose." This paradox, according to Holt, "marks the lives of all African-Americans because all experience racial alienation in some form — social, economic, or political."[15] Such alienation exacerbated the contradiction; African Americans had to learn to hide the "self" and pretend in order to work within the mainstream. Contradictions and inconsistencies are thus part of living conditions. According to philosopher Lewis R. Gordon, contradiction and paradox are for African Americans not dilemmas in the mundane sense; they are, rather, existential issues "for a being whose ontological structure is contradictory."[16] Existence was a daily struggle with competing pressures and desires, creating a world in which contradictions were a way of life. Paradox brings with it the social manifestation of cultural dislocation, one that African Americans became especially familiar with during the period.

Among the most significant of the paradoxes in art throughout the period was the demand, on the one hand, for artistic autonomy, and the insistence on racial solidarity by social critics on the other. The rise of individualism as a guiding motif in American life influenced both African American and European American culture and art. Yet the need for racial unity in the face of lynchings, segregation, and economic alienation placed enormous pressure on black artists. They attempted to uphold a commitment to autonomy in the context of group solidarity. Historian David Levering Lewis captures this dual emphasis when he describes the Harlem Renaissance as "divided between those who saw the value of the arts primarily in terms of service to civil rights and those who believed that artistic and literary freedom were the only civil rights worth having."[17] In response to this tension, individual creativity and group solidarity coexisted in an uneasy relationship. Many performers and playwrights felt pressure to act and write in ways that conformed to "New Negro" dictums, yet they strained against these restrictions in an act of artistic liberty.

In these circumstances, New Negro artists embarked on a reconstruction of their social and cultural identity. Some sought affiliation with white theatres while others rejected the allure of mainstream success, opting instead to work in and among their own communities. Performers of the Harlem Renaissance, like all performers, required an audience. For African American performers, however, the looming issue was whether to appeal to fellow blacks, to "cross over" and perform for whites, or attempt to appeal to both. Many experienced the pressures to create for several audiences—white, black, middle class, and working class—and tried to accommodate as many groups as possible simply in order to survive. The artists were by no means unified in their approaches; performers rarely, if ever, speak with a single voice. What they shared was their enforced segregation. In one way or another, they had to confront racial stereotyping and the reality of performing before audiences that labeled them as "black," "Negro," "Negroid," "colored," "Ethiopian," "African," or "mulatto."

Race was a principal factor in forming identity at the time, and figured in new ideas that transformed African Americans. New ideas arising from racial self-awareness were elicited by social realities. Segregation, for instance, was on the increase. As Eunice Roberta Hunton wrote in 1925 in *Survey Graphic,* "Harlem is a modern ghetto," with "prejudice" ringing "this group around with invisible lines and bars." Kelly Miller added that the "most gigantic instance of racial segregation in the United States is seen in Harlem." Despite the fact that

there is "no local law prescribing it," under the "normal operation of race prejudice" there were "200,000 Negroes shut in segregated areas as sharply marked as
the aisles of a church."[18] Racial consciousness was a constant reminder to
African Americans that their skin was a determining factor of their being.

Race onstage illuminated the forces at work at the time. Philosopher and social scientist Lucius Outlaw posits that although "race" is "without scientific basis
in biological terms," that does not mean that it is "without any social value."[19] In an
age when an emphasis on racial differences and Jim Crow segregation were a constant in daily life, African Americans could not escape its consequences. During
this period, the freewheeling Jazz Age and the interest in "race" as an insignia of
modernity surfaced alongside Prohibition and the rising popularity of the Ku Klux
Klan not only in the South but in the North as well. The interest in black literature,
music, and culture coincided with the high tide of Jim Crow and lynching, while
primitivism, modernism, and industrialism coexisted alongside a heightened American nationalism and xenophobia. This schizophrenic period exhibited a social gai-
ety replete with flappers, colorful speakeasies (called "blind pigs" in some black
communities), and giddy prosperity, as well as a stream of social conservatism,
which influenced black performance and theatre during the time.

THE EARLY HARLEM RENAISSANCE

*All human relations have shifted. Let us agree to place one of these
changes about the year 1910.*   —Virginia Woolf (1924)[20]

The term "Harlem Renaissance" itself has been subject to much controversy
among cultural historians, who have debated its merits, shortcomings, distinctive
characteristics, and temporal boundaries ever since it first appeared. Few agree
as to what actually took place during the Harlem Renaissance or how its outcome affected the world. I shall avoid challenging each commentator.[21] Rather,
by "Harlem Renaissance" I understand the period of African American history
beginning around 1910 and ending approximately at the conclusion of World
War II. Though periodization is problematic, since events overlap, I will maintain that the initiation of the Harlem Renaissance was marked by three important events. The first two are owing to W. E. B. Du Bois: his cofounding of the
National Association for the Advancement of Colored People (NAACP), and his
inauguration of the journal, *Crisis* (both in 1910), launched the era. But the most
significant moment was Jack Johnson's defeat of "white hope" Jim Jeffries in
1910 (see chapter 2). The Harlem Renaissance continued through the period of
the Great Migration and post–World War I, often referred to as the "Swing Era"

or "Jazz Age." It reached its zenith during the literary and cultural renaissance of the 1920s. It continued through the Depression (though changing considerably) and had concluded by the end of World War II, at a time when the Civil Rights movement was poised to replace the ideas and events that defined the Harlem Renaissance.[22]

Seventeen crucial years are discussed here. They represent a considerable shift in African American life. There has been reasonable disagreement regarding the extent and timetable of the New Negro–Harlem Renaissance era, but it is evident that it brought with it a burgeoning movement in theatre and performance. The Great Migration, America's intervention in World War I in 1917 in which 370,000 African Americans participated,[23] and the rise of Harlem brought a new complexity that ramified throughout African American culture. The shift from rural to urban society was essential to this transition. The relatively settled relationships of the rural era gave way to modern industrialization. Not only did urban African American performers, artists, and intellectuals radically change the perception of African American identity, but they also constructed the particular "New Negro" social identity—urban, sophisticated, and progressive—that came to characterize African American people through much of this epoch.

Change was inextricably bound up with the Great Migration.[24] Social critic Kerry Candaele has made clear that during the time "a deep loathing for the segregation and racial violence of the South" impelled more than a million African Americans "to heed the radical *Chicago Defender*'s call to 'leave that benighted land' and migrate North."[25] Although 75 percent of black people resided in the South as late as 1930, beginning in 1910, African American population showed greater urban increase than did the white population.[26] In the 1910s, nearly half a million African Americans left the rural South for the urban North. By the next decade, three-quarters of a million headed northward, increasing the black northern population from 1910 to 1930 by 300 percent. But the change amounted to more than mere demographics. The Great Migration was explained primarily in terms of what Locke referred to as "a new vision" that looked toward opportunity, social and economic freedom, and "a spirit to seize, even in the face of an extortionate and heavy toll, a chance for the improvement of conditions."[27] African American migration north was motivated by better wages; better treatment; better cultural and educational opportunities; better living conditions; and the mass psychology underlying the freedom to move.[28]

Despite changes, not all African Americans shared in the "new optimism." Many, in fact, still resided in the impoverished South, cut off from the benefits of education and industrial growth, and subject to Jim Crow segregation and the threat of lynching. For many northerners, the situation was just as bleak. Urban centers were ghettoized and steeped in squalor. Harlem was becoming the geographic center of African American culture; it would, however, also emerge as a "slum."[29] Infant mortality was double that of whites; tuberculosis was three to four times more common; syphilis nine times higher; and unemployment for black Americans hovered at 50 percent.[30] Moreover, urban overcrowding led to corruption and exploitation, and segregation continued unabated.[31] Black migrants from the South and West Indies paid exorbitant rent to live in overcrowded tenements and confined to certain neighborhoods. Black women in particular suffered from the hardships of poverty, including the constant threat of rape and abuse, and the difficulties of traveling alone.[32] Langston Hughes put it best when he said: "The ordinary Negroes hadn't heard of the Negro Renaissance. And if they had, it hadn't raised their wages any."[33]

African Americans endured a collective diasporic experience. Their misfortune penetrated the culture itself: theatre and performance conspired to encourage the stereotypes. As late as 1937, poet and literary historian Sterling Brown recognized that in drama large areas of black experience "remain unexplored." Broadway, he lamented, "is still entranced with the stereotypes of the exotic primitive, the comic stooge and the tragic mulatto."[34] In addition, the issue of writing and performing for two audiences, one black, one white, was an ongoing problem. The dilemma of the "double audience," wrote James Weldon Johnson in 1928, was more than merely the doubling of spectators; it was "a divided audience, an audience made up of two elements with differing and often opposite and antagonistic points of view." For Johnson, when black writers wrote, they were "immediately called upon to solve, consciously or unconsciously, this problem of the double audience."[35] Performers experienced this problem, too.

Nevertheless, changes were taking place. By the 1920s, many African Americans were better educated, wealthier, and had greater access to the media. The number of black newspapers had increased significantly and colleges were enjoying expanded enrollment. The creative outpouring far surpassed any previous era. In 1927, critic Benjamin Brawley could say with confidence that to be black "ceased to be a matter for explanation or apology; instead it became something to be advertised and exploited: thus the changed point of view made for increased self-respect."[36] Urban life afforded African Americans the opportunity to share a new outlook. The most well-known cultural center, Harlem, epitomized the new, urban African American. More than merely a place where black people lived, Harlem, in historian James De Jongh's words, "posed a challenge to contemporary limits and cultural terms within which personal being for both blacks and whites were imagined and defined."[37]

Harlem, though not the only major area to boast a large African American population, came to symbolize modern black society. After the New York race riots of 1900 and 1905, and the destruction of many homes to make way for Pennsylvania Station, black communities in the Tenderloin and San Juan Hill districts, which were part of this new redistricting, no longer felt secure. They began to desert midtown for Harlem. In 1904, the completion of New York's IRT Lenox Avenue subway line improved access throughout the city. Traveling uptown was now only a matter of minutes. By 1910, encouraged by real estate entrepreneurs and the "On to Harlem" movement, "central Harlem" came into existence. It emerged as an area that contained African Americans from the South and the West Indies, as well as New York natives.[38]

With the emergence of Harlem as a "race capital" came "spatialization." Race remained significant in the formation of identity, but location affected people as well. Cut off from the mainstream, Harlem was rich in *communitas* (community fellowship) and cultural spontaneity. For the first time, large segments of the African American population lived in close proximity; no longer divided by plantations and farms, African Americans were now living in closely knit communities. Proximity was a cathartic social redefinition. As early as 1923, drama and social critic Lester A. Walton stressed Harlem's "diversity"; one finds there, he said, "members from Africa, Asia, Europe, South and Central America, as well as all parts of the United States, speaking different tongues yet held together by a community of interests."[39] This concept of community of interests arose as an essential definition of culture. To be black not only meant the color of one's skin, but one's residence as well. One identified "place" with "race."

BLACK MODERNITY AND PERFORMANCE

1910, that is indeed the year when all scaffolds began to crack.
— Gottfried Benn (1955)[40]

Much more will be said here about modernity and performance from 1910 to 1927. But because the terms "modernity" and "performance" are easily misunderstood, some definition will prove valuable. By "black modernity" I mean the cultural milieu beginning around 1910, brought on by industrialization, a concomitant desire for self-determination, and resistance to racism. No doubt African Americans had resisted racism prior to 1910. However, by 1910 a shift in circumstances had occurred, bringing with it a new call for new strategies. With the collapse of Reconstruction, the rise of Jim Crow, the steady stream of lynchings, and the migratory movement north commonly referred to as "goin' up south,"[41] African Americans were forced into a new self-awareness.

"Black modernity" was a humanist vision incorporating the contradictory impulses of autonomy and solidarity. "Humanism" builds on the principles of human action viewed as autonomous reasoning and will; racial solidarity affirms the belief in consensus-building among certain groups as a prelude to social change. During the period from 1910 to 1927, African American modernity surfaced through the paradox of autonomy and solidarity. Furthermore, black modernity was a complex mixture of ideas and movements—migratory, urbanized, intellectualized, fragmentary, literary, oral, folk, jazz, blues, rhythmic, Western, and Afrocentric—that created a complex, hybrid form. But one thing remained constant: black modernity represented a desire to *transform the image of black culture from minstrelsy to sophisticated urbanity.*

Entering into the new mainstream while building a separate culture was a paradox for which black modernity was the antidote. However, different social leaders sought different antidotes. For example, during the period, Black Nationalist Marcus Garvey sought black separatism and recognition of a unique black culture, while Alain Locke, James Weldon Johnson, and others pursued new images of African Americans fully integrated into the mainstream. Contemporary scholar Gerald Early calls attention to this division, noting that the New Negro Movement split into distinct, "though not necessarily antagonistic, groups: the chiliastic, nationalistic, visionary remnant of Garveyites" on the one hand, and "the secular, modernist, assimilationist elite" on the other.[42] As a result, there was no single defining black modernity, but an intersection of ideas and movements seeking ways to end racism and assert self-determination.

Rich in cultural activity, black "New Negro" modernity sought new ideas in art and performance; new standards of literary and dramatic theory; new artistic expressions; a new self-awareness; and a new explanation of the reality of life removed from the stigma of minstrelsy. Like their European counterparts, African American modernists possessed an urge to control their art. Each artist, in varying degrees, sought autonomy. However, many Europeans sought autonomy through art for art's sake (*l'art pour l'art*). They wanted to remove art from social reality. African American modernists were trapped in a defensive position and were continually made aware of their "place" in society. Hence, rather than eschew social realism, their art was informed by it. Black identity during the era was also an expression of individual style tied to group values. It was not a unified response, but a family of responses designed to conceptualize unity in diversity. Some sought a self-contained world, while others reached out to form bonds with mainstream society; many attempted both.

Broadly speaking, "performance" includes any live act (not film) created for a public audience. It may involve theatre, music, poetry reading, dance, ritual, parade, ceremony, pageantry, sport, public speaking, or any combination of these. Performance is not limited to stage acting. It may include non-dramatic, non-textual, and ceremonial activities. "Performance" denotes a public art that stresses the expressive power of voice, body, and gesture; performers also make use of cultural codes that reveal the social lexicon of the times. The "social scene" is where performer and audience interact by means of words and gestures, thereby establishing a public identity within a social context.[43]

For many African Americans, performance is often more than public expression; it communicates thoughts, ideas, and desires to and from a culture denied access to other forms of communication. Cut off from the free use of written language and restricted from expressing cultural identity during slavery, performance became a primary, and sometimes the sole, mode of communication. During the cross-Atlantic journey known as the Middle Passage, Africans entered a world of varied languages and cultures. Difficulty in communicating with white slave traders as well as each other was a state inviting chaos. Enslavement was anxiety ridden and brutal enough; the inability to communicate with fellow slaves or enslavers added to the intensity of emotions. Historian Michael Gomez observes that these circumstances forced African slaves to communicate through other means, primarily by the "tone of the delivery, the lilt of the voice, the cadence of the words, [and] the coordinated body language." These communicative skills were needed in order to make sense of the experience and to share "the ideas, emotions, and sensibilities of persons of African descent."[44] Performance arose as a significant means of communication. It was not a "natural" phenomenon, but one borne from social conditions that made performing imperative for survival. It was this condition that caused performance to take root in African American culture and resurface throughout its history.

The Harlem Renaissance incorporated performance as one of the most effective means of communicating black identity and the development of black modernity. It was a watershed moment because it built on the concept of performance as a cultural means of expression. Jazz and the blues played a significant role, but drama and performance were another venue of cultural expression. Alain Locke encouraged dramatists to take stock of the African American experience, because the black group experience in America "has plumbed greater emotional depths, or passed so dramatically through more levels of life or caught up into itself more of those elements of social conflicts and complication" than the other group's experience, enabling the modern dramatist to mine these depths for creative purposes.[45] For Locke and others, theatre and performance became an outlet for expression and social change. Performance might challenge familiar perceptions and begin the effort to correct injustices.

The modern age involved, among other things, a process of fragmentation that denied persons their place as whole subjects. In other words, "modernity" entailed the fragmentation of consciousness and identity.[46] Black performance was a healing process against dispersion and diaspora; by singing spirituals in church or performing the blues in nightclubs, performers and audiences created a perspective on the world, one holding together what the modern age had fragmented and shattered. Performance gave life meaning; it promoted a social cohesion through communal rites and ritual practices. It strengthened traditions while creating new bonds. Performance, social critic Manthia Diawara says, takes into account "the way in which black people, through communicative action, engender themselves within the American experience," and interpret their own traditions "in such a way that the individual or group of people invent themselves for [their] audience."[47] Black performers, reinterpreting their ancestral culture, played out the process of original cultural formation in the Americas, while simultaneously building new forms that worked against the enduring restraint of racial bias.

CONCLUSION: CULTURAL LEGITIMACY

Yes, there is a New Negro. And it is he who will pilot the Negro through
this terrible hour of storm and stress.   —*The Messenger* (1920)[48]

Black artists of the New Negro Renaissance sought cultural legitimacy. Setting its sights on this objective, the renaissance exemplified what historian James C. Scott calls "high modernism," an attempt to impose a rational order on society and standardize its forms. For Scott, high modernism is a "version of the self-confidence about scientific and technical progress, the expansion of production, the growing satisfaction of human needs, the mastery of nature," and most importantly, "the rational design of social order commensurate with the scientific understanding of natural law." Originating in the West, high modernism was "a particularly sweeping vision of how the benefits of technical and scientific progress might be applied" in every field of human endeavor.[49] However, whereas Scott condemns "the imperialism of high-modernist, planned social order,"[50] black high modernists envisioned a planned social order that demanded an image distinct from minstrelsy. African Americans lacked political influence, and images of blacks as "Aunt Jemimas," "Sambos," and "coons" dominated the larger culture. Performers used drama, dance, the pulpit, and sports to offset the offensive paradigms. If Scott's definition is correct, black artists and intellectuals, though not imperialists, were high modernists to the core. They attempted to correct injustices by imposing an alternative perception of African America through a planned social order.

Contemporary attacks on modernism have cast a negative light on its efforts at culture formation. If the post-structuralist equation of truth-claims, scientific objectivity, and reason were intrinsically linked to the desire for power, then African American modernists at the time in question were indeed seeking power and legitimacy. Powerless, black intellectuals sought to unify the plethora of standards in black art. Social critic Yvonne Ochillo is most likely correct when she asserts that Alain Locke and others were committed to the idea that black artists "would have to strive to achieve spiritual unity through the healing balm of art." Locke's desire for unity and aesthetic order, Ochillo says, "lay at the heart of his evaluation of Negro art."[51] For Locke, the central task of the artist and intellectual was to transform folk art into modern art by creating a new vision for African Americans. The desire for a new perception and racial solidarity was based on the need for legitimacy.

Cultural legitimacy and social ordering became necessary tools in the face of racism and the demand for group redefinition. By unifying the period through a planned social order, black artists thought they could begin to validate their own work. Today this seems naïve, given postmodernism's skepticism toward unifying "truths." Unity required constraints on individual representation, favoring standardized forms. It often produced derivative and predictable art, tolerating little, if at all, works beyond restrictive boundaries. However, for the black intellectual and artist of the time, unity and solidarity were essential in defeating incipient racism. The period reflected the modernist motif of the belief in the vision of one idea, or leader, who sets the tone and standard for others to follow. The "talented tenth," a term coined by Du Bois in 1903 and frequently used by others, was the impetus that influenced many writers and performers.[52] Black art served in the capacity of guidance, defining the moral and ethical order and boundaries for a society fragmented, dislocated, and detached from the mainstream. Modernist historian Astradur Eysteinsson's description of modernism as "aesthetic heroism" has significance for black modernity. As Eysteinsson explains, "aesthetic heroism" is a modernity in which, "in the face of the chaos of the modern world (very much a 'fallen' world)," art is seen "as the only dependable reality." The unity of art is an ordering principle that is "supposedly a salvation from the shattered order of modern reality."[53] For black modernity, art would provide the ordering principles required for cultural survival.

During the early Harlem Renaissance, black artists and performers would sometimes expose black and white America to a romanticized, almost idealized black culture in the hopes of ending racism. Their efforts fell short, and by the

1950s and 1960s, the Civil Rights movement had divested itself from the need for cultural legitimacy in favor of social activism and confrontation. Martin Luther King's non-violent movement, Malcolm X's revolutionary stance, student activism, urban uprisings, and the militant discourse combined to cast aside incrementalism. Nevertheless, the events from 1910 to 1927 deserve recognition.

What transpired during the era was a beautiful pageant, a mosaic of ideas, performances, plays, dramatic theories, dance, and self-expression, which eventuated in a tapestry that converged throughout African American life and art. Black intellectuals and artists at the time argued for the most part that self-determination was an essential component for justice, and that a rational society must be based on the view that the capacity for freedom and mutual respect was fundamental. Racism, they claimed, was irrational and empirically without defense. In 1922, James Weldon Johnson said that the status of black people in the United States "is more a question of national mental attitude toward the race than of actual conditions." For Johnson, "nothing will do more to change that mental attitude and raise his status than a demonstration of intellectual parity by the Negro through the production of literature and art."[54] It was believed that once mental attitudes changed, parity would be achieved, cultural legitimacy would be acquired, and whites would come to realize the universally negative consequences of racism for everyone. This strategy for the most part fell short, insofar as segregation failed to abate, lynching remained a constant threat, and racism gained a stronger foothold in the minds of many white Americans. But the underlying motives that informed black theatre, drama, and performance helped set the course for future generations, and it is this directive that will capture our attention.

PART ONE

1910-1918

Negro life is not only founding new centers, but finding a new soul.
—Alain Locke (1925)[1]

The New Negro–Harlem Renaissance has come to symbolize an era of unprecedented musical, artistic, literary, and dramatic outpourings. It was a time in which black people began to liberate themselves from a past fraught with minstrelsy and degradation, turning instead to what art historian Richard Powell calls "an unprecedented optimism, a novel pride in all things black and a cultural confidence that stretched beyond the borders of Harlem to other black communities in the Western world."[2] This new sense of selfhood was blossoming in all areas of art and life. Social critic Hubert H. Harrison observed in 1920 that the "new situation" for black people in the United States was evident "in the mental attitude of the Negro people." African Americans, Harrison maintained, "have developed new ideas of their own place in the category of races and have evolved new conceptions of their powers and destiny."[3] This newly discovered pride and optimism would find expression in philosophy, medicine, science, education, and the arts.

The cultural efflorescence of the 1920s grew out of events in the 1910s. Dance historian Jacqui Malone raises the salient point that between 1910 and 1920, black theatre developed away from Broadway, permitting it "to grow without the constraints of white critics."[4] Harold Cruse has it right when he asserts that the 1920s Harlem Renaissance "was actually a culminating phase of a previous renaissance that had emerged with the initial growth of black Harlem around 1910."[5] Theatres operated by African Americans for an African American audience began appearing throughout the decade of the 1910s. Moreover, black people were finding new ways to express their creativity. In what follows, three important genres of performance—sports, dance, and pageantry—are examined in order to investigate their influence on culture and impact on race.

CHAPTER TWO

MEN IN BLACK AND WHITE: RACE AND MASCULINITY IN THE HEAVYWEIGHT TITLE FIGHT OF 1910

This fight was the greatest event that had happened to the black race since the Emancipation Proclamation. No other day since the "Day of Jubilee" had had such a positive effect upon the black American's self image and his ability to compete on an equal basis with the white man. When Jack Johnson met Jim Jeffries they were representing the hopes and fears of their respective races. —William H. Wiggins, Jr. (1973)[1]

INTRODUCTION

[Jim Jeffries] in his prime no greater fighter ever lived. May he still be man enough to lick Johnson. —Richard Barry (1910)[2]

On Independence Day, 1910, Jack Johnson fought "white hope" Jim Jeffries for the heavyweight title. The title fight was a major event, attracting twenty thousand spectators and a press corps of six hundred. Thousands waited outside press buildings in cities across the country to hear round-by-round reports of the fight from the wire service.[3] More was at stake than the heavyweight title. Johnson's victory would inflame white sentiment, and provoked the first nationwide race riot in United States history. According to the *New York Times*, riots "occurred in all parts of the country"; it added that "scores of negroes were injured seriously, and eight negroes were killed outright." The *Chicago Tribune* reported:

> There were battles in the streets of practically every large city in the country. Negroes formed the greater number of those who were victims of the outbreaks. They were set upon by whites and killed or wounded because of cheers for Johnson's victory.[4]

Literary Digest added that the announcement of Johnson's victory signaled "brutal clashes between negroes and whites, in which the latter were almost always the aggressors." From sites in "Texas, Georgia, Arkansas, Illinois, New York, Virginia, Pennsylvania, Louisiana, Missouri, Maryland, West Virginia, Colorado, Delaware, Ohio, Kentucky, and the District of Columbia," there totaled "eighteen dead and hundreds injured."[5] When Johnson entered the ring, a band played the song, "All Coons Look Alike"—Ernest Hogan's 1895 minstrel show's theme song.[6] Throughout the preliminary and the fight itself, the white spectators jeered at Johnson with the usual epithets. As Roi Ottley observed, when Johnson met Jeffries "he was in fact fighting the white community."[7]

Jack Johnson (1878–1946) had soundly defeated Tommy Burns in December 1908 to obtain the heavyweight crown at a time when social scientists and psychologists portrayed African Americans as less than human. The so-called innate inferiority of African Americans was advanced in virtually every field of science and culture. Herbert Croly, for instance, wrote in *The Promise of American Life* (1909) that "Southern slave owners were not unclean beasts," but were "right in believing that the negroes were a race possessed of moral and intellectual qualities inferior to those of the white men."[8] According to Johnson biographer Sal Fradella, "the heavyweight crown was the symbol of American manhood," and the fact that "this symbol should now pass to a member of a so-called inferior breed was considered an outrage."[9] Jeffries himself made this point clear when he said, "I am going into this fight for the sole purpose of proving that a white man is better than a negro."[10] Johnson's flamboyant lifestyle heightened tensions. Not only did he date and marry white women at a time when interracial marriage was socially denigrated and even illegal in many states, Johnson often taunted his opponents in the ring.[11]

Among whites, few fighters carried Jeffries's aura of invincibility. With his menacing scowl, reputation as a hard puncher, and his ability to absorb punishment, he appeared even bigger and more terrifying than his six feet, one-and-half inches, 225-pound frame indicated (compared to Johnson's "mere" six-foot, half-inch, 215 pounds). Jeffries (1875–1953) inspired awe: his virility, strength, en-

durance, and intelligence were overwhelming. From 1897 till his retirement in
1904, the undefeated champion had never been knocked down. His reputation
was based on his crouching style and relentless attack. What he lacked in flash
he made up for in brute strength; always plodding ahead, he could endure long
bouts and administer powerful punches. He defeated two former champions,
Bob Fitzsimmons and Jim Corbett, twice—each time by knockout (Fitzsimmons
in 1899 and 1903, Corbett in 1900 and 1903). Arthur Ruhl described Jeffries's
menacing entrance into the ring as "stamping like a bull pawing the ground before the charge."[12] During what was considered the "Golden Age of Boxing"
(1899–1904), Jeffries met every challenger and defeated him. After being
coaxed out of retirement to fight Johnson, Jeffries spent almost a year getting
into shape (he had ballooned up to nearly three hundred pounds). Despite the
fact that Jeffries was 35 (Johnson was 32), out of shape, and had been retired
for six years, white fight critics were confident of victory. Bob Fitzsimmons predicted "Jeffries will hit that nigger once and Johnson'll turn white. Why, Jeff
can kill him."[13]

Johnson had also established an impressive career, winning 40 bouts and
losing only 3 times, from 1901 to 1910. Often unable to find white fighters to
fight, Johnson fought other gifted heavyweight black fighters: Sam MacVey,
Sam Langford, and Joe Jeannette. Johnson defeated MacVey three times (twice
in 1903 and once in 1904), Langford in 1906, and fought Jeannette six times
from 1903 to 1906 (Johnson won once, lost once on a foul, and fought to a no decision or draw four times). But these fights yielded less financial gain than fighting white fighters, and Johnson sought fights primarily for money. Johnson was
a product of an age that promoted self-sufficiency, independence, and wealth. He
also needed money to fuel his extravagant lifestyle.

After following the champion to Australia and demanding an opportunity
for the heavyweight championship, Johnson defeated Tommy Burns (real name
Noah Brusso) decisively in fourteen rounds in December of 1908 to obtain the
title. He knocked Burns down in the first round; for the remainder of the fight
Johnson held a boxing clinic, striking Burns at will.[14] The *Australian Bulletin* reported that Burns was "outgeneraled, over-reached, overmatched in strength, in-
sulted and treated like a helpless mouse by a great black cat."[15] Johnson often
fought long bouts. He seemed reluctant to fight for early knockouts, opting instead to showcase his ring generalship and defensive skills.

Following his fight with Burns, Johnson fought five times before facing Jeffries. Ignoring the requests by black fighters to fight him again, Johnson sought
out more lucrative fights with whites. Three of the fights were uneventful; his
fights with Jack O'Brien, Tony Rose, and Al Kaufman resulted in no decisions

(at the time prizefighting was not left to decisions, which resulted in a fight without a knockout being recorded as "no decision"). Johnson finally agreed to fight Stanley Ketchel, a good middleweight but significantly lighter than Johnson. Rumors suggested that the fight was fixed. Johnson was expected to arrange for a no decision, and both fighters would collect considerable money. In the twelfth round Ketchel surprised a lackadaisical Johnson with a roundhouse right that sent the champion to the canvas. Johnson, who had indeed fought half-heartedly, rose before the count was finished and met a charging Ketchel head on. He threw a right uppercut that landed with such force that Johnson's forward momentum and the blow itself sent both men to the floor, with Johnson falling on top of Ketchel and continuing to roll nearly out of the ring. Johnson rose and stood against the ropes, as Ketchel lay helpless on the floor.[16] Johnson won, leaving the sport devoid of legitimate contenders with any hope of defeating him. Johnson's biographer Randy Roberts wrote that the fights with Ketchel, Kaufman, Rose, and O'Brien "were just preliminaries." The real fight was to be with Jeffries. Roberts noted:

> About the call for Jeffries's comeback there was a smug confidence, a belief that the big, grizzly-strong white fighter would not disappoint the race. There would be no more grim picture like the one taken with Ketchel spread out on the canvas while Johnson, one hand on hip, the other touching the upper ropes, looked on. . . . Once Jeffries returned, boxing enthusiasts assured each other, racial superiority would be restored.[17]

Despite the hype, the Johnson-Jeffries fight was a one-sided affair. Johnson was in command from the beginning. As Johnson himself put it, "I hit Jeff at will."[18] For more than half the fight Jeffries clinched, holding Johnson and resting his head on his shoulders. The accumulation of blows mangled Jeffries's face. Despite considerable efforts, Jeffries failed to reach Johnson with a decisive punch and Johnson grew more confident with each round. Between fierce blows Johnson toyed with Jeffries, laughing and chatting with him and ringside luminaries. By the fifteenth round Johnson had hit him repeatedly with left hooks, sending Jeffries through the ropes three times. After the first knockdown, Jeffries barely gained his footing before Johnson sent him to the ropes again. Jeffries's assistants climbed into the ring to throw in the towel, but the referee pushed them back. Johnson then sent Jeffries reeling to the canvas across the ring. Jeffries, tangled in the ropes and exhausted, remained on the ground. As Johnson said: "Jeffries at no time made the going very difficult for me, and in the fifteenth round I knocked him out," adding: "Hardly a blow been struck when I knew I was Jeff's master."[19] The predominantly white crowd was visibly stunned and disappointed.

The film of the fight, albeit grainy, evinces the style of each fighter.[20] From the outset it appears nothing could stop Johnson. Johnson fights with his hands held relatively low, below the waistline. He checks every move Jeffries makes; his balance and precision move in unison with Jeffries, parrying each of Jeffries's attacks. If Jeffries advances, Johnson circles away; if Jeffries lunges, he blocks and counters. Johnson often pushes Jeffries's punches aside. Throughout Jeffries crouches, moves forward, and probes for an opening, but fails to land a solid punch. His strategy is predictably straightforward. Johnson anticipates Jeffries. His punches are swift, often snapping Jeffries's head backwards.

Under the sweltering, Fourth-of-July Reno summer sun the spectators in the backdrop, virtually all white and in straw hats, continually wag their hand-held fans. For the most part they sit motionless. In the opening round Jeffries lunges at Johnson; Johnson moves backward gracefully. Countering his advances, two right uppercuts snap Jeffries's head backward. The fight carries on this way for the first five rounds: Jeffries lunging, Johnson countering by snapping Jeffries's head with uppercuts and straight punches from both hands. Johnson demonstrates his skills in jabs, straight rights, and counterpunches, but the uppercut is his most effective weapon since it is a punch that works best when an opponent leans in, crouching and holding. By the third round Johnson's punches are delivered with greater intensity; by the sixth, Johnson steps backward, planting his right foot for leverage and throwing a straight right hand that lands on Jeffries's jaw with the force of a projectile. Jeffries lurches backward and appears dazed. By the seventh, Johnson begins moving forward, using feints with either hand while blocking Jeffries's jabs. There is little vitality in Jeffries's punches, while Johnson continues to snap his opponent's head. In the middle rounds, six through ten, Jeffries begins to miss wildly, stalking Johnson without success. Johnson doubles up his punches, throwing combinations and clearly hurting Jeffries. In the later rounds Jeffries stumbles backward and defensively grabs Johnson for self-protection. The twelfth round proves decisive, with Johnson throwing tremendous right uppercuts and straight rights. Following thirteen rounds, Jeffries is leaning to his right, off-balance and wounded. He probes Johnson for a body blow, but Johnson covers his torso with his right elbow and forearm.

At the end of the thirteenth, Johnson again steps back, plants his right foot, and hurls his right fist into an onrushing Jeffries. By the fourteenth, Johnson is jabbing with his left, swirling his hands in front of Jeffries's face, smiling, feinting, and having fun. He laughs off all attempts by an exhausted Jeffries. Between rounds Jeffries's assistants fan him with towels and shade him from the sun with a large, leaf-shaped awning. Johnson is left uncovered in the sun, and by the middle rounds his aids do not even bother to fan him with towels. The end comes swiftly in the fifteenth round. Jeffries charges toward Johnson and Johnson jolts him with a stiff left jab. Johnson hits the clutching Jeffries with a right uppercut, sending him backward and into the ropes. Then Johnson, circling his hands in front of Jeffries in order to confuse him, stops advancing and backs up. Jeffries, predictably moving in a straight line toward his opponent, is lured into the trap. He stalks forward, weight on his forward left foot, trying to find an opening in Johnson's superb defense. With his weight forward, Jeffries dangerously leans toward Johnson. Johnson unleashes a perfect left jab against the forward-leaning Jeffries that sends him into the ropes again. Jeffries clinches, holding onto Johnson for protection, but Johnson lands a right uppercut, his full weight behind the punch. The blow lifts Jeffries off the canvas and when his feet return to the ground he staggers backward. Johnson follows with two left hooks, sending Jeffries to the floor. Although he tries to rise, Johnson knocks him down two more times (see figure 1).

Former heavyweight champion John L. Sullivan, reporting on the fight for the *New York Times*, said "Johnson didn't receive a blow during the whole encounter that would have hurt a 16-year-old boy. From the time Jeff got his right eye closed in the sixth round it was all over."[21] Fight critic Rex Beach declared the fight a "pitiful tragedy."[22] Some tried to put a good spin on the fight; Harry C. Carr, for instance, reported in the *Los Angeles Times* that when the fight began, "Johnson was so frightened that his face was a deathly, ashen gray." Johnson's eyes, Carr claimed, "were staring with a sort of horrified terror."[23] But such reporting was rare; for the most part, white critics acknowledged an anti-climatic fight. One newspaper tried to show Jeffries in a good light, drawing a portrait in which Jeffries appears to be backing up Johnson into the ropes. The caption underneath reads: "Jeffries forcing the negro a little" (see figure 2).[24] However, Finis Farr makes vividly clear what happened. Prior to the third round, the crowd took Johnson's "solemn and thoughtful approach" as "evidence of fear"; but in the third "Johnson suddenly flicked out his left glove in a jab that brought the crouching Jeffries up straight as though he had run into the edge of an open door."[25] From this point onward it was clear who would win. The *Omaha Bee* reported: "After the third round Johnson treated his opponent almost as a joke."[26] As the fight progressed, Johnson toyed with Jeffries; it has even been suggested that he let the match continue in order to prolong the filming of the fight.[27] Writing two days after to the fight, Jackson J. Stovall wrote in the *Chicago Defender*:

> Johnson, being a past master of feints and guards, has exceptional cleverness,
> great speed and almost impenetrable defense, enabling him to wage battle the

full limit of scheduled rounds, winning by a narrow margin, whereas a quick victory over his opponents would have put his future interests in jeopardy. Hence the public was misled as to his real form.[28]

Jeffries admitted on his way back to California after the fight: "I could never have whipped Jack Johnson at my best. I couldn't have hit him. No, I couldn't have reached him in a thousand years."[29] Johnson had turned the "color line" on its head.

THE COLOR LINE

Now that Mr. Johnson, the Texas dinge, is the Champion face smasher in the world, the color line question is receiving an unusual amount of public attention. —*New York Morning Telegraph* (1909)[30]

White hostility toward Johnson had been growing since the fight between Johnson and Tommy Burns was set to commence on 26 December 1908 in Australia. One reporter's comment typifies the prevailing sentiment: "Citizens who have never prayed before are supplicating Providence to give the white man [Tommy Burns] a strong right arm with which to belt the coon into oblivion."[31] Johnson, however, defeated Burns easily, setting the stage for Jeffries as the "white hope." The intense desire to regain the title for the white race prompted famed author Jack London to initiate the call for former undefeated champion Jim Jeffries to return from retirement and avenge Burn's defeat. Following Johnson's victory over Burns, London enjoined Jeffries to "emerge from his alfalfa farm and remove that smile from Jack Johnson's face. Jeff, it's up to you."[32] The prizefight prompted many civic leaders and cultural critics to weigh in with advice. Two-time Democratic presidential candidate William Jennings Bryan, for example, went so far as to telegram Jeffries: "God will forgive everything you do to that nigger in this fight" Bryan assured the white fighter; "Jeff, God is with you."[33]

If, as W. E. B. Du Bois asserted in 1903, "the problem of the twentieth century is the problem of the color line,"[34] then the heavyweight championship fight of 1910 between Johnson and Jeffries sharply defined the problem. The *Plessy v. Ferguson* decision of 1896 legalizing Jim Crow segregation had become fully operative by 1910, with institutionalized segregation strictly enforced. The racial divide was drawn everywhere; however, because of Johnson's publicly acknowledged abilities, it became evident that the color line had denied a talented individual an opportunity to excel in his field. The pressure to break the color line in professional prizefighting was intensified, given the desire by African Americans to demonstrate their worth, Johnson's obvious talent, and the fact that any fighter refusing to compete with Johnson might be perceived as cowardly.[35] Despite opposition to black participation in professional boxing, many social critics were confident that natural selection would eventually weed out Johnson. The *San Francisco Examiner,* for example, reported that the "spirit of Caesar in Jeff ought to whip the Barbarian."[36] James Weldon Johnson noted that "the security of the white civilization and white supremacy depended upon the defeat of Jack Johnson," and in the "red-blooded style of the day" Jeffries "was bound to win" because "the Negro had nothing but the jungle; that the Negro would be licked the moment the white man looked him in the eye."[37] Max Balthazar, a white writer for the *Omaha Daily News,* claimed that Jeffries would "restore to the Caucasians the crown of elemental greatness as measured by strength of brow, power of heart and lung, and withal, that cunning or keenness that denotes mental as well as physical superiority."[38] As sports historian John Hoberman observed, the "inhumanity of this sort of reasoning was rationalized in accordance with the social Darwinism of the era and its ethos of a competitive racial fight to the finish."[39]

The fight became a laboratory for social critics eager to prove their racial hypotheses. Writing days before the fight, columnist Alfred Henry Lewis maintained that Jeffries would win because "Jeffries has imagination; Johnson has none." Johnson, Lewis posited, is "essentially African" and "feels no deeper than the moment, sees no further than his nose," and is "incapable of anticipation."[40] According to *Fairplay Magazine,* Johnson was nothing more than a "huge primordial beast,"[41] whose brute strength might provide some success but only early in the bout. During the last decade of the nineteenth and first decade of the twentieth century, concepts of race classified peoples and categorized ethnicities according to biological "traits." Books such as Frederick L. Hoffman's *Race Traits and Tendencies of the American Negro* (1896), Charles Carroll's *The Negro as Beast* (1900), Thomas Nelson Page's *The Negro: The Southern's Problem* (1904), Thomas Dixon's *The Clansman* (1905), Robert Shufeldt's *The Negro: A Menace to American Civilization* (1907), Alfred P. Schultz's *Race or Mongrel* (1908), and William P. Pickett's *The Negro Problem* (1909) advanced the theories of racial supremacy.[42] According to historian Richard Hofstadter, the "Darwinian mood" surfacing in the late nineteenth and early twentieth century "sustained the belief in Anglo-Saxon racial superiority which obsessed many American thinkers."[43]

By 1910 the science of racialism had gained considerable credibility in academic and intellectual circles.[44] Scientists maintained the assumptions that there were divergent strands of human genetic development and that genes—commonly referred to as "blood" lines—manifested in race, with one gene (black) deemed degenerative while the other (white) was considered progressive. For instance, John W. Burgess wrote in 1902:

> The claim that there is nothing in the color of the skin from the point of view of political ethics is a great sophism. A black skin means membership in a race of men which has never of itself succeeded in subjecting passion to reason, has never, therefore, created any civilization of any kind.[45]

Sociologist George W. Stocking contends that turn-of-the-century concerns with antediluvian analysis of the "blood" of a culture—and by extension the "race"—promoted the investigations of cultural atavism's racially transmitted characteristics.[46] By the early twentieth century, biologists, sociologists, anthropologists, historians, journalists, and novelists lent support to the doctrine that races were separate entities, with the Anglo-Saxon or Caucasian superior to them all.[47] Social scientists and fight analysts went along with these ideas and used the fight as a paradigm that would prove racial difference and superiority. "Utter opposites," Waldemar Young reported in the *San Francisco Chronicle*; the fighters, he claimed in 1910, possessed "differences of disposition," dependent upon "that heritage which is of ancestry ages old."[48] This view, supported by social Darwinism and the vogue of biological ethnology, epitomized the racial divide surrounding the fight.[49]

The problem of the color line surfaced in terms of gender as well as race. Both Johnson and Jeffries embodied, by proxy of their respective races, the era's conception of black and white manhood. They became larger-than-life figures, symbols of masculine prowess. Publicity had endowed both with folk-hero status.[50] Men throughout the United States vicariously identified with the fighters, affixing their concepts of masculinity to them.[51] One example of this identification was in music. Songwriter Dorothy Forrester penned song lyrics that paid homage to Jeffries. "Jim-a-da-Jeff," using a stereotypical and condescending Italian dialect, urged Jeffries to beat the "coon" and wipe "Africa" off the "map."

Commence right away to get into condish,
An' you punch-a da bag-a day and night,
An'a den pretty soon, when you meet-a de coon,
You knock-a him clear'a outa sight.
[. . .]
Who give-a da Jack Jonce one-a little-a tap?
Who make-a him take-a one big-a long nap?
Who wipe-a da Africa off-a de map?
It's da Jim-a-da-Jeff.[52]

As the fight drew near, newspapers and magazines projected a Manichean battle between the best of the races. Because of their legendary status—the fighters' alleged sexual prowess, their skills and talents in the ring, and their reputation for unprecedented courage—interest in the fight was greater than usual.

The fight and its social context were inseparable. Most significant was the concept of white supremacy, which was one idea behind induced segregation. This social division insured diverse, culturally defined meanings of "identity," yielding differences in circumstances, life conditions, and worldviews. These differences existed not only in the South; the rise of black urban populations in the North created cities within cities. Prior to the fight, two secretaries of the National Negro Political League, Alexander Walters and Monroe Trotter, declared at a league meeting: "race persecution infects the North," and "color prejudice is on the increase." Racial discrimination in "civil rights and in economic opportunities," they observed, was "gaining ground." They concluded:

> Jim Crow [railway] cars have reached the borders of the nations capital, [and] color disenfranchisement has raised its horrid head above the Mason and Dixon line, while bloody race riots and barbarous lynchings have reached up to Illinois, even to the home of the martyred Lincoln.[53]

Throughout Jack Johnson's and Jim Jeffries's adult lives, segregation resulted in distinctively different living conditions. These social divisions led to differences in standards and values. Days before the fight, novelist Rex Beach wrote that when "these two gladiators" enter the ring, "they will represent not only the highest physical types of their respective races, but also two utterly different and distinctive patterns of the human animal."[54] Beach's comments, while based on biological assumptions, are not entirely wrong. His comments resonate because of the environments from which these fighters emerged, producing different ideas about masculinity and identity. These ideas, in turn, affected both the way the fighters were perceived, analyzed, and incorporated into the body politic, as well as the attitudes of the fighters themselves. By linking the fight to these ideas, we can better understand how the era's culturally constructed identities developed.

By "culturally constructed identities" I mean a collection of gestures, attitudes, and locutions that exist separately from individual qualities such as genetic makeup. The distinctions between black and white cultures at the time reflected different worlds and ways of knowing. These differences led to antagonism: this was manifest in the spurious doctrine of racial superiority and the reactions against its effects by social movements pursuing equality and justice. The division was held up to scrutiny by many whites and found to be morally sound and legally justifiable; many blacks found it unjustified and immoral. In 1901, W. E. B. Du Bois made note of the fact that in many cities and towns, particularly in the South but in the North as well, it was as if there was a "straight line drawn down the middle of main street," separating the races and ensuring that "the best of the Negroes almost never live in anything like close proximity" with whites.[55] Despite protests by some, these two cultures, separated by clearly marked borders, inevitably created distinct lifeworlds. Rather than "imagined communities," as historian Benedict Anderson would have it, where social groups formed discrete subcultures imaginarily,[56] the results of segregation created real differences with real consequences, producing different values by exclusive local consensus that expressed different relationships. Cultural conditions defined the whole way of life for these groups as living social bonds, saturated with shared beliefs and interests, that linked knowledge, art, morals, and customs into social rules, symbolic structures, and systems of meaning.

Culture itself is a construct based on gestural and lexical codes that supply meaning in social intercourse. It defines identity to varying degrees; codes of behavior are consolidated by individual routine and reinforced by habits, customs, and traditions.[57] By definition, culture is not the individual but the collective values describing group attitudes that inform everyday life. In the social world of 1910, Jim Crow segregation affected every aspect of cultural and daily life. The concept of the color line ensured that spatial divisions would be enforced. This cartographic logic was justified by the argument that, since continents, zones, and climates already separated the races, regions within the United States should be similarly bound by geographic distinctions. Racial differences were spatialized as "natural" divisions according to human sciences and regional mappings. Since races allegedly originated in difference parts of the world, it was deemed fitting that the laws should continue to enforce these borders. For instance, in *The Spirit of America,* Henry van Dyke rationalized the racial division in 1910:

> Nine millions of Negroes, largely ignorant and naturally ill-fitted for self-government, are domiciled in the midst of a white population which in some sections of the South they outnumber. How to rule, protect, and educate this body of colored people; how to secure them in their civil rights without admitting them to a racial mixture—that is the problem.[58]

At the same time, African Americans were reminded at every turn that they had no more rights than beasts of burden, lacking access to public facilities beyond those marked "colored," and denied admittance to economic opportunities.

The white majority defined the boundaries within which African Americans could live, with African Americans, for the most part, fearing to cross these boundaries. This fear, Leon F. Litwack observes, "haunted black men and women in their daily routines, compelling them to act with extreme caution in the presence of whites."[59] In streetcars, restaurants, libraries, athletic fields, hospitals, hotels, restrooms, drinking fountains, parks, cemeteries, schools, saloons, telephone booths, theatres, prisons, brothels, clubs, and churches, blacks were reminded daily of their "proper" status.

For black Americans, segregation was not merely a betrayal of Reconstruction and conscription to the ghetto; it restricted hope by denying their participation in the new American economy. In the transition from the Gilded Age to the Progressive era (circa 1900 to 1910), the mass production of steel, coal, and other manufacturing items such as automobiles, as well as emerging urbanization, created an abundance of consumer goods. Entrepreneurial opportunities abounded, but only for some. Even the ordinary citizen, enjoying newfound status in middle management, seized opportunities to expand their monetary base by creating investments. With this came leisure activities and middle-class life. But for black people, the new prosperity was not feasible; cut off from America's wealth, many blacks turned to restricted areas of employment: domestic service, Pullman porters, farmers, and manual laborers. The highest levels of attainment were artisanship and professions internal to the black community: teachers, barbers, morticians, artisans, ministers, lawyers, doctors, and shopkeepers. Due to segregation, few gained access to higher education and the more lucrative professions. For many, performance areas such as entertainment and sports were limited but enticing roads to success; yet even these would be restricted by segregation.

Prizefighting, however, became the one sport where blacks gained entry, albeit minimally. This was due, in part, to the interest of the white public in boxing and often in certain all-black fights held in controlled arenas, known as the "battle royale." The "battle royale," surfacing in the late nineteenth century, was a "sport" where several black fighters were placed blindfolded in a ring, and fought until one remained standing. Coins were often tossed in the ring; the lone fighter remaining upright would pick up the coins as "profit." Johnson himself experienced the "battle royale" as a teenager.[60] This brutal entertainment for white audiences became part of the early "training" of black fighters. As more black fighters participated in the battle royale, their fighting skills gained recognition. Gradually, black fighters, by insisting on fighting white fighters, broke the color barrier in the lighter professional divisions, winning titles and gaining recognition. In addition, the black fighters slowly emerged as a symbol of success and social achievement in the black community. As the heavyweight champion,

Johnson's significance as a symbol of accomplishment and defiance was evident in his victory parade in Chicago days after the fight. Despite the race riots that pervaded the country, the black urban neighborhood of Chicago was overflowing with pride. According to one black newspaper:

> Jack Johnson came to town with the "blare of trumpets." The citizens clung to the wheels of his chariot; drew from there the horses and bore him on broad shoulders high above the shouting multitudes. Not since the gladiator days of Rome has there been a scene enacted as that which greeted Johnson's return from Reno. His pathway was strewn with flowers; rich and poor alike lost distinction in the crushing throng to seize his hand.[61]

The *Richmond Planet* reported: "no event in forty years has given more genuine satisfaction to the colored people of this country than has the signal victory of Jack Johnson."[62] Jack Johnson had begun to change the perception of African Americans, a perception that had complicated and lasting ramifications.

BOXING, PROFESSIONALISM, AND MASCULINITY

Johnson has shown that he has only the instincts of a nigger — pure nigger.   —Post-fight review (1908)[63]

If, as Terry Eagleton asserts, the aesthetic "is born as a discourse of the body,"[64] then the black and white bodies in the boxing ring became cultural symbols of masculine athletics and aesthetics. In boxing, the body is not only visible, demonstrating brawn and fluidity of muscle and flexibility, but it is also said to reveal style, courage, and identity *through performance*. Nearly all the embodiments of physical manhood — strength, reflexes, bravery, endurance, speed, technique, concentration, strategy, and the ability to administer punishment while withstanding pain — are legitimized in boxing. Boxers possess "weapons" (hook, jab, straight punch, counterpunch, footwork, defense, and combinations), move with "grace," and demonstrate "aggressive" behavior that, in the formal representation of boxing, combines numerous qualities, among them the art of warfare, the mobility of a dancer, the strategic planning of a chess player, and underlying psychology.

By the late nineteenth century, attention to boxing as a sport had risen rapidly. Although many viewed it as barbaric and sought restrictive laws to prohibit it, its popularity was undeniable.[65] Through prizefighting, the male body was itself a symbol. Not only did the sport demonstrate individual skill and courage, it also represented performative technique. A fighter was deemed aggressive or defensive, a puncher or a counterpuncher, skilled in footwork or devastating power, and fight fans would vicariously link their own sense of identity to these individualistic styles. Boxing became metaphoric, as writers waxed poetic and readers identified with fighters who best exemplified various attributes of fighting skills. Moreover, in an era obsessed with ethnic categorization, race entered the discourse and fighters became associated with styles according to race. White fighters, for instance, were allegedly "thinking fighters," while black fighters were mere "naturals" possessing instinct but no intelligence. The body of the fighters would, it was claimed, demonstrate these "truths" by revealing the ways in which they fought. Thus a fighter might be called a "legitimate white man" because he fought in a particular style attributable to white men. Consequently, boxing became the paradigmatic struggle over what Pierre Bourdieu calls "the definition of the *legitimate body* and the *legitimate use of the body*" (emphasis in original).[66] The legitimation of bodily "style" became a central objective; boxing would provide visible "proof" of race-based theories through the performative style.

Prize fighting became popular during the turn of the century as a sport because it fell in line with a nation infatuated with masculine prowess and physical hardihood. The pugnacious President Theodore Roosevelt helped transform "the doctrine of the strenuous life" into a national obsession. In promoting a more vigorous lifestyle, Roosevelt enjoined American men in 1905 to throw off the "life of ease" and embrace "the life of strenuous endeavor," so that they would not miss the opportunity to "win for themselves the domination of the world."[67] Roosevelt himself boxed as a Harvard undergraduate, reportedly demonstrating "coolness and skill" in the ring despite his slight frame.[68]

Boxing offered the theatrical display of adolescent masculinity in a controlled environment. Cities across the country hosted boxing clubs where men trained during the day in the art of fisticuffs and participated at night in rituals of drinking, carousing, and letting off steam. These clubs provided a release from the era's constraining gentility. Boxing was also the focus of a new professionalism, the "sweet science" where fighters "plied their trade," using brute strength, hand speed, feints, psychology, strategy, and mental will. While the machine replaced the artisan who was unable to compete with the efficiency of the assembly line, at least boxing—the "science" of boxing—retained the concept of craftsmanship that had been the bailiwick of the artisan. Thus, the image of a "fighting machine" emerged, with Jeffries as its principal symbol. As Michael Kimmel reminds us, newspapers reported boxers who "went to work" or "made good work" of their opponents, converting the nineteenth-century terminology of "craft," "labor," and "work" into the boxing metaphors.[69] Moreover, growing approval of individualism bolstered boxing as a sport; prizefighting's one-man showmanship showcased strength, courage, identity, cunning, and individual style. In 1910, Richard Barry wrote:

> In our complex civilization, where it is sometimes difficult to tell whether the man with whom you have been neighbor all your life has or has not a yellow streak, where interests are so refined and occupations so highly specialized, the prize-fighter stalks forth as a crude but glaring type of the individual.[70]

In the face of criticism that boxing remained barbaric no matter how many regulations were imposed, boxing's proponents, such as Duffield Osborn, defended prizefighting; he maintained in 1888 that the "manly art" countered the "mere womanishness" of modern, over-refined society. Boxing's rigorous training and demand for courage in the face of pain and fatigue would advance "high manly qualities" over the "mawkish sentimentality" that had become the era's "shibboleth of progress, civilization and refinement."[71] Along similar lines, E. D. Cope argued in 1893 that the "effeminisation of man" could be countered with lessons in boxing. Boxing would teach men calmness under duress: "a cool head is essential to success in all conflicts," Cope explained, "and the training which develops this trait, which is nascent, if not well developed in most men, is of great value to them."[72] Boxing replaced bare-knuckle fighting as the main attraction in popular sports, unsullied by the barbarism of bare knuckles. It now had rules, regulations, and structure provided by the Marquis of Queensbury Rules (drafted in 1865 to replace the London Prize Ring Rules, and widely adopted in 1892 to include gloves, discourage wrestling, and limit rounds to 3 minutes). These rules brought to boxing a semblance of dignity, form, and some of society's tacit approval. In his important study, *The Manly Art*, Elliot J. Gorn observed that boxing's toughness, ferocity, prowess, and honor became "the touchstone of maleness" upholding the "definition of manhood." By the turn of the century, heavyweight champion John L. Sullivan had come to symbolize what Gorn called the "growing desire to smash through the fluff of bourgeois gentility and the tangle of corporate ensnarement to the throbbing heart of life."[73]

Throwing off the gentility of the Victorian period, boxing became the symbol of the new, progressive American male who had returned to nature, embraced physical combat, showed mental toughness, tossed aside the trappings of civilization, and demonstrated the ability to use the mind in combat. It was one way of developing the skills essential to manhood since it served to strengthen both mind and body equally, establishing what John Boyle O'Reilly called a "sound mind in a sound body." In his book, *Ethics of Boxing and Manly Sports*

(1888), O'Reilly claimed that boxing "exercises the whole man at once and equally—the trunk, the limbs, the eyes—and the mind." Many at the time agreed with O'Reilly that a boxer in action "has not a loose muscle or a sleepy brain cell. His mind is quicker and more watchful than a chess-player's."[74] Boxing helped counter the fears of the emasculating effects of modern, corporate culture and the challenges surfacing from the New Woman, inspiring in men an ideal of revitalized manhood.

However, if boxing existed as the testing ground for male superiority, then Johnson challenged the racial superiority of whites. When Johnson won the title in 1908, white men, writes Gail Bederman, "clamored for Jeffries to ameliorate the situation and restore manhood to what they believed was its proper functioning."[75] Johnson had not only defeated Burns in 1908 to obtain the heavyweight title; he flaunted his position as a superior male, mocking the ineptitude of white fighters. His provocative style, relationships with white women, and confidence became unbearable for white supremacists. According to Johnson's biographer Al-Tony Gilmore, one of his most daring and provocative acts came during sparring sessions when Johnson "wrapped his penis in gauze bandages, enhancing its size for all onlookers, and strolled around the ring."[76] His behavior provoked envious hostility among whites, inspiring one newspaper editorial to produce a photo of a young white girl pointing a finger at Jim Jeffries, imploring: "Please Mr. Jeffries, Are You Going to Fight Mr. Johnson?" (See figure 3).[77] The photo suggests that Jeffries must fight to secure the safety of civilization and children. People looked to Jeffries as the last resort; as Jeffries put it in 1908, days before the Burns–Johnson fight: "If that coon comes around here with a challenge," he said, "I'll grab him by the neck and run him out."[78] In 1910, Jeffries was called upon to live up to his word.

White Americans considered the usurpation of the heavyweight title a contravention of the social fabric. According to social critic Jarvis Anderson, not only had the "championship—one of the most prized possessions in the trophy room of white supremacy—passed into the hands of the Negro race but the agent of its passing was a man who seemed to have no sense of his place in American life."[79] Fearful of the repercussion of a Johnson victory, John Callan O'Laughlin reported in the *Chicago Tribune* on the day of the fight that if "the black man wins the fight ignorant members of his race may feel like conquerors." Johnson's potential victory, O'Laughlin warned, would "increase the confidence" of black people, "cause them to be less respectful of the power of the whites," and might encourage African Americans "to acts which formerly they would dare not commit."[80] This breakdown of the social hierarchy led to a demand for redress.

WHITE MANHOOD: "BURROWING IN" AND "MIND OVER MATTER"

Jeff is an aggressive fighter, and he will necessarily be the aggressor in the coming battle. . . . Johnson is trained to fight on the defensive. He has always fought on the defensive, and he doesn't know how to fight offensively unless he has a much smaller and weaker man in front of him.[81]

As the "white hope," Jim Jeffries's symbolism for white culture went beyond the sport of prizefighting. As the fight drew closer, white manhood was on the line; what emerged in the discourse surrounding the fight were two "characteristics" of whiteness: the white man's so-called bullish bravery and his alleged mental superiority. Bullish bravery meant an unflinching, straight-ahead style that mirrored white attitudes toward life. Jeffries's method, exaggerated by the hyperbolic imagination of writers and critics, symbolized white masculinity's ability to *hold ground*. White manhood, unyielding and dependable, was conceived as stalwart, fearless, and lacking frivolity. Jeffries would also represent, in the words of his contemporaries, a "thinking man." White masculinity would be shown to remain undaunted in a crisis; through Jeffries's victory, mental superiority and a straight-ahead, no-nonsense approach would vicariously personify white manhood.

Jeffries's style was relentless. Critics maintained that he would "burrow in" and march forward, "determined" and "undaunted." Jeffries, said Jack London, "will force the fight and persistently hunt his man from gong to gong."[82] Jeffries, argued Bob Fitzsimmons, "bores right into the thick of it, shuts his jaw and takes what is coming and gives a little bit more."[83] Johnson was perceived as a defensive fighter, always talking, smiling, and oblivious to the pressures of the fight. White critics noted Johnson's behavior as frivolous, undisciplined, and confirming the clichés associated with African Americans. Jeffries, by contrast, was steady and dependable. He charged forward in a straight line and this charge would symbolize fearless white men. As Jeffries himself put it:

> It is my intention to go right after my opponent and knock him out as soon as possible. I intend to take a large amount of punishment in order to get to him quickly. But you may depend that I'll deliver a greater and more severe amount of punishment in return.[84]

It was supposed that Jeffries would prevail if only because of his superior endurance. Social scientists supported the view that African Americans lacked the ability to endure. Charles E. Woodruff, for instance, wrote in 1907 that in tropical climates "the excessive light prods the nervous system to do more than it should, and in time such constant stimulation is followed by irritability and finally by exhaustion."[85] In addition, Johnson's alleged indolence was supposed to prove that his race lacked the mental fortitude to endure in a long bout. The *New York Times* reported on the eve of the fight that Johnson is "care free and cool. He seems to take to the game with indifference and not the slightest sign of worry appears in his demeanor." Jeffries, by contrast, "is a different type of man. He is far-seeing and undoubtedly possesses the worrying qualities of the white race."[86] Tip Wright, covering the pre-fight events for the *Omaha Daily News*, admitted that Johnson put in "strenuous road work, gymnasium work and boxing," which would indicate Johnson's dedication. Nevertheless, Wright offered stereotypical definitions of black men, calling Johnson "just a great big, good-natured darky, out for a frolic, with little real work to do once in a while."[87] Fight analyst Mike Murphy was more blunt, saying that Johnson was "loose," having no "concentration." He added: "If he don't wake up, he might get knocked out in the first round."[88] Former fight trainer and football player Tom Shevlin summed up the prevailing view; Johnson, he claimed, has "no concentration. He's going up against a locomotive for two hours, and he don't know it."[89]

There was nothing deceptive in Jeffries; no mask hid the "authentic" man. He would win not by trickery but by the force of his "locomotive" will and brute strength. Jeffries was a "real" fighter who "bored in" like a "bull." Johnson's performance, in the final analysis, was deemed cowardly. He might hurt Jeffries early but this would be a mere distraction.[90] As fight trainer Pat Kenrick put it, Johnson was "too cowardly"; Johnson, he said was "undoubtedly clever," but "he isn't going to outbox Jeffries."[91] In his pre-fight analysis, Mike Murphy reported in the *New York Herald*: "Personally I know that Johnson is going to be a pretty much scared fighter before he goes into the ring."[92] Along similar lines, James Corbett emphasized Jeffries's relentlessness: "Jeffries is the embodiment of all that is powerful and brutish in the white man," while Johnson, in contrast, belonged to a race that "feared the white man." Corbett predicted that after Johnson "has pounded Jeffries in every conceivable place and then repeated it all over again, and Jim keeps stalking in, always coming, never receding," then "Johnson's heart will just evaporate."[93] Corbett considered Johnson a "careless child," and said Jeffries's fighting abilities would "paralyze Johnson's arms and faculties."[94] Arthur Ruhl best represents the prevailing white view:

> The betting was 10 to 6 or 7 on Jeffries and the talk about 1,000 to 1. You
> couldn't hurt [Jeffries]—Fitzsimmons had landed enough times to kill an ordi-

nary man in the first rounds, and Jeffries had only shaken his head like a bull and bored in. The Negro might be a clever boxer, but he has never been up against a real fighter before. He had a yellow streak, there was nothing to it, and anyway, let's hope he kills the coon.[95]

Jack London, reporting the fight for the *New York Herald*, summed up the disposition of both fighters at the opening:

Dark and somber and ominous was [Jeffries's] face, solid and stolid and expressionless, with eyes that smoldered and looked savage. The man of iron, grim with determination, sat down in his corner. And the care free negro smiled and smiled. And that is the story of the fight.[96]

Jeffries symbolized for whites all that was powerful and manly. He could, at times, explode, but his explosive power was a manifestation of fierce pride and untamed individualism. "Had Jeffries lived thousands of years ago," Corbett claimed, "when strength and courage made kings, he would have reigned supreme among his fellow men."[97] He personified the imperial might of the white race. Even in defeat, white style was defended. Richard Broome, for instance, observed that in the Johnson–Burns fight, Burns's "boxing brain and courage were the attributes most journalists stressed," and that the fight "was portrayed as a contest between the brains and dedication of Burns and the brute strength and flashiness of Johnson."[98] Johnson was all "flash" but no substance, a mere "brute" who had to be contained.

Jeffries was represented as possessing superior mental ability as well. As one journalist put it: "I do not think Johnson is equal in the all important matter of brains."[99] It was believed that a white fighter's superior intellect would enable him to defeat a black fighter. Excuses were made that Burns's defeat was the result of his smaller size rather than his lack of brainpower. Randolph Bedford expressed the view of many when he wrote, "the white beauty [Burns] faced the black unloveliness, forcing the fight, bearing the punishment as if it were none." Despite the fact that Johnson's "weight and reach were telling against [Burns's] intrepidity, intelligence, and lightness," Burns's "courage still shone in his eyes."[100]

Newspapers and social scientists helped perpetuate the myth of Jeffries's mental superiority by drawing caricatures of Johnson as primitive and ape-like, incapable of thinking or planning. In a cartoon in the *New York Times* on the eve of the fight, Johnson is depicted as apish, while Jeffries appears barrel-chested, muscular, and imposing (see figure 4).[101] Jeffries is posed sideways and is staring at Johnson, his weight on one foot, giving the appearance of calm before the storm. What is significant is the size of Jeffries's chest, symbolizing his large "heart," or courage. Johnson, in contrast, faces straight ahead, with long primate arms draped to the canvas, his head bowed in fear. A white woman with an American flag held high seems to be applauding the inevitable outcome. William H. Wiggins describes the cartoon as "contrasting stereotypes" in which Jeffries is "positively portrayed as the strong white champion, complete with bowed belt tied around his trim waist," while "disdainfully glaring" at Johnson.[102] The black body in the drawing represents African Americans as animals located somewhere on the chain of being between man and ape. Johnson became the timeless "primitive," a stereotype in which the black man is denied dignity and self-expression. Displayed for the gaze of whites, Johnson is stripped of his humanity; he is, as psychiatrist and cultural historian Frantz Fanon put it succinctly, "*fixed*" and laid bare for whites to "objectively cut away slices" of African American existence.[103]

Johnson doubtlessly possessed talent and ring savvy; white critics realized this fact. What critics *needed to prove* was his inferiority to Jeffries. Jeffries victory alone would not suffice; the styles of each fighter had to be evaluated and critiqued, for it was in the body and its performance that such theories were tested. An essay entitled "The Psychology of the Prize Fight" in *Current Literature* went the furthest in defending the presumption of white mental superiority demonstrated in performance. The article reported that the "superiority of the brain of the white man" would triumph because the "white man's brain is a finer intellectual instrument than is that of the black brother." The essay asserted that the "psychological factor" would enable Jeffries to beat Johnson because if Johnson were "faced by an antagonist only slightly his inferior physically and much his superior intellectually he would go down to defeat—other things being equal." Despite the fact that Johnson would have the upper hand in the early rounds, due to the "fact" that the "negro is more emotional than the white man," the white man's alleged intellectual superiority "will emerge from the emotional crisis . . . much ahead of his black rival." The article concluded that the "enormous advantage of the white man should consist in his ability to make a fight last." Johnson's victories came only in shorter fights. This, the article concluded, "is the black man's psychology. He fights emotionally, whereas the white man can use his brain after twenty rounds."[104] Three years after the fight, white critics persisted in these same notions of white mental superiority. The *Cleveland Leader*, in manufacturing an excuse for Jeffries, reported that Jeffries's "Caucasian mind," replete with "vast concentration of thought, was overwhelmed. So he blundered through the fight and lost."[105] Johnson, by implication, lacked depth of thought to worry and won as a result. Along similar lines, an editorial from *Current Opinion* reported that Jeffries was "always intellectual in his methods," whereas in Johnson "we have what is called the artistic temperament, likewise valuable in the modern prize ring, although less useful than the scientific attitude."[106]

The devices invented by white culture to explain identity and fighting style eventually turned to the subject's fixed sense of self as a source for self-actualization and social representation. White culture searched for a principle of self-identity in a consciousness that remained steady, reliable, grimly determined, and iron-willed in the face of change. The need for steadiness became a protocol for identity. White masculinity would remain unflinching and straightforward in the face of modernity's rapidly changing, industrialized world. Jeffries was said to pulverize his opponents, while Johnson often out-boxed them. Johnson, to be sure, was quite capable of brutal infighting; but this was not the basis of his reputation. Jeffries was a one-dimensional fighter who would smash his opponents relentlessly in "locomotive" fashion and emerge the victor based on "brutish" and "intellectual" merits rather than nuance and finesse.

The architects of white masculinity—particularly social scientists, novelists, and journalists—defined "fixity" of self as an unwavering sense of purpose and "courage." The quest for a stable and unchanging notion of masculinity was part of the need among white men to solve the problems of fragmentation and rapid change that accompanied the industrial age. "Civilized" white men of the era were thus said to be firm in character, self-reliant, and self-controlled. Other virtuous roles included protectors of women and children and bearers of stalwart morals in the face of instability created by rapid social change. When technology brought change, the white man's inner moral strength would counterbalance these changes with steadiness of character. White men were fathers and breadwinners who held firm to values in opposition to supposedly whimsical wives who were held hostage to fashion and caprice. This hegemonic construction of white manhood balanced unflinching stability and dependability against the allegedly skittish behavior of women and people of color. Within this identity formation, masculine silence and strength represented a monadic consistency and fundamental rigidity, which would provide assurance that men—real men—guaranteed security amid transitions.

Rigidity avoided all determinants of social history, fads, and trends that came with the changing times. Jeffries symbolized these attributes. The fact that, at the time of Burns's defeat in 1908, Jeffries was in poor shape—"very fat and entirely out of condition," reported one newspaper—was of little consequence.[107] Jack London summed up the conception of Jeffries and the white man's "mental superiority" versus Johnson's characteristics:

[Jim Jeffries] is a thinker. A silent man is usually a thinker, and because Jeffries does not blurt out all he knows to the first chance comer is no sign that he does not know a great deal back behind those searching black eyes. Quite in contrast is care-free, happy Jack Johnson. Nobody was ever more gregarious than he, ever happier to greet old friends and make new ones.[108]

London maintained that as the fight progressed Johnson "will talk less and less, and his famous smile will fade from his lips."[109] This dichotomy between silence and gregariousness, private versus public, "thinking" Jeffries and the alleged "non-thinking," carefree, and smiling Johnson, established a deeper division.

The scrutiny of the fight by intellectual spectators such as London symbolized a Cartesian paradigm of analysis, where mental activity (*res cognitas*) identified the mind with what is inner, and the body with outward sensations (*res extensa*). While the Cartesian model of the mind argues that the external world is the source of many private sensations, confirmation of these sensations is less objective, and therefore less reliable, than pure mental activity. The gap between the internal and the external is thus firmly grounded. "I recognize only two ultimate classes of things," Descartes contends: "first, intellectual or thinking things, i.e., those which pertain to mind or thinking substance; and secondly, material things, i.e., those which pertain to extended substance or body." The mind is the thinking and perceiving "being," which involves both perception and volition. Minds are referred to as "thinking substances,"[110] with mental activity incorporeal and non-spatial. The mind, as Descartes put it, is "entirely distinct from the body and is even easier to know than the body,"[111] because the mind exists as a separate substance unrelated to outside influences that complicate matters. It was this notion of the mind as separate and manageable that lent support to the belief that Jeffries, by his awareness of such distinctions, could overcome retirement and defeat Johnson.

The mind-body duality expressed by social scientists and cultural critics surfaced in various descriptions of the fight. Rex Beach, for instance, asserted that Jeffries "possesses a mentality lacking in his antagonist." For Beach, "mind is stronger than matter," adding that the "man of education will outlast the man of ignorance in any test of endurance, be they evenly matched in strength."[112] The concept of mind over matter, specifically the mind's ability to overcome fatigue, was made to reflect in a fundamental way the Cartesian duality, and many fighters shared the belief that the mental could be psychologically detached from the physical. For example, middleweight prizefighter Stanley Ketchel, who lost to Jack Johnson in 1909, explained his fighting philosophy this way:

I say to my body, "Come on now, we've got to lick this fellow." I treat my body just as if it were another person, a friend of mine, a pretty good friend, too. So my body gets up and comes into the ring with me, and I say to my body, "Now don't get anxious; he's worse scared than you are! And don't get in a hurry; just take your time."[113]

Ketchel's use of the inner-outer metaphor is emblematic of the dual substance theory of reality. The body exists in space, subject to laws of mechanics and the deterioration of age; but the mind operates independently, known through intro-spection, and functions privately. Ketchel and Jeffries thus personified the fight-ers who employed the interiorized mental will, "thinkers" whose thoughts are hidden but whose behavior exemplifies quiet, internal dignity and prowess as ex-emplars of whiteness.

After Jeffries's defeat, the status of boxing in the public mind lost its nobility and deteriorated to mere brawling. Sports historian Frederic Cople Jaher con-tends that the mass media that had built up the fight as a contest of racial su-premacy now "proclaimed that it merely proved that 'the best fighter comes from the lowest and least developed race' and that boxing was a brutal sport that should be outlawed."[114] Prior to the fight, the subject was white superiority; after the fight, the discourse turned to the brutality of the sport. To be sure, many protested prize-fighting's brutality prior to the fight; however, for many their sentiment and sup-port for Jeffries overcame misgivings. It was only *after Jeffries's defeat* that the importance of prizefighting truly diminished. For instance, following a plethora of columns devoted to prizefighting as a paradigm of mental ability in sports, the *Chicago Tribune* reported in an editorial following the fight that it was "an ignoble pursuit."[115] President Theodore Roosevelt, who had previously endorsed prize-fighting, declared after the fight that despite being "always fond of boxing," prize-fighting "will, as it ought to, be stopped in every State in the Union."[116] Anti-boxing sentiment, coupled with riots, forced many city and state governments to ban the film of the fight. An editorial in the *Washington Evening Star* warned African Americans that they "must realize that it is a discredit rather than a matter of congratulations that one of their number has proved himself the greater brute in the professional prize ring."[117] A *New York Times* editorial was one of the few occa-sions where Johnson was treated sympathetically, albeit patronizingly:

> Let us admit that Johnson has borne himself decently and modestly, that, al-though the pugilist does not represent the highest type of physical manhood, by any means, yet he is an uncommonly fine specimen of his abnormal kind, and that he is, after all, an American citizen.[118]

The *Los Angeles Times*, however, was not so kind. In one editorial, it stated that soci-ety should not "pin too much racial importance" on the fight, since it was a victory of "brawn over brains." White concepts had been reversed, and now it was believed that "pugilism and civilization bear no direct connection, but are in inverse ratio." The *Times* warned African Americans to remember their "place" in society:

> Do not point your nose too high. Do not swell your chest too much. Do not boast too loudly. Do not be puffed up. Let not your ambitions be inordinate or take a wrong direction. Let no treasured resentments rise up and spill over. Remember, you have done nothing at all.[119]

At the conclusion of the fight, riots broke out in virtually every city in the United States. In New York, the *New York Herald* reported that "more than thirty thousand white men took possession of Eighth Avenue early in the evening" demanding, "let's lynch the first negro we see." When seeing a black man, many shouted "hang him to a lamp post!"[120] The *Times* reported that gangs of whites "formed for apparently the sole purpose of beating up whatever Negroes they could get their hands on," and in several instances African Americans "retaliated."[121] It would be many years before an interracial heavyweight championship fight would be staged again in the United States.

JOHNSON AND BLACK CULTURE

> *While Jack Johnson was clearly a source of pride to many blacks, and to some an alter ego, a man many blacks wished they could be—reckless, independent, bold, and superior in the face of whites—to many other blacks he was a source of embarrassment and resentment.*
> —Jeffrey T. Sammons (1990)[122]

Despite the fact that many African Americans held Jack Johnson in great esteem, the fight engendered mixed feelings. Johnson forced African Americans to confront two compelling issues: to live independently or to live in solidarity with the community. Freedom meant living autonomously; but it also meant turning away from the group. Johnson created a paradoxical situation in the African American community, where the issues of independence and solidarity clashed.

Johnson was simultaneously praised and condemned. For instance, the *Richmond Daily Planet* extolled the moment, noting, "no event in forty years has given more genuine satisfaction to the colored people of the country than has the signal victory of Jack Johnson."[123] Prior to the fight, Lester A. Walton, drama critic for the black newspaper the *New York Age,* called the "coming contest" the "all-absorbing topic for discussion everywhere."[124] By 1910 the segregation of blacks had labeled them "inferior." This system cut them off from opportunities and sent a humiliating message. The fight, then, was seen as vindication; if boxing were to be deemed a "manly art" denoting style and courage, then Johnson's victory ought to be perceived as setting the record straight. Learning of the impending fight, the Reverend Reverdy C. Ransom, prominent leader of the A. M. E. Church, said in 1909:

> The greatest marathon race of the ages is about to begin between the white race and the darker races of mankind. What Jack Johnson seeks to do to Jeffries in the roped arena will [do more for] the ambition of Negroes in every domain of human endeavor.[125]

Along similar lines, Walton reported following the fight that

> The result of the fight had a peculiar effect on the populace. . . . Seldom was a white brother seen to smile and appear as if pleased. The only people whose faces were bright and who went about in a light-hearted manner were the colored folks.[126]

Still, reaction was mixed; there was elation but also caution. A principal from a black industrial college warned that if Johnson won, "the anti-negro sentiment will quickly and dangerously collect itself ready to strike back at any undue exhibition of rejoicing on the part of negroes."[127] There was certainly cause for concern. *Current Literature* reported that within a "half hour after the result of the fight was announced to the country, race trouble broke out in New York and elsewhere."[128] In an effort to stem the violence, George L. Knox, publisher of the black newspaper *Indianapolis Freeman,* wrote the following editorial:

> We should not take Johnson's victory over Jeffries too seriously; it was a man to man fight . . . and not a matter of races. The promoters got it up, not as a race question, but purely as a financial scheme of their own. . . . Neither the white [n]or black should take this great prize fight seriously.[129]

Knox later warned Johnson to tone down his excessive lifestyle and urged him to behave like "a man."[130] Knox, a close associate of Booker T. Washington, did not want Johnson's victory to instigate trouble. Instead, he advised Johnson to "save his money," and "not go scattering it around the country and die in poverty as most prizefighters of our race have died."[131] Washington, who disapproved of Johnson and prizefighting in general, had himself said: "Jack Johnson has harmed rather than helped the race."[132] Washington, Knox, and other black leaders placed a premium on decorum; behavior that might have been regarded as "deviant" could play into the hands of those touting Johnson's extravagance as "typical" of the race. An editorial in the *New York Age* (which, like the *Freeman*, owed its allegiance to Booker T. Washington) reflected this sentiment as well, reporting that they were glad "that a Negro was the winner," but that "this does not mean that we approve of prize fighting." The editorial continued: "We cannot, from our point of view, see that prize fighting has ever pushed forward the civilization of any race." Johnson was urged to "conduct himself in a modest manner," since he "can hurt the race immeasurably just now if he goes splurging and making a useless, noisy exhibition of himself."[133] Johnson's conceit was seen as a danger to blacks wanting to curry white favor, but his antics were also viewed as a menace to African Americans seeking entry into the mainstream. It was important to the black bourgeoisie that his behavior not be emulated.

Yet his escapades were gaining appeal in the black community, and not all black leaders expressed disapproval of Johnson. Many felt that downplaying the fight's racial angle would depreciate Johnson's accomplishments and significance. Others sought to use his victory as an assault on white prejudice. Black newspapers such as the *Chicago Defender* and the *Chicago Broad Ax* attempted to show Johnson's victory as exemplary and to focus on his achievements. For instance, the *Chicago Broad Ax*, a black newspaper independent of Washington's influence, reported that Johnson was "the new gladiator, whose sledgehammer blows" and "scientifically directed" fighting skills "can wing any giant on the face of the earth."[134] The *Chicago Defender* and its publisher, Robert Sengstackle Abbott, also did their best to use Johnson for the cause of equality. In a drawing that ran for several months, the *Defender* depicted Johnson and Jeffries as decent men shaking hands. Jeffries, however, is surrounded with ghost-like apparitions who represent "Jim Crow delegations, Negro persecutors, race-hatred, and prejudice."[135] (See figure 5.) If Johnson wins in the face of all these obstacles, the caption says, "he is truly entitled to a Carnegie Hero Medal." Johnson forced the nation to reckon with his dominance in the ring, and his reputation was emulated by the African American masses.

Still, Johnson was not a willing "hero," and hardly the "New Negro" that Alain Locke would later envision in his book of the same name. He fought for himself, and in many important respects this made him more of a threat to the status quo than had he accepted the role that had been assigned to him. His strongly independent, almost anarchistic sense of freedom captured the imagination of the black public. His defiance was less a stance for civil rights and more an individual act of self-assertion. He could be "his own man," and in doing so became a cultural symbol. Johnson's popularity with the black masses was not based so much on his *resistance to racism* but rather on his *independence of racism*. This is a subtle yet meaningful difference; Johnson was not so much in opposition to white culture as he was attempting to assert his agency and individuality *despite racism.* It was Johnson's independence, and not his race consciousness, that made him popular with many black men; his autonomy embodied their ideals, or at least the hope that they, too, could forge self-assertion. However, such behavior defied racial solidarity.

The paradox that arose between the desire for independence, the pressures of group allegiance, and the realities of segregation cut deeply into the souls of many working-class and poor black people. Many African American leaders had so far failed to galvanize fully the new, urban community; frustrations with racial roadblocks were not entirely removed by black social leaders and their plans for improvements. The accommodationism of Booker T. Washington, while useful, failed to resonate with the concepts of independence and self-reliance. Washington's emphasis on industrial education, with his specific attention to the development of independent artisans, was, according to John Hope Franklin, "outmoded at the time he enunciated it, by the increasing industrialization of the country."[136] Others perceived the radical New Negro ideals of Du Bois and Locke as being for the elite, who often patronized the underclass. Johnson offered an alternative to accommodationism and elitism; he was perceived as an outward projection of an individualistic spirit and the source of an identity that sought opportunistic self-assertion devoid of group affiliations.

Adding to his "individualistic" spirit was the fact that Johnson's monetary successes were well publicized in the black newspapers. This bolstered his reputation and helped to establish his popularity among the masses. According to Walton, the black race could now be "in a position to boast of having one [Johnson] who can look down with some indifference on the office of chief executive of the nation when the question of earning power is made the topic of conversation." Johnson, Walton reported, "can now command a salary of over $100,000 a year in vaudeville." He had signed a contract with Oscar Hammerstein for "$2,500 a week to appear in the Victoria Theatre the week of July 11 [1910]."[137] In addition, he received $75,000 for the fight (Jeffries, as loser, received $25,000), $50,000 for the motion picture rights, and $135,000 through bets.[138] Johnson was rich, which aided his flamboyant lifestyle and earned him recognition everywhere he went. For working-class African Americans, Leon F. Litwack observed, "no other black person had displayed so impressively the ability to outwit, outthink, and outfight white folks."[139]

Independence and self-assertion, however, were beyond the means of most African Americans in any significant sense. In order to achieve the most minimal level of political efficacy, blacks had to accept either incremental processes or seize the initiative and risk social opprobrium. Johnson pursued the latter course and became a social hero. A hero, cultural historian Roger D. Abrahams informs us, "is a man whose deeds epitomize the masculine attributes most highly valued within such a society." Because of historical differences, however, black culture, he writes, "has a folklore of a very different dimension and character than that of any other group in the country." These dimensions are exemplified by "warlike and precarious behavior"; the black hero always must be "ready for a fight." However, given his tenuous connection with a group, he "fights for himself."[140] In many ways this definition fits Johnson; his aggressive and precarious behavior (he enjoyed driving and living fast) became the reason for his heroic status among many African Americans, yet his aims were completely self-serving.

For blacks at the time it was a hostile world. Jim Crow was not merely an abstraction that denied the spirit and blocked social advancement; the black body was marked and confined. The alienation of African Americans was related to body and space; it was the body that was spatially restricted and subjugated. Access to restaurants, water fountains, and restrooms was divided along racial lines. As a result of strictly enforced separation, blacks violating the rules were deemed potential outlaws. The act of the body moving from one spatially defined area to another was a possible act of lawbreaking. Any desire related to food, restrooms, sleep, etcetera, came precariously close to criminal trespass. "Blackness" thus teetered on the edge of criminality. Lewis R. Gordon astutely observes that, "in limiting the options available for blacks in every negotiation of social life," Jim Crow segregation "increased the probability of blacks breaking the law on an everyday basis." These limiting options, Gordon adds, "forced every black to face choices about the self that placed selfhood in conflict with humanhood."[141] Blacks literally walked a very fine "color" line of legality whenever they moved through social spaces.

In a world that established conditions of criminality by mere existence, Johnson was a realization of the existential outsider who lived by his own rules. Simply put, the body caught in the wrong place at the wrong time was in danger. Recognizing this condition of his life, Johnson accepted as well as ignored his "outlaw" status. Many emulated him because he lived and represented his own person yet refused to embrace the social implications of blackness. Like many African Americans, Johnson was adept at code switching, what is referred to in the black community as the ability to shift modes of speech in several different ways. Moving from "ordinary" speech to "in-group" talk is a function of daily life for many in African American communities, where the need to assert oneself in different conditions requires different modes of communication. These practices of survival were learned from trial and error, observation, imitation, and improvisation, and forged by the pressures of everyday existence. Johnson, however, defied these rules, choosing to marry whom he pleased, live the way he wanted, and speak as he wished. He put his body in jeopardy, fundamentally disregarding the potential for danger. Rather than the role of victim lashing out at society—a portrait of Johnson drawn by Howard Sackler's 1967 play, *The Great White Hope* (staged on Broadway in 1968 and filmed in 1970 with James Earl Jones in the title role)—Johnson's public persona more or less conveyed indifference to racial stereotyping, whether it be resistance or victimhood. He was well educated, fluent in French, and versed in literature. He would hold forth on many subjects (especially automobiles), refusing to kowtow to anyone, black or white. His refusal to heed labels and boundaries was something of an act of courage, what is referred to euphemistically as the "bad nigger."

Al-Tony Gilmore defines "bad nigger" as "the personality type who adamantly refuses to accept the place given to blacks in American society, and who frequently challenges the outer perimeters of expected behavior."[142] Johnson's disregard of danger, emphasis on sexual virility, extravagance, and insatiable love of the good life, elevated him to cult-like status. As a cult hero, the glorification of his outsiderness—his badness—was in part recognition of Johnson's refusal to submit to racist presumptions. Johnson defied all codes of conduct, choosing to live self-sufficiently and independent of external pressures. Despite constant harassment and occasional incarceration, Johnson became symbolic of an individualized life.

Johnson asserted his identity in defiance of what Frantz Fanon has dubbed the "fact of blackness," which, under the gaze of whites, is seen as a fixed and objectified "thing"; the "fact" of blackness is inescapable. Fanon recalls a child pointing him out to his mother and saying: "'Dirty nigger!' Or simply, 'Look, a Negro!'" He then adds:

> I came into the world imbued with the will to find a meaning in things, my spirit filled with the desire to attain to the source of the world, and then I found that I was an object in the midst of other objects.[143]

The passage eloquently expresses felt objectification; blackness is held prisoner to the gaze, and the fact of blackness snares him in a bind, giving him "two frames of reference within which he has to place himself": dirty nigger or self-effacing Negro.[144] Fanon's will to self-assertion is thwarted at every turn by objectification, with the whole history of African America bearing down. This relationship to history is rooted in everyday life. Every black person, Lewis R. Gordon explains, "*faces* history—*his* or *her* history—every day as a situation, as a choice": of how to stand in relation to oppression, whether to live as a being subsumed by oppression or to actively pursue liberation, or to live with mere indifference.[145] To be oneself outside of racial identity is to transcend racial "history" and thereby assert self-determination. This was an achievement nearly impossible for African Americans in Johnson's world. Yet that is precisely what Johnson set out to attain. To the degree that he accomplished this, it was a result of his being flexible, protean, and improvisational.

Johnson lived in a world that required near instantaneous decisions: how to negotiate the white world, how to react to the police, and how to function in a hostile environment required rapid evaluation. In Jim Crow America, the need to make choices and split-second decisions created a demand for flexibility and adaptability. The body was in constant danger of arrest, abuse, or humiliation. Even middle-class blacks were hardly immune from racism. It is thus no surprise that when Frantz Fanon refers to *l'expérience vécue du Noir* ("the lived experience of the black"), he means the experience of blackness in a racist world where the "body is surrounded by an atmosphere of certain uncertainty."[146] Because the spotlight was not generally focused on white people as it was on black people, the world of white people allowed them release from historical consciousness. The black body, by contrast, always stands for blackness in every conceivable way.

Improvisation, then, emerged as a means of coping with the historical condition of racism. Improvisation is not a definitive attribute of a group as a result of biology and genetics; such totalizing "essence" is blatantly false. Instead, improvisation is used in this case to define a "reactive device," with flexibility acting as a means of survival—flexibility is imperative in an antagonistic world. It is first of all the logical response to fixity, especially in reaction to a rigidity that deemed the self as less than human. The emphasis on spontaneity and the moment fostered process and creativity; this moment-by-moment life informed Johnson's worldview. Jeffries, it was argued, knew in advance how he was going to fight; his fighting strategy was usually pre-planned. As an experienced fighter, Jeffries no doubt accepted contingencies and knew that plans often need revision;[147] however, the extent of his flexibility fell far short of Johnson's. Johnson, too, had a plan, but his fighting style was less predictable, improvisation being a necessary function of his existence as well as of the fight itself. Black Americans did not perceive Johnson as lacking a sense of self, but it was of an improvisatory nature, and that is what helped him achieve victory.

Improvisation is, in fact, a mechanism expressive of individuality. It creates moments in performance that go beyond the predictable, asserting agency and self-awareness. It need not be a defiance of the rules; it may in fact be merely a way of performing within guidelines while being productively innovative in its execution. Quality improvisation respects the integrity of the game; it balances individual style with the game's rules, yet it offers an occasion for original expression. It amounts to a balancing act combining independence and interdependence; a performer must adhere to and play within the structures of the game, yet redefine the game according to individualistic and stylistic additions. Improvisation resists fixity by being both *proactive and reactive,* i.e., it is assertive, antiphonal, and cognizant of changing perceptions and circumstances. It thrives on change, adjustment, and flexibility.

For Johnson, the movement of the body paralleled a need for flexibility in social and cultural spheres. His bodily dynamic was a cultural insignia, creating what Ralph Ellison calls a "fluid style that reduced the chaos of living to form."[148] This style was one of improvisatory action and reaction; not merely strategy but strategies; and not merely pre-arranged plans but an intelligence that can willingly abandon all prior plans and adjust in the moment. Cultural historian Gena Dagel Caponi makes this point clear when she says that black style "evolved from a cultural willingness to improvise, from a cultural imperative to adapt, and in reaction to a rule change."[149]

Johnson gained the reputation as a "defensive" fighter.[150] But this is something of an oversimplification. For black people, having a fixed plan could be dangerous. Johnson as a fighter represented a sense of self that eschewed strict and rigid orthodoxies; instead, he epitomized temporal changes as part of life's processes. To be sure, Johnson fought at times with determined fixity just as Jeffries fought at times with flexibility. These strategies were not so much "facts" as they were concepts combined to define the fighters. What is significant is how the fighters incorporated the cultural identities of their respective groups. Johnson's self in action certainly displayed consistency of purpose; he differed from Jeffries to the degree that his knowledge of give-and-take of events and the emphasis on improvisation added to his style of fighting and plan of attack.

Improvisation is based on the moment of performance, but performance of any sort has rarely received intellectual acceptance. Performance is typically made to appear "instinctive," unshaped and devoid of strategy and intelligence. It is something that simply happens intuitively without design. Considered wholly spontaneous and aleatory, it is viewed as more luck than skill. African Americans are often derogatorily depicted as people invested in "impulse" and "instinct" over "reason." This is false as well as misleading. Rather than antithetical to reason, improvisation embodies reason to its fullest extent. Improvisation requires thought as well as impulse; it simultaneously demands experience, intelligence, and creativity. African American music, for example, is often recognized for its reasoned improvisation and this improvisational capacity is seldom ignored. However, less attention has been paid to African American improvisation in other areas of performance, which has shortchanged significant analysis of this phenomenon. The development of improvisatory principles in black culture is actuated by what Zora Neale Hurston calls the "characteristics of Negro expression,"[151] characteristics that correspond to what literary historian Kimberly W. Benston terms the "will to self-enactment" embedded in "the dozens, toasts, the call-and-response patterns of musical and religious performance, and the signifying improvisations of the streets."[152] Modern black performance arises from "the signifying improvisations of the streets," where the historical northward migration and the rise of black urban culture intersected in Chicago's South Side, Harlem, Detroit, Roxbury, Newark, and Philadelphia and incorporated southern lifestyles derived from rural traditions. Benston's term "improvisations of the streets" encompasses hybrid forms expressive of the rhythms of industrial life, urban lifestyle, rural roots, and black cultural expression.

Improvisation becomes a key element in black experience and performance, one that builds on the blues, jazz, religious services, and community discourse. Houston A. Baker, Jr.'s, analysis of African American vernacular literature and the blues aptly describes the emergence of improvisation as a "nonlinear, freely associative, nonsequential meditation" on lived experiences.[153] The everyday social existence of African Americans amounted to a back-and-forth relationship between desire and not having, goals and thwarted goals, dreams and dreams deferred, a need for communication and being set apart. Despite racist efforts to label blacks with a single and degrading "truth," there was in fact no single truth about the self because the self was in motion. Identity was therefore a far-reaching and temporally unfolding web of relations, and Johnson was exemplary of this style.

Johnson's performative style contained a contradiction compelled by life; he appeared one way, when in fact he was another. His laxity was in fact concealed seriousness; it masked the ferocity of his purpose. The ability to appear one way and be another was a realization of the improvisational style and the paradoxes inherent in it. It is a style that is judged by the ability to understand and utilize the exterior phenomenon of the mask (the disguise), and the interior phenomenon of intentionality. In his introduction to Jack Johnson's autobiography, the sports writer and cartoonist Tad Dargan, who coined Johnson's nickname "Li'l Arthur," wrote:

> It was his easy-going manner in the ring that fooled many. He smiled and kidded in the clinches and many thought he was careless, but all the time he held his opponent safe, knew every move the other made and was at all times the boss in the ring.[154]

For black people at the time, deception was essential. It was imperative that African Americans wear the smiling mask of laziness in order to deflect hostility and assure whites of a non-threatening presence. In the ring, Johnson's appearance of frivolity and lack of seriousness was that same mask but one which disguised the fierceness of his intent. Jack London observed that Johnson was play-acting throughout the fight with Jeffries. London said:

> Johnson played, as usual. With his opponent not strong in the attack Johnson, blocking and defending in masterly fashion, could afford to play. And he played and fought a white man, in the white man's country, before a white man's audience. And the audience was Jeffries' audience. . . . The greatest battle of the century was a monologue delivered to twenty thousand spectators by a smiling negro, who was never in doubt and who was never serious for more than a moment at a time.[155]

What London failed to realize was that Johnson was quite serious, with the "smile" merely the surface manifestation that shielded his inner complexity. Rex Beach had also mistaken Johnson's appearance of playfulness, calling him a "joyrider." Couching his remarks in the racism that typified the era, Beach stated that "nature designed [Johnson] for a chauffeur and while he is the master of the greatest defensive system any fighter of his weight has been equipped with, he seems to look upon this battle as a joke."[156] What London and Beach could not comprehend was Johnson's ability to joke and be serious simultaneously, incorporating the paradox of both concepts within one mindset. Ralph Ellison, who coined the phrase "change the joke and slip the yoke," maintained that black people "wear the mask for purposes of aggression as well as for defense; when we are projecting the future and preserving the past." The motives beneath the mask, Ellison explains, "are as numerous as the ambiguities the mask conceals."[157] The appearance of playfulness and indolence is a complex appearance drawn from multiple levels of awareness. The mask of playfulness disarms an opponent but also deceives.

Johnson's style was imbued with playful improvisation. His body in performance demonstrated an intelligence that emphasized the moment of existence rather than preplanned strategy. This is not to say that Johnson eschewed planning; on the contrary, improvisation requires extensive planning and multiple strategies. Improvisation, however, means a willingness to change or even abandon plans if necessary. Throughout the fight, Johnson shifted his strategy. In the early rounds he fought defensively, countering Jeffries and attempting to unbalance him. As the fight progressed he became increasingly aggressive, attacking his opponent and initiating contact. In many ways Johnson practiced a style equivalent to call-and-response; his actions in the ring were in response to Jeffries and his verbal jousting was due in part to the influence of African American oral history. Call-and-response is the alternation of voice (call) and refrain (response). It is the verbal and non-verbal interaction between speaker and hearer in which the speaker's statements are punctuated by responses. While rooted in African music, vernacular traditions, and black religious services, its genealogy can also be traced to slave life. Slaves would frequently communicate across plantation fields with other slaves by call-and-response. One slave would call to another either through song or the rhythmic cadence of sound and motion. Since education was denied to African Americans, many newly arriving slaves did not know English, and since communication between slaves was often curtailed, it took the form of humming, singing, and chanting. African Americans during slavery developed a sophisticated method of communication. Sounds indecipherable to plantation masters drifted across cotton and tobacco fields. As English became the accepted language, words replaced sounds, but the form of call-and-response remained, eventually developing roots in black vernacular and churches. According to Jane Duran and Earl L. Stewart, call-and-response was highly influential "in the shaping of African American notions of form, structure, and timbre," featuring "the alternation of solo passages with choral passages or choral refrains." More importantly, from "the Reconstruction era onward," call-and-response "became more creative and sophisticated."[158] It is within this time frame that Johnson emerged as a fighter and his relationship to this phenomenon and its specific historical moment is undeniable.

Johnson's call-and-response banter enraged Jeffries, broke his concentration, and made him lose his game plan. Johnson's biographer Robert H. deCoy maintains that Johnson's "back-chat" with ringside notables "infuriated Jeffries so that he mustered the daredevil recklessness of a madman."[159] Throughout the fight Jeffries lunged and clinched, hoping to disable Johnson's punching power and allow Jeffries time to clear his head. Johnson finally said, "All right, Jim, I'll love you if you want me to," and proceeded to kiss Jeffries on the cheek.[160] Such banter—termed "playing the dozens"—unbalanced Jeffries, who was unused to an oral tradition where verbal tactics and quick responses are commonplace. Johnson kept this up throughout the fight. At one point Jim Corbett stood at Jeffries's corner and yelled to Johnson, "Why don't you do something," to which Johnson replied, "Too clever, too clever like you."[161] At other times Johnson would say, "Package being delivered, Mr. Jeff," "Wishing for the old days, Mr. Jeff," "Come on, you Jeff," and called out to Jim Corbett, "Too late to do anything, Jim; your man's all in."[162] In the interval between the fifth and sixth round Johnson said to John L. Sullivan, "John, I thought this fellow could hit." Sullivan replied defensively, "I never said so, but I believe he could have six years ago." Johnson replied, "Six years ago ain't now."[163]

William H. Wiggins, quoting fighters he knew, relates the details of Johnson's legendary ability to upset other fighters with verbal play and joking:

Man, Jack [Johnson] was too smart for them white fighters. He'd get them in a corner and pin their arms at the elbow joint between his thumb and index finger. Then he would smile sweetly and kiss them on the cheek. Man, this would make these fighters so mad they would forget about boxing and come out swinging wild. And that was all old Jack wanted. He'd step inside their leads and counter punch them to death![164]

In observing the film of the fight, we can see that Johnson patted Jeffries playfully on the back of the head after the seventh round ended as both headed to their respective corners. Jeffries, reacting quickly to the "friendly tap" on the head, turned briefly and scowled at Johnson as he walked to his corner; he was clearly upset. Throughout the fight Johnson would anger Jeffries, making him push Johnson and thus expend energy that should have been conserved.

Verbal banter directed at a powerful figure is one of the significant aspects of African American oral expression. Johnson's experience at the nuances of verbal strategy aided him in two ways: by softening the effects of the jeers and hostility he faced from the crowd, and as a tactic. Throughout the fight, Johnson kept up the verbal assault on Jeffries, his corner's associates, and the crowd as well. Rarely did he fail to respond to a jeer or insult. He taunted Jeffries, saying, "Come on now, Mr. Jeff. Let me see what you got. Do something, man. This is for the cham-*peen*-ship." After repeatedly hitting Jeffries, Johnson said, "I can go on like this all afternoon, Mr. Jeff."[165] Johnson's reference to "Mr. Jeff" parodied the black-white relationship of master-slave, with African Americans referring to whites as "Massa." How much Johnson actually said can be disputed; it probably has been exaggerated over time, embellished for the sake of storytelling. But we can ascertain for a fact that he talked to his opponent throughout, making Jeffries poorer in judgment.

To be sure, Johnson's improvisational style was not the only reason for his victory. His ability to improvise must be seen in correlation with a number of skills working simultaneously. Johnson's style had a pragmatic as well as cultural justification. Still, his improvisatory skills are evident in the fight, and were related to his freewheeling lifestyle, which was seen as brazen, confident, and self-assertive. He drew from life's experiences for his style, and he had an enormous effect on the black community.

After the fight Johnson returned to his home in Chicago, where black civil leaders planned a celebration and parade. Robert Motts, director of the Pekin Theatre on 27th and State Street, one of the first successfully run African American theatres, was the chairman of the reception committee. According to the *Chicago Tribune,* the impresario Motts and his fellow actors from the Pekin were denied a permit for a victory parade. Motts, in defense of the celebration, said that the plans were for a dignified procession, adding, "if Mr. Jeffries had won the fight and a demonstration had been arranged here in his honor there would have been no attempt on the part of the city administration to block the plans or stop the exhibition of the fight pictures, either."[166] Instead of a parade, Motts astutely organized an "impromptu procession" of 40 automobiles from the train station to Johnson's home at 3344 Wabash Avenue. A more modest celebration was attempted on the seventh of July. However much city officials attempted to deny the celebration, thousands of African Americans turned out to greet Johnson. A dinner at the Pekin Theatre followed the victory parade and celebration at his home. Motts, who orchestrated all ceremonies, kept a strict vigil to prevent violence. The *Chicago Defender* reported "no evidence of hostility" between blacks and whites.[167]

What is perhaps most significant is the large number of white participants in the processions from the Pekin Theatre to Johnson's home. According to the *Defender*, whites "generously cheered their fellow American, fellow Chicagoan, in recognition of skill and physical prowess, and in disregard of the oversight of Providence in wrapping it up in a black package." The *Defender* added:

> That whites who crowded to meet Johnson were actuated either by friendly enthusiasm, gratitude for filled pocketbooks, or mere curiosity, and not by anger, was amply demonstrated at the Northwestern station where they outnumbered the blacks four to one.[168]

In a scene hardly imaginable today, let alone in 1910, the *Defender* reported that many white policeman stopped Johnson's black motorcade, not for the purposes of harassment, but rather "to shake Johnson's hand." Most of the nation had been torn by racial conflict. Yet in Chicago, a city known for its racial animosities, blacks and whites celebrated together. Johnson's victory had a friendlier effect on white society in Chicago then one could imagine. Briefly, racial discord subsided and people joined in celebrating the accomplishments of one talented individual.

CONCLUSION

In an age when conformism was fortuitous for the Negro, Jack Johnson dared to be an individual.   —A. S. (Doc) Young (1963)[169]

Money, the *New York Times* reported, "has been the sole object of this brutal and vulgar contest."[170] Indeed, much money was made, especially for the promoter, George Lewis "Tex" Richards, whose total earnings were an estimated $400,000.[171] Playing the "race card" helped box office receipts, with Johnson and Jeffries going along with the hoopla in order to sell tickets. Richards encouraged promoters to publicize the fight as a racial Armageddon. Given the large amounts of money made, both Jeffries and Johnson understood that interest in the fight transcended "mere" sport and that instigating racial discord could only enhance their earnings.

However, the impact of Johnson's victory on the black community cannot be underestimated. Lucille B. Watkins's poem, written following the fight, revealed the sentiments of many:

> Jack Johnson, we have waited long for you,
> To grow our prayers in this single blow
> Today we place upon your wreath the dew
> Of tears—the wordless gratitude we owe
> We kiss the perspiration from your face
> And give—unbounded love in our embrace.[172]

Other folk odes to Johnson were penned, as in this tongue-in-cheek paean:

> Amaze an 'Grace, how sweet it sounds,
> Jack Johnson knocked Jim Jeffries down.
> Jim Jeffries jumped up an' hit Jack on the chin,
> An' then Jack knocked him down agin.
> The Yankees hold the play,
> The white man pulls the trigger;
> But it make no difference what the white man say,
> The world champion's still a nigger.[173]

The significance of Johnson's victory did not escape the front-page article in the *Chicago Broad Ax*. The consequence of the fight and its relationship to the larger social scene is succinctly placed in context with other events of the time. If Jeffries had won, the paper conjectured,

> he would be hailed by the so-called Christians throughout this country, as divine evidence of the superiority in every respect of the white race over the black race. But as it turned out the other way, it is very galling indeed to hypocritical Christians, who roll up their eyes Heavenward, in holy horror, at the very idea of permitting the exhibition of the moving pictures [of the fight]. But if a lynching bee was on tap, of a Negro . . . thousands and thousands of this same class of Christians . . . would attend the lynching bee with their sweet innocent little children to witness the Negro being burned at the stake and gladly pay out their money for slices of his quivering flesh, and the preachers would have exclaimed

from their pulpits that such demoralizing scenes have been productive of much wholesome and moral influence.[174]

The popularity of the fight was no doubt the result of clever marketing, which played a large role in getting people interested in it. Still, Johnson's victory created a wholesale paradigm shift in what it meant to be an African American. Sports columnist John Lardner wrote in 1949 that there were two reasons for the intensity of feelings against Johnson: first was the reluctance to accept an African American as heavyweight champion, and second, that Johnson was a "headlong defier of convention." Johnson insisted on his rights at a time "when most people believed that Negroes should know what was called their place and should live their lives as discreetly."[175] Johnson was contemptuous of such restrictions, living his life as he wished. In 1912, Johnson was convicted under the Mann Act, accused of kidnapping. He skipped bail and lived in Paris for two years, until his money ran dry. He accepted a few fights, but his high living had taken its toll. His fighting skills had diminished, and in 1915 he lost his championship to Jess Willard in Havana.

Johnson's victory over Jeffries would have lasting ramifications and his impact endured well after his fighting skills declined. His legacy resides in his inspiring independence, but it came at a price. In the following decades the marketing of race became vogue, with Harlem emerging as the Mecca, a race capital. Johnson's independence inspired other African Americans toward a self-definition that rejected not only racial stereotyping, but also racial unity. Social critic Everett H. Akam has correctly identified the emergence of Harlem in the 1920s as both a "spiritual center for cultural renewal" and "corrupted into a kind of forerunner of Club Med, the self-styled 'antidote for civilization.'" Johnson's "style" helped contribute to the creation of what Akam terms "a new stereotype" based on "black instinctual spontaneity that complemented, rather than challenged," perceptions.[176] His self-reliance and autonomy not only helped to establish the image of the "bad nigger" who defied repression, but also bolstered the exaggerated and falsified stereotypes that have haunted African Americans. Johnson, perhaps more than anyone, established the ideals of self-assertion that were read as mere "selfishness" for the sake of material gain alone. Yet Johnson's ability to transcend the animosities of race, and his defiance, helped to bolster the spirit of a people caught in the clutches of prejudice.

CHAPTER THREE

EXOTICISM, DANCE, AND RACIAL MYTHS: MODERN DANCE AND THE CLASS DIVIDE IN THE CHOREOGRAPHY OF AIDA OVERTON WALKER AND ETHEL WATERS

[The black female] is there to entertain guests with the naked image of Otherness. They are not to look at her as a whole human being. They are to notice only certain parts. Objectified in a manner similar to that of black female slaves who stood on the auction blocks while owners and overseers described their important, salable parts, the black women whose naked bodies were displayed for whites at social functions had no presence. They were reduced to mere spectacle. Little is known of their lives, their motivations. Their body parts were offered as evidence to support racist notions that black people were more akin to animals than other humans.

—bell hooks (1992)[1]

ABSENCE AND PRESENCE IN EARLY MODERN BLACK DANCE

Though a sizable body of literature on dance has been generated in the past two decades [1975–1995], none of it has focused on the socio-historical context from which African-American secular social dance has emerged.

—Katrina Hazzard-Gordon (1996)[2]

Though black women played a pivotal role in the development of modern choreography, dance scholars have largely ignored their contributions.[3] Yet the evidence is unequivocal: black women contributed significantly to the origins of modern dance. The Charleston, turkey trot, Texas Tommy, fox trot, and shimmy emerged in black communities and made their way into the world of white middle-class dance halls. In addition to inventing new forms of social dancing, black women choreographed "classical" modern dance during the early twentieth century. Their choreography represented an act of empowerment; despite the exploitatively sexual overtones of dancing at the time, many black women fought against stereotyping, attempting to maintain their creativity and self-expression. Black women dancers were forced to maneuver through narrowly prescribed paths, yet despite restrictions, some still managed to carve out innovative careers.[4] No doubt African American women choreographers experienced many of the same conditions that affected all dancers at the time; black dancers sought ways of creating a style that reflected modern society and trends. However, without downplaying the significance of social trends, black women faced unique issues that influenced their choreography.

In order to understand better the conditions under which black female choreographers worked, and how they communicated to different audiences, this chapter will focus on the choreography of two important performers: Aida Overton Walker (1880–1914) and Ethel Waters (circa 1896–1977). Walker and Waters shared many common issues during the 1910s, yet they also differed in a number of interesting ways. In examining the careers of Walker and Waters, we discover how it was that early twentieth-century black female performers negotiated their creativity within a complex era of racism on the one hand, and amid rising interest in modern dance on the other. Rooted in their choreography is the expression of the black woman's struggle, a struggle to gain control over her artistic expression by adapting, absorbing, and challenging the prevailing stereotypes of the period. Neither their choreography nor their response to stereotypical caricatures was uniform: while Walker moved in middle-class circles and performed in theatres aimed at bourgeois ideas of culture, Waters gained early fame in working-class dance halls where her shimmy attracted large followings.

Aida Overton Walker's performance of *Salome* (a popular "classical" modern dance performed by white dancers) in 1908 and 1912 represented "high art" available to middle- and upper-middle class society.[5] She performed *Salome* in cabarets and Broadway theatres, playhouses attended by largely bourgeois audiences. In this environment, Walker enjoyed the critical attention of reviewers and culturally influential people. In contrast, Ethel Waters arose from a working-class background, where the emphasis was less on critical evaluation and more on the momentary release of everyday tensions and the physical expressions of the proletariat. Her shimmy dance of the late 1910s became popular in cellar clubs and jook joints, areas largely known for their plebian clientele. Though Waters's singing was, as American historian Ann Douglas put it, "sweeter and smoother" than the "earthy" blues of her fellow jazz singers Ma Rainey, Alberta Hunter, and Bessie Smith, her dancing was provocative yet within the bounds of social accept-ability.[6] Waters was one of the earliest black female performers to work in black, northern, working-class cellar clubs, helping to shift popular social dance from a predominantly southern and rural environment to a northern and urban setting. Walker, too, kept her choreography within the bounds of decorum, enabling her to gain a large audience, which appreciated her risqué dance that enticed yet did not move beyond current notions of respectability.

At the risk of over-simplification, one could say that Walker represented mid-dle-class "concert halls," while Waters epitomized working-class "dance halls." This distinction enables us to begin an analysis of social class as forms of cultural production and receptivity. To be sure, Walker and Waters were not alone; Dora Dean, Florence Mills, and Josephine Baker were among several early popular black choreographers.[7] However, Dean's cakewalking and Baker's cabaret per-formances developed primarily in Europe, and Mills gained fame during the 1920s, a period outside the scope of this chapter (more on Mills in chapter 11). Walker and Waters performed in the United States in the 1910s, and it is this backdrop under which Walker and Waters worked that will begin my analysis.

MODERNISM, PRIMITIVISM, AND BLACK DANCE

She who "happens" to be a (non-white) Third World member, a woman, and a writer is bound to go through the ordeal of exposing her work to the abuse of praise and criticisms that either ignore, dispense with, or overem-phasize her racial and sexual attributes. —Trinh T. Minh-ha (1989)[8]

During the 1910s a change was taking place in American society. The rise of im-migrants to the urban scene brought new ideas about social relations and the im-portance of social dancing as a means of interpersonal contact. Dance historian Ann Wagner has commented on this transition, noting that shifts in urban living and class distinctions "fostered the unprecedented popularity of dancing be-tween 1910 and 1914."[9] Working-class women and men frequented new public dance halls and all social classes enjoyed the growth of cabarets. Dancing en-couraged both sexes in either heterosexual or homosexual environments to use dance as a venue to enjoy each other's company. In addition, despite the prevail-ing racism of the time, enthusiasm for dance encouraged whites to look to black culture for examples of modern, innovative choreography.

As a result of both the emerging interest in dance and the rise of stereotyping of African Americans during the early twentieth century, black culture took shape as a resistance to, and appropriation of, racism. According to film historian Mark Reid, black culture developed "within and around the competing tensions created by the intermittent desire to appropriate, negotiate, and resist mainstream American and European cultures."[10] In his designation of Booker T. Washington (circa 1895 to 1915) as the "quintessential herald of modernism in black expressive culture," Houston A. Baker, Jr., maintains that Washington maneuvered through Jim Crowism and racist stereotyping by "crafting a voice out of tight places."[11] The notions of "competing tensions" and "tight places" were certainly applicable to the conditions facing black female modern choreographers who had to contend with a host of stereotypes and cultural codes that influenced their artistic choices.

The concept of feminine beauty associated with whiteness was something black women, and black female performers in particular, struggled against. In her 1925 contribution to *The New Negro*, Elie Johnson McDougald makes the point clear: black women, she observed, realize "that the ideals of beauty," bolstered by the fine arts, have excluded black women "almost entirely." Instead of blackness being a signifier of beauty, in the cultural lexicon it became "the grotesque Aunt Jemimas of the street-car advertisements," existing merely "to serve, without grace of loveliness."[12] For black women dancers the deck was clearly stacked: stereotypes, the usual obstacles of culture-bound racism, often prevented them from enjoying success even during a period of newfound interest in dance. Notions of sexuality in dance worked to reinforce the negative image of black women as "primitive" and "inferior."

Historically, black people were sold on the auction block as specimens of "primitive" physicality. This attitude of display and fascination did not recede following slavery; blacks continued to be mythologized as hyper-lascivious and sexually debased. In addition to minstrelsy and white folklore depicting black males as sexual predators and black females as permissive, stereotyping gained further ground during the late-nineteenth century as Anglo-Europeans put more stock in social science. For white ethnographers of the late nineteenth and early twentieth century, the economic and social position of African Americans served as "proof" that all black people were, as Richard J. Powell put it, "cut from the same coarse, 'biologically-determined' cloth."[13] Such views were held even among liberal factions of white culture. For example, a white patron of black artists, Albert C. Barnes, wrote in 1925 that black art is "sound" because it arose "from a primitive nature upon which a white man's education has never been harnessed."[14] Primitivism functioned as an effective definition of black art, collapsing notions of authenticity and the raw, untrammeled "talent" of black "natural" abilities into a single and easily digestible concept.

At the turn of the century, Social Darwinism found a new way of packaging racism. It was argued that a duality in human species pitted "advanced" white civilization against "primitive" people of color. For ethnologists, Western advances in science and technology suggested that other races were still clinging to a primitive past. According to art historian Colin Rhodes, by an insidious rationale, "tribal societies were often not even credited as emerging civilizations, but as an evolutionary cul-de-sac," arrested in their development and "fixed" in the evolutionary ladder, where they "could be viewed as the sociological 'missing link,' preserved, living examples of the 'childhood of humanity.'"[15] As a consequence, primitivism began to represent a number of aesthetic and cultural myths—demonism, fauvism, masks, voodoo, cannibalism, exoticism, eroticism—that evoked images of unrestrained sexuality, wildness, and passion. Building largely on the Enlightenment, specifically Rousseauian celebrations of natural innocence and the "noble savage,"[16] racial ideology gained further prominence in the early twentieth century owing to the rise of what cultural historian Marianna Torgovnick calls the "primitive trope."[17] The primitive is represented as a series of childlike tropes, a combination of our rebellious selves and the id, exhibiting a libidinous and violent social group, allegedly in tune with nature's harmony. This allowed for the reduction of black culture to either inferiority or idealization; primitives may be childlike and violent, but they may also be "noble savages." Literary historian Hayden White emphasizes the point when he states that savages were "either a breed of super animals (similar to dogs, bears, or monkeys)," or "they were a breed of degenerate men (descendants of the lost tribes of Israel or a race of men rendered destitute of reason and moral sense by the effects of harsh climate)."[18] Thus, people of color were caught in a culturally manufactured double bind: relegated to the lowest rung of the evolutionary ladder, yet looked to as a source of visceral originality as well.

Despite the negative connotations, primitives were thought to enjoy a closer relationship to subconscious impulse, childish innocence, and sexuality. In an increasingly mechanized world, primitivism, rooted in simple "nature," offered an alternative to urban, progressive life. Primitivism emerged as a reaction to an escalating alienation born of an industrialized world, and served as an alternative to modern technological society; hence, the primitivist cult developed into new artistic premises. Primitivism allegedly supported the case for artists and social theorists who attempted to inculcate simple values to a culture suffering from industrialization, dehumanization, and exhaustion. This led to a "fetishization" of the primitive: primitivism's relation to the supposed early evolutionary stages of human development afforded Western society a sense of superiority to other groups while simultaneously encouraging an analysis of primitivism as a way of learning the roots of evolution. White ethnographers, despairing over the lack of "nobility" in modern white civilizations, began to search for it in black "primitivism." But there was more underlying their motives; it was a reach for the primeval mysteries and the jungle depths exemplified by what historian Harold Isaacs termed "the naked black man in his natural state and setting."[19]

During the late nineteenth and early twentieth century, primitivism offered whites an alternative to puritanical mores. The moral dichotomy of the Victorian era—humanity and civilization on the one side, primitivism and savagery on the other—was intermingled during the modern era. If American Victorians of the 1870s and 1880s described cultures as either civilized or savage according to whether they were black and white, maintaining a rigid separation of the two, then American modernists of the early twentieth century enjoyed this distinction by embracing the exoticized black—but only up to a point. Segregation remained enforceable law, but white pirating of black culture emerged as part of the hip social scene. Primitivism evolved into myth, with the common thread being the symbolically sexualized representation of the nonwhite body. Ethnic historian Sander Gilman's essay on the iconography of female sexuality contends that the perception of the prostitute "merged with the perception of the black," and that this perception created the "commonplace" notion that the "primitiveness" of the black woman "was associated with unbridled sexuality."[20] African American women symbolized the exotic, erotic, and sexually lascivious side of "primitivism." For many white men (and black men as well), black women represented an image of foreignness and a "colorful" panacea for an overworked, over-industrialized culture looking to spend its disposable income on entertainment.

The vertical arrangement of ethnicities—whites on top, others on the bottom—created new taxonomies. While the bottom rung was considered inferior, it also placed blacks closer to impulse, spontaneity, and nature, and therefore made them attractive. By the end of the 1920s, many psychologists and social critics warned of this attraction as a prognostication of civilization's demise. For example, in 1930, the influential psychologist Carl Jung cautioned that the "inferior man" exerts a "tremendous pull upon civilized beings who are forced to live with him, because he fascinates the inferior layers of our psyche." As Jung put it, to the subconscious mind "contact with primitives recalls not only our childhood, but also our prehistory," adding that it would be easy to see why "the Negro, with his primitive motility, his expressive emotionality, his childlike immediacy, his sense of music and rhythm, his funny and picturesque language, has infected American behavior."[21] This "infection" gained root around the early 1910s when whites, enjoying the rising interest in dance, began to go "slumming" in black cabarets in order to absorb the "expressive emotionality" and "childlike immediacy." While the invasion of Harlem and other black communities by whites had yet to reach the popularity of the 1920s, the 1910s saw the seeds of this phenomenon.[22]

By the twentieth century, primitivism had become a catchall phrase defining blacks, and with it came the implication that primitivism was an artistic attribute. The notion emerged that black writers, performers, and artists were capable of primitivism expressing a racial uniqueness that incorporated authenticity, untarnished amateurism, and aesthetic beauty. The combination of alleged authenticity and primitivism validated the abilities and talents of African Americans, who were supposedly unencumbered by formal training. Black artists were supposedly "raw" talent, "naturals" at creativity as opposed to the so-called stilted, overrefined art of Europeans. By the 1910s, the amalgamation of amateurism, primitivism, and atavism into a unified concept of black art, literature, and performance had taken root; by the 1920s and 1930s, it had become conventional wisdom. No matter how manipulative and misleading, the alleged validity of these ideas afforded some African American artists and performers an opportunity to take advantage of the situation. For many, primitivism provided an entry into mainstream culture. Left with little choice but to conform to inaccurate and exaggerated representations or be denied opportunities, some black artists, writers, and performers accentuated the so-called "jungle rhythms" of their artwork in order to accommodate the demands of their white audiences. White patrons, eager to associate with what they perceived to be the "real thing," paid for black art and entertainment. For black women, the problem of sexism added to the racism of the time, making it difficult for black female artists to find creative outlets that went beyond the limitations of stereotyping.

The assumption that black women were "primitive"—sexually obsessed and erotically out of control—was undoubtedly a canard. The falsification involves the attempt to subordinate racial groups and control them. In response to primitivism, the black middle class eschewed depictions of black sexuality. The early twentieth century began as a period of "racial uplift," in which the black middle class, among other things, undertook a campaign against erotic displays and performance. Feminist scholar Evelyn Brooks Higginbotham explains that given the limitations on educational and income opportunities imposed on African Americans, "many black women linked mainstream domestic duties, codes of dress, sexual conduct, and public etiquette with both individual success and group progress."[23] Showered with sexual and racial stereotypes, black women campaigned for respectability and moral authority. Performing was equated with opprobrious behavior; respectable women considered the stage beneath their dignity. In 1904, Fannie Barrier Williams wrote that the black woman's "grave responsibility" to maintain bourgeois respectability was essential because

> the Negro is learning that the things that our women are doing come first in the lessons of citizenship; that there will never be an unchallenged vote, a respected political power, or an unquestioned claim to a position of influence and importance, until the present stigma is removed from the home and the women of the race.[24]

We see, then, that black female dancers faced additional prejudices not only from without, but fostered within by bourgeois values inside the black community itself.

Yet, however much primitivism carried the stamp of inferiority, many also used the primitive trope to promote an aesthetic. No excuses will be ventured on behalf of primitivism; it was part of a racist ideology and must be seen as such, contributing to a mendacious epistemology of racial identity. Moreover, dancing's eroticism, which the male gaze fostered at the time, adds to the already excessive reification and objectification of the female body. By objectifying women, the gaze enables the dominant society to turn sexuality into a commodity. Black women once again become bartered flesh, to be observed and mastered. Simply put, since black women were mythologized as oversexed, many white and black males were attracted to their stage performances.

Many dancers, black and white, exploited the notion of "fetishized" sexuality to varying degrees for commercial gain. The fact that certain performers took advantage of prevailing ideas can neither be ignored nor absolutely condemned. Those living in communities and circumstances where biases restrict advancement cannot always depend on the ethical high ground for sustenance; to survive, oppressed people often realize that only a diverse and sometimes compromising axiology of existence can guarantee material subsistence. It is easy to dismiss dancers who capitalized on primitivism as exploitative by their capitulation to racism; it is more difficult to accept the fact that the oppressed must often turn adverse conditions to their advantage. Feminist critic and historian Hazel Carby observes that there is "a touchiness among feminists about representing black women as complex." For Carby, it is easier to portray black women as "morally superior because of suffering or victimization." But in doing so, Carby insists, feminist scholars "deny their complexity, their dangerousness, their refusal to be policed."[25] This is not to say that critiques of primitivism are invalid. Instead, critiques ought to be broad enough to include observations on how oppressed people made innovative use of the narrow frames allotted them.

Caught in the paradoxical bind between competing urges to express creativity and to thwart stereotypes, black female choreographers were also under considerable scrutiny for their erotic movements, and under pressure to choreo-graph according to the current vogue. It is perhaps for this reason that Josephine Baker, rejecting American morality, departed for Europe. Baker constructed a persona that followed the paradigm of the black exotic in the context of white society. Free from Puritanical morality, Baker exploited a European primitivism that was no less racist, but simply less inhibited. Baker was not, however, the first choreographer to come to grips with the primitive trope. Walker and Waters not only endured the idea of primitivism in America, they continued to choreograph within an American cultural framework replete with racial codes. Walker and Waters negotiated a minefield of representations, each developing a unique choreography.

AIDA OVERTON WALKER:
"BAREFOOT CLASSICAL DANCER" AND MIDDLE CLASS RESPECTABILITY

It took a long time for the disreputable creativity of black artists to climb down from the plinth of primitivism and natural spontaneity and win a different status as modern art.   —Paul Gilroy (1995)[26]

Aida Overton Walker's objective was to lift black women's choreography into the modern world.[27] At a time when black women were compelled to rein in their expectations and bridle their imaginations, Aida (sometimes spelled Ada) Walker did the opposite. During her career she made her presence felt in several ways: she was an accomplished cakewalker, teaching the cakewalk to elite, white society; she established herself as the highest paid and most popular female actress, singer, and dancer of the Williams and Walker vaudeville company; she choreographed all of the Williams and Walker shows, including *In Dahomey* (1902–1905), *Abyssinia* (1905–1907), and *Bandanna Land* (1907–1909); and she was considered one of the brightest stars on the vaudeville stage. Despite the overwhelming presence of the male stars in her company—the famous comedian Bert Williams and her husband, George Walker—she managed to gain recognition as a consummate performer during the first decade of the twentieth century.

Walker defended the stage against criticisms that performing led to an ignoble life. Drawing on her experiences as choreographer and lead performer of the Williams and Walker company, she contended that middle-class black people as well as white critics misunderstood the goals of African Americans in the performing arts. In her 1905 article, worth quoting at length, she hoped to set the record straight about performers and their significance in the field of civil rights:

> Some of our so-called society people regard the Stage as a place to be ashamed of. Whenever it is my good fortune to meet such persons, I sympathize with them for I know they are ignorant as to what is really being done in their own behalf by members of their race on the Stage.
>
> In this age we are all fighting the one problem—that is the color problem! I venture to think and dare to state that our profession does more toward the alleviation of color prejudice than any other profession among colored people. The fact of the matter is this, that we come in contact with more white people in a week than other professional colored people meet in a year and more than some meet in a whole decade.[28]

As the above makes clear, Walker fought a rear-guard action against a black middle-class eager to condemn the performing arts. She attempted to illuminate the situation of African American performers caught between competing urges. Walker explained that black performers "are often compelled by sheer force of circumstance to work at a disadvantage," because they are criticized by whites "as severely as white actors and actresses, who have every advantage." When black performers "fall short" in comparison to whites, white critics "cry out and think it strange that our acting is inferior." Yet these critics frequently acknowledge that it is "wonderful" that African Americans "have done so well and accomplished so much in spite of overwhelming difficulties that do not overwhelm."[29] Continually seeking parity with white actors and dancers, Walker framed her career along the lines of others in her profession. Yet she never lost sight of the fact that in the eyes of many she represented her race.

Walker wanted recognition as a consummate choreographer; in order to achieve this, she needed the approval of critics and the acceptance of a black middle-class audience. To this end she joined the *Salome* craze, the vogue in the United States and Europe for choreography and literature based on the biblical story. By aligning herself with the popular dance of modern white female choreographers, she raised the stakes in her quest for legitimacy and critical recognition. In 1908, Percival Pollard of the *New York Times* dubbed the *Salome* craze itself as "Salomania."[30] By adding it to the Williams and Walker production of *Bandanna Land*, Walker challenged the accepted notion that only white women could dance the "classics." Nevertheless, she had to suppress the erotic component of her dancing. As a result, her choreography, although notable for its grace, was also known for its propriety. Walker had to be especially careful not to offend black audiences, while refusing to succumb to prudery. She affected the bourgeois norms of good taste, which meant she submitted her costume to a regime of concealment and restraint. Yet she also wore exotic and provocative costumes frequently modeled after modern white dancers. As a well-known member of the Harlem community, Walker was under considerable pressure to conform to a middle-class society caught up in social propriety and racial uplift, while simultaneously she felt compelled to join her fellow white female dancers by presenting her version of "Salomania." The cultural influences that informed her performance exerted contradictory pressures, creating a unique style, which, as the following reviews will reveal, might have been misinterpreted as obtuse. On the one hand, she stressed the abstract, hiding her sexuality and casting off the visibility of her body. On the other hand, she emphasized the sensual and exotic, which puts the body in full view. Her dance probably changed often, given the improvisatory nature of her work, the touring circuit she followed, and the diverse demands of each city and town she performed in. Some cities had strict puritanical codes of conduct, while others loosened restrictions. The rising imposition of Jim Crow laws also made performing a complicated affair; some cities she toured had lax racial restrictions while others imposed strict curfews and boundaries for African Americans. In other words, sometimes her expressions of sexuality were conveyed, while at other times a modest approach was required. The racial and sexual codes of each city compounded for Walker the difficulties involved in the dance.

Beginning in 1908, versions of the *Salome* dance were performed throughout New York. *Current Literature* reported in October 1908 that there were "no less than twenty-four vaudeville dancers in New York alone who give their interpretation of the daughter of Herodias, and from the Empire City the Salome epidemic is spreading over the rest of the country."[31] Around the turn of the century, the popular figure of *Salome* epitomized the inherent sensuality and, according to some, perversity of women. *Salome* became the image of "women as serpents, as brute nature's virgin dancer," whose only reason for existence "lay in the movements of the arms, the legs, of the supple body and the muscular loins, born indefinitely from a visible source, the very center of dance."[32] The erotic was linked to dancing itself, with *Salome* collapsing both the sexual impulse with the movements of the dancer's body as a single entity. Moreover, the image of *Salome* represented the archetype of a "terrible femininity and fin-de-siècle femme fatale," symbolizing the "obscure paradoxes of unconscious desires and fears" associated with women.[33] In the minds of many, *Salome* was both "the virgin and the devouress," whose popularity was closely tied to the myths that accompany the "decadent femme fatale."[34] Many dancers capitalized on the myth, using the *Salome* dance to promote their careers.

In addition, Walker had to contend with a parody of her *Salome* dance by her co-star, Bert Williams, in the same show. Williams viewed the *Salome* craze as an opportunity to burlesque the dance in *Bandanna Land*—cross-dressing and imitating the gestures commonly associated with the choreography. This was intended to add levity to the show, but it also had the effect of undermining the seriousness of Walker's intent. Still, Walker introduced her version of *Salome* in 1908, working it into *Bandanna Land*. Despite the implication of her *Salome* as both femme fatale and primitive, Walker likely considered the dance as the perfect opportunity to align herself with both modern dance and highbrow art. It was highly unusual for a Broadway musical, and a black Broadway show in particular, to include modern dance, but Walker was determined to position herself within the establishment of modern dancers.

Critical response to Walker's *Salome* was predictably mixed. The fact that she was a black woman dancing a provocative character probably influenced Walker to downplay the erotic, or so it would appear, judging from the reviews of her choreography, which emphasized her modest costume, lack of vulgarity, and gracefulness. According to Lester A. Walton, Walker's *Salome* costume and dance "all come up to expectation, but in comparison with some of the other dancers Miss Walker's interpretation showed to a disadvantage." For Walton, white choreographers "danced more with their body" than Walker, and this, he notes, led them to be more "vulgar." Walton praised Walker's "desire to make 'Salome' a cleaner dance and void of suggestiveness, but in so doing she gives a version that is mild in comparison."[35] Perhaps because of her restraint, Walker chose to emphasize the dramatic elements over the suggestive in her choreography. One reviewer remarked that in Walker's version of *Salome*,

> [the] feet began to move, and the arms to sway, and the limbs to portray the
> passion of motion. And suddenly, at the height of the mad, intoxicating dance, a
> curtain was drawn and a ray of light fell on the head of the Baptist. The effect
> was electric, and so was the vision of the head for the dance. It struck her wild
> joy as with a blight, crushed her consciousness of power and flung her to the
> ground in defeat.[36]

In the 1908 version (see figure 6), her persona is audacious, with her hair projecting an African style and her dress bejeweled and spangled. Her appearance in Boston (see figure 7) suggests a similar approach: exotic jewelry and defiant stance. At least one Boston reviewer was particularly struck by Walker's creative interpretation and, at the same time, the modesty of her costume. Walker, the reviewer reported, "does not handle the gruesome head, she does not rely solely upon the movements of the body, and her dress is not so conspicuous by its absence." The reviewer praised Walker for "the fact that she acts the role of 'Salome' as well as dances it. Her face is unusually mobile and she expresses through its muscles the emotions which the body is also interpreting, thus making the character of the biblical dancer lifelike."[37] Another reviewer commented on Walker's modest costume, writing that her dance "is a very properly draped Salome, but the dance is interesting because of the rare grace and skill of the performer."[38] Still, another critic emphasized Walker's restraint, noting with some condescension that

> Miss Walker's Salome is something like the others, being more modest, but quite as meaningless. Grace it has in abundance, but most of the weirdness and barbaric grandeur is supplied by the trap man of the orchestra, who beats with vigor upon what we assume to be a large dishpan. There are a few wild figures, and much is made of the sinuous parade which most dancers conceive to have been characteristic of the foul-minded daughter of Herodias, but there is nothing of the hoocha-ma-cooch effect which adds a suggestion of sensuality to the exhibitions of other Salomes.[39]

It is clear from the caricature by Moe Zayas (figure 6), the photograph (figure 7), and available reviews that Walker wanted a *Salome* that was more dramatic but less erotic than those of her contemporaries.

In considering Walker's second, 1912 version of *Salome* (see figure 8), a comparison can be usefully made between Walker and one contemporary, Isadora Duncan. Although Duncan has received considerable attention, Walker, who continually broke new ground in choreography, has not. Like Duncan, Walker saw herself as a modern classical dancer in a quest for innovative ways of using the body to express her creativity. It is also likely that Duncan's presence in the United States influenced Walker. In her essay "Isadora Duncan and the Male Gaze," Ann Daly writes that, when Isadora Duncan "toured America in 1908, 1909, and 1911, her reputation as the 'Barefoot Classical Dancer' had preceded her from Europe."[40] Daly maintains that, whatever audience expectations of Duncan there were, "they were confounded by [Duncan's] actual performance" and its resistance to current conventions.[41] Daly asserts that Duncan was one of America's "first self-made women," who was "constantly re-imagining herself, both onstage and in her interviews."[42]

Much the same can be said of Aida Walker. Before Duncan became famous, Walker, a self-made performer, re-imagined herself from vaudeville star to cakewalker and from actress to modern dancer. She was, in fact, a self-made woman at a time when black women had neither power nor agency. Yet she found ways to express her creativity. Her dance, for example, was less entertainment (showing off her legs, for instance), and more artistry. Rather than emphasizing the show of body parts, Walker sought to convey her imagination and emotional conviction as an expression of her aesthetic values and artistic ideas. As the drawing of her 1912 *Salome* choreography shows (figure 8), Walker, like Duncan, was a "barefoot classical dancer" dressed in a loose-fitting outfit, projecting her swaying arms and feet lightly and with grace. Walker executed her second version in flowing movements in which improvisation and spontaneous emotions were marked features. From the drawings and photographs, we can see a departure from her 1908 version. By 1912, she was free of the presence of Bert Williams, who parodied her performance and undermined her interpretation, and she was free of the Williams and Walker Company in general. Since the death of her husband George Walker in 1911, Aida Walker was on her own, performing solo acts that toured throughout the country. After appearing in Bob Cole's production of *The Red Moon* (1909–1910) and nursing her husband during the final year of his life, Walker traveled the United States singing, dancing, and performing comedy. In 1912, she had revised her *Salome* dance, making it the unique feature of her one-woman show. The 1912 image portrays her as light, airy, and energetic. Her hands are expressive and her body appears to be in fluid motion. Her costume was similar to the outfits worn by Duncan—a chemise that flowed—but it also covered much of her body, unlike that of other *Salomes*. It is conceivable that Walker was attempting to imitate Duncan's performance while adding her own, considerably more modest, interpretation. In the second version, Walker appears to be rising into the air, in contrast to the earth-oriented, hip-centered choreography in the first version. In both, her lithe body conveys poise and passion, and there is strong emphasis on the face.

Walker crafted her interpretation in other ways. The 1908 version incorporates the garish jewelry and Jewish emblems bound up with *Salome*'s Biblical representation, while the 1912 image represents Walker with "traditional" modern dance costume and gesture. In both figures, there is an impression of individuality and awareness of the current scene; she is presenting her own version of *Salome*, incorporating the work of white dancers as well. Close examination of the drawings reveals that Walker's spine is not the center of her gesture, but merely one of many movement possibilities, and that the body appears in motion, not static. The arms, legs, hips, head, and torso move independently, creating a plethora of angles, curves, and shapes, each moving in separate directions.

Despite Walker's efforts to gain acceptance, her choreography was given little attention. The reasons have to do with race, and emanated not just from the usual expected sources, but also from her fellow dancers. Some white choreographers, particularly Isadora Duncan, were especially racist, deliberately designing their choreography antithetically to the so-called primitivism of black dancers.

For example, in her autobiography, Duncan claimed that black jazz rhythm "expresses the primitive savage" and that "the ape-like convulsions of the Charleston," like the "inane coquetry of the ballet, or the sensual convulsion of the Negro" are antithetical to the noblest forms of dance.[43] Elsewhere, Duncan notes that, if America had adopted her school and theories of dancing, "this deplorable modern dancing, which has its roots in the ceremonies of the African primitive, could never have become dominant."[44] By incorporating the popular dance of *Salome* into her repertoire, Walker may have been seeking an artistic response to the demeaning impressions held by many. *Salome* represented modern dance, and Walker sought the legitimacy that a modernist aesthetic might offer.

In the summer of 1912, after a 16-week tour of her vaudeville show across the Midwest, Walker returned to New York, where impresario Oscar Hammerstein offered her the opportunity to reappear in the role of *Salome* at his Roof Garden theatre (also known as the Victoria Theatre) on Broadway. Robert Speare reported that in her new version of *Salome*, Walker "is the only colored artist who has ever been known to give this dance in public." For Speare, "Miss Walker fully lives up to expectations and gives a graceful and interesting version of the dance."[45] Commenting on her 1912 performance, *Stage Pictorial* said that Walker "shows that she had studied the part and perhaps had also seen several other women in it. She was good without being great."[46] *Vanity Fair* published a précis to Walker's 1912 production that identified her "pantherine movements" as having "all the languorous grace which is traditionally bound up with Orient dancing."[47] The reference to "Orient dancing" reflected the vogue of Orientalism, which was symbolic of exoticism, otherness, and mystery.[48] One reviewer went so far as to consider Walker's *Salome* as a revival of ragtime. A "ragtime Salome" by "Miss Aida Overton Walker," reported the *New York Herald*, is the result of "the characteristic dance of her race." Judging from the applause, the reviewer wrote, "the revival pleased the spectators":

> Miss Walker was most effective in her dance when the curtain rose, showing her in Oriental costume standing at the top of a short flight of steps. She was graceful and wore her costume well.[49]

Walker danced in Broadway theatres and major theatrical playhouses throughout the United States. Although there are no extant playbills of her 1912 performance of *Salome* at Hammerstein's Victoria Theatre, the production was probably attended by a crowd eager to witness her interpretation of the sophisticated modern dance. Walker's dancing attempted to express a story, a plot, and aesthetic representation commonly found in middle-class theatres.

At a time when black women's expectations were severely limited, Walker knew what she wanted and set out to obtain it. She was in conflict, with dominant society's established expectations frustrating her desire for creative expression. She dared to take her dance into the domain of white dancers, crossing the racial divide and courageously encountering all the dangers such crossings implied. For the black community, Walker was recognized as a leader in her field. In *Colored American Review,* R. G. Doggett wrote in 1916 (two years after her death) that, in observing Walker dance *Salome,* "one is led to feel the true power and fascination of a real danseuse."[50] Five years following her death, Howe Alexander praised her in *Half-Century,* a middle-class African American journal that catered to black professionals and entrepreneurs. For Alexander, Walker "was the apogee of dancing as done by Colored dancers," and added that she "had the power to dilate the vision and stretch the imagination."[51] Vaudeville actor and writer Salem Tutt Whitney was Walker's colleague in several theatrical endeavors. In 1920 he wrote the following eulogy:

> Aida Overton Walker was one of the brightest, sweetest, most loveable, sagacious, talented and intelligent women who ever graced the ranks of show business. By force of ability, diligent study, strenuous work, tenacity of purpose and an almost superfluity of talent, she climbed to the top-most rung of the theatrical ladder, without a white or colored peer in her line. And then, she ran afoul of the color line. . . . Where her white sisters flourished she was not permitted to lead, nor would she condescend to follow.[52]

Walker chafed against the limitations imposed upon her and sought ways to circumvent, resist, and defy convention. Ethel Waters, too, sought to defy the restrictions imposed on her; but she danced in locales where an entirely different set of values and expectations were in play.

ETHEL WATERS: SWEET MAMA STRINGBEAN AND THE WORKING CLASS

[Ethel] Waters reveals a consciousness of being a part of a world in which women were under surveillance and has little hesitation in declaring her allegiance. —Hazel Carby (1995)[53]

Ethel Waters was born around 1896 (no one knows for certain her birth date) in Chester, Pennsylvania, where she was raised for a time by her maternal grandmother.[54] For the most part, she was shuttled from one home to another, living in extreme poverty. Her only way out was dancing and singing. "I love to dance,"

Waters maintained in an interview with the *New York Herald Tribune*. Her grandmother, she said, arranged "for me to go to a dancing school three times a week." While living in the "red-light section of Philadelphia," her grandmother "fixed it for a policeman to bring me home every night after school" because "the men around there would go for anything in skirts."[55] From an early age, dancing and singing became a way for her to circumvent poverty and express her independence. She performed in tent shows, singing popular minstrel, ragtime, and coon songs.

Waters began singing and dancing in vaudeville theatres in black neighborhoods, first in Decatur Street in Atlanta, and later in Philadelphia and Baltimore around 1917. Along the way she sang the blues and ragtime songs, learning much from Bessie Smith and Ma Rainey.[56] While the glamour of show business was attractive, show business was also an opportunity to work beyond domestic service. An article in the 1910 *Chicago Defender* reported that a singer engaged at Chicago's Pekin Theatre enjoyed a salary that provided her with "an honest living" wage rather than work "as a washroom maid."[57] Limited opportunities prompted Waters to join the Hill Sisters, a vaudevillian act she met while on tour. She entered the TOBA circuit around 1917, perhaps even earlier. The term "TOBA" meant the Theatre Owners Booking Association but was also euphemistically referred to as "Tough on Black Actors," because "it paid so little money, except to headliners."[58] Despite being a busy route for black vaudevillians, "reaching from Chicago to Florida, and from Oklahoma to New Orleans, with Memphis, Toledo, Chattanooga, Atlanta, Pittsburgh and other towns in between,"[59] the TOBA circuit was also a low-wage, catch-as-catch-can arena of vaudeville performance where entertainers were offered little in the way of assurances of schedule or pay (more on TOBA in chapter 11). In addition, the clubs on the circuit were frequently boisterous bars, juke joints, and honky-tonks.

It was in the touring circuit that Waters procured the nicknamed "Sweet Mamma Stringbean" because, as she put it, "I was so scrawny and tall."[60] Her work was arduous and dangerous. "When I was a honky-tonk entertainer," Waters said, "I used to work from nine until unconscious. I was just a young girl and when I tried to sing anything but the double-meaning songs they'd say: 'Oh, my God, Ethel, get hot!'"[61] Double-meaning songs contained sexual references, innuendoes, and parody, providing Waters with an early understanding of vocal and physical gestures that can mean several things at once. She learned at an early age how to manipulate the slippery slope of divvy bars and rough honky tonks while gaining a foothold in show business.

By 1919, Waters was appearing regularly at the Lincoln Theatre in Baltimore as well as Edmond Johnson's Cellar (known as Edmond's Cellar) in New York. According to Waters, Edmond's Cellar, on 132nd Street and Fifth Avenue in Harlem, was "the last stop on the way down in show business." After anyone worked at Edmond's, she sardonically remarked, "there was no place to go except into domestic service." Edmond's "drew the sporting men, the hookers, and other assorted underworld characters." Waters also appeared at the Bank's Club on 133rd Street, between Lenox and Fifth Avenues, which, as she described it, "was in the same low-down category" as Edmond's nightclub.[62] Edmond's and Bank's were juke joints frequented by bootleggers, hustlers, and drug dealers. It was also where working people went seeking music, dance, intoxication, gambling, fellowship, sex, and respite from the veneer of "respectable" life. It was markedly different from the middle- and upper-class Harlem clubs at the time, especially since most of the wealthier nightspots barred African Americans from attending except as servants, waiters, and performers. The interracial clubs were clearly marked and designated. Waters noted that the most popular club "for Negro sporting men and big shots was Baron Wilkins' famous night club, which also drew the white trade from downtown." However, "the ordinary working colored people weren't wanted there and knew better than to try to get in."[63]

The "ordinary working colored people," as Waters's put it, constituted her audience, at least during her early career (circa 1917 to 1920), before her recordings and rise to Broadway and film stardom. Waters performed in Edmond's, "a small place" that "seated between 150 and 200 people." The patrons sat at tables "jammed close together" and maneuvered around a "handkerchief-size dance floor."[64] As she bluntly put it, "I don't think it can hurt anybody if I say there were many junkers, gamblers, and thieves down in that cellar at all times."[65] Rudolph Fisher describes the scene at Edmond's in detail:

> It was a sure-enough honky-tonk, occupying the cellar of a saloon. It was the social center of what was then, and still is, Negro Harlem's kitchen. Here a tall brown-skin girl, unmistakably the one guaranteed in the song to make a preacher lay his Bible down, used to sing and dance her own peculiar numbers, vesting them with her own originality. She was known simply as Ethel, and was a genuine drawing-card. [Ethel] would stride with great leisure and self-assurance to the center of the floor, stand there with a half-contemptuous nonchalance, and wait. All would become silent at once. Then she'd begin her song, genuine blues, which, for all their humorous lines, emanated tragedy and heart-break.[66]

Zora Neale Hurston described Waters as an "open fire," because "the color and shape of her personality is never the same twice." Her "extraordinary talent" lacked formal education, but her gifts for performing were "in abundance."[67] Her alluring and simple entrances—standing at center stage with barely any motion—

indicated that she "knew" her audience and her audience had certain expectations of her. Waters discovered that intimacy and innuendo could prevail over excess and overacting. Her subtle gestures, nuanced voice, and restrained manner resulted from a talented, intelligent, and insightful entertainer realizing that within this cramped environment, filled with spectators eager to forget their daily burdens and indulge in music and drink, small gestures and vocal tones could be made to imply intimacy and sensuality.

With virtually no acoustical support (cellars are hardly musically conducive atmospheres), Waters was aware of the limitations of her stage; yet she overcame these limitations by accepting the environment she sang in and the people she sang to. Her performance style captured both the spirit of southern honky-tonks and the excitement of urban nightlife; the easy, smooth flow of the blues mixed with the inner, racy pulse of city vibrancy and jazz. She was a product of the ghetto, familiar with its dangers as well as its pulsating excitement; she was also savvy, attuned to the needs of the men who frequented the bars. Waters knew that in her world, dancing involved the treatment of women as objects for visual delectation. Her performance exuded sexuality and the expected "primitivism," but with something more: a sensibility that made her aware of her audiences' conditions. Her style evinced an empathy that evoked more by gesturing less.

For Waters, lowly bars like Edmond's Cellar and the TOBA circuit were venues where she honed her craft as a singer and shimmy dancer. "I love to dance," she said, adding that her "specialty was the choreography of the body shakes," or "shimmy," and referred to herself as the "best shimmier in our neighborhood."[68] Irene Castle described the shimmy in condescending terms:

> We get our dances from the Barbary Coast. Of course, they reach New York in very primitive condition, and have to be considerably toned down before they can be used in the drawing-room. There is one just arrived now—it is called "Shaking the Shimmy." It's a nigger dance, of course, and it appears to be a slow walk with frequent twitching of the shoulders.[69]

Cultural historian Kathy Peiss adds that the emergence of "tough" dancing on the social scene "ranged from a slow shimmy, or shaking of the shoulders and hips, to boisterous animal imitations that ridiculed middle-class ideas of grace and refinement."[70] Analyzing Waters's shimmy requires consideration of her dance movements, her relationship to the working class, and the recognition of the tropes of spontaneity and the various movements that define her style.

As a witness to her performances, James Weldon Johnson described Waters's choreography as lacking the versatility of one of her contemporaries,

Florence Mills, the star of the Broadway musical *Shuffle Along* (1921). For Johnson, Waters was without Mills's "vivacious energy" and "elusive charm." But what gave Waters charisma was the shimmy dance, in which she revealed the "innate poise that she possesses," made evident by the "quiet and subtlety of her personality." Waters's movements, he said, are "languorous," adding, "she is at her best when she is standing perfectly still, singing quietly." She "never over-exerts" her voice or movement, but rather "creates a sense of reserved power that compels the listener."[71] Her subtle movements and voice conveyed sexuality more by way of imagination than overt indication. It caught on with the black working-class audiences frequenting these clubs; the reasons underlying her success with this group bear significance beyond surface appearances.

Conditions for the black working class at the end of World War I were bleak. The industrial revolution engaged workers in high-risk jobs and the war machine of 1917 and 1918 needed employees. While many white men were off fighting the war, blacks and women filled the labor force. When the war ended, African Americans were, in the words of C. Vann Woodward, "pushed out of the more desirable jobs in industries that they had succeeded in invading during the manpower shortage of the war years."[72] Returning white workers from Europe demanded their jobs back, creating a vast pool of unemployed black workers. By 1919, this tension led to a series of race riots. Historian Herbert Shapiro alerts us to the fact that after the armistice and during the "Red Summer" of 1919, violence against blacks in Elaine, Arkansas, Chicago, Omaha, Washington, D.C., and other major cities uncovered a society "in which antagonisms of race and class were sharper, more explosive, than ever."[73] Chicago's riot in July was particularly brutal, lasting for five days and leaving over 500 people killed or injured.[74] The riot began during a hot summer's day, when the segregated beaches on Lake Michigan were overflowing and containment of each group's territory became impossible. A few black swimmers accidentally drifted into the unofficially designated white area, where they were subsequently pummeled with rocks and other objects while still in the water. One black youth drowned, either from being struck by rocks or fear of swimming to shore. The incident inflamed deeper resentments; much of the hostilities were attributable to the conflicts between returning white soldiers seeking the jobs they held prior to the war and black workers losing the hopes and dreams such jobs had provided. In this climate, black urban workers searched for nightclubs where the blues and suggestive dancing offered an alternative to the frustrations of unemployment and the tensions of racism in the workplace and everyday life. Waters's shimmy dance became one of several focal points for the release of tensions.

In addition to race riots, the black working class of the late 1910s and early 1920s experienced other violent transformations. Black farmers, fleeing from the oppressive conditions of tenancy, debt peonage, and crop liens common in the South, moved north in record numbers.[75] The peonage laws were particularly stressful; the *New York Age* reported in 1921 that in Georgia,

> any farmer can go to a city stockade or county prison where Negroes are impris-
> oned for misdemeanors and, if a Negro assents, can buy him out by paying his
> fine and take the Negro to his farm with the understanding that the Negro will
> remain there till the amount of his fine and debt to the farmer are worked out.[76]

From 1910 to 1920, New York City's black population grew from 91,708 to 152,467 (a 66.3 percent increase); Chicago's rose from 44,103 to 109,458 (148.2 percent); Cleveland from 8,448 to 34,451 (307.8 percent); Philadelphia from 84,859 to 134,339 (58.9 percent); and Detroit from a population of 5,741 African Americans to 40,838 (611.3 percent).[77] With the hope of freedom and the possibilities of work, African Americans during the Great Migration trekked northward in large numbers, only to find alienation and detachment from family, friends, and home. The hopes fueled by migration soon turned to disappointment. Forced to reside in the segregated communities of Harlem, Chicago, Detroit, Newark, Baltimore, Philadelphia, Roxbury, and East St. Louis, many black laborers also lived isolated from mainstream society and middle-class blacks, as well as families and friends left behind. In addition, work, if it was to be had at all, was hard, dull, arduous, and sometimes dangerous.

Cellar clubs, rent parties, and juke joints emerged as important social locations in the community. Black men who habituated jukes and cellar clubs often arrived after failing to find work or a hard day at low-wage jobs, where daily indignities and humiliations were the norm. Many were single men away from home; often driven by loneliness, they came to the "joints" not merely to anesthetize their emotional pain, but also to bolster self-esteem and socialize with others who had shared many of the same conditions. Caught in jobs with little or no opportunity for advancement, many sent money back to their families in the hope that they might join them in the North. For those coming from the West Indies, the lack of documentation made it all the more impossible to enter banks and build savings accounts. They spent their "extra" money, what little was left, in the jukes and cellars where singing and dancing enticed them with the promise of liquor, music, and camaraderie. The nights of leisure for the working class were, according to historian Robin D. G. Kelly, keys to "the private worlds of black working people where thoughts, dreams, and actions that were otherwise choked back in public could find expression." For African Americans, "whose days consisted of backbreaking wage work, low income, long hours, and pervasive racism," bars and clubs enabled them "to take back their bodies for their own pleasure rather than another's profit."[78] In a world where education and the elite environments were off-limits, cellar clubs, honky-tonks, and rent parties represented a panacea for life and a form of social cohesion. Moreover, for many black workers, cellar clubs were reminiscent of the southern juke joints they left behind. Dance was for these workers not only a release; it also became a form of continuation, a way of remembering distant family and friends.

Furthermore, dancing in bars provided movements and rhythm that was antithetical to the pace of the factory. The rhythms of these joints, coupled with liquor, endowed participants with feelings of impulsiveness and spontaneity that countered the monotony and repetition of industrial and domestic labor. Taylorism, the theory of mass production and the assembly line that reconceptualized the workplace into specialized tasks, induced a repetitiveness that denied outlets for individuality and inventiveness.[79] Routinized movements established a sameness between humans and machines; along with wages came drudgery and mechanized gestures. Dance, however, replaced the monotonous movements of the factory, establishing a site for the accepted release of stress and an outlet for personal creativity. For many African Americans, dancing was cathartic, a social expression that, as historian Tera W. Hunter notes, "embodied a resistance to the confinement of the body solely to wage work."[80] Searching for self-empowerment and socialization, workers attending bars and clubs experienced self-expression, fellowship, and physical release. In the bars and cellars, the black body expressed pleasure rather than being an instrument of labor for the satisfaction of industrial productivity. Waters's shimmy became the nexus of visual attention; her movements were attuned to celebration and release from the daily routine.

Having lived among them, Waters was acutely aware of her audience. She was one of many blues singers who, in the words of musicologist Daphne Duval Harrison, spoke "directly of and to the folk who have suffered pain," assuring them that "they are not alone."[81] While she frequently assumed the veneer of toughness offstage, onstage her dancing did not intimidate. Waters's biographer William Gardner Smith notes that although Waters "did the hottest dance shake of her day," wearing "tassels on her hips" and a "large buckle on her belt, to accentuate the movement of her body," she never conveyed a sense of "vulgarity."[82] Waters's dancing was unthreatening yet erotic, sensual but never vulgar. Her posture ingratiated her to audiences who often suffered from low self-esteem.

She provided a sense of dignity in her gestures and voice, even while her movements suggested sexuality. Waters sang and danced ribald songs without vulgarity. Through her vulnerability, she allowed herself to become the object of male desires, but through her decorum, she maintained the distance necessary for respect and survival. She drew a subtle line between allure and self-protection; she enticed, but kept her spectators at arm's length. Her decorum gained her the admiration of her audiences.

Waters learned to improvise by dividing her intentions between outward appearances and inward purposes. She was not an overly confident dancer, performing with the exuberant guile that might be attributed to Aida Overton Walker, Florence Mills, or Josephine Baker. Rather, her small movements suggested a measure of timidity, humility, and empathy with her audience. This enabled Waters to forge a bond with bruised egos and the disappointed. She did not cater to whites or the middle class like Aida Walker, at least not during her early career; instead, she allowed her vulnerability and subtlety as a dancer to connect with her working-class audiences. She was "one of them," born in poverty and hardship, sexually attractive yet also able to command a degree of reverence.

Waters, like Aida Walker, danced for self-definition, for selfhood; dancing offered her the best way of achieving an identity free of the forces that dictated what a black woman was supposed to be. But whereas Walker lived in a middle-class world and aspired to cultural recognition, Waters during her early career danced and sang in nightclubs and juke joints that existed in a world less conscious of middle-class intervention and requirements. For the middle class, a visit to the theatres and concert halls was "enriching" as well as entertaining. Watching dance in bourgeois theatres was deemed "cultural enlightenment," an opportunity for intellectual as well as pleasurable reflection. Dancing in Edmond's Cellar offered different aims and purposes. Waters's surroundings established an atmosphere of illegality, transgression, and defiance; those performing and those in attendance knew that their presence was an act of rebellion against the moral codes of the day. Illegal liquor (Prohibition was in full force) and drugs provided an atmosphere of transgression and rebellion, creating an aura already rife with sexual edginess and raw language.

In the early 1920s, Waters moved away from the working-class "joints" and into the mainstream. She recorded her first two songs on the Cardinal record label in 1921.[83] During the same year she became the first black recording artist for Black Swan Records, one of the most important recording companies for blues singers during the time. By the late 1920s she was a major star on Broadway and later in Hollywood. Unlike her friend and mentor, Bessie Smith, Waters ventured beyond the world of juke joints and speakeasies. By the mid-1920s, she headlined the celebrated Cotton Club, where she introduced her keynote song, "Stormy Weather," with the Duke Ellington Orchestra. In 1927, she appeared in her first Broadway musical, *Africana,* and by the early 1930s she was featured in Lew Leslie's *Blackbirds.* She had turned away from the rough clubs and bars to become a featured player.

Waters had learned to move fluidly from black audiences, which were frequently vocal and boisterous, to white audiences, where restraint and composure were commonplace. Bessie Smith's biographer Elaine Feinstein reports that Waters's early appearances before white audiences appalled her, owing to their seeming under-reaction to her performance. She believed she failed because the audience "received her only by clapping their hands."[84] As Waters explained, nobody "stomped as they always do in colored theatres when I finish my act." Because nobody in the white audiences "screamed or jumped up and down" or "howled with joy," she was skeptical of success with whites.[85] However, she quickly learned to understand and accept differences in audience appreciation. Eventually, Waters's flexibility enabled her to move from cellar clubs to mainstream theatres.

Waters's early years in show business as a dancer and blues singer at Edmond's affords us a glimpse into the black working-class entertainment milieu of the late 1910s. Before the influx of white patronage, Harlem's entertainment world featured African American performers for African American audiences. Langston Hughes describes the audience transition of the early 1920s in terms of "the growing influx of whites toward Harlem after sundown, flooding the little cabarets and bars where formerly only colored people laughed and sang, and where now the strangers were given the best ringside tables." These new white patrons, Hughes lamented, would "sit and stare at the Negro customers—like amusing animals in a zoo."[86] Prior to the change, Waters was one of the most popular entertainers in the late 1910s. There were many other black women who danced and sang in Edmond's Cellar and other equally low-paying, dead-end nightclubs. Waters represented only a fraction of performers who, by dint of their courage and perseverance, successfully climbed out of Edmond's Cellar to become featured players. Many more performers are forgotten, and little will ever be known about them. But it is important to recognize that black women who danced in places like Edmond's (before the rising tide of white interest) created choreography that was mimicked by popular dancers everywhere. The contributions of black women in these clubs had considerable social impact on popular entertainment.

CONCLUSION: CREATING DANCE OUT OF PATCHWORK QUILTS

*History is more than the accumulation of new data and facts. It is not
enough to simply add a few black women to the existing story and stir.*
—Darlene Clark Hine (1996)[87]

Dance was one of few professions available to black women that allowed for
creativity while offering the slight hope of escaping poverty. During the 1910s
and 1920s, domestic service was the largest source of employment for black
women. According to Chicago historian Allan H. Spear, approximately two-
thirds of African American women were employed in domestic services, with
"over 30 per cent as household servants and almost 14 per cent as laun-
dresses."[88] Performing provided one of the few options available to women
seeking a way out of this predictable life. Walker and Waters represented different ways of dancing, reflecting the demands of the environment that each inhab-
ited. But both sought recognition as choreographers, albeit in different settings.
Walker sought to express her choreography in the evolving modernist culture;
Waters was content, at least during her early career, to perform within the black
community's local clubs. Yet they shared similar conditions and obstacles: both
desired to shape their artistic expression within the context of primitivism and
all its trappings.

As a result of the multifarious influences on their work, Walker and Waters
developed their choreography in patchwork fashion, borrowing elements from
white dancers, drawing on black traditions of dance, accepting the role of primitive, resisting that role, and fusing these conflictual notions together, sometimes
rehearsed, sometimes not, but always with a combination of instinct, reflection,
and meticulous awareness of their precarious position as black women in a racist
and sexist atmosphere. Every gesture they incorporated into their choreography
had double, sometimes triple meanings, and they not only had to weigh the consequences of these meanings, but also to consider their ramifications for the
image of black women collectively.

Angela Y. Davis makes the point that given "the long history of slavery and
segregation in the United States, it is understandable that black social consciousness has been overdetermined by race."[89] This over-determination is mul-
tiplied by gender and the performance of the black female body. The
performances of Walker and Waters were double-edged: they played into
gender/racial stereotyping, and simultaneously worked against it. Black women
struggled against the constant imposition of being the Other—the "black"

Isadora Duncan, the "objectified" sexual object, and the marginalized dancer unrecognized by both peers and critics. As black female dancers, they remained on the outside. Yet as black women they did not passively accept the limitation society sought to impose upon them; they fought for legitimacy and the right to perform. When black women were denied the means to produce and express their history through written texts, they seized access to oral texts (singing) and the body (dancing). The rise of the blues and jazz recording industry afforded black women a venue of expression. Dance provided another venue, but one more difficult to assess.

The lack of historical records persistently overshadows our abilities to evaluate the important contributions these women made. Yet, there is enough to suggest that their performances were neither a *tabula rasa* nor free of constraints; rather, their choreography negotiated within the interstitial tensions of sexuality, self-expression, and cultural templates. Despite a divergence in emphasis, their choreography was complementary. Walker sought to enter the master's house, as it were, of "high-brow" art, while Waters enunciated the grass-roots life of the black working class. The contrast between Walker's modernist aesthetic and Waters's cellar club expression was striking. But they shared the precarious status of black women's choreography in the early twentieth century.

CHAPTER FOUR

"THE PAGEANT IS THE THING": BLACK NATIONALISM AND *THE STAR OF ETHIOPIA*

Colonialism is not satisfied merely with holding a people in its grip and emptying the native's brain of all form and content. By a kind of perverted logic, it turns to the past of oppressed people, and distorts, disfigures and destroys it.

—Frantz Fanon (1968)[1]

INTRODUCTION

The claims of no people . . . are respected by any nation until they are presented in a national capacity.   —Martin Delany (1852)[2]

W. E. B. Du Bois's production of the pageant *The Star of Ethiopia* opened at the 12th Regiment Armory in New York on 22 October 1913 (see figure 9).[3] It was not without controversy, for it raised significant issues concerning the portrayal of African Americans during a period of heightened racism and its antithesis, Black Nationalism, in the United States. Subsequent productions continued to portray African American history quite differently than it had been depicted by white ethnologists, novelists, and playwrights. *The Star of Ethiopia* stood in stark contrast to the depictions one finds, for example, in Thomas Dixon's *The Clansman: An Historical Romance of the Ku Klux Klan* (1905), and later, in D. W. Griffith's film based on Dixon's book, *Birth of a Nation* (1915). In the film, according to Du Bois, the black man was portrayed as a "fool, a vicious rapist, a venal and unscrupulous politician or a faithful but doddering idiot."[4]

The Star of Ethiopia, writes Du Bois biographer David Levering Lewis, "was the most patent, expansive use yet made by Du Bois of an ideology of black supremacy in order to confound one of white supremacy."[5] In *The Star of Ethiopia*, Du Bois sought a cultural representation of the black diaspora, a collective consciousness among black people centered upon a common history and ancestry. Confronted by racist propaganda that African Americans were devoid of culture, Du Bois set out to prove them wrong. His concerns in *The Star of Ethiopia* were to show first that African Americans have contributed to the rise of civilization; second, that this cultural contribution was, and is, as rich and diverse as that of Europe; and third, that African Americans have what historian Arnold Rampersad calls "a capacity for cultural regeneration even where they seemed to be in permanent social disarray."[6] The influence of colonial slavery was, in fact, to be viewed as a historical conflict testing the fortitude of black people. For Du Bois, the invocation of black collective history was to be seen in a positive light, inspiring the black community to higher stages of development. He believed that historical pageantry provided a useful means of encouraging black solidarity. After surveying some of the background to *The Star of Ethiopia*, I will examine the significance of Du Bois's production within the historical context of emerging Black Nationalism.[7]

A pernicious effect of racism is the internalization of negative stereotyping. George Parker observed in 1908 that "it has been constantly affirmed and reaffirmed that races of African blood have contributed nothing to humanity's store of knowledge and civilization." This persistent point of view "has produced a conviction of truth not only in the minds of those who affirm it, but also in the minds of those whom it wrongs."[8] Du Bois noted that in propaganda against blacks, African Americans "face one of the most stupendous efforts the world ever saw to discredit human beings, an effort involving universities, history, science, social life and religion."[9] In reaction to racist misrepresentations, Du Bois wrote the pageant in order, he said, to achieve three goals: to "get people interested in the development of Negro drama"; to teach "the colored people themselves the meaning of their history and their rich emotional life through a new theatre"; and "to reveal the Negro to the white world as a human, feeling thing."[10] As *The Washington Bee* acknowledged in 1915, *The Star of Ethiopia* was

> a serious effort by our most distinguished scholar to use the drama in a large form to teach the history of our origin, to stimulate the study of the history of the peoples from whom we have sprung, to ennoble our youth and to furnish our people with high ideals, hope and inspiration.[11]

Du Bois believed that historical pageantry provided a means to achieve black solidarity. *The Star of Ethiopia* attempted to situate black theatre in the realm of high art, while simultaneously bringing the same high art to the masses. In doing so, Du Bois sought a black national theatre based on both intellectual and folk-cultural roots. Frederic J. Haskins wrote in 1915 that the dual purpose of Du Bois's pageant was "to stimulate the pride of the colored people in historical process of their race, and to develop their natural dramatic talent."[12] As a consequence, the pageant ushered in an early form of black aesthetics, preparing the way for Du Bois's vision of a didactic folk theatre. He wrote that *The Star of Ethiopia*, "with masses of costumed colored folk and a dramatic theme carried out chiefly by movement, dancing, and music, could be made effective."[13] For Du Bois, "pageantry among colored people is not only possible, but in many ways of unsurpassed beauty and can be made a means of uplift and education and the beginning of a folk drama."[14] *The Star of Ethiopia*, Du Bois hoped, would serve as a powerful catalyst for the creation of a black national theatre fostering interest in racial uplift and indigenous black culture. "Art is propaganda," he wrote, "and ever must be, despite the wailing of the purists."[15] As propaganda, the pageant would illuminate black self-determination and cultural enlightenment. As art, it would provide a thrilling spectacle.

Ultimately, the aim of the pageant was to bolster an African American moral regeneration that would promote black culture. Each episode was designed to inspire admiration for black history by both entertaining and calling attention to the historical record. The production joined dance, music, and historical reenactments of African history, the Middle Passage, slavery, emancipation, and Reconstruction in order to celebrate black uniqueness. Directed by Charles Burroughs,[16] the pageant's four productions were altered slightly; broadly speaking, however, it consisted of a prologue and five scenes in thirteen episodes: Scene (1) The Gift of Iron; (2) The Dream of Egypt; (3) The Glory of Ethiopia; (4) The Valley of Humiliation; and (5) The Vision Everlasting.[17] Du Bois inserted activist Mary Church Terrell as Harriet Beecher Stowe in the pageant, and Montgomery Gregory, director of the Howard Players, appeared as an abolitionist.[18] *The Star of Ethiopia*, Du Bois explained,

> begins with the prehistoric black men who gave to the world the gift of welding iron. Ethiopia, Mother of Men, then leads the mystic procession of historic events past the glory of ancient Egypt, the splendid kingdoms of the Sudan and Zymbabwe down to the tragedy of the American slave trade. Up from slavery slowly . . . the black race writhes back to life and hope and with Touissant and Douglass builds a new and mighty Tower of Light on which the Star of Ethiopia gleams forever.[19]

The Star of Ethiopia was, up to that time, the most impressive history of pan–African Nationalism on the American stage. The *New York Outlook* called it "an impressive spectacle both from [a] historical point of view and as a forecast."[20] The *Washington Bee* observed that *The Star of Ethiopia* "covers a period of 10,000 years and more in the mythology, history and development of our race. It vividly tells the story of its work, its suffering, triumphs and hopes as an integral part of the human family."[21] Except for two selections from Verdi's *Aïda*, all facets of the production—music, costume, lighting, set design, and stage direction—were conceived and produced by African Americans. Two songs were drawn from the well-known musical theatre team of Cole and Johnson.[22] Despite the fact that each production met difficulties in overcoming financial shortages,[23] scheduling problems (the show contained over a thousand actors), and production obstacles,[24] Du Bois proudly proclaimed that the pageant "sweeps on and you hang trembling to its skirts. Nothing can stop it. It is. It will. Wonderfully, irresistibly the dream comes true."[25]

The Star of Ethiopia demonstrates that African Americans, like all Americans other than native indigenous peoples, bring their culture from foreign soil into the fabric of American life. The concept of pluralism and difference informed Du Bois's outlook. Historian David W. Blight argues that in Du Bois's collection of historical writing, he stressed "how multiple parts could make a new whole, how pluralism might be a new conceptual framework for American history."[26] Du Bois's consideration of African Americans in relationship to American history, philosopher Anthony Appiah explains, sought an "acceptance of difference," in which "the white race and its racial Other are related not as superior to inferior but as complementaries; that the Negro message is, with the white one, part of the message of humankind."[27] *The Star of Ethiopia* looked emphatically to Africa in conveying the play's ideology, in much the same way that several white pageants at the time looked to Europe. In fact, Du Bois hoped that white America would collectively share in the splendor of his pageant, seeing it as co-existent with white historical pageants. However, in disappointment he wrote that *The Star of Ethiopia*, "with thousands of actors, was given by Negroes for Negroes in three great cities for audiences aggregating tens of thousands—but the white American world hardly heard of it despite the marvelous color and drama."[28] The *Washington Bee* reported that "'The Star of Ethiopia' was undoubtedly the biggest thing in the drama that Washington has ever had, yet only a very few white persons came to see it."[29] But despite the difficulties in attracting white audiences, the pageant laid the groundwork for a black indigenous folk aesthetic.

Saginaw Valley State University ®

7400 Bay Road • University Center, MI 48710

Marc Gordon, Ph.D.
Assistant Professor
Department of Theatre
189 Curtiss Hall
Office: (989) 964-7496
E-mail: mgordon@svsu.edu

I'll try to get
the how to pay. $35.00

Have a great holiday!

Love to Jesse, Mark(?) and Mike

Marc

PAGEANTRY, NATIONALISM, AND ETHIOPIANISM

"Semper novi quid ex Africa," cried the Roman proconsul; and he voiced the verdict of forty centuries. Yet there are those who would write world-history and leave out this most marvelous of continents.

—W.E.B. Du Bois (1915)[30]

The significance of Du Bois's *The Star of Ethiopia* can best be understood within the context of the more general pageant movement, which reached the height of its popularity during the 1910s. Broadly speaking, pageants extolled the virtues of American history through historic reenactments of major events and actively participated in a burgeoning spirit of cultural nationalism through their enactments of immigrant identity—often juxtaposed with the assimilationist or melting-pot ideologies of their institutional sponsors. In 1914, William Chauncy Langdon wrote in the *Bulletin of the American Pageantry Association* that pageantry is "the drama of a community, showing how the character of that community as a community has developed."[31] Pageant historian Steve Grolin noted that pageants were being used throughout the country "to promote patriotism and civic pride, by dramatizing the integration of immigrants and other workers into the American community."[32] Nonetheless, Du Bois moved cautiously into the field of pageant drama, having little experience in playwriting.

Du Bois held that historical pageantry would supply the needed framework for African American cultural renewal. In June 1913, Du Bois wrote to Ellis P. Oberholtzer, member of the Board of Directors of the American Pageantry Association, that he was "going to have in New York a celebration of Emancipation, and among the things which we have planned is a pageant of Negro history."[33] For Du Bois, historicism—"Negro history"—was critical in understanding black culture and society. As Du Bois saw it, history was not merely evidence on which data rests; rather, it becomes both the way to apprehend the spirit of a community and the way of learning the culture of a particular society. According to Frederic J. Haskins, the purpose of Du Bois's pageant was similar to other historical pageants, "except that it is confined in scope to the interpretation of the highest ideals of Negro life."[34] The advance guard of African American people, Du Bois wrote in 1897, "must soon come to realize that if they are to take their just place in the van of Pan-Negroism, then their destiny is not absorption by the white Americans." Rather, African American destiny "is not a servile imitation of Anglo-Saxon culture, but a stalwart originality which shall unswervingly follow Negro ideals."[35] Pageantry, it appears, would be instrumental in conveying these "Negro ideals."

Du Bois's greatest fear, it seems, was the extinction of Africanism through apathy and cultural impoverishment. The underlying purpose of *The Star of Ethiopia* was to instruct and enlighten people of both races, and to use the pageant's theme, in Freda L. Scott's words, as a "valuable weapon in the Black cultural and political propaganda arsenal."[36] Pageantry was a political instrument that could bring together visual spectacle and dramatic performance, amounting to a useful device for creating a sense of community. Art historian Linda Nochlin maintains that a pageant could function in the style of "participatory dramatic action" in much the same way as "Diego Rivera's Mexican murals did in the realm of public, visual art," facilitating "a sense of contemporary purpose, self-identity and social cohesion out of a vivid recapitulation of historical fact heightened by symbolism."[37] While Du Bois doubtlessly borrowed structural arrangements from white pageants—emphasizing episodic scenes, historical reenactments, music, grand spectacle, and generalized rather than detailed dramas—his pageant would stress Black Nationalist themes.

Du Bois's Black Nationalist ideology emphasized not only the advancement of black economic and political independence, but inner pride as well.[38] Black Nationalism, in general, surfaced from a desire to reverse an intolerable situation; Black Nationalism viewed the basis of social life as a strategy for the promotion of cultural and economic power. Du Bois desired equality and empowerment for African Americans in the American system. He wrote in *Dusk of Dawn* that the "plan of action would have for its ultimate object, full Negro rights and Negro equality in America," with one method of attaining this being "continued agitation, protest and propaganda."[39] He also stressed aesthetic goals. Music, drama, and dance could unite a nation's folk heritage, thus encouraging a sense of social cohesion. For Du Bois, folk nationalism challenged the popular belief that blacks have failed to contribute culturally to American life.

Black Nationalism is the search for, and the establishment of, an identity in a society that has always viewed African Americans and their achievements as minimal at best. This nationalism attempts to correct this error on the part of the majority of white America by (a) recognizing black achievements in all areas of life; (b) establishing organizations that acknowledge black pride and accomplishments; and (c) seeking to identify those achievements as emanating directly from African American people. In her book *Nationalism: Five Roads to Modernity*, Liah Greenfield tells us that nationalism locates the source of identity "within a 'people,' which is seen as the bearer of sovereignty, the central object of loyalty, and the basis of collective solidarity." It is, fundamentally, "a matter of dignity," giving people "reasons to be proud."[40] Nationalism, for Du Bois, is more conceptual than factual; it resides in the realm of ideas, although it must be rooted in the actual achievements of a common people. Du Bois believed that the pageant would serve as a sign symbolizing a new identity paraded before the American public.

The roots of Du Bois's nationalism are also closely tied to Hegelianism and the German folklore movement spearheaded by Johann Gottfried von Herder (1744–1804). Du Bois's nationalism combined African traditions with European forms, representing what historian Wilson Jeremiah Moses describes as "the culmination of a tradition that conceived Black Nationalism in European terms."[41] Du Bois argued that each ethnic or racial group raises the collective consciousness of its members not individually but by a pursuit of its "Volksgeist," their spirit, soul, and genius.[42] Du Bois increasingly viewed racial conflict in America as resolvable through a *Sturm und Drang* struggle ("storm and stress," the German Romantic movement of the 1770s, which stressed passion and social commitment). Blacks and whites would eventually advance toward an apprecia-tion of one another, ultimately finding the Hegelian *Geist* in a cooperative World-Spirit.[43] Du Bois would follow Herder's advice that only "amid storms can the noble plant flourish: only by opposing struggle against false pretensions can the sweet labor of man be victorious."[44] Du Bois, writes Bernard W. Bell, believed that Herder's theory of folk art laid the foundation "for high art and the corollary conception of folksong as a spontaneous, indigenous expression of the collective soul of a people."[45]

In many ways, Du Bois belonged to a line of thinkers inculcated in the ideol-ogy of African American liberation movements that developed from needs felt by African Americans in their subordinate status in the American racial hierarchy. Building on initiatives that had their antecedents in the nineteenth century, Du Bois reconstructed African history as proof of Africa's contributions to human-ity. His focus on Black Nationalism prompted Du Bois not only to stage black history, but also to document it in his short but important work, *The Negro* (1915). There he wrote that race "is a dynamic and not a static conception," yielding "a social group distinct in history, appearance, and to some extent in spiritual gift."[46] *The Negro*, like *The Star of Ethiopia*, should be viewed as evidence of Du Bois's continuing intellectual development as a historian and social critic. Prior to these works he also established *Crisis* in 1910, a pioneering journal whose fundamental aim, says Arnold Rampersad, "was to defend, praise, and in-struct black people; more simply put, its goal was black power."[47]

American pageantry and German Romanticism were not the only agendas that characterized Du Bois's nationalist commentary. Broadly speaking, he sought a form of Black Nationalism he dubbed "Ethiopianism."[48] In fact, Du Bois originally titled the pageant *The Jewel of Ethiopia: The People of Peoples and Their Gifts to Men*. Ethiopianism began as an independent Church movement inspired by black religious secessionists who, according to historian J. Mutero Chirenje, used the terms Ethiopianism and Ethiopia in the Greco-Roman and biblical sense, "that Africa was the land of black people (or people with 'burnt faces')."[49] In the Bible, Psalm 68:31 says: "Ethiopia shall soon stretch out her hands to God." This biblical passage was not only a message of hope; the passage was also "echoed and re-echoed in all Black Nationalist literature" as "a metaphysical black heaven."[50] History, wrote B. F. Lee in 1904, supplies accounts of Ethiopian people "who reached a high state of civilization long before the Christian era."[51] Ethiopia symbolized for many a coming black cultural renaissance. The fact that, along with Liberia, Ethiopia managed to escape European colonization provided the symbol with richness of content. In 1896, Ethiopians defeated an invading Italian army at Adowa, and the Italian government subsequently sued for peace. The impact of the Ethiopian victory, writes African historian Edmond J. Keller, "was profound, sending shock waves throughout Europe." European powers, Keller adds, realized for the first time "that Ethiopia was an African power to be reckoned with."[52]

Ethiopianism was also a late-nineteenth-century movement seeking an independent Africa rooted in African Christianity and, in particular, based on the African Methodist Episcopal Church. Its purpose was threefold: to retain African cultural values for blacks worldwide, to instill racial pride, and to promote a mystical belief that Africa's redemption would be accompanied by a declining West. Ethiopianism provided the significant ingredients for the foundation for early African nationalism.[53] The Ethiopian tradition emerged from the shared political and religious experiences of English-speaking Africans during the late eighteenth and early nineteenth centuries. It eventually found its expression in Du Bois's pageant.

Du Bois was not alone in extolling the virtues of Ethiopianism. In varying degrees, Black Nationalists such as Martin Delany (1812–1885), Henry Highland Garnet (1812–1882), and Alexander Crummell (1818–1898) preceded Du Bois in espousing Ethiopianism. In 1848, Garnet wrote that Ethiopia is "one of the few nations whose destiny is spoken of in prophecy."[54] In 1879, Delany remarked that there is "little doubt as to the Ethiopians having been the first people in propagating an advanced civilization in morals, religion, arts, science and literature."[55] For the most part, Ethiopianism represented to black Americans what European history meant to white Americans, Asia to Asian Americans, and South America to Hispanic Americans: a cultural link to the past that served to nurture pride and identity. Poets such as Frances Ellen Watkins Harper (1824–1911) and Paul Laurence Dunbar (1872–1906) joined the nationalist cause. Meta Warrick Fuller's sculpture *The Awakening of Ethiopia* (circa 1914) depicts a proud African woman dressed, as art historian Richard Powell observes, "in the classical headgear and apparel of an ancient Egyptian pharaoh."[56]

By the late nineteenth century, many African American publications used Ethiopia as symbolic both of the unity and the diversity of black cultural experience in the United States. In an *Indianapolis Freeman* essay entitled "Ethiopia Shall Stretch," Charles Alexander wrote in 1898 that

> [the] Negro of today is up to every new art, every strange device, every new invention, every important discovery in the scientific world, every new religious thought, every social and economic movement—every important public question is of question to him, and he is working his way into every position of honor and worth to which the white man aspires.[57]

Du Bois presented in his pageant a diversity of African Americans from all walks of life, including "the symbolic figures of the Laborer, the Artisan, the Servant of Men, the Merchant, the Inventor, the Musician, the All-Mother, who begins as the Veiled Woman, who is now unveiled."[58] The stage directions note: "Enter 20 [African American] women in modern dress: doctor, nurse, teacher, musician, actress, hairdresser, book-keeper, stenographer, merchant, reporter, cook, artist, photographer, dressmaker, milliner and 5 women of fashion."[59] The pageant brings together ideas of nationalism and Ethiopianism in a broad display of African American cultural diversity.

THE PAGEANT IS THE THING

The Pageant is the Thing: That is what the people want and long for.
—W.E.B. Du Bois (1915)[60]

The Star of Ethiopia was first staged in New York, in six scenes using 350 actors, with a reported total audience of some 30,000. In *Dusk of Dawn*, Du Bois wrote:

> Encouraged by this response I undertook in 1915 to reproduce this in Washington. We used the great ball field of the American League, a massive background of an Egyptian temple painted by young Richard Brown, and a thousand actors. A committee of the most distinguished colored citizens of Washington co-operated with me. Audiences aggregating fourteen thousand saw the pageant.[61]

While productions in New York (1913), Washington, D.C. (1915), Philadelphia (1916), and Los Angeles (1925) enjoyed a high attendance, they were not financially successful. The venture was costly in the extreme: the Washington pageant of 1915 alone cost over $5,000. The 1916 Philadelphia pageant cost a "mere" $4,100. These costs were comparatively expensive, considering Du Bois's fledgling budget and the insufficient funds required for such an undertaking. The economic burden on Du Bois as well as the Hudson Guild, an organization run by Du Bois to sponsor the production, was enormous. Du Bois promoted the Philadelphia pageant by offering prizes to those selling the largest number of tickets.[62] Despite the cost, the pageants were, according to advertisements, "a great human festival and may be of singular beauty and lasting impression."[63]

In the opening moments of *The Star of Ethiopia*, the prelude sets the stage with four banners declaring the four gifts African Americans present to the world: iron, the Nile, Faith in Righteousness, and Humiliation. The Herald proclaimed at the opening performance:

> Hear ye, hear ye! All them that come to know the truth and listen to the tale of the Wisest and Greatest of Races of Men whose faces be Black. Hear ye, hear ye! And learn the ancient Glory of Ethiopia, All-Mother of men, whose wonders men forgot. See how beneath the Mountains of the Moon, alike in the Valley of Father Nile and in ancient Negro-land and Atlantis the Black Race ruled and strove and fought and sought the Star of Faith and Freedom even as other races did and do. Father of Men and sires of Children golden, black and brown, keep silent and hear the mighty word.[64]

Each succeeding episode portrays different periods of black history. The first episode, "The Gift of Iron: 50,000 Years B.C.," depicts Africans "fleeing from beast and storm, pray[ing] to Shango, and receiv[ing] from his daughter, Ethiopia, the Star of the Fire of Freedom."[65] Ethiopia, portrayed as the Veiled Woman, appears, "commanding in stature and splendid in garment, her dark face faintly visible, and in her right hand Fire, and Iron in her left."[66] Africans, as the pageant suggests, invent the welding of iron. For Du Bois, this episode established Africa as the regional source of iron smelting, illustrating one of Africa's many contributions to civilization.[67]

The second episode, "The Gift of the Nile: 5,000 B.C. and Later," depicts Egypt coming to worship the Black Sphinx. One reviewer wrote: "priests and worshippers file out of the temple. They are in the midst of their worship when the Kushites, having conquered all of their neighbors, rush in, but are appeased by the friendliness of the Egyptians and perhaps dazed by the splendor of the civilization and culture before their eyes. The two peoples fraternize and finally blend."[68] This episode illustrates human cooperation and establishes Africa as an early center of art and commerce.

The third episode, the "Gift of Faith: 1,000 B.C. and Later," portrays the Queen of Sheba, who "visits Solomon and shows him how Ethiopia has triumphed."[69] The episode also depicts the rise of Mohammedanism through battles with the Songhay. Gradually, war depletes the strength of the Africans, providing white slave traders their opportunity. One reviewer wrote, "The third scene depicts in the strongest dramatic manner how 'Ethiopia' was blotted out by fire and smoke and pillage by slave hunters, how they sought to get possession of the 'Star of Freedom.'" In the end, "Christians and Mohammedans chain and enslave all the people. At last the traders set fire to the Black Rock. Ethiopia burns [while] lifting the Cross to God and the Rock becomes her tomb. There is darkness."[70] This episode depicts the evolution of human conflict, with Africans struggling against external and internal strife.

Diaspora and slavery were the themes of the fourth episode, "The Valley of Humiliation: 1500 A.D. and Later." Ethiopia appears "on the West Coast in an African Village."[71] Blacks are subsequently enslaved. The abolitionist John Brown appears, Toussaint Louverture leads the Haitians, and Nat Turner inspires a slave revolt. The fourth episode portrays black humility and fortitude in their heroic resistance to oppression. The Herald declares:

> Hear ye, hear ye! All them that know the sorrow of the world. Hear ye, hear ye, and listen to the tale of the humblest and mightiest of the races of men whose faces be black. Hear ye, hear ye, and learn how this race did suffer of Pain, of Death and Slavery and yet of this Humiliation did not die.[72]

The final scene emphasizes "Freedom" and "The Vision Everlasting." African Americans are also seen in various professional roles. A reviewer wrote:

> When all these different groups are quietly enjoying their freedom . . . they are continually and most viciously attacked by the "furies" of race prejudice, envy, gambling, idleness, intemperance and the ku klux. . . . At first some of the groups give way, but others stand their ground. The "furies" try to seize the "Star." The freedmen appeal to "Ethiopia" with the sorrow song, "Nobody Knows the Trouble I See."[73]

The episode ends optimistically with victory for Ethiopia over greed, indolence, and intolerance. Burroughs's stage direction suggests a closing dance, "at the end of which, the world sings." Ethiopia, taking position "in front of [the] throne chair, extends her hands in benediction."[74]

According to Du Bois, the pageant was forced to close owing to a lack of funds and the advent of the motion pictures.[75] While neither a financial success nor recognized by white critics, *The Star of Ethiopia* served Du Bois's immediate purpose: to draw black people into the theatres and raise interest in a national black folk drama.

CONCLUSION

We believe that the Negro people, as a race, have a contribution to make
to civilization and humanity, which no other race can make.

W.E.B. Du Bois (1897)[76]

In *The Star of Ethiopia*, writes cultural historian Sterling Stuckey, Du Bois "attempted to use the past, in Négritude style, to erase self-hatred among his people, to inspire in the present and ennoble in the future."[77] In another important study, Stuckey calls Du Bois's form of Négritude a celebration of blackness that attempts to turn "negative attributes into positive ones."[78] If one assumes that Stuckey is correct, it may then be argued that, in applying Négritude taxonomies (i. e., turning negative attributes into positive signifiers), Du Bois may have oversimplified Black Nationalism, thereby compromising, in some respects, the very goals he sought. Stuckey's identification of *The Star of Ethiopia* with Négritude, however, is flawed.

Négritude, wrote poet and statesman Léopold Senghor (1906–2001) in his *Négritude et humanisme* (1964), "is the whole of the values of [black] civilization" that characterizes black people as "essentially instinctive reason."[79] Négritude defined the essence of blackness by deploying a dialectical response to whiteness: it signaled black intuition, what Senghor calls *l'homme de la nature* (the man of nature), in opposition to white rationalism. For Senghor and the Martinican poet and fellow Négritudist Aimé Césaire, the restoration of the primacy of intuition over reason was essential to their efforts to resist racism and recover their cultural identity. Frantz Fanon observes, however, that the poets of Négritude, while contrasting "the idea of an old Europe" to "a young Africa, tiresome reasoning to lyricism, oppressive logic to high-stepping nature," created a bipolar universe: "one side stiffness, ceremony, etiquette, and skepticism, while on the other frankness, liveliness, liberty, and . . . luxuriance: but also irresponsibility."[80] Consequently, the Négritudists trapped themselves into what playwright and philosopher Wole Soyinka calls "the defensive role, even though its accents were strident, its syntax hyperbolic and its strategy aggressive." Négritudists found themselves defending the idea that blacks were instinctual rather than intellectual. In doing so, they failed to incorporate a multifaceted system of values, stereotyping black people even if the stereotypes reflected positively. Négritude, Soyinka asserts, "accepted one of the most commonplace blasphemies of racism, that the black man has nothing between the ears."[81] It adopted the European Manichean tradition and borrowed Euro-American symbols of racial identification.

Du Bois's project avoided Négritude by promoting a plurality of black contributions to civilization through commerce, science, and the arts. By presenting black cultural diversity in *The Star of Ethiopia*, Du Bois created a polyphony of black voices. In doing so, he would eschew any call for a monolithic black culture. No doubt Du Bois constructed the pageant as a response to white nationalism, depicting black evolution from irrationality to rationality. Arnold Rampersad is most certainly correct when he asserts that Du Bois affirmed Georg Lukács's nineteenth-century historicist-positivist vision of art as "the product of social development."[82] Du Bois's black aesthetics had little choice but to borrow from the dominant culture; as Edward W. Said reminds us, one of the first tasks of cultural resistance is "to reclaim, rename, and reinhabit" the space reserved initially by and for the dominant society.[83] Moreover, Du Bois's notions of a racialized Africanism moved towards essentialism through identity politics. In concentrating on Africanism as the nexus of his aesthetic plan, however, Du Bois's pageantry acknowledged the significance of a shared, communal experience. Rather than inverting racial logic in Négritude fashion (suggesting that black intuition counters white rationalism), Du Bois intended a more subtle attack on racist presumptions, paying homage to African American cultural diversity. The pageant, wrote Du Bois, was a folk play "based on the history, real and legendary, of the negro race."[84] *The Star of Ethiopia* was the source of a new, reflexive black consciousness, which looked toward an African past that was synonymous with the black diaspora, while simultaneously affirming the plethora of black contemporary contributions.

Anthropologically, colonialism has, as part of its intent, to homogenize the world, to shape other cultures according to its images. Du Bois resisted hegemony by facilitating a new Afrocentricity from the hybridization of African and African American aesthetics. To be sure, Du Bois's pageant reflected Eurocentric patterns and forms, projecting them onto African American theatre. Yet Du Bois critiqued traditions that stereotyped all nonwhite cultures as creatively unsophisticated. He hoped to endow Africa symbolically through pageantry. For Du Bois, Africa's heritage should be a source of pride and the basic ingredient of racial solidarity. By representing Africa as the matrix of cultural reunion, Du Bois set in motion a healing process for African Americans denied cultural roots.

Moreover, Du Bois's views on drama sounded the challenge of a black national theatre (more on this idea in chapter 10). African Americans, he argued, would not realize the true potential of black drama until black theatre turned toward nationalism and African roots. Throughout Africa, Du Bois observed, "pageantry and dramatic recital [are] closely mingled with religious rites and in America the 'Shout' of the church revival is in its essence pure drama."[85] Du Bois recognized early on that patterns found in black churches were central to African American dramatic art. He also advocated historical fidelity and verity, which would ultimately reveal African American cultural worth. The pageant, he said,

> is not a tableau or playlet or float. It is a great historical folk festival, staged and conducted by experts with all the devices of modern theatrical presentation and with the added touch of reality given by numbers, space and fidelity to historical truth.[86]

In performing black pageantry, Du Bois challenged the master narrative of United States history. He realized that early twentieth-century pageantry was contributing to an American mythology that would establish the United States as a dominant society. Conscious of this emerging modern American identity, Du Bois sought to include African Americans in the discourse of nationalist rhetoric. David W. Blight notes that the "endless dialectic between the beauty and the pain" that lies at the root of American history "is just what Du Bois sought to capture by bringing the black experience to the center of the story."[87] Despite the odds, *The Star of Ethiopia* projected the diversity of the black experience onto the fabric of American life.

PART II

BLACK DRAMA

You can make this a real Negro theatre, maybe the best in the world. You could do it. If there aren't any plays get somebody to write them for you. Within your bodies and souls lie the immense possibilities of your race, and it is up to you to make successes of everything you essay.

—Charles S. Gilpin (1923)[1]

During the Harlem Renaissance, black playwrights searched for new representations of African America. The idea of drama, and of a national theatre, began to possess a special place in African American culture when Ridgely Torrence's *Three Plays for a Negro Theatre* opened on Broadway in 1917. In this context the claims that black intellectuals, playwrights, and performers made for an indigenous drama as a kind of redemptive cultural ritual became understandable. Harlem Renaissance drama, writes theatre historian Freda Scott Giles, was first an "effective counterattack against the overwhelmingly powerful minstrel stereotypes," and second it helped open a "window of opportunity" that would "enable African-Americans to internally and externally value the culture they had created."[2] The place of drama in the life of the black community was inspired by the rise of national dramas throughout Europe and the United States, and the desire to create an expressive drama that spoke to the hearts and minds of African Americans.

Not every cultural historian, however, has reacted enthusiastically to Harlem Renaissance drama. In the late 1960s, critic Larry Neal decried Harlem Renaissance drama as "essentially a failure" because it failed to address "the mythology and the life-style" of the black community and "to take roots, to link itself concretely to the struggles of that community, to become its voice and spirit."[3] Largely because

Neal's view has become conventional wisdom, scant attention has been paid to the dramas of the Harlem Renaissance. The editors of the *Norton Anthology of African American Literature* confirm this dismal perception, encouraging the view that, despite the success of the musical *Shuffle Along* (1921), the Harlem Renaissance period "produced few new plays of quality."[4] Notwithstanding the entreaties of Kathy A. Perkins and Judith L. Stephens,[5] many critics concur that Harlem Renaissance plays were overwrought and unsuccessful, exerting little if any influence over future generations of playwrights.

However, a close examination of several plays will provide some basis for challenging the received opinion. The plays discussed here may not have been box office successes, but the playwrights did attempt to link their messages to the community and its struggles.

CHAPTER FIVE

WALTER BENJAMIN AND THE LYNCHING PLAY: MOURNING AND ALLEGORY IN ANGELINA WELD GRIMKÉ'S *RACHEL*

That is their rite of colored male passage: having to drag all those lynchings around with them, around their necks: those are their ancestors. Too bad when violent deaths define who you are.

—Hilton Als (2000)[1]

INTRODUCTION

To read the details of lynching is to be reminded of the torture of the Middle Ages.   —Thomas F. Gossett (1963)[2]

From the mid-1910s through the 1920s, several anti-lynching plays by African Americans were presented. The plays were in response to the violent tactics of mobs terrorizing African Americans not only throughout the South, but also in many northern states as well. The authorial efforts were by writers and social critics who, firm in their conviction, believed drama capable of evoking social change.[3] Angelina Weld Grimké's play *Rachel* (1916) represented one of these attempts and it is this drama that shall be the focus of this chapter.[4]

Drama critics have tended to frame most anti-lynching plays narrowly, seeing them through the prism of melodrama and realism. For example, Patricia R. Schroeder argues that Grimké and another anti-lynching dramatist, Mary Burrill, "used naturalistic settings, vernacular language, realistic characters, and linear causality in their plots to depict the conflicts over motherhood faced by African-American women of their era." In this way, they hoped "to use realism's mimetic power to question stereotypes and illustrate social injustice."[5] There is certainly much truth to this observation. Realism revealed the consequences of lynching and the conditions under which black people endured. Judith L. Stephens also adds credibility to the alleged realist connection when she claims that anti-lynching plays "graphically depict lynching as both a violent crime and a pervasive influence in daily life."[6] This "graphic depiction" was meant to provoke awareness of mob violence and its affects. Grimké's realistic purpose, according to Will Harris, was "to stage substantive, independent African American female presences" in the midst of violence.[7] Realism helped describe in human terms how lynching cast a shadow over the lives of people, and thus assisted in efforts to abolish the heinous practice.[8] This interpretation is accurate up to a point; however, it offers a narrow outlook, whereas an alternative perspective to realism can be taken.

Melancholic in tone, Grimké's *Rachel* ought to be understood as a highly subjective response to the violence of the time. The protagonist of the play, Rachel, suffers from acute melancholia. Responding to the horrors of her environment, Grimké uses mourning, lamentation, and melancholy as the modes of her protagonist's expression. The critic most closely attuned to these modes in drama is art and social commentator Walter Benjamin, whose theories on dramatic criticism have influenced many contemporary critics. In view of their parallel interests in dramaturgical construction, Grimké's *Rachel* can be interpreted along the lines of Benjamin's theory of mourning and allegory.

Benjamin (1892–1940) and Grimké (1880–1958), despite being contemporaries, wrote about different epochs. Whereas Benjamin's most extensive and complex work, *Ursprung des deutschen Trauerspiels* (literally, "The Origin of German Mourning Plays," 1925), emphasizes seventeenth-century baroque drama, Grimké's play, *Rachel*, takes its point of departure from the late nineteenth- and early twentieth-century crime of lynching in the United States. There are undeniable difficulties in comparing an African American lynching play and the theories underlying German baroque dramas written nearly three centuries earlier. Notwithstanding the obvious drawbacks, there are worthwhile comparisons to be made. In response to Judith L. Stephens's question—can lynching plays "be evaluated from 'purely artistic' criteria, without regard to their social/historical meaning and function"[9]—it will be argued here that an artistic criterion is not only possible but also justifiable. In aligning *Rachel* with Benjaminian themes, I hope to shed a different light on a play frequently dismissed as one-dimensional.

Written and produced in 1916 in Washington, D.C., and published in 1920, *Rachel* was the first full-length extant anti-lynching drama.[10] Originally titled *Blessed Are the Barren,* this three-act play depicts an educated and overly sensitive African American woman confronted with the horrors of lynching and racism. Rachel lives in a well cared for but humble apartment with her mother and brother. Grimké describes her in the play as "the spirit of abounding life, health, job, youth."[11] Rachel is a sensitive and exuberant young woman who hopes someday to marry her brother's friend, John Strong, and raise a family. Her wish to be a mother is unequivocally stated: "And, Ma dear, if I believed that I should grow up and not be a mother, I'd pray to die now." Shortly thereafter, she expresses her need to protect "little black and brown babies" more than others, since they are put "in danger" by racism.[12] Her mother decides it is time to reveal the family's past. Ten years earlier Rachel's father, editor of a black newspaper, criticized whites of a southern town for lynching an innocent black man. Incensed, a white mob broke down the door, dragged him and his oldest son from the home, and hung them from the nearest tree. At the end of the act, Rachel must, as Grimké explains, "come suddenly and terribly face to face with what motherhood means to the colored woman in the South."[13]

Four years lapse between Acts I and II. Rachel has received a Jim Crow education and endured the economic realities that awaited many blacks heading North. But she also comes to learn that John Strong's feelings for her are genuine. It is her great misfortune, however, to witness racism's effect on children and she is unprepared for its cruelty. The experiences of her adopted son, Jimmy, and those related by visitors convince her that the neighborhood schools and the environment are rife with racism. Torn between what Grimké calls "this desire for motherhood," and the vow "never to bring a child here to have its life blighted and ruined," Rachel, according to the stage directions, ends the second act by "fiercely [snatching] the rose buds from the vase, [grasping] them roughly, and [grinding the roses] under her feet."[14]

A week passes between Acts II to III. Although Rachel vows never to have children, she is still driven to protect her adopted son, Jimmy. In the end, Strong makes his final offer to marry, but Rachel is determined, as Grimké explains in her synopsis of the play:

> Every night since Jimmy has undergone that searing experience in the previous act [of racist taunts] he has dreamed of it and awakens weeping. With that sound in her ears and soul she finds that she cannot marry [Strong]. . . . Although her heart is breaking she sends him away. The play ends in blackness and with the inconsolable sounds of little Jimmy weeping.[15]

Grimké's biographer Gloria T. Hull maintains that the greatest fault contemporary readers are likely to find with the play is its sentimentality. She asserts that, although one may be sympathetic toward Rachel and convinced of her message and its truth, Rachel comes across as "extreme." For Hull, Rachel is "too sensitive, too good, too sweet—almost saccharine," leading to treacly melodrama and lachrymose sentiments.[16] While modern audiences might find *Rachel* excessive, the opulence of her imagery, the overabundance of her passion, and the repetitiveness of her language are appropriate to Benjamin's concept of *Trauerspiel*. Understanding Benjamin's theories as they pertain to Grimké's play will make this evident.

RACHEL AND *TRAUERSPIEL*

> *Southern trees bear strange fruit,*
> *Blood on the leaves and blood at the root,*
> *Black body swinging in the Southern breeze,*
> *Strange fruit hanging from the poplar trees.*
> —Abe Meeropol (1937)[17]

Benjamin's most important work, *Ursprung des deutschen Trauerspiels* (translated for English publication as *The Origin of German Tragic Drama*) focuses on the period of baroque drama, particularly during the Thirty Years' War (1618–1648). The playwrights Benjamin refers to—Opitz, Gryphius, and Lohenstein, among others—were writing at a time of immense, violent destruction. Benjamin examines these plays and playwrights, but his real intent is to reflect not only on the era's bloody reign, but also on Judeo-Christian philosophy and the dichotomy between history and myth, tragedy and mourning, and symbol and allegory. One of the most important points he raises is that the baroque period was an epoch of destructiveness, decay, and ruination, crucial aspects that must be considered along with the plays. Lynching plays require a similar contextualization against a background of mob terrorism. In both worlds, catastrophic violence threatens daily existence. While baroque plays deal primarily with the failure of sovereignty in the face of violence, there are similarities between the protagonists of baroque dramas and *Rachel:* in both, the protagonists respond to the violence with excessive lamentations, desolation lurks ubiquitously, and the plays mock the pretense of human action. Above all, Benjamin's analysis eventuates in the term *Trauerspiel*, which marks this type of genre.

Trauerspiel describes a drama in which symbolic representations of real-world destructiveness fail in two ways: first, they fail to create in the drama a cohesive social whole, and second, they fail to bring the horrors of the world to some form of dramaturgical comprehension and closure. Instead of cohesion and lucidity, *Trauerspiel* (literally "mourning play") are "plays for the mournful,"[18] where grief and excess are characteristic motifs. Continuous and excessive mourning is the proper response to a specific period of unimaginable destruction, where the blood of corpses washes away any illusion of myth, hope, and symbolic aestheticism. The experience of unprecedented violence is not merely commented on by the plays; violence itself is incorporated in the work through three dramaturgical devices: lamentation, ostentation (opulent language and excessive emotion), and allegory. The German plays of this genre try to come to grips with the reality of historic catastrophe and unparalleled physical violence; lynching plays attempt to come to terms with similar circumstances.

The opulent sorrow of *Rachel* can be said to exemplify Benjamin's term *Trauerspiel*. In fact, the concept of *Trauerspiel* is particularly well suited for examining lynching dramas as an art form. Beginning in the post-Reconstruction period and continuing through the 1930s, lynching of African Americans was commonplace. *Crisis* maintained statistics and data on lynching victims according to place (states where the crimes occurred) and justification (what motivated the lynchings). Reports also emerged clarifying in blunt terms the brutality of lynching itself. For example, in 1905, Mary Church Terrell, honorary President of the National Association of Colored Women, provided the following account of a lynching in the *Atlantic Monthly*, which characterized the sadistic nature of the act.

> When two Negroes were captured, they were tied to trees. . . . The blacks were forced to hold out their hands while one finger at a time was chopped off. The fingers were distributed as souvenirs. . . . The most excruciating form of punishment consisted in the use of large corkscrews in the hands of some of the mob. The instruments were bored into the flesh of the man and woman, in the arms, legs and body, and then pulled out, the spirals tearing out big pieces of raw, quivering flesh every time it was withdrawn.[19]

The above description was not unusual. The accounts were well documented. The mobs themselves boasted of the act in an effort to instill fear. Lynchings were more than mere facts of hanging; they were, in Leon F. Litwack's words, "slow, methodical, sadistic, often highly inventive forms of torture and mutilation,"[20] designed to send a clear message against any attempts at social transgression.

For Benjamin, historic periods of extreme violence require an extreme form of drama to represent them. Unimaginable violence cannot be cloaked in the pristine dignity of "tragedy." Tragedy corresponds to linguistic purity, semantic lucidity, and spoken eloquence. It is a refined art form, best suited to represent myths and legends rather than the sullied and muddled events of history. In arguing his case for mourning plays as a unique genre, Benjamin compares tragedy and *Trauerspiel*. In an essay, "On the Significance of Speech in Trauerspiel and Tragedy," he writes that the tragic "is based on the legitimacy of the spoken word between humans."[21] Language helps illuminate tragedy; more importantly for Benjamin, in tragedy "the word and the tragic arise together, simultaneously, each in the same place."[22] Language, as Benjamin sees it, clarifies the world, and tragedy is formulated around the need to make sense. Tragic language provides understanding of myths of heroic proportions, eventuating in a cathartic experience. *Trauerspiel*, by contrast, offers neither order nor finality; in *Trauerspiel*, expressions of grief are continuous, logic is unfulfilling, and the echoes of mourning rather than relief from catharsis are the only appropriate responses to the mundane reality of incomprehensible injustice. Although in *Trauerspiel* grieving takes the form of an endless outpouring of words, the words are essentially repetitious, overstated, and ultimately meaningless (or, at the very least, ineffectual). However, they are significant in that they serve, through sound, to keep the horrors of the world at the forefront of the drama. In *Trauerspiel*, sound and lamentation — mourning — are more significant than words, since it is the voice in abstraction, apart from structure or meaning, that serves as the most immediate response, in a purely emotive sense, to terror. Yet sound, by itself, threatens to dissolve into a distant echo. For Benjamin, the baroque "echo," which is literally a free play of sound, is harnessed for dramatic effect. However, like an echo, it runs the risk of dissolution. Sound therefore has to be manufactured continuously, which makes this type of drama appear contrived. Still, the sound of mourning and its eventual dissolution is for Benjamin the basis of *Trauerspiel*'s ambiguity and fascination.

Benjamin is, to a certain degree, describing opera. The language of *Trauerspiel*, specifically its sound or lamentation, is linked to music and the continual cadence of sound. Benjamin explains that *Trauerspiel* "describes the route from the sound of nature through the lament [*Klage*] to music." Sound, he says, "reveals itself in *Trauerspiel* symphonically, and this is at once the musical principle of its language."[23] Benjamin notes that baroque tragedy must find its expression in the "mystery of music," because *Trauerspiel* "rests not on the basis of realistic language," but rather "on the consciousness of the unity of language through feeling, which unfolds itself in the word." Within this unfolding, he says, lost feelings, forgotten passions, and historical events rise "to the lament of mourning."[24] In *Trauerspiel* the meaning of words alone cannot capture feelings or adequately express the significance of events; the expressiveness of sound — its musicality — must buttress the words, giving them visceral authority to convey pain and suffering. As Benjamin explains, "mourning is merely a sound in the scale of feeling," because in *Trauerspiel* "everything arrives from the ear of lament"; whereas in tragedy, "the eternal rigidity of the spoken word asserts itself [*sich erhebt*], *Trauerspiel* aggregates in the endless resonance of sound."[25]

Rachel is based on sound, on the melodramatic overflow of words. Literary historian Nellie McKay calls it "an angry play," revealing Grimké's outrage at the sadism and banality of lynching.[26] Anger describes the play to some extent; but the play is also an oral lament. Rachel is an educated, middle-class African American woman whose overt sensitivity and linguistic facility chafes against the crude primitivism of oppression. Like the sound of opera, the protagonist hurls her words at the brick wall of lynchers, hopeful that the repetition of her voice will chip away at insensitivity. Her long speeches and excessive melancholia are artistic devices that convey her overwrought sorrow. Rachel's lamentation is a gateway into the abyss of her soul and *Trauerspiel* is the artistic device that grants us a glimpse into this chasm.

In *Trauerspiel* there are neither resolutions nor conclusions, but only a profound gulf between words and meaning. Unlike tragedy, with its rational coherence and concise beginning, middle, and end, *Trauerspiel* questions our confidence in making sense of the world; it rejects the certainty of the world as false, since time will eventually erode things and their meanings. Instead of certainty, *Trauerspiel* favors a ghostly or haunted presence in drama that bears the effects of time and decay, conveying an irrationality that "pervades existing society."[27] Rachel's sustained, painful lament moves past the point of rationality, becoming a repetitive cascade of sounds spoken in a murky void. In its heavy-handedness, Grimké's *Rachel* attempts to find the root of pain and express it through an outpouring of words and emotions.

For Benjamin, *Trauerspiel*'s extremes are a response to the extremes of confusion and decay, excess and nothingness, and bemoaning of the incomprehensibility of *Weltschmerz* (world-pain).[28] Thus, the "awkward heavy-handedness [*Schwerfälligkeit*]" of *Trauerspiel* is "essential" to the nature of the genre.[29] Confronting violence directly is deemed senseless; instead, the violence is internalized in the protagonist. But the act of internalizing merely invites sorrow, unhappiness, and chaos. This internalization leads to a dramatic display of groping anguish and incessant grief. George Steiner explains that for Benjamin tragic feelings "refine, enrich and bring into tensed equilibrium the inchoate muddle or incipience of the spectator's emotions." In contrast, *Trauerspiel* "signifies sorrow, lament, the ceremonies and memorabilia of grief"; literally and in spirit, *Trauerspiel* is "a play of sorrow, a playing at and displaying of human wretchedness."[30] In *Rachel*, the continual display of the protagonist's anguish is the resonance of *Trauerspiel*.

Traurigkeit (sorrow) is at the foundation of *Rachel,* with mourning reverberating throughout. An anguished lament signals the protagonist's self-denial and her speeches are stamped by an overflow of excess and sound. In one passage, she speaks to God with disdain, anger, and passion, but her purposes seem indeterminate and random, as if God and not humans ordained her suffering. At the end of Act II, Rachel remarks mournfully:

> Why, God, you were making a mock of me; you were laughing at me. I didn't believe God could laugh at our suffering, but He can. We are accursed, accursed! We have nothing, absolutely nothing.... You God!—You terrible, laughing God! Listen! I swear—and may my soul be damned to eternity, if I do break my oath—I swear—that no child of mine shall ever lie upon my breast, for I will not have it rise up, in the terrible days to be—and call me cursed.[31]

The above passage expresses Rachel's rage, but it also captures her threnody. Her invocation of God reflects her dispirited dirge, her disturbing unhappiness, and vocalization of continuous pain. Her frustration is everywhere in the play. Characters in *Trauerspiel* are engulfed by an indeterminate inwardness and uncertainty, forced to confront, as Benjamin says, "the tense polarity" between sound and words.[32] *Trauerspiel* is conceived as the proper self-expression of what literary critic Ferenc Feher calls Benjamin's "godforsaken world."[33] In *Rachel,* Grimké creates a godforsaken world filled with inward mourning and indeterminate grief. Rachel's *Traurigkeit* is an all-consuming sorrow; her anguish is directed broadly at racism and the absurdity of violence. Her melancholia is, by and large, a Freudian pathology; she is an individual who, as Freud explains, moves from a "process of regression" to "isolated actions and innervations" based on narcissistic "reaction to the loss of a love object."[34] Based on her feelings of loss, Rachel's sorrowful expressions are rooted in the sound of her lament, not merely in the syntax of her language. Her mode is operatic; opera is the aesthetic form that might well describe the play, for it is in opera where sound will predominate over spoken words.

Fredric Jameson notes that Benjamin's *Trauerspiel* may best be characterized as a "funeral pageant."[35] For Rachel, the ritual lynchings mark an anguished procession of moral and social decay, and her responses echo the incomprehensibility of such events. In Benjaminian terms, Rachel's introspectiveness and melancholy are expressed ostentatiously through sorrow. Rachel is, in fact, steeped in melancholy, shrouding everything in despair. At the close of Act I, Rachel poignantly expresses the thoughts of a black mother who has lost children to a lynch mob:

Then everywhere, everywhere, throughout the South, there are hundreds of dark mothers who live in fear, terrible suffocating fear, whose rest by night is broken, and whose joy by day in their babies on their hearts is three parts—pain. . . . Why—it would be more merciful—to strangle the little things at birth. And so this nation—this white Christian nation—has deliberately set its curse upon the most beautiful—the most holy thing in life—motherhood![36]

Grimké's Rachel builds her sacred world around her decision to be childless. For Rachel, motherhood is an all-or-nothing proposition: either she will bring children into a world safe from terror, or she will have none of it. In her notes, Grimké explains her intent: if anything can make all women sisters, "it is motherhood." She then surmises that if "I could make the white women of this country see, feel, understand just what [effect] their prejudices . . . were having on the souls of the colored mothers everywhere," then "a great power to affect public opinion would be set free and the battle would be half won."[37] Grimké's gambit banked on the empathetic response of white women to a shared identification with motherhood.

Grimké uses childlessness as an artistic representation emphasizing the effects lynching had on black women; lynching becomes the obstacle to normalcy and joy. Grimké, note Perkins and Stephens, "has structured her play" so that lynching is the "overarching symbol for all injustices experienced by African Americans." In *Rachel*, they maintain, "lynching is inexorably linked to the daily indignities faced by African Americans and emerges as the ultimate symbol of injustice against black people."[38] Viewed in this way, lynching represents the "symbolic" underpinnings of the play. However, close inspection of *Rachel* will reveal that Grimké's dramaturgical effects are, according to Benjamin's definition, *allegorical* rather than symbolic.

RACHEL AND ALLEGORY

That people could see and hear about these events far away from and long after the fact of their occurrence is part of the act of lynching itself, for representations not only function to preserve the act in perpetuity, they also allow the act to be committed again.

—Angelina Weld Grimké (n.d.)[39]

According to Benjamin, allegory has the potential to express historical epochs in their ruin and decay. Whereas the symbol nobly aspires to an immediate unification with that which it is intended to represent, encapsulating the subject within the object it wishes to depict, allegory is profane in its affinity for ruin, chaos, and redemption. Benjamin states that "whereas in the symbol destruction is idealized and the transfigured face of nature is fleetingly revealed in the light of redemption," in allegory the observer is confronted with history that is a "petrified, primordial landscape," that everything about history "has been untimely, sorrowful, unsuccessful," and that history is expressed in a "death's head."[40] Symbolism points beyond itself toward some transcendent, idealized realization, ascribing clarity and purity to the meaning of its object. Allegory, in contrast, is a process of signification that calls forth negation, corrosion, and death. Allegories, says Benjamin, are "in the realm of thoughts, what ruins are in the realm of things."[41] Allegory has the power to express confused and inarticulate passions of oppressed people living amidst violence. For Benjamin, symbols are pristine images of harmony, simplicity, and tonality. Allegory, by comparison, is abundant, overflowing with images of death and ruin, a muddle of signs that Hans-Georg Gadamer calls allegory's "overload."[42] It is this overload that provides the raw material for artistic expression in an age of ruin.

Benjamin attempts to rehabilitate allegory, a literary and dramatic device that lost its authority during the late eighteenth and early nineteenth centuries.[43] Spearheaded by Goethe's later works, Weimar neoclassicists based their aesthetics on theories that rejected allegorical interpretation in favor of the symbolic. According to the Weimar school, symbolism provides an aesthetic of absolute transcendence, a totality of artistic expression representing beauty, wholeness, and enduring representation. In symbols, writes Benjamin, what is deemed "beautiful is supposed to merge with the divine in an unbroken whole."[44] For Goethe and Weimar neoclassicists, allegory was considered a weak artistic mode belonging to a debilitated period of German art and literature. Its degraded status as an art form was due primarily to its profane and commonplace quality; its supposed banality lacked the noble stature of myth. Benjamin wanted to restore artistic integrity to allegorical dramas, especially German baroque dramas that expressed an age of decay, catastrophe, and discontinuity. He believed the baroque plays merited the same attention as classical tragedy, but for different reasons. Allegorical dramas epitomized historic periods where the dignity and elevation of mythic tragedy was incomprehensible and therefore nonexistent. Instead of nobility, the violence and decay caused by moral erosion and collapse needed an artistic device to represent its condition. Pure realism would prove unsatisfying; mimetic representations of horrible events do a disservice to the actual events, because they merely attempt to recreate death and destruction through artificially staged gimmicks. Audiences would see through the artifice, diminishing the dramatic effect. Only allegorical representations would best express the condition of the times.

Rachel represents a similar situation and similar aesthetic relations to its time. How can a writer or artist represent lynching, and how can such depictions onstage carry the weight of symbolic representation? The play attempts to evoke the pain of lynching, its torture and its aftermath. But like Benjamin's German baroque plays, the mimetic representation of an actual lynching could not satisfactorily capture the proper emotional response. First, "lynching" an actor onstage would automatically fail to evoke what the mimetic act tries to induce. It would merely result in a falsified theatricality. Second, white mobs often photographed lynching, with the pictures used as mementos, postcards, and documentation of the alleged "justice" it enforced on African Americans.[45] White lynch mobs had seized the symbolic realism of the event; the horrors of it were graphically framed and displayed in the photos, much to the delight of the lynchers and observers. Rather than call attention to the event of lynching itself, Grimké focuses on its repercussions. In this way, Grimké represents the lynching allegorically, as an aftereffect that resonates like an echo.

More importantly, lynching is not a ritual practiced by black people; it is a white racist ritual and as such cannot bear the weight of representative symbolism.[46] Its brutality cannot be reproduced "cleanly" for black audiences because it is not an act by black people, but an act *done to* black people. How, then, does a playwright capture the event's emotional experience for a theatrical purpose? Mere brutality onstage can, at best, only numb. For Benjamin and Grimké, the device suited to this purpose was to portray such horrors allegorically; not the event itself, but its aftershocks had to reverberate.

Lynching was frequently an act of visceral hatred by white people that occurred in a picnic or carnival atmosphere. As the quote by Mary Church Terrell earlier in this chapter made clear, people in the crowds often took part in the torture, scrambling afterward to gather bits of clothes or body parts as souvenirs. Portrayals of such acts onstage might pose the possibility of becoming absurd, or even comic, undermining the intended purpose (though realism might have greater success on film). The lynching rope took root as a symbol; the rope conveyed clarity of purpose, becoming throughout the twentieth century the pure signifier of terror. Eventually, the mere act of showing a rope to an African American would successfully accomplish its racist purpose: to instill fear. Ropes were, and are, symbolic: white communities often hung them at the edge of town as a "symbol" to African Americans who might attempt to transgress racial boundaries, signifying what Robyn Wiegman terms "the panoptic power of whiteness."[47] For lynch mobs, the rope represented a relation between the signifier and the thing signified. Its clarity and lucidity was unmistakable; mistaking its purpose was life-threatening.

Historian Trudier Harris has criticized black women playwrights of the era for "shying away" from depicting the horrors of lynching, to the degree that "we might ask whether these are truly anti-lynching plays."[48] However, recording a lynching dramatically is mere data through which its visceral responses can hardly come to light. The effects of lynching's brutality on the victims resonate with chaos, and chaos is difficult to contain symbolically. As a frenzied act of extralegal mob violence, lynching itself is beyond expression for those suffering from it. For African Americans, there cannot be the slightest pretense of "symbolism."

Rather than portraying the violence *per se*, the authors of anti-lynching dramas chose to show its reverberations. In the case of *Rachel*, Rachel's reaction to this violence is reflected in her allegorical "childlessness." In Benjaminian terms, her refusal to bear children evokes the allegorical figure of the *Via Dolorosa*, the baroque projection of crucifixion and redemption. Rachel is systematically crucified and then redeemed. She is stripped of her right to bear children without fear, to enjoy freedom without danger, and to experience family life without indignities. Critic Bainard Cowan defines Benjamin's *Trauerspiel* as the temporal stripping away of "natural dignity" from the protagonist, thereby "anticipating the conferring of an infinitely more glorious dignity from above."[49] Rachel's extreme, Christ-like act of sacrifice first conveys her suffering and then imbues her with a new sense of dignity. In expressing Rachel's sacrifice, Grimké also creates an atmosphere heavy with endless sorrow, the "piling-on" of ruin upon ruin (epitomized by the protagonist's long speeches), in which Rachel's anguish is repeatedly dragged into the open. The endless repetition of Rachel's struggle is characterized by overflow, haunted grief, and endless lamentation. As one reviewer put it, *Rachel* is "morbid and overstrained." However, the review adds, "there is a basis of crushing reality for this painful drama."[50] The depiction of an "overstrained, crushing reality" is akin to the allegorical representation of crucifixion and decay brought about, over time, by the recurrence of sorrow.

For Benjamin, allegory has a temporal dimension that links it to the process of aging and decay. The temporal process of chipping away at the protagonist reflects the melancholic state of endless grief, yet this grief takes on a profound dimension. This is true of *Rachel*: the play depicts the hopelessness of earthly existence and Rachel's Christ-like redemption over time. In Rachel's action there is no catharsis, no closure as such, but only an epiphany of endless, temporal mourning, which eventually bestows dignity upon her. As allegory, her gesture amounts to defining what Benjamin calls history's "immense sorrow."[51] This sense of sorrow and temporality is most explicit in Rachel's final speech; after saying goodbye to John forever, she invokes a darkness that epitomizes a series of grievances to come:

(Strong goes out. A door opens and shuts. There is finality in the sound. The weeping continues. Suddenly; with a great cry) John! John! . . . Oh! John,—if it only—if it only—(breaks off, controls herself. Slowly again; thoughtfully) No—no sunshine—no laughter—always—darkness. That is it. Even our little flat—(in a whisper). John's and mine—the little flat—that calls, calls us—through darkness. It shall wait—and wait—in vain—in darkness.[52]

Above all, *Rachel* is a play about melancholy. Rachel's grieving is motivated by several factors. Her decision to be childless and her rejection of Strong compound her feelings of sadness, but it is the inability of human action to stop the horrors of the world that underlies the root of her despair. In Benjamin's allegorical way of seeing the world, the subject, recoiling with horror from the inability to stop the violence, descends into a form of madness. The ineffectuality of action is redirected toward an inner melancholic condition; the protagonist thereby comes to understand the world as a place of chaotic meaninglessness. As Max Pensky describes it in his book, *Melancholy Dialectics*, melancholia is a "retreat from and a total rejection of society," due to the effects of society, "which the melancholic experiences as suffocating." When all avenues of effective action have been closed off, "the melancholic rebel recedes into a resigned interiority, brooding over the very conditions of the impossibility of action themselves."[53] This description applies to Rachel, who has retreated inwardly and into a form of madness owing to her realization of the ineffectuality of action. Her refusal to live in hope creates a condition of paralysis and *acedia*, or torpor, which cuts against the grain of "active" dramatic action. Yet, according to Benjamin's theory, this anti-active drama is a manner of expressing a particular reaction to sadistic and banal terror.

Grimké sets up the protagonist's grieving in a calculated, somewhat manufactured way. This seems at first glance to contribute to the play's contrivance. But as Benjamin explains, grief and endless sorrow need to be pushed along to create the ceaseless sound of anguish. Allegory, Benjamin claims, is a "form of expression [*Ausdruck*]" that, like other forms, is an intentional way of seeing the world.[54] It reflects a particular philosophical-historical juncture of baroque fragmentation and wretchedness, where life is distanced from significant meaning. However, unlike symbols, allegory is not a self-sufficient relation to the images or ideas that carry on adjacent to the objects they represent; instead, they are in need of help from the allegorist. The allegorist's manipulation of the artwork completes the picture, thereby conjuring a relation to meaning in a chaotic cosmos of miscellaneous fragments. For Rachel, lynching's deadly signification is not symbolic, since, as Benjamin's epistemological point makes clear, symbols are artistic devices with clear relations to the event being represented. Lynching's allegorical representation is exemplified in the play by the aesthetic device of mourning. But mourning by itself remains ambivalent, and will eventually lose resiliency; as allegory, it continually needs an author's manipulation, a sort of "push from behind," to justify its presence. The author engineers the theme of mourning, manipulates and persists at it, because, like an echo, the power of the protagonist's voice will eventually fade from fatigue and exhaustion. Hence, the allegorical dramatist must continually push the play's mechanisms—even at the risk of melodramatic contrivance—through repetitive dialogue and abundant sorrowful lamentations.

The work's persistence and repetitiousness risk appearing artificial.[55] The sudden appearances of outside forces that weigh against Rachel (her father's lynching, racism against children, news of other lynchings, and denial of economic opportunities for blacks) mark the play's predictability, jeopardizing the balance of events necessary for realism. Yet, *Trauerspiel* is not realism *per se;* for all its surface appearance of reality, *Trauerspiel* is defined by an irregular rhythm. Marxist literary critic Terry Eagleton asserts that if we are to believe that the action of such melancholic dramas progresses with a heavy-handed slowness, "it is also true that situations can change in a flash." Objects, characters, and events in such texts repulse "any suave linearity of presentation for a syncopated rhythm that oscillates endlessly between swift switches of direction and consolidations into rigidity."[56] This description applies to *Rachel:* sudden disasters arrive unexpectedly, undermining the seamless linearity and melodramatic flow of the play. Thus, the allegorical form captures in art the signs of oscillation, expressing a sorrowful way of seeing the world.

CONCLUSION

Every part of you becomes bitter. —Marita O. Bonner (1925)[57]

No doubt reading *Rachel* as a play compatible with seventeenth-century German baroque drama might appear strained. The discrepancies of time, culture, and circumstances work against such comparisons, suggesting that applying a Benjaminian template to *Rachel* is a mere exercise in academic criticism. Yet, the similarity between lynching in the first three decades of the twentieth century and the brutality of the European baroque age are undeniable. Both eras were rife with terror, violence, and the threat of mutilation. Each had their uniqueness and differences, but the works of artists attempting to find a mode of expression for these chaotic, horrific worlds bear striking similarities. Grimké's *Rachel* constructs the spiritual quest of redemption for those seeking answers to indescribable terror and fear. Despite the risk of over-generalization, mourning and allegory are evident in *Rachel*.

Ultimately the logic of *Rachel* is neither realistic nor symbolic. The deployment of its elements does not aim primarily at sustaining the illusion of verisimilitude, though the play does provide a narrative situated in a recognizable social setting. Instead, Grimké's treatment of lynching is designed above all to intensify audience reactions to the horrors by raising the stakes through a sustained lament, an echo that reverberates like music. (The play, in fact, incorporates several "sorrow" songs into the text, as well as the image of Raphael's *Madonna* over the piano.) Both Benjamin and Grimké are aware that mere realism will not suffice; the protagonists have to demonstrate extreme martyrdom in order to make the meaning effective. In *Rachel*, Grimké manipulates the play's episodes so that the intended effect, as Grimké explains, is "not primarily [on] the colored people, but [on] the whites," in order to show them "how a refined, sensitive, highly-strung girl, a dreamer and an idealist, the strongest instinct in whose nature is a love for children and a desire some day to be a mother herself," was affected by lynching.[58] Grimké wants *Rachel* to be recognized not merely for the character's individual suffering, but as a drama that incorporates the inchoate existence of black women living during times of fear. She hoped that by situating Rachel's pain in the context of motherhood, all women would empathize with her character's perpetual mourning. Allegory, with its ambiguities and contradictions, has the power to express the amorphous aesthetic of lynching's effect on a sensitive and overwrought character.

The sentiments elicited by *Rachel* spin out of control with passion and vertigo; they move toward anguish and outrage. Sentimentality and sorrow set up a vortex, building on the horror. *Rachel* is therefore an allegorical lamentation that, like opera, is based on sound, not word. The sound is continuous, piled on by words but with words that are effective only by dint of their cumulative repetition and rhythm. The words become sound, like an echo of pain. Rachel's outcry reverberates from the body and the voice, pitched like a tuning fork that resonates from the depths of human sorrow.

CHAPTER SIX

MIGRATION, FRAGMENTATION, AND IDENTITY: ZORA NEALE HURSTON'S *COLOR STRUCK* AND THE GEOGRAPHY OF THE HARLEM RENAISSANCE

The location is not already there before the bridge. . . . a location comes into existence only by virtue of the bridge.

—Martin Heidegger (1954)[1]

INTRODUCTION

I must be the bridge to nowhere / But my true self / And then / I will be useful.
—Donna Kate Rushin (1981)[2]

Geography and migration played a key role in the description and formation of the Harlem Renaissance–New Negro era. The Great Migration, which began just prior to World War I and continued well after, had a profound effect both on the cities of the North and the southern, rural communities left behind. Indeed, during the 1910s, nearly half a million African Americans left the rural South for the urban North.[3] Within a decade, more than three-quarters of a million would follow, increasing the black northern population from 1910 to 1930 by 300 percent.[4] Swept up by what Alain Locke called the "wash and rush of this human tide on the beach line of the northern city center," black people were rejecting the South's history of racial violence and lynching, embracing the mass psychology underlying movement, escaping from poor rural farming, and seeking a better future.[5]

In contrast to the image of the migrating African American is the work of Zora Neale Hurston (ca. 1891–1960). Hurston was a playwright and anthropologist who felt that migration, while affording some positive opportunities, was also violent and costly. She saw the results of the Great Migration as terrifying and spasmodic, unbearably inhumane and devastating to those left behind. For Hurston, rural black people were being forgotten, disappearing amidst the heady enthusiasm of the urban New Negro Movement. Hazel Carby makes the claim that Hurston wanted to represent "rural folk" and their cultural forms as measured "against an urban, mass culture."[6] Analyzing Hurston's play, *Color Struck* (1925), as both a document of dramatic literature and an anthropological study reveals some of the tragic and devastating implications of the Great Migration.[7] In what follows, I will examine the relationship of African American women and the Great Migration on the one hand, and focus on the author's personal expressions of fragmentation as they relate to the play's protagonist on the other, making use of what Crispin Sartwell calls Hurston's "bits and pieces" of self-identity, which inform her fiction.[8] Significantly, Hurston shifts the locus of the Harlem–New Negro Renaissance from the urban North, with its relatively positive, upbeat outlook, to the impoverished rural South, where she attempts to depict a tragedy of epic proportions.

Rural culture among black southern women was for Hurston what Hazel Carby calls the artistic representation of the folk; that is, "not only a discursive displacement of the historical and cultural transformation of migration, but also is a creation of a folk who are outside history."[9] In *Color Struck*, Hurston creates a world made up of those who are "outside history," having fallen through the interstices of social recognition. Emma is Hurston's creation taken to the level of symbolic representation: by dint of the fact that she is black, poor, disenfranchised, and rural, she epitomizes the outsider in every way. She is not the "New Negro" fashioned by the doyens of the Harlem Renaissance. Rather, she defies commodification as a cultural artifact made for the amusement of whites and the progressive faction of the black elite. Literary historian Barbara Johnson emphasizes that Hurston both "deplored the appropriation, dilution, and commodification of black culture" typical during the Roaring Twenties–Jazz Age, and constantly tried to define the difference between "a reified 'art'" fixed in the minds of her audience and "a living culture" that is neither unyielding nor simplistically understood.[10] Johnson's point can be extended. Hurston was in revolt against a black northern elitist culture that rejected the values of the black South as well as its people, and she was embarking on a creative process of reclaiming southern, poor, black women from the dustbin of history. Black women of the South had been deemed out of step with the progressive elements of an urbanized, sophisticated, and for the most part masculine New Negro culture. And they were allegedly unfit to represent the "new woman," fully self-sufficient and modern. Hurston's project of anthropological recovery combined with dramatic intensity permeates *Color Struck*.

Much has been written about Hurston's creative writing in relation to her anthropological study, particularly through her association with Franz Boas (1858–1942).[11] In 1925, Hurston entered Columbia University's Barnard College to study anthropology under Boas. According to him, cultures, races, and languages have distinctive individualities, which are expressed in their modes of life, thought, and feeling, and it is the aim of the anthropologist to document and collate the empirical evidence of cultures and races objectively and scientifically. Under Boas's tutelage, Hurston absorbed the concept of anthropology as a body of research following scientific laws that exist in nature and not in the mind of the scholar. Cultures assessed by anthropologists do not arise from subjective assertions, Boas said, but rather reflect "external truth."[12] His brand of anthropology rejected the perspective of race and culture as linkages to a single, grand system of evolutionary sequence. Rather, he thought, anthropology must endeavor to focus on the society in which the subject lives, take inventory of material artifacts, and examine the detailed patterns, symbols, and myths that characterize various "cultures."[13] The Columbia School of anthropology initiated by Boas instituted two significant changes in the discipline that had a direct bearing on Hurston's research and creative output: the emergence of the "fieldworker archetype" and the study of culture as the "focal concept and subject matter."[14] Rather than as a vertical arrangement of "cultures," Boas and his protégées (with Hurston among them) viewed anthropology horizontally, as a commitment to social contingency rather than matters of biology or cultural hierarchy.[15] Field research, contact with the subject, impartiality, and the expression of "laws" defining reoccurring modes of historical events were the principal objectives of Columbia School anthropologists.[16]

Hurston's commitment to Boas's anthropology was ambivalent. On the one hand, she embraced the critical distancing demanded of the fieldworker archetype, which required onsite research, detached objectivity, and gathering empirical evidence. In *Mules and Men* she confessed that her prior experiences within African American rural culture fit her too closely, "like a tight chemise." This familiarity inhibited her ability to collect folkloric data unclouded by subjective interference. Boasian anthropology enabled her to make use of what she called the "spy-glass of Anthropology" to "stand off and look at my garments."[17] On the other hand, Hurston was an artist who drew from her personal experiences. Southern black rural folklife was grist for her writer's mill, the primary source of her imagination, and the most influential part of her creativity. In both her roles as fieldworker and creative writer, she sought to preserve black folklore by advancing what anthropologist Lee D. Baker terms her "vindicationist concern for debunking stereotypes while promoting African American culture by using the Boasian idea of culture."[18] However, juggling objective anthropology and subjective creativity caused an internal rift, making her dual identity as academic folklorist and creative artist difficult to reconcile. As biographer Robert E. Hemenway observed, by balancing her energies "between art and science, fiction and anthropology," Hurston "searched for an expressive instrument, an intellectual formula," that might accommodate her twin interests.[19] But the inductive reasoning of Boasian anthropology chafed against the deductive assertions and subjective partiality Hurston needed to instill an emotional content in her art. The ambiguities and tensions between "detached researcher" and "impassioned artist" failed to be resolved.

Color Struck was completed just prior to Hurston's entrance into Barnard.[20] Having not yet come under the Columbia School influence, Hurston was free from the pressures associated with Boas and his demanding impartiality. Hurston wrote the play using her objective knowledge of folklore *and* her empathetic imagination. As a pre-Boasian text, the play is a vindication of black folk culture and a dynamic drama that is informed by the thoughts and feelings of the author.[21] It combines Hurston's anthropological research and creativity in the invention of the protagonist. Through Hurston's research and aesthetics, Emma becomes a representative of her milieu, drawn from the author's external observations and, to a certain degree, autobiography. Hurston's balancing act of docudrama and melodrama—research and cultural analysis on the one hand, and dramatic art on the other—yields a text that is multifaceted, immersed in anthropological study yet unburdened by the rigorous scientific objectivity Boasian anthropology required. In other words, Hurston had already entered into meta-anthropological research earlier than scholars have indicated, creating a drama that looks through "spyglasses" at the poverty and ennui of southern black women. Yet this drama also imbricates the author's imagination and personal experiences of fragmentation and dislocation.[22]

The play can be summarized this way: Emmaline (called Emma throughout the play) is a dark-skinned African American woman from Jacksonville, Florida. Her lover, John, pursues light-skinned women, thus keeping Emma in a constant state of jealousy. The play is set in an all-black region of rural Florida during the first two decades of the twentieth century. In four scenes, Hurston explores the disintegration of Emma and John's relationship. The first three scenes take place in 1900, the fourth twenty years later. The opening scene occurs in a railway car where John, Emma, and others from various parts of Florida—Jacksonville, Augustine, and Eatonville—are en route to a cakewalk-ing dance contest. Scene two takes place right before the contest, while scene three occurs during the contest itself. The final scene, twenty years later, depicts John's return from the North and his attempt to reconcile his differences with Emma. Emma, however, rejects John's overtures as much too little and too late. Emma embodies the circumstances of rural, southern black women of the time, making a "happy" conclusion based on romantic reconciliation untenable.

While it won second prize in the drama division of the 1925 *Opportunity Mag-azine* contest for best play, *Color Struck* has, with few exceptions, received scant critical attention. Critic Pearlie Mae Fisher Peters summarily dismisses the play, calling the protagonist a "clinging-vine woman obsessed with the dynamics of intra-racial color prejudice."[23] Other studies have emphasized the play's "col-orism."[24] Colorism within the African American community makes use of the de-gree of blackness or whiteness to assign privileges. There is considerable evidence to support this claim. Hurston wrote in her autobiography, *Dust Tracks on a Road*, that "the blackest Negro" is often "the butt of all jokes, particularly black women."[25] Certainly colorism is part of the play; both Emma's self-effacement and racial prejudice add to her tragedy.[26] Emma's inferiority complex creates a twin condition, one that both internalizes a self-depreciating identity *and* externalizes it by focusing on the color prejudice of others. There is more in the play, however, than a study of color bias and self-pity; there is a statement about regionalism and the dislocation of character.

Cultural historians Sandra L. Richards, Anthea Kraut, and Michael North provide an analysis of *Color Struck* that examines regionalism and the significance of identity. In her reading of *Color Struck*, Richards makes the point that "because the body onstage, through its carriage, gesture, and spatial relationships to other bodies, resonates with social history, the viewing experience is considerably dif-ferent."[27] She rightly points out that Hurston intended to place the black body in visible proximity to other bodies onstage, and in so doing establish the "potential interlocking" of characters, which depends not so much on "the written structur-ing elements" but instead on the "dynamic triangulation between these formal el-ements, performers, and spectators."[28] The visual presence of Emma becomes a performative strategy, creating a potential for receptivity that *must be considered to-gether* with the written text.

Richards is also right to weigh the importance of historical circumstances and locale. She notes that the opening scene in the Jim Crow railway car, which because of segregation shows an all-black cast of characters, is a stage picture that black audiences at the time would no doubt immediately recognize. She calls attention also to the presence of whites in the audience, since Hurston, she says, "wanted to speak to white Americans, too"; Richards suggests that the opening scene of the play, with its characters carrying on rambunctiously, fell victim to "primitivism." The presentation of rowdiness, says Richards, served as a "site of the irrational," creating "negative signifiers on the scale of civilization," and revealing "examples of the primitive who unself-consciously provide salvation models for white sophisticates, chafing at the stultifying materialism and positivism of American culture."[29]

Little evidence is adduced, however, to substantiate the claim that the play was written for white audiences.[30] The evidence, in fact, suggests that the play was specifically written for a black audience. To begin with, the play was originally published in *Fire!*, a radical black journal intended primarily for African Americans.[31] While the journal was certainly made available to whites, it was specifically a work by writers and artists who rejected stereotypes and discussed African themes, jazz, the blues, and black folk culture, which would be familiar to blacks but anathema to whites. The journal also represented an alternative to middle-class "New Negro" audiences, particularly those of Locke's book, *The New Negro* (1925), and Du Bois's magazine, *Crisis*, where tastes were inclined toward urbanity and alleged assimilationism.[32] Locke himself dubbed the short-lived (one issue) *Fire!* "left-wing literary modernism" containing a "charging brigade of literary revolt, especially against the bulwarks of Puritanism."[33]

Furthermore, an African American company may have produced the play for a black audience in Hurston's lifetime. Hurston's letter to Annie Nathan Meyer (10 November 1929) provides some evidence, though it is hardly conclusive. Hurston wrote, "The Negro Art Theatre of Harlem is fairly launching now and the first program will include my 'Color Struck.'"[34] The publication in *Fire!* and the potential production suggests, in this instance, that Hurston neither curried white favor nor sought to publish in white journals. Finally, the play's ambiance lies wholly within black culture, invested in what Anthea Kraut astutely terms a "circumscribed, southern black space."[35] The play's cakewalking contest, for instance, a plot device dominating the first three scenes, is exclusively of an African American milieu.

The cakewalk was a high-stepping dance that emerged through a combination of black vernacular culture, minstrelsy, and the cultural exchange of black and white.[36] Yet in *Color Struck* the dance is completely devoid of a white presence; in fact, throughout the play the subject of white people hardly arises. A white doctor does appear at the end, but his presence is brief and insignificant. Michael North raises the significant point that in *Color Struck* the cakewalk "is a black rural ritual that has no reference to anything outside itself." Thus, says

North, by removing the "white frame around the cakewalk," the play "recommends its own sublime indifference to white opinion as a way of redeeming black folk culture from its popularized and vulgarized white versions."[37] For Hurston, the cakewalk is no longer a dance influenced by or connected to whites, but a self-enclosed community ritual. In *Color Struck*, Hurston draws from her experience of growing up in an all-black rural region of Eatonville, Florida. She creates a world of black southern folklore through her protagonist, Emma, who is rejected both by mainstream society and by her own community.

MY PEOPLE!

> *Implicit in her desire was racial self-loathing. And twenty years later I was still wondering about how one learns that. Who told her? Who made her feel that it was better to be a freak than what she was? Who had looked at her and found her so wanting, so small a weight on the beauty scale?*   —Toni Morrison (1994)[38]

The friction between emerging urban "New Negroes" of the Harlem Renaissance and rural, working-class southern African Americans provides a useful point of entry for the opening scene of *Color Struck;* but rather than beginning with the play itself, it will prove more illuminating if we first turn our attention to Hurston's 1942 autobiographical study, *Dust Tracks on a Road.* In this work, she revisits the class divisions within middle-class African America that appears in a similar way in the opening of the play. First, *Dust Tracks:*

> My People! My people! From the earliest rocking of my cradle days, I have heard this cry go up from Negro lips. It is forced outward by pity, scorn and hopeless resignation. It is called forth by the observations of one class of Negro on the doings of another branch of the brother in black.[39]

The term "My People" brackets certain African Americans who experience the prevailing class-division. Hurston draws an example:

> For instance, well-mannered Negroes groan out like that [My people!] when they board a train or a bus and find other Negroes on there with their shoes off, stuffing themselves with fried fish, bananas and peanuts, and throwing the garbage on the floor. Maybe they are not only eating and drinking. The offenders may be "loud talking" the place, and holding back nothing of their private lives, in a voice that embraces the entire coach. The well-dressed Negro shrinks back in his seat at that, shakes his head and sighs, "My people! My people!"[40]

In the opening of *Color Struck*, actors represented "loud-talking Negroes," while the audience was likely to be "well-mannered" middle-class African Americans. This observer-and-observed dynamic appears 17 years later in *Dust Tracks*. The play's stage directions state:

> Before the curtain goes up there is the sound of a locomotive whistle and a stopping engine, loud laughter, many people speaking at once, good-natured shrieks, strumming of a stringed instrument, etc. The ascending curtain discovers a happy lot of Negroes boarding the train dressed in gaudy, twdry [sic] best of 1900. They are mostly in couples—each couple bearing a covered-over market basket which the men hastily deposit in the racks as they scramble for seats. There is a little friendly pushing and shoving. One pair just miss a seat three times, much to the enjoyment of the crowd. The women are showily dressed in the manner of the time, and quite conscious of their finery. A few seats remain unoccupied.[41]

The play's opening is conceived with the spectator in mind. The black audience Hurston may have had in mind might have reacted to the "loud-talking" characters on the railcar with the refrain, "My People! My People!"[42] In addition, the place—a railway car—has numerous significatory ramifications. The car sets the stage for movement, which implies freedom and mobility. Being able to move freely is important in African American culture, particularly in the South, where freedom to travel during slavery was nonexistent. Yet movement was, as we shall soon see, not an option open to everyone at the turn of the century.

In the opening scene, Emma's rival in the cakewalking contest and for John's affections, Effie, a "mulatto girl," enters the car looking for a seat. She is "greeted" immediately by the men seated in the car. One says "Howdy do, Miss Effie, you'se lookin' jes lak a rose."[43] Effie spurns his advances. This opening contains a frequently overlooked theme, one that will continually resurface: John's attraction to Effie. Critic Lynda Marion Hill asserts that the conflict in the play "escalates as Emma convinces herself that John is 'carryin' on with the light-skinned Effie." For Hill, Emma is jealous as well as fearful that Effie will steal John away because she is more friendly, attractive, light-skinned, and a better cakewalker.[44] Yet John encourages Effie, suggesting either a prior affair or John's philandering nature. John's behavior is hardly innocent: his words and the speed with which he embraces Effie at the dance indicate involvement and desire on a deeper level than surface observations imply.

When we first see Emma and John, they are late in boarding the railcar. John explains the reasons for their lateness, claiming that Emma "says I wuz smiling at Effie on the street car and she had to get off and wait for another one." Emma replies furiously: "You wuz grinning at her and she was grinning back jes like a ole cheesy cat!" John denies this, but Emma insists: "You wuz. I seen you looking jes lake a possum." She adds: "Jes the same every time you sees a yaller face, you *takes* a chance. (*They sit down in peeved silence for a minute*)."[45] In this exchange, the question of who is telling the truth is not obvious; for the most part, critics have accepted John's words. The next dialogue from John is to Effie.

> John: (*looking behind him*). Hellow, Effie, where's Sam?
> Effie: Deed, I don't know.
> John: Y'all on a bust?
> Emma: None ah yo'bizness, you got enough tuh mind yo' own self. Turn 'round!

Emma has warned John not to talk to Effie, yet John almost immediately turns to Effie and asks why her dance partner, Sam, is missing. This is not innocent banter; rather, John is obsessed with Effie. His approach is bold. He ignores completely Emma's plea to avoid her. Emma thus has every reason to fear John's betrayal. It is John who initiates conversation with Effie, not the other way around.

After John and Emma strut the cakewalk through the aisle of the train, Effie takes her solo turn. John comments:

> John: (*applauding loudly*). If dat Effie can't step nobody can.
> Emma: Course you'd say so cause it's her. Everything she do is pretty to you.[46]

John is applauding loudly, despite Emma's protest against his flirtation. At the very least, he should show restraint and a little sensitivity toward Emma. His relationship to Emma is tenuous at best and appears likely to be severed at any moment. John is, in fact, less than subtle; though he does what he can to caress Emma and assure her of his love, his gestures smack of "hedging his bets." Applauding loudly for one woman and caressing another is slim evidence of loyalty; Emma has every reason to be jealous.

The second scene takes place outside the dance hall just before the cakewalking contest. Emma is now so enraged that she refuses to join in the cakewalk. Since Emma refuses, John takes on another partner, who happens to be the light-skinned mulatto Effie. John and Effie win the contest and bring honor to their town—and just as Emma predicted, John leaves with Effie for parts north. The haste of his embrace of and elopement with Effie suggests that Emma was correct all along.

In the final scene of *Color Struck*, John has returned twenty years later from the North. John's departure was not only a betrayal; it also symbolized his newfound mobility. Despite urban poverty and overcrowding, northern cities produced hope. His unfaithfulness, as the play suggests, had consequences beyond romance. Emma must live with the understanding that not only is her ex-lover now enjoying life with her rival, but also enjoys the possibilities opened by a new life in the North.

For black women travel was risky business and few cared to take their chances. A black woman traveling alone was a tempting target for any predator. Moving through unfamiliar terrain presented dangers. In *Dust Tracks on a Road*, Hurston makes us aware of this; in her own anthropological search for what she called the "knowledge of things," her life "was in danger several times." As she says, if "I had not learned how to take care of myself in these circumstances, I could have been maimed or killed on most any day of the several years of my research work."[47] Hurston's research was based on the desire to reveal the life of rural black women trapped in stultifying conditions. Rather than focusing on those who escaped, Hurston turns her attention to those left behind. In *Color Struck*, Emma is left to fend for herself. Emma's tragedy resides in the fact that she lacked what critic and cultural historian Carole Boyce Davies calls black women's agency, which is based on "migration, mobility, movement, departure, return, re-departure and transformation."[48] Mobility, however, was seldom an option available to African American women at the time.

Black women avoided northward travel for a number of reasons.[49] Not only did women traveling alone face numerous dangers; there was also little opportunity of work. For women, work was far from guaranteed, even during industrialization. Factories were often closed to black women, and European and Asian immigrants competed with African Americans for domestic labor. Moreover, black women had little or no assurance of hotel residency. Forced sometimes to sleep outside in wooded areas or alleyways increased the potential for rape and robbery. Added to this was minimal and sometimes nonexistent legal protection. Unfamiliarity with the surroundings also complicated the search for a safe haven. Travel for men represented privilege, freedom, and a chance to start fresh and make over mistakes. By contrast, women travelers were, as anthropologist James Clifford puts it, "forced to conform, masquerade, or rebel discreetly within a set of normatively male definitions and experiences."[50] Women faced more frequent bias and danger, forcing them to sometimes "act tough" in the form of masculine norms of behavior. Often belligerent behavior was used to establish a protective aura. Given the pioneering spirit of American life that began to flourish in the nineteenth century, a man traveling alone was not unusual; but a woman alone was often met with either disdain or sexual advances.

According to Houston A. Baker, Jr., African American literature is marked by "transience." Baker maintains that the railway juncture, with its implication of movement, way station, migration, and the blues, represents "the liminal trickster on the move." Black literature is symbolized by a lineage that is "nomadic," the crossing signs of a railway station signifying "change, motion, transience, process."[51] Yet Hurston's Emma is the very opposite of change; while she desired the results accompanying movement, she was denied access to it. Hazel Carby says succinctly that migration for black women "often meant being left behind: 'Bye-Bye Baby' and 'Sorry I can't take you' were the common refrains of male blues."[52] Hurston's Emma lives amidst uncertainty, fearful that John may leave at any moment—and indeed, that is what happens.

Hurston's Emma turns against the big city, with all its emphasis on efficiency and productivity, its culture of expediency and novelty. Instead, she looks toward the provincial, inner world of her rural black community for spiritual sustenance. Yet her own community, as portrayed in the play, rejects Emma as well. Emma, as a woman of color, uneducated yet knowledgeable to her limits, holds on to what is most tangible: home. However, because of her dark skin, she remains an outcast in both the black and white worlds; even "home" becomes unsatisfying. Emma's darker hue and the social conditions that are imposed on "blackness" make her subject to exclusion both externally and internally.

As a refugee of sorts, Emma exists in what Edward Said calls the "perilous territory of not-belonging," a territory where "people are banished."[53] Throughout the play, Hurston's protagonist exemplifies displacement and dislocation. Emma's diasporic condition is one of homelessness, fragmentation, and nonidentity. Hurston has created a female character existing in social limbo. Emma's dilemma resides in instability, of knowing and not-knowing, dwelling and notdwelling, presence and absence. Emma's classification as black, female, poor, powerless, and disenfranchised leads to dislocation. If her reaction seems extreme, it is owing to the extremes of her condition.

It is for this reason that her actions seem irrational. In her study of the geography of modern drama, Una Chaudhuri raises the point that homelessness and displacement "constitute the insistent and pervasive challenges to home," which transform "the apparently simple figure into a powerful irreality, something on the order of a fantasy, fable, myth, or impossible dream."[54] In *Color Struck*, not only does homelessness lead to a condition of extreme anguish, it creates instability and a detachment from others.

Emma's alienation is apparent in every scene. In scene one, Emma and John are on the Jim Crow railroad car headed to Eatonville and the cakewalk contest. Despite his flirtations with Effie, John is frustrated by Emma's accusations of betrayal; Emma replies, in essence, that she can only love a man if he is faithful. Her love is, moreover, expressed in her jealousy, but jealousy is all that she can claim. Jealously, at least, reflects a feeling of "ownership"; given a world that limits her possession of "things," jealousy is an emotional possession, providing a fixed point in life:

> Emma: (*sadly*) Then you don't want my love, John, cause I can't help mahself from being jealous. I loves you so hard, John, and jealous love is the only kind I got.
> (*John kisses her very feelingly*)
> Emma: Just for myself alone is the only way I knows how to love.[55]

The "self alone," cut off from place *and* movement, expresses an autonomy that is nothing more than a prison house of flesh. In such a condition, self-assertion often becomes a matter of boisterous public display. For example, in scene two, John again flirts with Effie and Emma admonishes him. When he tries to hush her up, she replies with bravura:

> Ah-Ah aint gonna bite mah tongue! If she don't like it she can lump it. Mah back is broad—(*John tries to cover her mouth with his hand*). She calls herself a big cigar, but I kin smoke her![56]

This sassy reply or put-down in a public space is part of Emma's assertion of self-worth in a world that offers her little. When faced with betrayal, Emma lashes out satirically. Her irrepressible rage is always just below the surface, triggered by the slightest inducement. Yet beneath her rage lies a deeper, more poignant signification.

MELANCHOLIA AND FRAGMENTATION

> *Why do they see a colored woman only as a gross collection of desires, all uncontrolled, reaching out for their Apollos and the Quasimodos with avid indiscrimination?*   —Marita O. Bonner (1925)[57]

The unpredictability that from the outset dwells in the relationship between Emma and John results from John's disloyalty and Emma's displaced condition. Emma's effort to keep John from leaving takes the form of reaching out, yet her intimacy risks ridicule and rejection. Her fears extend throughout her everyday life; every prospect of social engagement becomes a potentially dangerous emotional encounter. At the end of the scene two, John and Emma are called to the dance floor as the representatives of Jacksonville, but Emma refuses. She is now alone.

> Emma: (*She stands and clenches her fists*) Ah, mah God! He's in there with her—
> Oh, them half whites, they gets everything, they gets everything everybody

else wants! The men, the jobs—everything! The whole world is got a sign on it. Wanted: Light colored. Us blacks was made for cobble stones. (*She muffles a cry and sinks limp upon her seat.*)[58]

The final line reminds us of Emma's condition, that she is nothing more than cobblestones for others to walk on. Her desperation is not mere self-indulgence, but something more relevant: melancholia.

Melancholia as a dramatic conceit has significant value. It has an honored history in Western aesthetics and philosophical traditions. When, as literary historian Juliana Schiesari points out, "women fall into the depths of sorrow," they "are all too easily dismissed with the banal and unprestigious term 'depression.'" Cultural expressions of melancholia, or loss, are not given the same "representational value as those of men within the Western canon of literature, philosophy, and psychoanalysis."[59] Properly understood, melancholia provides a clear understanding of the protagonist, placing Emma within a complex emotional matrix of social conceptualization. From the point where John leaves her, Emma says little. Paucity of speech is highly unusual in melodrama, where the tendency is toward effusive dialogue. In *Color Struck*, melancholia could all too easily lead to verbal excess resulting in satiation. Hurston avoids this, with the consequences that her technique becomes theatrically rich and somewhat unique. In strong contrast to the melodramatic overflow of words in Angelina Weld Grimké's *Rachel* (discussed in the previous chapter), Hurston rejects verbal cascades and grand speeches, opting instead for silence, evasiveness, and indirection. Both Grimké and Hurston experiment with different dramatic forms to emphasize their points.

Hurston's employment of dashes, ellipses, and circumlocution in the text are indices of what both literary historians Saidiya V. Hartman and Claudia Tate call "textual enigmas." These markings embody black women's discourse. Hartman asserts that the dashes and elisions are "literal and figurative cuts in the narrative," displaying "the searing wounds of the violated and muted body" acting out its remembrances without the linguistic and symbolic tools to articulate its history of injury.[60] The violated body in *Color Struck* is represented as a fragmented soul, separated from community and respect. Claudia Tate argues along similar lines, maintaining that the ellipses are "enigmatic illocutions" indicative of a "surplus" of unattainable desires.[61] Emma's halting words, inarticulate responses, and enigmatic behavior require dashes and ellipses in their textual representation. They are emblematic of the body acting out a speechless articulation of desire and pain. The "melancholy moment,"[62] a term coined by psychoanalyst and cultural historian Julia Kristeva, reveals a condition frequently misinterpreted as mere self-effacing "rage" typifying exaggerated jealously and little else. This view of mere rage and exaggerated jealousy, however, misses the main point of the play.

Emma's anguish transcends language because her world is too fragmented for conceptualization. Words as signifiers of felt experiences are, in this case, inadequate. The structural relationship between the signifier (language) and the thing signified (event) falls apart in the face of multiple and contradictory meanings. The play reveals this complexity in strong theatrical terms. For example, at the end of the third scene, John and Effie have won the cakewalking contest. While the dancing inside is joyful, Emma stands outside, alone, listening to the announcer declare John and Effie the winners. A man approaches Emma, and says, "You're from Jacksonville, ain't you?" Then there are the following stage directions: *"He whirls her around and around."* "Ain't you happy?," he says; "Whoopee!" The final stage direction notes that he releases her, and *"she buries her face in the moss."*[63] John, dancing inside, will soon leave with Effie for parts north, abandoning Emma.

The striking juxtaposition of the lively dance inside and Emma being thrust to the ground with her face in the moss outside is Hurston's visual projection of a powerful content. Emma's silence during the moment of her greatest humiliation is Hurston's way of making the action carry meaning within the unfolding theatrical process. The audience must see Emma alone and face down while the black community in the background dances with joy; only through the visual, not the verbal, can we grasp the tragic dimension of Emma's existence. Emma, cut off from lover and culture, is diminished in value. Hurston's folk tragedy depends on a background of folk life (dance and celebration) displayed against the foreground of isolation. The author has juxtaposed a world fragmented between two opposing images. The image of Emma thrown to the moss epitomizes her being thrown from house, home, and community. Lying there in silence, she bespeaks a tragedy beyond words.

VOICING VOICELESSNESS

Essentially, Hurston is saying that her becoming a writer is tantamount to a rock learning to talk. In fact, the rocks will talk through her. And who are these "dead-seeming, cold rocks" but the tens of thousands of rural black women, considered less than beasts and denied a voice in history and letters. —Susan Willis (1987)[64]

Silence is often something evoked rather than contained. Emma's silence is a nonverbal expression of the complexity of her social circumstances arising from lack of, or disengagement with, language itself. Silence is frequently misunderstood; a character's lack of speech is simply ignored, with the assumption that there is "nothing" but silence. But onstage, where the body remains even if words do not, presence is a critical component in the formation of meaning. Once we recognize Emma's silent presence onstage as significatory, we can understand her condition.

In the final scene, John returns. Emma lives, as the stage directions explain, "*in a one-room shack in an alley.*" Hurston describes the interior as containing a "cheap" rocker and bed. As the curtain rises, a woman—Emma, though we are not told it is her and the stage is in virtual darkness—"*is seen rocking to and fro in the low rocker.*" Hurston may have described her as "a woman" in order to endow her with universal meaning. There is "*dead silence except for the sound of the rocker and an occasional groan from the bed.*"[65] Then, the woman rises in response to a "faint voice" that says "water"; she gives water to the child. She is on her way to the doctor again when John enters. It is John's entrance that distracts her; he interferes with her care of the child. He reports that he lived "up North" in Philadelphia, but his wife died and he now has returned to Emma permanently. John persists in trying to light the oil lamp, but Emma won't have it, preferring to sit by herself in the dark. He tries to soften her by recalling their youthful romance. He finally lights the lamp, only to see the ill child for the first time. He bends over for a closer look. Emma tries to shield the child from him. The stage directions are as follows:

> *He turns in his chair and Emma rushes over to the bed and covers the girl securely, tucking her long hair under the covers, too—before he arises. He goes over to the bed and looks down into her face. She is mulatto. Turns to Emma teasingly.*
> John: Talkin' 'bout *me* liking high-yallers—*yo* husband musta been pretty near white.[66]

John realizes that the child is feverish. Emma assures him that she has tried to find the best doctors within her limited means. John urges Emma to seek the doctor. A worried but defeated Emma says "She'll be all right, Ah reckon, for a while." Then she says: "John, you love me—you really want me sho' nuff?"[67] Before going for the doctor again, she tries to find out exactly why John has returned.

Critics have assumed that Emma's self-hatred is at the root of her neglect of the child. However, she never actually neglects the child, but rather pauses briefly in order to probe John's sincerity. In the next exchange, John declares his love, and Emma even suggests that they marry the following day. John agrees, urging her once more: "run after the doctor—we must look after our girl." As Emma readies herself, John says, looking at the child: "Gee, she's got a full suit of hair! Glad you didn't let her chop it off."[68] Hurston makes it clear: for John nothing has changed. He is enamored by the child's long, straight hair, symbolic of whiteness, femininity, beauty, and everything that in his eyes Emma is not.[69] But Emma, instead of going for the doctor, returns to her rocker. John sits next to her. He enjoins her yet again to find a doctor, offering money for the taxi. At last, Emma agrees.

The doctor arrives shortly after Emma returns, suggesting that Emma summoned him. Before he arrives, she enters the room, finding John helping the child. She rushes furiously toward him, threatening to "kill him." John struggles to free himself of Emma's grip and exclaims before leaving: "So this is the woman I've been wearing my heart like a rose for twenty years! She so despises her own skin that she can't believe any one else could love it!"[70] Emma's self-hatred drives a wedge between them and her delay costs the child her life. On the face of it, John and the child appear to be the ones wronged. Emma, it might seem, has unjustly accused John of unfaithfulness. Yet, during John's twenty years of "waiting" he was married, probably to the light-skinned Effie. Despite his protestations, he hardly wore his "heart like a rose." Instead, he only returned after twenty years and the death of his wife. More important, his attention to the child may have suggested to Emma John's lust for "mulattoes," and most likely she would not be entirely wrong in this.

During the play's final moments, the doctor arrives. He asks Emma why she had not summoned him sooner. She replies that she had. He remarks that she waited too long, and that this procrastination will prove fatal. "An hour more or less is mighty important sometimes," he says, adding: "Why didn't you come"? Emma replies: "Couldn't see."[71] The doctor offers pills sympathetically and leaves quietly.

Emma's final words in the play are, "couldn't see." What is it that she failed to see? There are several possible answers, none of them adequate. Hurston, like Chekhov, resists easy explanations. With guarded certainty it might be said that she delayed in responding to the child's turn for the worse because she had to "see" John's sincerity. Or, perhaps it is also the fact that she "couldn't see" her own hatred for the child because it reminded her of John's desires, about whom and which she may have thought angrily about while conceiving it, given John's skin tone preferences. Or, it may in fact be Hurston's use of melancholia raised to a symbolic level.

The play closes in silence.[72] Emma is rocking in her chair next to the now dead child. The audience sits with her in silence. The experience of sitting and observing her rocking is more theatrically basic than dialogue. There is nothing

verifiable with certainty, and this is how it should be. Explanations reduce meaning to mere descriptions, and these descriptions often fail to delineate the unspeakable reality. Emma's story cannot be explained; it is essentially unfinished
and without resolution.

The play's disjointed structure reflects the protagonist. It presents Emma in
fragments because there is no whole "Emma." Crispin Sartwell realizes that in
many of Hurston's literary figures, there is contained a "miscellaneous self, or
nonself," which is "precisely the self that could not be spoken." Sartwell sees this
as an extension of Hurston's autobiographical input into her fictional characters;
Hurston's own sense of self is neither a "racial self," nor is it "culturally constructed." At the deepest level, he explains, the self Hurston creates "exceeds or
is incomprehensible to any construction," because "it is bits and pieces; the self
Hurston asserts is in a sense not anything in particular."[73] Emma is also bits and
pieces and nothing in particular.

In 1928, just three years following completion of *Color Struck*, Hurston wrote
"How It Feels to Be Colored Me":

> I feel like a brown bag of miscellany propped against a wall. Against a wall in
> company with other bags, white, red, and yellow. Pour out the contents, and
> there is discovered a jumble of small things priceless and worthless. . . . In your
> hand is the brown bag. On the ground before you is the jumble it held. . . . A bit
> of colored glass more or less would not matter.[74]

This may serve to explain *Color Struck*. Hurston may have inserted her own feelings into the creation of Emma. The stage picture ends in the following way:

> *She seats herself and rocks monotonously and stares out of the door. A dry sob now and then.*
> *The wind from the open door blows out the lamp and she is seen by the little light from the*
> *window rocking in an even, monotonous gait, and sobbing.*[75]

The image of Emma in fragments can be explained as an expression of
Hurston's own experience. The final moment onstage reveals Hurston's talent
for documenting the social conditions of black women in the South, but it also
shows her talent for seamlessly inserting her thoughts and feelings into the fabric of her fictional characters. Emma's isolation may be both a symbolic representation of black southern women and a personal experience drawn from the
author's imagination.

The door onstage represents the outside world, with its opportunities of emigration. "Outside" belongs to the community, realized in cakewalking, mobility,
socialization, and the "renaissance" up North. Inside, Emma sits monotonously

alone, presenting the audience with the spectacle of her uneventful life. Left alone, she rocks. There is, as Toni Morrison informs us, a "loneliness that can be rocked." This rocking, says Morrison, is expressed in silence and the body: "Arms crossed, knees drawn up; holding, holding on, this motion, unlike a ship's, smooths and contains the rocker. It's an inside kind—wrapped tight like skin."[76] At the end of the play Emma is left with a life like "a bit of colored glass," which, as Hurston notes, "more or less would not matter." She rocks and waits, like a Beckett character, for nothing. In the process, the "black woman" is granted tragic dignity.

Hurston limns Emma as a representation of black women who have slipped through the cracks of history. Hurston's anthropological act of recovery follows Boas's precepts of "fieldwork" and "objective study," while simultaneously fashioning the research into dramatic form. As a fictional yet carefully documented representation of black women at the time, Emma deserves recognition as a significant figure within the New Negro–Harlem Renaissance literature. Although the protagonist stands outside the traditional depictions of Harlem Renaissance fiction and documentation (which may be why the play has been largely ignored), she nonetheless reflects the social conditions of a great many caught in similar circumstances. It is the fact that Emma stands as a creative representation of so many people now forgotten, and because the protagonist is portrayed as a profound characterization of voicelessness and fragmentation, that Hurston's play represents an important document of its era.

CHAPTER SEVEN

THE WAGES OF CULTURE: ALAIN LOCKE AND THE FOLK DRAMAS OF GEORGIA DOUGLAS JOHNSON AND WILLIS RICHARDSON

America should not be a "melting-pot" for the diverse races gathered on her soil but that each race should maintain its essential integrity and contribute its own special and particular gift to our composite civilization: not a "melting-pot" but a symphony where each instrument contributes its particular quality of music to an ensemble of harmonious sounds.

— Montgomery Gregory (n.d.)[1]

INTRODUCTION

Every civilization produces its type.   — (Alain Locke (1916)[2]

White supremacy during the first quarter of the twentieth century was especially virulent. One of its advocates, Thomas Pearce Bailey, wrote in 1914 that the "more white men recognize sharply their kinship with fellow whites," the more "the negro is compelled to 'keep his place'—a place that is being gradually narrowed in the North as well as in the South."[3] In *Race Traits and Tendencies of the American Negro*, a book written in 1896 and widely read at the time, Frederick L. Hoffman held that "a low standard of sexual morality is the main and underlying cause of the law and anti-social conditions of the [black] race at the present time."[4] James Kimble Vardaman was even more pernicious, declaring that the African American is a "lazy, lying, lustful animal," which "no conceivable amount of training can transform into a tolerable citizen."[5] William Hannibal Thomas was likewise a good example of overt racism, claiming in 1901 that African Americans have "no ethical integrity, no inbred determination for right-doing, and consequently no clearly defined and steadfast aversion to wrong-doing."[6] Thomas Nelson Page, who alleged in 1904 that black people "appear not only to have no idea of morality, but to lack any instinct upon which such an idea can be founded," also put the moral argument forward.[7] In his history of the United States, Ellis Paxson Oberholtzer wrote in 1917 that the "laziness and immorality" of black people is a belief grounded "in a good deal of truth."[8] Lothrop Stoddard was no less insistent when he wrote in 1927, "White America will not abolish the color-line, will not admit the Negro to social equality, will not open the door to racial amalgamation."[9]

African American writers and social critics made it a priority to counter precisely these stereotypes, particularly those evident in the theatre, where the depiction of black immorality was vivid. Carter G. Woodson, historian and for a time artistic director of the Howard Players of Howard University, lamented in 1933 that black people "have been recognized by the white man only in purely plantation comedy and minstrelsy." He remarked that the "American Negro has all but ceased to attempt anything else."[10] Woodson's point notwithstanding, dramas attempting to show black people in a "different sphere" in fact existed. Georgia Douglas Johnson (1877–1966) and Willis Richardson (1889–1977) were playwrights who, during the 1920s, created dramatic representations of racial pride, moral virtue, and resistance to oppression. Through their plays, they made a compelling case for an indigenous black theatre and supplied empirical evidence that ordinary black people have values, conscience, and the skills to make these facts evident.

Johnson and Richardson, who were the most prolific African American playwrights of the 1920s, shared numerous attributes.[11] They were dubbed "Harlem Renaissance" playwrights, yet they lived most of their adult lives in and around Washington, D.C. Both had southern roots: Johnson was born and raised in Atlanta, Georgia, and Richardson in Wilmington, North Carolina. Upon graduating from Atlanta University's Normal School in 1893, Johnson became a schoolteacher. She remained in that capacity until 1902, at which time she resigned to pursue a musical career at the Oberlin Conservatory. She married Henry Lincoln Johnson in 1903, a lawyer and civil employee, abandoning music to raise their two children. By 1910 she had relocated with her family to

Washington, D.C., where her husband established a law firm and forged ties with the Washington establishment (he had been a Georgia delegate-at-large to the 1896 Republican national convention).[12] In 1912, President Taft appointed him as the Recorder of Deeds, placing the family squarely within Washington's black middle class.[13] Henry Johnson held to rigid views about marriage, expecting his wife to remain housebound. Despite this restriction, Georgia Johnson, although preoccupied with raising a family, managed to author two books of poetry during their marriage: *The Heart of a Woman* in 1918 and *Bronze: A Book of Verse* in 1922. Her biographer, Gloria T. Hull, described Johnson's husband's death in 1925 as a "turning point" in her life, one that would free her creative impulses.[14] Her play, *Blue Blood*, received honorable mention in the 1926 *Opportunity* play contest, and another of her plays, *Plumes*, would take first prize in 1927.

Following the 1898 race riots in their hometown of Wilmington, the Richardson family moved to Washington, where Willis obtained his education.[15] Richardson attended the city's well-known M Street High School (later renamed Dunbar High), where he studied drama, rhetoric, and English under playwright Mary P. Burrill (1884–1946), whose plays, *Aftermath* (1919) and *They That Sit in Darkness* (1919), dealt with the topics of lynching and birth control. Richardson was accepted into Howard University; unable to pay the tuition, he declined to enroll in order to support himself, working as a government clerk in the department of Engraving and Printing. From 1916 to 1918, he studied playwriting by correspondence. In 1923, his play *The Chip Woman's Fortune* became the first non-musical drama by an African American to receive a Broadway production. He would twice win the *Crisis* playwriting award (in 1925 and 1926), and in 1928 he won Yale University's Schwab Cup award for playwriting.

Living in Washington provided Johnson and Richardson with a life removed from Harlem. Many African Americans in Washington enjoyed government service employment, resulting in a black middle class. Despite a lack of resources in some schools, Washington had one of the best school systems in the nation. There were segregation and poverty, especially in areas known as the "alley";[16] but within the black community, there was a commitment to education and self-respect. Howard University in Washington had become a leading institution, with a distinguished faculty that included Alain Locke, Montgomery Gregory, and many others. In 1915, the *New York Age* went so far as to report that Howard was "one of the landmarks of Negro-American civilization," with an influence that "ramified into every community in the nation."[17] Historian Herbert Aptheker described the period from 1910 to 1930 as a "great leap in higher education" for African Americans, with enrollment in colleges growing from 355,215 in 1910 to 597,682 in 1920, and then to 1,188,532 in 1930.[18]

The city had a sizeable African American population and by 1920 had replaced Chicago, which at one time had the second-largest black population
(Washington 109,996, Chicago 109,458) in the United States. New York City
had a greater African American population than either (152,467); however, this
tally combined Harlem with New York City as a whole.[19] Baltimore came in
fourth with 108,322 African Americans in 1920, and was but a short distance
from Washington. Given the ease and frequency of travel between Baltimore and
Washington, the Baltimore-Washington corridor had the largest concentration
of black people (over 200,000) in the United States. Thus, during the "Harlem"
Renaissance, a larger number of urbanized African Americans lived in the combined population centers of Washington and Baltimore.[20]

Despite poverty and the race riots of 1919, by 1920 black Washingtonians
came to enjoy an increasing standard of living. At the turn of the century, Washington was the site of the Negro elite, dubbed the "old cits." In 1900, poet Paul
Laurence Dunbar observed that Washington had become the "mecca for colored
people" and in 1901 he added that the area, with its "numerous literary organizations" and "reading clubs," showcased the city's cultural life.[21] In 1904 Mary
Church Terrell claimed that in Washington, "there are more colored people who
are well educated and well to do than in any other city in the world."[22] In addition,
during the 1910s the city would witness an influx of African American doctors,
lawyers, government employees, professors, and other professionals attracted by
Howard University, good high schools, and comfortable living conditions. By the
end of World War I, the elite guard of Washington's traditional families, the "old
cits," had joined the prospering middle class. By the 1910s the so-called "government official set," the traditional "social arbiters of the city's black community," had
welcomed the "educational set" arriving in Washington.[23] While Jim Crow segregation remained commonplace in public transportation, restaurants, schools, libraries, and hotels, the city's black middle class enjoyed bourgeois respectability
combined with southern gentility. Black Washingtonians at the time were some of
the most socially prominent and politically influential middle- and upper-middle-
class African Americans in the nation. In his book about Alain Locke's early years,
Jeffrey C. Stewart remarks that a "conspicuously high standard of living was
available to blacks who held political appointments generally reserved for the elite,
and many others filled clerical jobs in the federal government that were free from
segregated hiring practices and working conditions."[24] This middle-class contingent helped sustain drama and intellectual pursuits.

The intellectual and literary activity was vigorous—no doubt explaining
why, following the death of her husband in 1925, Georgia Douglas Johnson was
able to form a successful Saturday night discussion group for local writers, social

critics, and Howard University professors. In 1927, Gwendolyn B. Bennett would dub the group the *"Saturday nighters of Washington, D.C."*[25] Among the regulars who met at her home, which Johnson endearingly nicknamed her "halfway house," were Alain Locke, Jean Toomer, Jessie Redmond Fauset, Anne Spencer, Angela Weld Grimké, Carter Woodson, Mary Church Terrell, James Weldon Johnson, Montgomery Gregory, and Richardson.[26] Typically, when Langston Hughes, Zora Neale Hurston, W. E. B. Du Bois, and others passed through Washington, they would attend the Saturday night poetry and play readings. Every Saturday night at Johnson's home, says Richardson, "We used to meet at nine o'clock and stay until two or three in the morning," discussing "things like writing. Some would read their poems and they would discuss them."[27] There was a concentration on poetry, plays, and novels, with an emphasis on the written word rather than oral and musical traditions.

Broadway symbolized New York and its black musicals, with Harlem being the primary site of clubs and nightlife. While there were black theatres in Harlem devoted to non-musical drama, black musicals and club life came to dominate the image of the African American New York theatre scene. Washington had no such reputation; black writers, actors, and theatre patrons in Washington created and attended non-musical dramas, tending to avoid what was perceived of as minstrelsy. According to Montgomery Gregory, Harlem's musicals and clubs carried on "the old minstrel tradition."[28] By contrast, the "Washington aesthetic" sought parity with white writers. Drama, and more importantly its literary tradition, was accentuated. Dramas emerging from Washington would differ from Broadway musicals such as *Shuffle Along, Runnin' Wild*, and *From Dixie to Broadway*, which tended to pander to "commercial" tastes, while the Harlem nightclubs continued to cater to white patrons. In contrast, Johnson and Richardson, supported by a Washington-based audience, would come to represent a frequently forgotten strain of African American ecumenism and values.

Both Johnson and Richardson expected to reach people with their plays by conveying a sense of "truth" behind the phenomena of quotidian life. Theirs was a simple message, but one containing certain facts: African Americans were not primitive buffoons, but rather intelligent and empathetic people who consciously struggled to survive in a hostile world. Johnson and Richardson's values were motivated by a sense of justice. They aimed to universalize the black experience through the following aesthetic and grass-root activities:

1. They developed a rigorous idealism of black folk culture by taking its traditions seriously and building their dramas on a cross-section of middle- and lower middle-class "folk" life.

2. They incorporated the ideas of three notable figures in particular: W. E. B. Du Bois's notion of propaganda; Montgomery Gregory's belief that small, intimate theatres with black themes better served black communities than large-scale "Broadway"-style productions; and, primarily, Alain Locke's theory of black folk drama and realism.

3. They built on Locke's value theories, portraying African Americans as a people who advanced an ethical worldview in a world that offered them less than what they had hoped for (more on this point shortly).

4. They rejected what Winona L. Fletcher called "the stronghold of stereotypical images"[29] and the so-called "primal authenticity" that denoted the Harlem Renaissance.

5. They created a delicately wrought realism committed to recognizing the empirical realities of daily life through one-act plays rather than full-length dramas. Their dramas were intimate and were produced largely in churches, community meeting halls, college theatres, and people's homes.

6. They attempted to assert the commonplace over the poetic, even if this meant presenting philistinism and the banalities of everyday life. They portrayed black life along the lines of what the American realist William Dean Howells termed the "aesthetics of the common."[30]

7. They acted in the belief that drama's power of mimetic representation, combined with humanist values, can change the world.

Johnson and Richardson set out to provide common people with the means to see themselves onstage. Their "plain folk" aesthetics—what Richardson called "ordinary black people" and Johnson termed "average Negro life"[31]—stressed faith in the community. Although today their didactic dramas seem dated, at the time Johnson and Richardson produced important documents about black self-perception.

While there are discernable differences between them, Johnson and Richardson wrote with an essentially similar purpose. Johnson sought to present American audiences, white and black, with the consequences of lynching. She wanted people to observe how black people, especially mothers and grandmothers, suffered from lynching's brutality. Johnson realized that a play could never capture the effects of lynching with the vivacity and objective fidelity of a photograph; but she did feel obliged to remove the shroud of acceptance and expose the naked cruelty of the institution itself. Like Johnson, Richardson was a playwright whose realistic motifs reflected a dependence on standard melodramatic techniques. His was a self-conscious effort to live up to Gregory's and Locke's expectations of parity with Western drama and to convey black folk life.

Richardson's characters struggled with moral decisions of a religious and civic nature. He shared with Johnson the goal of presenting the details of a morally upright lifestyle, while dampening any overt political appearance. Yet his plays were political insofar as they conveyed "good" people struggling to come to terms with injustice.

Both Johnson and Richardson rebelled against the affectations of Washington's African American elite. Langston Hughes described this society as "pompous gentlemen and pouter-pigeoned ladies," whose "ideals seemed most Nordic" and "appeared to be moving away from the masses of the race rather than holding an identity with them." While Hughes appreciated Washington as "one of the most beautiful cities in the world" and spoke highly of Georgia Douglas Johnson's "charm" as she "poured tea on Saturday night for young writers and artists and intellectuals," the elites, he felt, were snobs of Victorian vintage.[32] Johnson and Richardson were bohemians of sorts, who rebelled against black elitism as well as white racism by writing plays about the "peasant class of the Negro group."[33] Richardson chastised African American audiences for disliking "dialect" and "unpleasant characters and endings," urging audiences to give attention to the underclass.[34] He further insisted that the black middle class "witness the interesting things in the lives of [their] kinsman, no matter what may be their condition of life, speech or manner."[35] In this way, black audiences would fulfill the required "duty to strengthen that weak link [rather] than to be ashamed of it."[36] Johnson believed writers should "depict the best" in African Americans,[37] but the "best" in her terms meant the best qualities of the poor.

Johnson and Richardson designed their plays for what was then termed the "Little Theatre Movement," writing against the grain of mainstream theatres.[38] Although Richardson's *Chip Woman's Fortune* was produced on Broadway in 1923, for the most part their plays were produced, if they were performed at all, by the Harlem Experimental Theatre and the Lafayette Players Theatre of New York, the Krigwa Theatre of New York and Washington, the Howard University Players Theatre and the Dunbar Players Theatre of Washington, the Ethiopian Art Theatre and the Folk Theatre of Chicago, the Dunbar Theatre of Philadelphia, the Dixwell Players Theatre of New Haven, and Karamu House's Gilpin Players Theatre in Cleveland (more on the Little Theatre Movement in chapter 10).

The need to write for black audiences was the result of a growing racial division combined with a growing sense of "race pride."[39] Segregation had entered every facet of life and black people saw little possibility of interracial harmony. In view of white hostility, Leon F. Litwack says that African Americans "drew inward, constructing in their communities a separate world," complete with "their own schools, churches, businesses, fraternal orders, cultural practices, and forms of activitism and expression."[40] Black theatre, too, drew inward. Furthermore, Johnson and Richardson rejected the ideas of abstract and experimental art such as surrealism and expressionism, with their focus on external form. Instead, they were interested in representations of their own community for the purposes of self-awareness and reform.

Notwithstanding the importance of Du Bois, the greatest influence on Johnson and Richardson was Alain Locke.[41] As a tutelary figure to many writers, Locke wielded enormous power. His prestige could leverage recognition; many sought his patronage and catered to his demands. Those who did not, or who chose to write against the grain of his opinions, were ostracized. Locke's importance to Johnson and Richardson cannot be underestimated. He sponsored the productions of both authors. Johnson became a sort of surrogate mother to Locke following the death of his biological mother in 1922.[42] As early as 1916, Johnson invited Locke to her home for advice on literary matters. By the 1920s he regularly read, critiqued, reviewed, and endorsed her poetry and dramatic works.[43] In 1928, Locke wrote in his "Foreword" to Johnson's third book of poetry, *An Autumn Love Cycle,* that her words were "pure lyric gold," having "gone straight to the mine of the heart."[44] Richardson also sought Locke's patronage. In 1925, he wrote to Locke thanking him for completing the ending to his play, *Compromise,* adding, "I am sure whatever you have done is an improvement on the play and your advice is always welcome."[45] Locke chose Richardson's *Compromise* to be published in the seminal work of the decade, *The New Negro* (1925) and, along with Gregory, produced Richardson's play *Mortgaged* at Howard University in 1924. Examining Locke's philosophy will provide the required understanding of underlying themes in the plays.

ALAIN LOCKE, ETHICAL VALUES, AND THE DRAMA OF RACE

Man does not, cannot, live in a valueless world.
—Alain Locke (1935)[46]

Born to schoolteacher parents in Philadelphia, Locke (1885–1954), a Harvard graduate (A.B., magna cum laude in English and philosophy, 1907), was the first African American to receive a Rhodes scholarship to Oxford. Following completion of his studies at Oxford in 1910, he moved to Germany, attending the University of Berlin, where he studied the works of Franz Brentano and Alexius Meinong, among others. In 1911 he returned to the United States and the next year began his teaching career at Howard University.[47] Locke would teach at

Howard until his death, creating and guiding the university's English, philosophy, and drama departments.[48] From the mid-1910s onward, he was a fixture in the Washington artistic community, providing encouragement, financial assistance, and reviews, referring to himself years later as "the philosophical mid-wife to generations of young Negro poets."[49]

Locke believed in art's vitalism, especially its energy and capacity to change the world. Foremost for Locke was drama, which he claimed could "penetrate the mind" in ways other art forms could not.[50] Representations onstage could demonstrate effectively the complexity and changing dynamics of African American life, expressing the elemental needs, desires, and roots of the black experience. He warned, however, against the "propaganda play." It was not the purpose of drama "to solve problems or reform society."[51] Instead of propaganda, he encouraged the "folk play," which, he claimed, "is really the promising path." Locke believed black people provided rich material for drama; the "Negro experience," he wrote, is "inherently dramatic," with folk drama offering the most effective means of conveying this experience.[52] The folk play, he maintained, is drama "of free self-expression and imaginative release," conveying "beautifully and colorfully the folk life of the race."[53] Locke opposed propaganda in art on the grounds that it contained the "sin of monotony and disproportion," perpetuating "the position of group inferiority even in crying out against it."[54] However, folk art, in Locke's terms, ought not to mean "primitivism," the "decadent cult" that according to him had blemished black musicals, art, and literature. Instead, folk art must show "the unbiased truth and the same angle of vision for all."[55]

Folk drama, being the dramatic enactment of text, music, dance, and shared myth, had the character of a collective religious performance, binding the community together as participants in a ritual rather than as mere spectators at a theatre. Locke's notion of folk drama, and the importance he attached to it, took hold in the Washington aesthetics embodied in the plays of Johnson and Richardson. The folk root of black drama, which finds in Johnson and Richardson their most ambitious embodiment, was an alternative to the Jazz Age musicals saturating Broadway. These musicals helped assist in the creation of black "primitivism," with fast-hoofing, show-girl attractions, and new rhythms establishing the myth of "black instinctualism." Locke's concept of drama exalted a counter-primitivism grounded in folk drama, yet devoid of the misconception that black people are happy-go-lucky dancers and nothing more. Many African Americans, especially in Washington, considered Broadway musicals unsatisfying and antithetical to the spiritual hunger of a people seeking transcendence from minstrelsy. Folk drama, spearheaded by Locke's conception of it, would be the panacea for a "New Negro" culture seeking roots and traditions.

Locke held that the age of the "New Negro" had been a critical break-through against sentimentalism and propaganda. He resisted propaganda not on the grounds that it was ineffective—he admitted that the "literature of assertion and protest did perform a valuable service," as it "encouraged and vindicated cultural equality." The problem with literature of protest was its costliness; it yielded mere "melodramatic sentimentalism" at the expense of "pure self-expression," thereby encouraging African American artists to curry white favor while at the same time inhibiting the growth "of folk forms and traditions."[56] He observed that a new phase of "Negro self-expression" created the "New Negro," who was contributing to the new social awareness. The spirit of the "New Negro" would liberate black people from "protest," allowing aesthetic forms to reveal past traditions as well as much that was new and of value.[57]

Still, the issue of race and how it informed "folk forms and traditions" had to be clarified before free self-expression, originality, and what Locke called the "simplicity, calm dignity, and depth of folk art" could flourish.[58] Speaking at his first major lecture at Howard University in 1916, Locke said that race was "in a paradoxical stage." The paradox amounted "to a social inheritance, and yet it parades itself as biological or anthropological inheritance."[59] De-emphasizing biological assumptions—what Locke termed the "biological fallacy"[60]—necessitated the examination of race as a cultural phenomena. According to him, the "entire scientific status and future of the consideration of man's group character rests upon a decisive demonstration of what factors are really indicative of race."[61]

For Locke, race and art required ten explanatory components: value theory, pluralism, cosmopolitanism, aesthetics, race loyalty, realism, culture, social reciprocity, civilization-type, and folk traditions. When comprehended, these ten factors would clarify and define "race drama" as "folk art." As Locke perceived it, "race drama" was a complex notion emerging from several influences. At Harvard, George Santayana and Josiah Royce had influenced Locke's philosophy of value, while William James instilled a respect for Pragmatism.[62] The world of Oxford imbued his thinking with a texture of cosmopolitanism, and Germany held for him a fascination with Herder's concepts of "folk culture" and a respect for the Austrian school of value theory (Brentano and Meinong). In addition, Boasian anthropology and Kant's theories of aesthetic judgment shaped his views. This mixture of influences provides the background to Locke's major theoretical contributions.

For Locke, everything begins with "values." Values determine decisions resulting from changing conditions.[63] Values, he claims in his seminal essay, "Values and Imperatives," are "philosophies of life and not of abstract, disembodied 'objective' reality; products of time, place, and situation, and thus systems of timed history rather than timeless eternity."[64] Following in the footsteps of Pragmatist William James, Locke averred that no single, unifying theory of value exists. He eschewed the absolutism of a fixed value theory, embracing instead a contextual conception of reality. As James had observed, absolutism claims that reality "stands ready-made and complete," where "our intellects supervene with the one simple duty of describing it as it is already."[65] Locke rejected this, too; he realized, however, that the world could not escape values as functional actions and objects of preference and choice. He thus set out to establish a normative principle of objective validity for values "without resort to dogmatism and absolutism."[66]

According to Locke, values incorporated relativism without succumbing to random subjectivism. Values occupied the point of equilibrium between "atomistic relativism" and the "colorless, uniformitarian criterion of logic."[67] Like his Harvard mentor Santayana, and to a lesser extent Brentano, Locke believed values were neither a free-for-all of feelings nor fixed and immutable entities; they were to be found in the processes related to evolving emotion and commonsense logic.[68] We react emotionally, but our feelings form a backdrop of reasonable application that can accommodate change. "Value-modes," as he called them, arise from a process of continual reevaluation and a temporal view of reality. There is "no fixity of content to values" because values, as the Pragmatists would have it, are subject to living, transforming experiences. Real-world circumstances demand the transformation of values, and thus values are influenced by real-world interactions.[69] "We are forced to conclude," he asserts, "that the feeling-quality, irrespective of content, makes a value of a given kind, and that a transformation of the attitude effects a change of type in the value situation."[70] All evaluations of truth, knowledge, morality, and virtue, the referential components that constitute values, refer back to the concrete details of the culture in which these concepts surface and develop.

Locke's philosophy of values underlies his views on dramatic art. His dramatic theories, likewise his philosophy, promulgate neither anarchic subjectivity nor rules of dramatic form. Dramatic art had to strike a balance between spontaneous creativity and attachment to interlocking values based on race loyalty. Locke recognized the importance of feeling in art, but he also insisted on a duty to racial solidarity. While this duty was by no means a categorical imperative, which demands rigid uniformity, aesthetic duty ought to advance cultural life. No doubt this was a byproduct of the "racial uplift" spirit (the notion of solidarity and help for all African Americans) that had prevailed during his time; however, Locke added to this the importance of pluralism, which acknowledges the contributions of each group in relation to society as a whole. Cultural pluralism, a term also used by Locke's friend and colleague Horace M. Kallen in 1924,[71] meant that different cultural groups should be granted equal respect, differences ought not to be prioritized, and each group expression should be shared and cross-fertilized with others. Building on the theories of anthropologist Franz Boas, Locke argued that racial differences were to be found in values and cultural products, not biology. Each race, Locke maintained, has its own cultural initiatives defining its people. Race is therefore a matter of what one does, having little or nothing to do with genetics. Races or civilizations (Locke uses these two terms interchangeably) develop over time, borrow from other cultures, and exchange the fruits of their labor. Instead of identity being self-evident, then, racial characteristics are to be perceived historically, as groups undergo evolution. Locke conceived this view from Pragmatism and German Romanticism, especially the conception of *Bildung*—culture as a developing idea—which has its roots in Herder's notions of folk life, or *Volksgeist* (folk spirit).

Locke rejected the belief in fixed racial attributes. Rather, the true meaning of black culture would reveal itself only in the process of social interaction. Each civilization has its distinct contributions to a pluralistic world in which understanding is based on mutual respect. Moreover, all aspects of culture should be explicated in terms relative to the culture's value systems and folk traditions, provided that these systems and traditions have internal coherence. In 1924, he unveiled his concept of "traditions," "traits," and "values," which define the features of race as a process of development:

> Race operates as tradition, as preferred traits and values, and when these things change . . . ethnic remoulding is taking place. Race then, so far as the ethnologist is concerned, seems to lie in that peculiar selective preference for certain cultural-traits and resistance to certain others which is characteristic of all types and levels of social organization.[72]

Cultural traits may separate groups, but Locke developed an idea of "cosmopolitanism" as a means of intercultural communication. "Cosmopolitanism" in Lockean terms meant group solidarity yet concomitant respect for others. In 1908, as a student at Oxford, he edited and wrote for several issues of the *Oxford Cosmopolitan*. In one of his earliest essays, he asserted the view that cosmopolitan culture "is a sense of value contrasts and a heightened and rationalized self-centralization." In a pluralistic world, race is mutual and reciprocal: "As *x* is to you, so is *y* to me," with x and y representing different cultures and traditions. He posited the only possible solution to static isolationism between races in comparative terms, as "an enforced respect and interest for one's own tradition, and a more or less accurate appreciation of its contrasting values with other traditions."[73]

While Locke's position on cultural pluralism would modify over the years, its fundamental principles were firmly in place by 1908. Each culture must develop its own self-conception, produce artworks that reflect its own traditions and values, and learn from, even borrow from, others as well. Common communicative practices, such as art, literature, and theatre, enable each culture to engage in mutually enriching and transformative exchanges. In 1930, he wrote that history sustains a continuous "reciprocity between cultures." The modern world, he continued, demands a "'free-trade in culture,' and a complete recognition of the principle of cultural reciprocity." For Locke, reciprocity (a term he frequently used) meant that each culture must relinquish its claim to "exclusive property," particularly in aesthetic production. Cultures must share their artworks, since they and their products "belong most to those who can use them best." Still, culture remains, despite its exchange value, a "folk-product, with the form and flavor of a particular people and place," which has "root and grows in that social soil which, for want of a better term, we call 'race.'"[74]

In the late 1910s and into the 1920s, Locke emphasized aesthetics.[75] He put forward the idea that African Americans have specific and demonstrable values in art, literature, music, and drama. Race, he said, is "a closer spiritual bond than nationality and group experience." In the case of African Americans, beauty is "born of long-suffering" and "truth" derives from "mass emotion and founded on collective vision."[76] This collective vision achieves its ultimate form through art and aesthetic evaluation. Locke's tastes were Whitmanesque, his style affectatious, and to a degree Kant had influenced his ideas on aesthetic judgment. While he rejected Kant's moral absolutism and categorical imperatives, Locke appeared to be guided by Kant's theory of aesthetic judgments based on subjective freedom and objective standards of beauty, the latter being what Kant called "the faculty of estimating formal purposiveness [*Zweckmässigkeit*]" through which an objective study "of nature by understanding and reason [*Verstand und Vernuft*]" might be attained.[77] Beauty in art is a coterminous relationship of subjective free will and objectivity. Kant refers to this relationship as the "conceived harmony of nature" and the "need of finding universality of principles."[78] This mixture is crucial for Kant; art must have a strict objective criterion, a universal yardstick based on reason by which to measure its value, yet it must permit indeterminacy and flexibility to allow for creative spontaneity, which nurtures aesthetic harmony (what Kant called a kind of "purposelessness without purpose").[79] For Locke, African American art combines the free spirit of subjectivism with objective, universal standards. In his "Introduction" to *Plays of Negro Life* (1927), Locke wrote that black dramatists "are beginning to seek vent and find free-flowing expression," while simultaneously creating dramas "with that reciprocity and universality of spirit which truly great art requires and itself helps to establish."[80] Looking to Irish dramatists as a paradigm, Locke called for an indigenous black drama, one that would stir audiences "poetically" as well as "universally." Rather than "anatomize and dissect," he called on dramatists to "paint and create." Most importantly, the new drama must "break down" the "false stereotypes in terms of which the world still sees us" and in its place "stimulate the group life culturally and give it the spiritual quickening of a native art."[81] This free expression of native roots and poetic life had yet to arrive; black dramatists first had to clear the ground of false stereotypes before they could arrive at what he termed "purely aesthetic attitudes."[82]

His aesthetic tastes notwithstanding, Locke understood the social importance of art and literature. Although he dismissed the stilted woodenness of social drama, he nevertheless offered qualified acceptance of protest art, provided that the "fire of social protest should flame, not smolder," and that the objective of the artist and writer "is not to ignore or eliminate the race problem, but to broaden its social dimensions and deepen its universal human implications."[83] He insisted throughout his life that black artists are obliged to maintain a loyalty to their race. In keeping with this theme of loyalty, Locke had little patience with black artists who exploited their talents for commercial gain. He chastised the "escapist escapades" of authors and performers whose "spiritual truancy and social irresponsibility" took advantage of primitivism and stereotypes. In his 1937 critique of poet and novelist Claude McKay's book, *A Long Way from Home,* Locke admonished the "decadent aestheticism" of certain "faddist Negrophiles," who failed to present black people as "soundly integrated with life."[84] For Locke, the "Negro Renaissance program" was "to interpret the folk to itself, to vitalize it from within; it was a wholesome, vigorous, assertive racialism, even if not explicitly proletarian in conception and justification." He would call for "Negro writers" to become "truer sons of the people, more loyal providers of spiritual bread and less aesthetic wastrels and truants of the streets."[85]

Locke argues for an aesthetic value, but not an aesthetic essence. This is because he stakes his claims on the ever-transforming idea of race, which prevents race, and in turn aesthetics, from hypostasizing into absolutism. As a consequence, the relationship of individuals to community continually transforms art and drama. However, Locke puts the artist in a difficult position; for him the admixture of artistic "free self-expression" and "race loyalty" is contradictory. It promotes creative autonomy yet requires a continual search for validation from the community. Drama and art subtend a relation between subject and community, liberated from the demands of propaganda yet bound by loyalty to the culture from which they originate. How can the artist be free to explore boundless options while constrained by group solidarity?

Locke's advocacy of "folk drama" was inherently problematic. Folk art is, for the most part, based on traditions and reenactments of rituals. It is rooted in native soil and developed through time and repetition. But African American drama had little if any tradition; slavery had robbed black people of an indigenous culture from which to draw folk traditions. Minstrelsy was the primary stage depiction of African Americans for over a century, creating a ritual that falsified rather than enhanced black cultural practices. As a consequence, Locke encouraged writers to build a new tradition that essentially lacked historical foundation. Tradition without history, however, is a paradox, because the meaning of "folk" without repetition and reenactments is devoid of "roots." Folk drama depends on chronological traditions and linear development; folk tradition lacking rituals and prior enactments is basically a transcendental idea without empirical grounding.

Locke sought to address this problem in three ways: first, African American drama must have high standards that transcend minstrelsy; second, dramatists must build new folk roots and traditions; and third, black drama ought to be acknowledged by mainstream America without having to sacrifice its roots. However, such demands cut against the grain of folk art, which develops from linear history and takes root in the community's native traditions—or risks losing its folk "purity." Locke's theory, therefore, advocated a radical adjustment to the concept of "folk": it replaced the horizontal (linear) conditions of folk chronology with a vertical arrangement. In other words, black drama had to aim downwards into the soil and upwards, transcending minstrelsy, hence avoiding minstrel history. Locke clarified these goals in a series of articles in two 1926 issues of *Theatre Arts Monthly*, where he wrote that the "finest function" of race drama "would be to supply an imaginative channel of escape and spiritual release," and through emotional reinforcement, "cover life with the illusion of happiness and spiritual freedom." However, because black drama lacked

> any tradition or art to which to attach itself, this reaction [of happiness and spiritual freedom] has never functioned in the life of the American Negro except at the level of the explosive and abortive release of buffoonery and low comedy. Held down by social tyranny to the jester's footstool, the dramatic instincts of the race have had to fawn, crouch and be amusingly vulgar.[86]

Locke expended much of his intellectual energies working through the competing urges of individual self-expression versus community ties on the one hand, and the formation of a folk drama and the development of its roots on the other. His search for a way to resolve the demands for autonomous, free self-expression and racial solidarity reflects the persistent need to make choices between the self and the world. He understood that pure aesthetic factors had to be put on hold until historical realities were confronted and resolved.

Although he rejected biological essentialism, Locke did not shy away from occasionally stating "truths" about black people. His assertion that the "Negro actor" brings "the gift of a temperament, not the gift of tradition," suggests naïveté.[87] Nevertheless, he understood these claims of "temperament" to be temporary and contingent. Black dramatic "tradition" had been upstaged by minstrelsy; hence, black actors and playwrights lacked "tradition" to fall back on; "temperament" was one way of filling the void, at least temporarily. Black dramatists, looking for roots to build on, must come to terms with a history of less than flattering depictions that were often absurd. To counter a century of minstrelsy, he called for black playwrights to connect with their roots, however new these roots were, and offer African Americans emotional freedom and spiritual uplift.

According to Locke, realism was one way to create new folk forms and counter stereotyping. Only realism, he said in 1934, can "painfully reconstruct from actual life truer, livelier, more representative" presentations of the folk.[88] For Locke, the New Negro—urbanized and sophisticated—had cast away obsequious behavior associated with the "Old Negro" and replaced it with resolute challenges to authority. He maintained that the post-Reconstruction philosophy that dominated the rural period from 1876 to 1910 would give way to a philosophy of objective rationalism, which might overturn Jim Crow. Locke, like Du Bois, believed that drama was a primary means of reversing minstrel images and the status quo; for both, only a realistic depiction of black life would counteract the damage done by minstrelsy. Samuel A. Hay has offered the opinion that African American theatre arose from Du Bois's plea for propaganda, and Locke's demand for folk drama. The Du Boisian theatre, he writes, "was strictly political," while Locke "wanted believable characters and situations that sprang from the real life of the people." The principles of the two schools, he asserts, "still inform African American drama."[89] While Hay is no doubt correct in saying that Du Bois and Locke held differing objectives, there is a danger in overstating their differences. Du Bois and Locke were absorbed in the bourgeoisie and both promoted realism. For them, drama, whether folk or propaganda, would be guided by realism. Art, considered as a vehicle of truth, expressed life as something unambiguous; it must convey real events and hold them up for public scrutiny. Realism aligned Locke with Du Bois. Charles Scruggs appears to concur when he says that Du Bois's emphasis on propaganda "was actually a plea for Locke's 'self-expression,'" and that Locke's emphasis on art "was itself propagandistic," since the truth in art "will set us free."[90] Self-expression and truth combined to create a realistic drama informed by political commitment.

Realism was a means to cleanse the stage of past stereotypes and begin the process of building folk roots and traditions. Believable depictions of African American life would set the stage for a new representation of traditions. For Locke, theatre flourishes only if there is a connection between what happens on-stage and the world. Because minstrelsy, with its exaggerated and misconstrued portrayal of African Americans, failed to portray the world accurately, realism might present something "real" as opposed to something "fake." Theatrical realism examines the link between private lives and the stage, illuminating reality by clarifying what lies beneath its surface. "Facts shouldn't be regretted," Locke said, "they should be explained."[91] Given the history of minstrelsy's exaggerations, reality was in need of clarification. What counts as real for African Americans—the traditions, folk forms, and values of the group—defines the "authentic" and the "real." The realistic play positions the audience as sympathetic observers who care about the lives of the characters. Thus drama, as Locke imagined it, should teach us something about the folk life of the people. Willis Richardson's biographer, Christine R. Gray, rightly observes that folk culture presented by black dramatists was "given dignity and thereby validated" through the depiction of struggles and virtues. However, the African American folk tradition in drama did not, as Gray maintains, repudiate "European aesthetics," but rather used its realism as basic to the form.[92] Locke held that African American dramatists should build on European realism, but revise the content to reflect black reality and experiences.

Although Locke emphasized folk traditions over propaganda, he never lost sight of the importance of reason, communication, and the ideals of Pragmatism. He claimed that for the New Negro, "reason and realism have cured us of sentimentality: instead of the wail and appeal, there is challenge and indictment."[93] For Locke, reason and realism were inextricably bound together through Pragmatism. The Pragmatist philosopher Charles Sanders Peirce contended that "information and reasoning" would result in a reality that is "independent of the vagaries of me and you." Thus, for Peirce, "the very origin of the conception of reality shows that this conception essentially involves the notion of a *community*, without definite limits, and capable of a definite increase of knowledge."[94] Peirce's definition of the "real" as an evolving interrelationship between the self and the community would be repeated in Locke's perspectives on race, culture, and drama.

Locke urged African American dramatists to convey folk life realistically, but also with passion. He saw the situation of the 1920s as a "dilemma of choice between the drama of discussion and social analysis and the drama of expression and artistic interpretation." He required drama to "grow in its own soil and cultivate its own intrinsic elements; only in this way can it become truly organic, and cease being a rootless derivative."[95] Realism would become the foundation of a truly indigenous and fecund African American drama. He wrote in his notes (ca. 1926) that "a peasant folk art pouring out from under a generation-long repression is the likeliest soil known for a dramatic renascence." From this fertile soil, "the supporters and exponents of Negro drama do not expect their folk temperament to prove the barren exception."[96]

Locke saw reality as a social process driven by the need to further objective knowledge about the structures of the world through education and acculturation. His opinions reflected Peirce's concepts of "information and reasoning" as the basis of reality, by which an evolving community might accrue knowledge and thus grow. As a consequence, the relationship of the individual to the community always transforms art and drama. Culture might reconcile the conflict between individual and community by "evolving" and "educating" (Peirce's concept of increased knowledge).[97] In his address to the incoming freshman class of 1922–23 at Howard, Locke firmly maintained that the "highest intellectual duty is the duty to be cultured." The objective of culture is to transcend self-interest; culture, he said, "begins in education where compulsion leaves off."[98] Culture sustains social ethics that, in turn, promote social conscience. This discipline in culture was not only a search for ethical perfection; he hoped it would resolve the contradiction between autonomy and solidarity. Through cultural enrichment, African Americans would be liberated from truculent egoism and rigid didacticism. In this context, the individual is no longer isolated from culture, but rooted in its soil.

Locke maintained that identity—the basic way we recognize each other—was inadequate to social individuation without cultural background, without knowing one's "roots." To be "Negro in the cultural sense," he said, "is not to be radically different, but only to be distinctively composite and idiomatic." Cultures, however, share their products "in the common cultural life," which, in turn, becomes "progressively even more composite and hybridized, sometimes for the better, sometimes not."[99] Through the analysis of plays, music, literature, science, and philosophy, the African American "race" would be identified, at each historic juncture, through its idiomatic and aesthetic productivity, creating a vernacular from a synthesis of African and Western traditions.[100]

While he took pride in his culture, Locke was influenced by European tastes. Jeffrey C. Stewart has criticized him for this, claiming that "European high art remained Locke's ideal throughout his life, clouding his vision of a native black and American culture."[101] To be sure, Locke was both a nativist and a Europeanist who sought indigenous folk art *and* European aesthetics. He attempted to preserve the primacy of racial identity without racial chauvinism, to keep racial distinctions without playing into the hands of biologism or reverse stereotyping, and to inculcate European aesthetics without losing African American uniqueness. Locke sought to balance "blackness" with Europeanism by maintaining a comparative method of criticism. For him, criticism of art and drama entailed the capacity of comparing one art form with another, not merely in juxtaposition, but as a self-critiquing activity that encouraged introspection and aesthetic improvement through the exchange of ideas. Only through reciprocity—borrowing, critiquing, and incorporating—can each culture dislodge internalized complacency and demonstrate growth and development. Locke thus juggled the dialectics of competing urges (self and world) and pluralistic empiricism through a Du Boisian "double consciousness," a dual trajectory situated in mainstream and African American cultures.

Despite similarities, Locke, contra Du Bois, placed less emphasis on cultural struggle than on social harmony and cultural reciprocity. In order to achieve harmony, attention must be paid to racial identities manifested in cultural productivity. Instead of promoting simplistic "essentialist" categories—the notion that groups or individuals have fundamentally biological and immutable "essences"—Locke pushed for recognition of social "types" through cultural accomplishments and collective values. These values and achievement are, however, *always subject to change.* He summarized the situation of African Americans and advised steps to alleviate racial oppression. Race pride was mandatory, yielding a mutable but meaningful common standard of what it means to be part of a social group. Yet a doctrine of racial solidarity must conform to standards of judgment that are historically contingent and expedient. Locke borrowed from Du Bois's "double consciousness," but he did not view it in terms of the interior struggle of the "soul"; rather, he identified the duality through external ethical choices, with race pride symbolic of an "individual moral life."[102]

Locke and Du Bois shared numerous opinions, particularly integrationism (as opposed to the separationism of Washington and Garvey), an emphasis on what Locke termed the "exceptional few" and Du Bois called "exceptional men" as representatives of the race before the world,[103] as well as the Hegelian belief that the world moves through stages of consciousness in which the core of humanity is altered by the external world. However, Du Bois remained, at least as a dramatic theorist, consistently Hegelian in his view that social conflict and the dialectical struggle lead to didactic drama, while Locke was more Kantian in that he lobbied for principles of cultural aesthetics and social harmony in dramatic literature. These subtle, albeit significant differences in their theories of drama also informed their positions on social justice and responsibility: whereas Du Bois viewed civil rights in terms of a dialectical struggle to attain social equality and mutual respect, Locke emphasized reciprocity, social harmony, and the reduction of conflicts, yielding cultural pluralism and a diminution of dogmatic certainty. Both shared a belief in the Hegelian dialectic as grounds for race relations and art; but for Locke, art hinged somewhat more fluidly on the Kantian idea of transcendent (hypothetical) idealism and creative individualism, rather than social conflict, on pluralism rather than struggle, and on the relativism of the one to the many—instead of a Du Boisian dyadic rivalry between races. Literary historian Dale E. Peterson makes the compelling case that, unlike Du Bois, Locke "was convinced that the aesthetic [itself] could be the political."[104] The depiction of aesthetic beauty might sufficiently convey the "truths" and ideals of each race, and through study races might achieve consensual understanding and mutual respect.

For Locke, race drama necessitated the recognition of "race type." This identity, however, must be seen through lifestyles and mutable cultural values; only then could African Americans be recognized onstage as participants in a "race drama" at a given historical juncture. What must be made discernible is what Locke called a "race type that expresses itself in terms of representative class or representative products." The product and not the person yielded one's race, ethnicity, and culture. This productivity entailed a "theory of social conservation" that "conserves the best in each group, and promotes the development of social solidarity out of heterogeneous elements."[105] Unless black drama portrays African Americans "for what we really are," Locke wrote in his notes, "it is not in any vital sense race drama."[106] But what African Americans really are depends on temporal, spatial, and contingent values.

Locke defined race drama, and by extension races themselves, in terms of "civilization-types." What defined civilization-types was "language, customs, habits, social adaptability, [and] social survival."[107] A civilization-type was based on having "the same manners and customs" as well as having the "same allegiance to the same social system" of a group during a specific historical period.[108] "Civilization-type" is a flexible term that accommodates a borderless albeit definable identity. Locke's claims to a specific black identity are based on shared values. Harlem, as Locke pointed out, was "not merely the largest Negro community in the world, but the first concentration in history of so many diverse elements of Negro life."[109] This diversity defined the contours and complexity of "Negro civilization."[110] A group's commonalities are historically specific and can be accounted for even in the case of changing cultural boundaries and pluralistic contributions. Race is civilization, and civilization, Locke observes, following

Herder, "isn't a smooth course"; instead, it "very often produces counter-currents," accommodating "these rough places, these antagonisms, these struggles, these actions and reactions," where cultures meet and come together.[111]

In the best of all worlds, Locke believed that the harmony of interracial relations would produce respective "culture-citizenships," where each group contribution was synthesized into a "joint civilization." Before such a synthesis could occur, each group would have to recognize its own and the others' aesthetic contributions. Drama for Locke was a civic responsibility creating what he termed "gateways" of cultural communication. Culture-citizenship, he said, is the "goal in which we can jointly accept whatever of value there is in the civilization's conception of itself."[112] He was a great believer in the power of "taking the initiative." Locke scholar William B. Harvey goes so far as to claim that the Harlem Renaissance "could properly be regarded as the realization of Locke's belief in the maxim that man's own initiative creates the culture of which he then becomes a major part."[113] Locke hoped the coming phase of dramatic development would lead audiences and writers to a kind of Kantian detachment of aesthetic judgments:

> Eventually the Negro dramatist must achieve mastery of a detached, artistic point of view, and reveal the inner stresses and dilemmas of these situations as from the psychological point of view he alone can. The race drama of the future will utilize satire for the necessary psychological distance and perspective, and rely upon irony as a natural corrective for the sentimentalism of propaganda.[114]

Locke would spend his intellectual life working through the paradoxical position of at once renouncing racism, while at the same time calling for an indigenous black aesthetic built on "cultural" characteristics. This is an argument that splits in two directions, and understanding Locke's aesthetic theories requires keeping both tracks of the argument in mind. Paradoxically, he wanted drama to be "racy" and "saturated with folk ways," yet he despised the pandering to the "decadent cult of the primitive" that many Harlem Renaissance authors succumbed to.[115] His defense of racial solidarity was sustained by a belief in the efficacy of cultural productivity. Race loyalty and folk life were to lead eventually to a distinct dramatic mode.

On one point, Johnson and Richardson affirmed what Locke rejected, that is, the use of drama for propagandistic purposes. Richardson made this clear when he wrote that a propaganda play "is a play written for the purpose of waging war against certain evils existing among the people," in order to promote social change and "to gain sympathy" among audiences who "have seldom, or never,

thought upon the subject."[116] Johnson's anti-lynching plays were meant for propaganda. However, theatre historian Margaret B. Wilkerson sees this inconsistency as part of the African American aesthetic, saying that the "two threads" of
propaganda and folk "joined in the plays of Georgia Douglas Johnson."[117] Locke
was, in fact, well served by Johnson and Richardson's desire to "identify" black
people as liberated from minstrelsy, to assert their cultural determinants, and to
ground their plays in aesthetic roots.

Locke tried to build a consensus for a deep spiritual life within the African
American community. In the face of racism outside the community, and even
selfishness within, Locke urged black artists to seek the higher ground. Johnson
and Richardson attempted, along with Locke, to forge a moral community and to
encourage a unifying frame of reference that would render the black experience
intelligible. Their short plays served as cultural "maps" of the African American
experience, reflecting the newly found roots of urban life and ethical values.
These "New Negro" characters had never been seen onstage before; they reflected intimately on "real," ordinary black people, which at the time was a
unique phenomenon. As Richardson stated, "my characters had dignity,"[118] a
dignity heretofore unseen in the theatre.

Johnson and Richardson exhibit Locke's emphasis on drama as demonstrating transitional values; as an agency that challenges familiar forms of perception; and as an initiative for reconstituting the world. Art and drama may be
imaginative experiences, but for Locke and his followers the materials of that
experience are as real as the concrete experiences themselves. Drama is not isolated from social and historical conditions, but rather represents the mutually
determining interrelatedness of the stage and the world. Johnson's three "anti-
lynching dramas," *A Sunday Morning in the South* (1925), *Safe* (ca. 1929), and
Blue-Eyed Black Boy (ca. 1930) as well as her two folk dramas, *Blue Blood* (1926)
and *Plumes* (1927), and Richardson's early plays of "Negro life," *The Chip
Woman's Fortune* (1923), *Mortgaged* (1924), and *Compromise, A Folk Play* (1925),
deal with Lockean themes of value, cultural productivity, race traits, and realism. By emphasizing folk roots, morality, and "Washingtonian aesthetics,"
Johnson and Richardson advanced Locke's goals. Their works copied Euro-
American classical realism in a formal sense, but they used this form to portray
the free self-expression of black life, warts and all. Kitchen settings, benign family bickering, friendships, superstitions, the dynamics of daily life, and ethical
judgments made in the immediacy of the moment are pervasive. The characters'
dialects are black and southern, but what is essential in the dialogue is "plain
folks talking." The talk is of things related to the black experience and is immediately recognized as such.

RICHARDSON AND THE POLITICS OF THE FOLK

*When I say Negro plays, I do not mean merely plays with Negro char-
acters. . . . [T]here is another kind of play; the play that shows the soul
of a people; and the soul of this people is truly worth showing.*

—Willis Richardson (1919)[119]

Richardson was inspired to begin his playwriting career after seeing a production
of Angela Weld Grimké's *Rachel* in 1916. Though he admired her drama, he felt he
could "write a better play."[120] From 1916 to 1918, he studied drama and poetry
through correspondence courses while working as a printer and engraver. In 1920
his first play, *Deacon's Awakening*, was published in *Crisis*, and received a modest
production in St. Paul, Minnesota, in 1921.[121] After a series of children's plays, he
made a breakthrough with his folk drama, *The Chip Woman's Fortune*, in 1922. First
produced by Raymond O'Neil, a white producer at Chicago's Ethiopian Art
Theatre, it then moved to Washington, and later to New York's Lafayette
Theatre. On 17 May 1923, the play opened at New York's Frazee Theatre, where
it became the first drama by an African American on Broadway. Alexander
Woollcott of the *New York Herald* called the production a "delightful one act,"
adding condescendingly that it was a "sketchy morsel of darky life which the company was able to present most engagingly."[122] John Corbin of the *New York Times*
was less enthusiastic, calling the play a "trifling and at times amusing piece."
However, he described the star, Evelyn Preer, as having "excellent comedy talent."[123] In Corbin's follow-up report for the Sunday *Times*, he praised the play as
an "unaffected and wholly convincing transcript" of everyday life in which "Willis
Richardson has limned half a dozen characters candidly, sympathetically,
truly."[124]

Richardson's plays countered negative stereotypes in literature and drama
by stressing drama's didactic and pedagogic power. In his essay, "The Negro
and the Stage," Richardson let it be known that drama should be considered
"as an educational institution side by side with the school," because the
"theatre has the ear of more reasoning people, more adults, than any other institution, not excepting the church."[125] He lamented that "most of the plays and
players [in black theatre] seemed to be put on the stage just to be laughed
at."[126] In his plays we observe black people facing ethical crossroads and making morally upright decisions. His folk plays of "Negro life" are concerned with
what theatre historian Leslie Catherine Sanders calls "the complex decisions
black people must make in painful circumstances," revealing "the integrity of

the black family."[127] Richardson's plays portray African Americans as being in possession of moral integrity.

Chip Woman's Fortune opens, as the stage directions indicate, in a "very plain dining room of a poor colored family."[128] The story revolves around Silas, a hard worker who has lost his job because he is overdue on his payments for his Victrola. Because of this, his boss lost faith in him and let him go. His wife, Liza, has taken in a friend named Mary (the Chip Woman). She offers Mary food and rent-free living; in return Mary, acting as a kind of nurse, assists the ailing Liza.[129]

Silas is fearful that his debt has cast a shadow of suspicion over him, making it difficult for him to find another job. He confronts his wife, complaining that having Mary around is just another mouth to feed. He threatens to evict Mary if she fails to contribute her fair share.

> Silas: Ah want you to understand Ah'm not actin' this way 'cause Ah mean to be hardhearted. Ah've just got to get out o' this trouble.
>
> Liza: (*discouraged*) Ah'm sorry everything turned out like this, cause I reckon Ah'll have to go back to bed if she goes.
>
> [. . .]
>
> Silas: If Ah can get her to do us this favor before the men come after that Victrola, everything'll be all right. (*There is a pause while they ponder over their situation*). And even if she will agree to help us, Ah'm tired o' this kind o' life. Ah'm sick o' livin' from hand to mouth.
>
> Liza: Ah reckon we ought to be thankful to be livin' any kind o' way with all the trouble we had. Some people get along better'n we do, but a whole lot o' others don't get along as good. Ah only got one consolation besides believin' in the Lord.
>
> Silas: What's that?
>
> Liza: That things ain't always been like this, and they might not always be like this.[130]

Silas needs to feel some control over his life. He is in danger of losing not only his livelihood and his Victrola, but also his self-esteem. Mary's presence poses a threat to him; he must choose his personal concerns and evict her, or stand behind her. Silas's situation can be read as a simple melodramatic device, but it may also be viewed as a circumstance that embodies Locke's value system. The contradiction between autonomy and social responsibility establishes the Lockean basis of self-expression and race loyalty. When individuals act autonomously they assert their individuality; but without a connection to society, the individual loses connections to culture and is severed from the community. The autonomous individual must therefore exhibit a consistency in judgment that coheres to social unity. Judgments must be spontaneous but cannot be made randomly, or without integrating considerations of ethical responsibility. As a result, moral judgments must be autonomous, yet never isolated. In this dynamic process each individual must reevaluate his or her relationship to the community. This takes place with each passing experience, and as a consequence, the entire culture undergoes a subsequent evolution. As Liza says, things "might not always be like this."

The Chip Woman proves to be the play's moral center. She has been saving her money for her son, Jim, who is shortly to be released from prison. When Jim arrives, he generously offers Silas the little money he has in return for the kindness of caring for his mother. When the Chip Woman gives Jim the money she has saved by selling wood chips, he turns it over to Silas, too. In the end, the Victrola is paid for and the Chip Woman is happily reunited with her son. Richardson's morality play, while somewhat saccharine, serves as a lesson in charity, cooperation, and the quiet dignity of ordinary people.

In *Mortgaged*, Richardson continues the theme of autonomy and group relationships. Produced for the Howard Players in 1924 by Locke and Gregory, the plot revolves around John Fields, a scientist on the verge of a research breakthrough, and his brother Thomas, a landlord and entrepreneur. Thomas's children are portrayed as spoiled and frivolous, while John's son, Herbert, is dutiful and studious. Herbert has been accepted to Harvard, but lacks the funds for tuition.[131] John approaches his brother for a loan, though he is already in debt to him. Thomas and his wife agree to help—provided John abandon his research and apply for well-paying jobs.

> Mrs. Fields: John, I think you could do more justice to yourself by giving up this research work and going into some first-class laboratory.
> John: (*starting as if struck*) Giving it up!
> Thomas Fields: That's what you ought to do.
> John: But I can't give it up! It means too much to me![132]

John finally agrees for the sake of his son, but calls it a "Shylock's bargain." His brother settles the issue, insisting that John "go West and get a place in some laboratory."[133] John replies:

> Yes, but first let me tell you something about yourself and your kind. You have your money and I have my science. Perhaps you think you're helping the race by piling up dollars, but you're not! It's not money that's going to make this race of ours respected, but what its men and women accomplish in science and

the arts—things that you and your kind know nothing about and care nothing about![134]

When Thomas defends his right to stockpile money as a way of gaining respect, John continues:

> In half of your wonderful country your dollars won't buy a first-class theater stalls, a first-class hotels accommodations, and never will until something is done to make the other fellow respect you! You can't buy his respect! You must earn it by accomplishing something![135]

In the clearest of terms, the above passages reflect Locke's notion of "cultural accomplishments" as one means, perhaps *the* means, by which a "race" is to be defined. John is spared having to make the decision when a letter arrives announcing that his research has produced startling results. He is given a big contract, and no longer needs his brother's money. He promises to repay his old debt with interest. A humiliated Thomas refuses, but John insists. In the end, John and his son leave, as the pretentious Thomas and his wife continue to watch their children play tennis.

Richardson's *Compromise* (1925) was selected by Locke to appear in *The New Negro*. It was a new kind of drama, illuminating the ethics and values of a new kind of African American. The play's protagonist, Jane Lee, is a poor widow whose son had "accidentally" been shot to death by a white neighbor the year before. The neighbor, Ben Carter, tried to "scare" some children from his orchard by shooting—he claims, "randomly"—but ended up killing Jane's son. The courts agreed that Ben had to pay Jane one hundred dollars for his "crime." Jane's husband used the money to drink himself to death from grief.

The play opens with the widow Jane and her three remaining children, Alec, Annie, and Ruth, trying to make ends meet. Ben Carter stops by for coffee and chitchat. While Ben enjoys the company of the Lees, he will never permit it to go beyond the superficial. Yet an intimate relationship is brewing between Ben's son and Jane's daughter, Annie. Alec, who harbors resentment against Ben for the killing of his brother, also discovers the details of the relationship (Annie is pregnant), and tries to exact revenge. Jane, anticipating all this, unloads the family shotgun. Alec takes the emptied gun, finds Ben's son, and breaks his arm with it. Alec returns home and describes his encounter with Ben's son. She urges him to hide. He leaves through the back window just as Ben arrives. He threatens to "put the sheriff on him." The play ends (an ending, as mentioned earlier, Locke wrote) with Jane reloading the gun, crying: "I oughtn't 'a' compermised. I oughtn't 'a' compermised."[136] Jane Lee pays dearly for compromising.

Locke was Richardson's mentor.[137] However, the relationship between Locke and Richardson was not always smooth. Locke's analysis of Richardson's *The Chip Woman's Fortune* leaves a lingering feeling of disappointment:

> Though the dialogue [of *Chip Woman's Fortune*] is a bit closer to Negro idiom of thought and speech [than Paul Green's plays and others by white authors], compensating somewhat for [Richardson's] greater amateurishness of technique and structure, there still [exists] the impression that the drama of Negro life has not yet become as racy, as gaily unconscious, as saturated with folk ways and the folk spirit as it could be, as it eventually will be.[138]

Some time after 1926, Locke and Richardson had a falling out, which proved devastating to Richardson. Locke, it seems, had produced Richardson's play, *Compromise*, without Richardson's permission. Richardson asked Locke for five dollars for compensation. At that point, says Richardson, Locke stopped speaking to him.[139] This episode and its result, says Christine R. Gray, "seems to have damaged Richardson" both "emotionally and creatively."[140] Few of his plays after this would receive comparable attention, and after 1930 Richardson's writing output slowed almost to a halt.

No doubt Richardson's plays often fell into the trap of melodramatic predictability. Moreover, he may have fallen victim to Locke's overbearing insistence on a particular type of "folk drama." Still, his work was an important contribution to African American theatre and his ideas would lay the groundwork for much that was to follow.

JOHNSON AND THE ETHICS OF THE FOLK

> *A minority is only safe and sound in terms of its social intelligence. . . . When you're up against the mass irrationality of racism, social sanity is the only antidote.*   —Alain Locke (1953)[141]

Georgia Douglas Johnson's first play, *A Sunday Morning in the South*, was written in 1925. Two versions of the play surfaced in the National Play Bureau of the Federal Theatre Project's Work Progress Administration, having been submitted somewhere between 1935 and 1939. Despite generally favorable project reviews, neither version was accepted for production or publication.[142] The first version is a one-act play in two scenes, while the second condenses all action into a single scene.[143]

In *A Sunday Morning,* Johnson begins by depicting the normalcy of black life. It opens in the kitchen, where the protagonist, Sue Jones, a grandmother of seventy, is preparing breakfast. She calls for her grandson to wake up and eat before the food grows cold. Church bells provide a backdrop. Tom, nineteen, enters and sits down to eat. He has slept late because he worked hard lifting boxes the night before. Tom had planned to go to church, but was overcome by fatigue. The opening establishes the ordinariness of the grandparent-grandchild relationship, church, and hard work. Soon Bossie, Tom's younger brother, enters and also begins to eat. Bossie declares that he will never do the backbreaking work of his brother, opting instead for the life of a preacher. Sue's friend Liza arrives, completing the cozy setting. Liza is on her way to church, just stopping by to share coffee and gossip. In the second version, the window is opened and both women listen as "Amazing Grace" is sung at the nearby church.[144] Liza relates the local news: "some po Nigger," says Liza, apparently "attacked" a white woman the night before last. Sue expresses her belief that the assailant should be punished. Liza agrees, but adds that law is the way to justice.

> Sue: (*drinking coffee*) I don't hold wid no rascality and I beleves in meeting out
>   punishment to the guilty but the fust ought to find out who done it and then
>   let the law handle'em. That's what I say.
> Liza: Me too. I thinks the law oughter hanel'em too, but you know a sight of
>   times they gits the wrong man goes and strings him up and don't fin out who
>   done it till its too late![145]

Although potential victims of injustice, Sue and Liza are nonetheless law-abiding. In Lockean terms, they believe in commonsense, rational "values." Johnson makes it clear through her characters that she is not opposed to justice that takes the form of punishment, as long as it is distributed fairly. Black criminals like anyone else need to be held accountable. No quarter is given to wrongdoers; but "laws," not lynch mobs, must dispense justice.

Conforming to the usual melodramatic style of the era, the police arrive. They are looking for the assailant; with them is the victim. She accuses Tom—he "fits" the racial profile—though it is made clear in the stage directions that the accuser is unsure of herself. Sue pleads desperately for her grandson, informing the police that he was home the night before. The police are dismissive. Tom, led away by the police, offers his grandmother reassurance. Liza pleads to Jesus. Sue also calls upon God all the while. Music continues from the church. A neighbor, Matilda, enters to report the coming of a lynch mob. In the end, Matilda exits briefly, only to return with the fateful news: Tom has been lynched. (In the first version, Sue goes to a nearby white church and begs to meet with Judge Manning, an allegedly sympathetic white man. But in the end, Manning fails to accomplish anything and two white men pass Sue by, joking about the lynching. One says: "Well we strung him up all right. But when he kept hollering, 'Granny, Granny,' it kinder made me sick in the belly".)

Johnson's realism negotiates the area between actual history and the stage. The frame that theatre provides brought to audiences a vision of the normalcy of black life and shows lynching's wrenching effect upon it. The onstage action is "ordinary" in contrast to the offstage violence. The play is streamlined for a purpose; as one reviewer from the Federal Theatre Project reported, the play makes its point "through simplicity and directness." Another wrote that the play "truthfully shows the futility of resisting the insane minds of a lynching mob with gentility," while another claimed that the two versions "are beautiful examples in simplicity in drama."[146]

For Johnson, theatre must realistically convey the Lockean "folk life" of black people. Focusing on the details of family relations, church, and community, juxtaposed with the brutal effect of a lynching, was an attempt to elicit an empathetic audience response. The play suggests that ordinary African Americans, left undisturbed, function socially in a rational and decent way, demonstrating their traditions of honesty and folk ways. Folk life is represented through the elemental roots (Locke's "cultural traits") of church, family, and ethical behavior. In this way, Johnson created what Locke referred to as drama that "must grow in its own soil and cultivate its own intrinsic elements." Only then, he maintained, "can it become truly organic."[147] From this would spring a sense of shared values.

Religion plays a dynamic part in Johnson's plays. The women in the play talk directly to God and plead to him as if he were present in the world. This relationship to God through dialogue and church music highlights African American Christianity. In African American culture, emotional vitality and verbal expression are often part of religious experience. In his 1929 essay, "The Negro Contribution to America," Locke maintained that African Americans borrowed Christianity from whites, but gave back to the religion "unique spiritual gifts—one emotional, and the other artistic." This unique contribution helped African Americans to bring "more spiritual and mystical values" to Christianity.[148] This is evident in the play, where the relationship to God is passionate, vocal, and spiritual.

Johnson makes the case that her characters—and by extension African American people—are "good." The characters may be ordinary, unexceptional, and sometimes frivolous, but they are, at the core, religious people who understand the value of right and wrong. These values are directly related to Lockean themes. Drawing on the Western philosophical tradition, Locke states:

> When Plato conceived the Good as the culmination of the Ideal world and as the principle which was to unify, systematize, and organize all other "forms," he was really putting "value" above "being," conceiving it as the supreme principle of explanation. . . . For he was proposing to view all being teleologically, and to make its relation to a "good" or end (an ethical notion) essential to its being.[149]

In *Sunday Morning,* Tom plans to "make good," helping people by furthering his education and studying law. Tom's being, as Locke would have it, is not a matter of biology, but something to be discovered in his teleological goals — hard work, education, and altruism — even in the face of violent racism.

> Tom: I been thinking a whole lot about these things and I mean to go to night school and git a little book learning so as I can do something to help — help change the laws . . . make em strong . . . I sometimes get right upset and wonder whut would I do if they ever tried to put something on me.[150]

Despite its good intentions, the play is stilted. The police arrive shortly after this speech. When characters assure Tom that the police will never harm him, Johnson telegraphs the fact that he will be lynched (one can almost hear an "uh-oh" in the background). However, Johnson captures succinctly the delineation of moral conundrums and her nuanced dialogue possesses a plebeian lyricism. More important is the point having to do with values and their centrality in Locke's principles of folk drama.

Johnson's other two anti-lynching plays of the 1920s, *Blue Eyed Black Boy* and *Safe,* and her two plays of black life, *Blue Blood* and *Plumes,* also showcase folk life and its values.[151] Like *Sunday Morning in the South, Blue Eyed Black Boy* and *Safe* are admonitory works, pleading seriously for a national acknowledgement of the destructive consequences of lynching. In *Safe,* the play opens in the kitchen where a husband, wife, and wife's mother live harmoniously. The wife, Liza, is about to give birth when she hears of a lynching. The young victim is a member of her church and the sole supporter of his widowed mother. At the play's climax, Liza gives birth, but strangles the child because she fears that he, too, will receive the same fate. Church and justice are once again thematically central.

A kitchen setting also begins the drama in *Blue Eyed Black Boy.* Pauline Waters is about to see her daughter, Rebecca, marry a doctor. A neighbor, Hester

Grant, soon arrives with the bad news: her son, Jack, has been arrested for allegedly "brushing against a white woman" on the street. A lynch mob gathers.
But Pauline turns up a certain ring and urges a family friend, Dr. Grey, to rush
to the governor's home and show it to him. Pauline and Hester pray to Jesus
while Dr. Grey rushes to the governor's mansion. The play ends with the arrival of state troopers to quell the mob. It seems the relationship between
Pauline and the Governor was an intimate union, one producing the "blue-
eyed black boy." Johnson once again conveys the senselessness of lynching.
Despite the contrivances, her three anti-lynching dramas reveal the crime's
devastating effects. In the words of Judith L. Stephens, Johnson's plays are
"an important part of a radical pride movement," whereby "artistic expression,
self-definition, social protest, and self-defense were united as fundamental
principles."[152] The plays attempt to provoke outrage against the randomness
and hectic violence of mob rule.

In 1927, Johnson wrote *Plumes,* which tells the story of a poor mother
who must decide whether to allow her ailing daughter to be operated on or to
use the money for the daughter's elaborate funeral. This play, too, opens in the
kitchen of a two-room cottage. The mother, Charity Brown, is concocting a
"medication" for her daughter, Emmerline, aged 14. Charity's friend, Tildy, assists her. Both share a belief in the medicinal value of roots and herbs. Dr.
Scott arrives and informs Charity that her daughter's only chance of survival
is an expensive operation, and even then success is not guaranteed. Charity
hesitates and in the end her hesitation costs her daughter her life. The conversation between Tildy and Charity and their superstition forms the core of the
play. Charity makes her decision based on the reading of "coffee grinds."
Tildy, experienced in reading the meaning of the grinds, concludes that the
operation will be pointless and the doctor, though insistent, confirms that
there are no assurances.

The play was produced twice in 1928: at the Harlem Experimental Theatre
and the Cube Theatre in Chicago. Johnson, it would appear, wrote this play for
an African American audience: using dialect, kitchen settings, folk superstitions, and ritual beliefs, Johnson created what linguist and literary historian
Jurij Striedter calls "polyfuctional polystructures," which provide an intended
effect if the reader, as an active "receptor," perceives the work "as a meaningful
whole."[153] For Johnson, the reader/audience can view her plays, apply the audience's system of values, and evaluate it in terms of existing realities. For the
reader or spectator, this evaluation will coincide with the author's values, creat-

ing a meaningful whole within a recognizable milieu. Johnson knew the black audiences of her time would grasp the play's meaning.

In *Plumes*, Johnson worked toward developing African American traditions rooted in what Locke would call the "native soil." Its realism is in the details of black life, but its message goes beyond mere facts. The characters are forging a "native tradition," even if these traditions rely on superstition and fantasy. Locke's point about race is worth repeating: race, he says, "operates as tradition, as preferred traits and values." Race-traits, then, "lie in that peculiar selective preference for certain cultural-traits and resistance to certain others which is characteristic of all types and levels of social organization."[154] The "race-traits" and folk traditions in *Plumes* would be recognizable to a black audience. Yet the play would also provide mainstream white audiences a glimpse into the world of working-class black culture.

As in her other plays, the sound of church bells hovers in the background of *Plumes*. Charity must decide whether to spend what little money she has on an operation or save it for her daughter's funeral. Her friend, Tildy, tries to comfort her, but Charity will not be consoled.

> Charity: I can't help it! Then little Bessie. We all jest scrooged in one hack and took her little coffin in our lap all the way out to the graveyard (*Breaks out crying*).
> Tildy: Do hush, Sister Charity. You done the best you could. Poor folks got to make the best of it. The Lord understands —
> Charity: I know that — but I made up my mind the time Bessie went that the next one of us what died would have a shore nuff funeral, everything grand, — with plumes! — I saved and saved and now — this yah doctor —.[155]

The doctor arrives and tries to dissuade Charity from trusting the wisdom of "coffee grinds";

> Dr. Scott: Why, my good woman, don't you believe in such senseless things! That cup of grounds can't show you anything. Wash them out and forget it.
> Charity: I can't forget it. I feel like it ain't no use; I'd just be spendin' my money that I needs — for nothing — nothing.[156]

The play ends with the death of Charity's daughter and preparations for a funeral complete with "plumes." Charity, as the name implies, "gives" in proportion to her quest for spiritual beauty. Here Johnson portrays ordinary people with religious values that are rooted in enduring traditions.

Johnson's plays went a long way in creating the basis for a modern African American drama. However, by 1930, she had begun to turn from drama, particularly drama associated with common folk. She wrote that drama "in the past has portrayed the Negro farthest down." Now she called for "plays of a different nature," conveying stories "that tell of the hopes, dreams, yearnings, [and] heartbreaks" of "our great middle class."[157] Despite these claims, her significance to the development of African American drama should not be underestimated.

CONCLUSION: DRAMATIC BEGINNINGS

> *We believe that no education is complete without art, and no art [is] truly educational without a practical experience with it in its creative aspects. The acting and writing [of] plays, therefore, becomes for us the natural and inevitable sequence, in a college community, of the new formal study of the drama.* —Alain Locke (ca. 1925)[158]

Johnson and Richardson's plays were documents of ethical and cultural evaluation. More than playwrights, they were theologians. For them, drama was a vehicle for social reform as well as morality, what Locke would describe as race "values." Delineating their characters in terms of humility, restraint, and civic virtue was a thought-out strategy of response to adversity and antagonistic misrepresentations. Richardson and Johnson attempted to create "community theatre" and to live up to Locke's expectations. The goal was to expose ordinary black life, to share the common intimacies experienced by black people, and to underscore the basic decency of black folk.

Yet, according to Locke, they never fully realized his intentions. Locke wanted "free self-expression," but only so long as it fit into his concept of "Negro art." Folk drama meant the celebration of African American traditions, provided it was a part of what Charles Scruggs aptly calls "the American tossed salad" of Locke's mixed messages and contradictory demands.[159] Locke's notes reveal the belief that African American drama was merely in its early stages:

> Somewhat under the inspiration of the Irish and Yiddish theatres, but also in part under a momentum of its own, our drama is reaching out toward two new channels of expression—the realistic folk-play, of which we have instances in the work of Richardson, and the poetic folk-play, of which we have as yet just the merest beginnings.[160]

Figure 1   Jim Jeffries and Jack Johnson (*Ebony Magazine* 17.3, January 1963, p. 67).

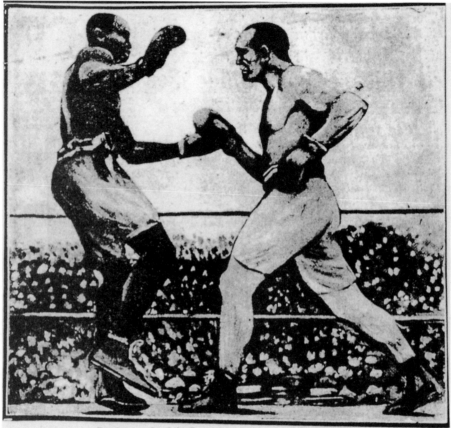

Opening rounds of the Reno fight. Jeffries forcing the negro a little.

Figure 2   "Opening rounds of the Reno fight" (*L.A. Times*, 6 July 1910, p. 7).

"Please, Mr. Jeffries, Are You Going to Fight Mr. Johnson?"

Figure 3   "Please, Mr. Jeffries, Are You Going to Fight Mr. Johnson?" (*Chicago Tribune*, 4 April 1909, sec. 3, p. 4).

Figure 4 Cartoon depiction of Jeffries–Johnson fight (*New York Times*, 3 July 1910, p. 14).

Figure 5 "The Fourth of July 1910–1776" (*Chicago Defender*, 2 July 1910, p. 1).

THE FOURTH OF JULY, 1910—1776.
(Republished by Request.)

Think, in 1776 the Colored Man Fought the British to Give the American His Freedom and To-Day
(1910), Which Should Be a Nation's Fight, the Colored Man Is Forced to Fight Jim Crow Delegations, Race
Prejudice and American Public Insane Sentiment—If He Wins in the Face of All This, He Is Truly Entitled
to a Carnegie Hero Medal.

Even Eighth Avenue Has Its Salome.

Willia. is and Walker, the Colored Comedians, Have Introduced THE Dance Into "Bandanna Land." Ada Overton Walker Does It, and the Critics Say That She Dances Better than Some of the Salomes That Wear Fewer Clothes.

Figure 6 "Even Eighth Avenue Has Its Salome" (*New York World*, 30 August 1908, Metropolitan section, p. 2.)

AIDA WALKER, WHO
WILL INTERPRET A
DANCE OF SALOME

left Figure 7 "Aida Walker, Who Will Interpret a Dance of Salome" (*Boston Herald*, September 1908, clipping file). Reprinted with permission of the Photographs and Prints Division, Schomburg Center for Research in Black Culture, The New York Public Library, Astor, Lenox, and Tilden Foundations.

right Figure 8 Drawing of Walker (*New York Age*, 8 August 1912, p. 6).

Figure 9 *The Star of Ethiopia*, unidentified performer (Special Collections and Archives, W. E. B. Du Bois Library, University of Massachusetts Amherst).

Figure 10   Parade through Harlem, 1920. Reprinted with permission of the Photographs and Prints Division, Schomburg Center for Research in Black Culture, The New York Public Library, Astor, Lenox, and Tilden Foundations.

Figure 11　Marcus Garvey. Reprinted with permission from the New York Daily News, 1 August 1922.

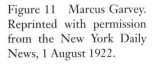

Figure 12　Black Star Line share.

left Figure 13 Charles Gilpin. Reprinted with permission of the Photographs and Prints Division, Billy Rose Theatre Collection, The New York Public Library, Astor, Lenox, and Tilden Foundations.

above Figure 14 Miller and Lyles in boxing gloves, ca. 1920s.

above   Figure 15   "And They Called It Dixieland" songbook cover.

right   Figure 16   Bert Williams in chicken costume. Photo: Hall, N.Y. Reprinted with permission of the Museum of the City of New York, The Theater Collection.

Mall N.Y.

121

JOSÉPHINE BAKER

above Figure 17 Josephine Baker, n.d. Reprinted with permission of the Photographs and Prints Division, Schomburg Center for Research in Black Culture, The New York Public Library, Astor, Lenox, and Tilden Foundations.

right Figure 18 Florence Mills in "Dixie to Broadway," 1924. Reprinted with permission of Joanna T. Steichen.

Figure 19 Portrait of Florence Mills, ca. 1920s. Reprinted with permission of the Photographs and Prints Division, Schomburg Center for Research in Black Culture, The New York Public Library, Astor, Lenox, and Tilden Foundations.

1918–1927

To "get along" and to obtain what he wanted from white people, he acquired the necessary demeanor and verbal skills. He learned "to humble down and play shut-mouthed."
                                        —Leon F. Litwack (2000)[1]

The rise of the "New Negro" from 1918 to 1927 was a response to prevailing racial stereotypes that existed throughout the nineteenth and even into the early twentieth century. The New Negro was, in short, the flip side of the racial coin, the "'New Negro' and his doppelgänger," in Henry Louis Gates's words. The "black Sambo" and the "New Negro," Gates explains, established an "antithetical relationship as surrogates in a simmering but undeclared race war." With "Sambo art" assisting white racists in expressing the negated black identity, the New Negro Renaissance sought to create an individual who was "a truly reconstructed presence in the face of white hostility."[2] Performers and playwrights facilitated the transformation of the image of African Americans from minstrelsy to a new, modern representation.

Minstrelsy, aside from being pernicious, was persistent, and had to be challenged. As James Weldon Johnson pointed out as late as 1930, minstrelsy was "a caricature of Negro life" that had "not yet been entirely broken." It reified the tradition of the African American as merely an "irresponsible, happy-go-lucky, wide-grinning, loud-laughing, shuffling, banjo-playing, singing, dancing sort of being."[3] The minstrel image that had dominated the stage became embedded in the American consciousness. In response to this minstrel image, the Harlem Renaissance experienced a concerted effort to end the stereotype. This assault did not always succeed; at times, images clashed within the same play, performance, or public event. Nellie McKay underscores the difficulty facing black actors on and off stage, noting that "in the white American mind," minstrelsy and its implications of "lazy, comic, pathetic, childlike, idiotic, etc.," codified "an image that was disastrous to the advancement of serious black theater, and one not easily reversed."[4] Performers unfortunately inherited a minstrel vocabulary and discourse that was thoroughly saturated with various forms of racial reductionism. Reversing pejorative depictions required a substitution of images through a unified approach. As one *New York Age* editorial reported in 1923, the "need for a real constructive program in building up racial solidarity is therefore insisted upon as a vital necessity."[5] Seeking security in collective identification, African American artists at the time sought control over cultural representations by establishing this "New Negro" ontology.

CHAPTER EIGHT

"IN THE WHIRLWIND AND THE STORM": MARCUS GARVEY AND THE PERFORMANCE OF BLACK NATIONALISM

It is but right that the Negro should strike out independently so as to insure his economic future. . . . There is a world to be conquered for the Negro. . . . The Negro must become a builder. He must become the architect of his own fate and, realizing that, the New Negro needs to be serious in his endeavors.

—Marcus Garvey (1919)[1]

INTRODUCTION: GARVEY AND THE WORKING CLASS

Yes, the black man is supposed to be a good nigger; once this has been laid down, the rest follows itself. —Frantz Fanon (1967)[2]

Marcus Garvey (1887–1940) and his Universal Negro Improvement Association (UNIA) surfaced as a major demonstration of Black Nationalism. By 1920, Garvey's large organization—according to reports by the organization, he had four to six million followers—sought a pan-Afro/Caribbeanism that was based on the triangular trade routes of Africa, the Caribbean, and the United States.[3] Garvey's movement was the first mass political movement of African Americans and played a significant role in the development of the Harlem Renaissance in general, and the emergence of Black Nationalism in particular. As a demonstration of the organization's success, Garvey staged a parade on the first of August 1920, beginning at

UNIA headquarters in Harlem, marching down Fifth Avenue, and concluding in a mass demonstration at New York's Madison Square Garden. The meeting at the Garden, which ran through the entire month of August, illuminated the strength and influence of Garvey and his group.

Garvey's movement, the parade, and the 1920 convention were important for several reasons. The movement was the largest organization to date to reach a large segment of the black working class. The parade was not only a demonstration of Garvey's success; it was in fact one of the main reasons for his popularity. As a performance, the parade captured the imagination of his followers, enlisting them to the group's cause. To understand the implications of the parade's impact for the black working class, I will examine the parade in light of Garvey's goals. As a significant figure during the Harlem Renaissance, Garvey used the theatricality of the parade to promote his agenda. By focusing attention on the parade, its theatricality, and the motives underlying it, we can observe the relationship between the black working class and Garvey's movement, the function of parades as a means to collectivize disenfranchised workers, and the way African Americans related to urban life at that time.

Garvey's rise has to be understood as resulting from a confluence of factors: the Great Migration of blacks from the South and the West Indies; unemployment among the black working class; and the fact that many ordinary black citizens were in despair. To be sure, many blacks and whites celebrated Harlem during the New Negro Renaissance, but for many others the hopes Harlem offered to black migrants would soon be dampened by unemployment, overcrowded tenements, tuberculosis, and job discrimination. Historian John Henrik Clarke puts the movement in perspective, saying that Garvey arrived on the scene during the years after the First World War, "when the promise to Black Americans had been broken, lynching [was] rampant, and when Blacks were still recovering from 'the red summer of 1919' in which there were race riots in most of the major cities and the white unemployed took out their grievances on the Blacks."[4] The outrage of lynching was compounded by the fact that many of those lynched were black soldiers. August Meier and Elliot Rudwick assert that Garvey's movement "provided a compensatory escape for Negroes to whom the urban promised land had turned out to be a hopeless ghetto."[5] African Americans arriving on the urban scene not only encountered racist practices, but also experienced an additional unease borne of disenfranchisement and displacement. A *Negro World* editorial in 1922 reported that with "inflated wages and prices" and "the tens of thousands of men who had flocked to the large cities consequently thrown out" of work because of the thousands of white soldiers returning to their previous jobs, "it is only natural that thousands of black workers would face unemployment."[6] Frustrated by unemployment and disappointed that urban life could fulfill few promises, many African American workers looked to Garvey for leadership.

Garvey's emergence took place not only in the midst of Jim Crow conditions, but also during a period of heightened class conflicts within the black community itself.[7] The rift that frequently divided the working class and the bourgeoisie was based not merely on economics, but also on skin tones. Many middle-class urbanites looked despairingly on the rural, migrant poor; and many light-skinned African Americans considered darker blacks, especially those arriving from Jamaica, the West Indies, and the South, to be inferior.[8] The tension between African Americans already living in northern cities and those immigrating north created considerable friction.[9]

Garvey's arrival on the scene quickly catapulted him into the role of a leader of the immigrant and working class. His political awareness was shaped by his experience as a printing shop foreman and leader of a printer's strike in 1909 in Jamaica, as well as by his experiences as a member of the editorial staff of the *African Times* and *Oriental Review* in London from 1912 to 1914 under the tutelage of radical Egyptian nationalist and editor Duse Mohammed Ali.[10] In addition, his dark complexion, his advocacy of racial "purity," and his fiery rhetoric helped convince many that blackness *per se* was a sign of superiority, not inferiority, and his plan to change the economic conditions of the poor appealed directly to those removed from America's prosperity. Political historian John McCartney describes the background from which Garvey emerged; Garvey, he says, "became aware of the severe economic exploitation of the Jamaican masses by the white oligarchy and of the debilitating color prejudice that prevailed among the non-whites of Jamaica." Along the way, Garvey discovered the hierarchical rigidity of class and skin distinctions: "the ruling minority was usually white, the middle class was most often brown, and the masses on the bottom were mostly black."[11] Garvey sought to reverse this arrangement of complexion and class by inverting its symbolic meaning. In so doing, his fervent rhetoric on behalf of Black Nationalism would attract a large following. Garvey's contemporary, E. Franklin Frazier, realized that what distinguished the Garvey movement was its "appeal to the masses," because working-class African Americans were "repressed and shut out from all serious participation in American life."[12] Garvey offered the hope of ameliorating intolerable conditions. His parades and organization satisfied a widespread need among African Americans, in particular the poorest among them, by providing them with what Pan-African historian Imanuel Geiss terms "psychological compensation for the tremendous inferiority complex from which they suffered."[13]

For many African Americans, the early 1920s represented a period of patriotism and cultural renaissance. The former was owed largely to the victory in Europe, and the latter arose from a newly acquired interest in black art, literature, and performance. However, to many ordinary black citizens, these developments were aimed at educated whites and the black middle class. For the working class, with little disposable income, the rising interests in entertainment and literature were cultural events unavailable to them. Such were the impressions of Garveyite Hubert H. Harrison, who announced in the *Negro World* that members of the black working class have swallowed the "cup of gall and wormwood to the bitter dregs." For Harrison, black laborers had built the nation, but were being denied its benefits; black people had been "jim-crowed, disenfranchised and lynched without redress from law or public sentiment."[14] The UNIA was not the only black organization in existence that sought black unity and self-sufficiency; the National Association for the Advancement of Colored People (NAACP) and the Urban League in the 1910s exerted a significant influence. Yet despite their importance, many African Americans, especially southern migrants, West Indian immigrants, and ex-servicemen, felt that the NAACP and the Urban League served the needs of the middle and upper classes exclusively. E. Franklin Frazier observed that the NAACP, which had fought uncompromisingly for African Americans, "had never secured, except locally and occasionally, the support of the masses." Its failure to secure support, he claimed, was owing to the fact that the middle-class organizations "lacked the dramatic element."[15]

Garvey's dramatic impact, especially manifested in his parade down Fifth Avenue and his visceral rhetoric, was the galvanizing element that captured the imagination of the black working class. Through pomp and ceremony, a resonant voice, superlative stage presence, and physical self-confidence, Garvey displayed a sense of pride and fashion to black people who had felt removed from the growing economic and cultural advances of Americans in general. The NAACP, in contrast, appeared stale, tepid, and disinterested in the proletariat. In 1921, one Garveyite reported in the *Negro World* that the NAACP "appeals to the Beau Brummel, Lord Chesterfield, kid-gloved, silk-stocking, creased-trousered, patent leather shoe element, while the UNIA appeals to the sober, sane, serious, earnest, hard-working man, who earns his living by the sweat of his brow." In contrasting two figureheads of their respective movements, the reporter said that the NAACP leader W. E. B. Du Bois "appeals to the 'talented tenth' while Garvey appeals to the 'Hoi Polloi.'"[16] Garvey filled a void in the minds of the black working class and his parade became the focal point by which this appeal could be demonstrated.

To a restless and disillusioned working class, Garvey promised a better life. His activities in the United States from 1916 to the time of his deportation in 1927 coincided with the rise of Black Nationalism and the New Negro movement. Garvey's significance, wrote Truman Hughes Talley in 1920, "lies in the fact that he embodies and directs a new spirit among Negroes."[17] However, this new spirit was different for the working class than it was for the elite. For many working-class blacks, the New Negro Renaissance was less a cultural and literary movement; instead, it was linked to economic conditions and to the music of ragtime, jazz, and the blues. Although Charles Johnson was correct to assert that a "new type of Negro is evolving—a city Negro," transplanted "from one culture [rural] to another [urban],"[18] class distinctions defined this new experience in relatively different terms. Cultural historian Paul Gilroy points out that for the poor and working class Garvey's emphasis on self-determination "would supply an angry voice and a timely militaristic style to the unprecedented political and cultural forces formed in this urban confluence of peoples and interests."[19] The mid- to late-1910s saw the urban black working class essentially leaderless. The black proletariat in general, critic Robert H. Brisbane has pointed out, appeared as "sometimes with a purpose and sometimes without a purpose." The desire to assert a black presence in the United States, Brisbane observes, was "often spontaneous and nearly always uncoordinated. In short, Black Nationalism was producing a cacophony. What was needed was a leader who could obtain harmony."[20]

Garvey would prove to be the right match for the working class. His nationalism was based on black pride, economic success, and an aggressive black business enterprise. His focus was global, not just local; he lifted and inspired people seeking a worldwide, race-based solidarity.[21] While some facets of Garvey's nationalistic policies were vague and abstract, other aspects were visceral and immediate. Garvey, in other words, was not always precise, with his rhetoric holding more promise than his delivery; but his promises arose from a deeply felt passion and an urgent desire for change. His ability to move a crowd was well known, and he used his oratorical skills to maximize his popularity and shore up UNIA membership. Garvey's oratory—literally his theatrical and deeply resonating voice, as well as commanding stage presence—was significant in promoting his popularity. Although critical of his anti-Marxist, anti-trade unionist position, C. L. R. James nevertheless recognized that Garvey "was one of the great orators of his time." For James, Garvey was a poorly educated demagogue, but he was also "a master of rhetoric and invective, capable of great emotional appeals and dramatic intensity."[22] Garvey's brand of nationalism took the form of a search for identity and pride in a society that viewed blacks and their achievements as essentially nonexistent and irrelevant. His success lay in his ability to tap into the frustration and disenchantment of ordinary black people who had been attracted to him because, unlike the black establishment at the time, Garvey was not under the thumb of whites. Rather, his outlook coincided with the masses. He was a dark-skinned, political activist immigrant and a down-to-earth leader who spoke bluntly yet with theatrical flare.[23] His parade would prove to be the right vehicle for his brand of nationalism.

PARADE

[Garvey's] pageantry drew thousands of onlookers and constituted a bold symbolic demonstration that African people had to stand up and stake their own claim for dignity and self-determination.

—Rupert Lewis (1988)[24]

Garvey's 1920 UNIA parade and convention was nothing short of a theatrical triumph. The parade leading up to the convention transpired on 1 August 1920, "in which over 5,000 members and delegates participated."[25] It began in UNIA Headquarters at Liberty Hall, where Garvey declared that the march would make "a complete circuit of the Harlem district."[26] August 1 was a symbolic date, chosen in recognition of the end of slavery in the British Empire in 1833, and it would remain the symbolic date for subsequent UNIA annual parades. Amy Jacques Garvey reported that legions of the UNIA moved in strict formation, as did "members of the Black Cross Nurses, with the insignia of the black cross on their caps." What drew particular attention "were the placards and banners carried by the marchers with the inscriptions, 'Africa for the Africans,' 'The Negro Wants Liberty,' [and] 'Negroes Helped Win the War.'"[27] At Madison Square Garden, delegates and UNIA members convened to hear speeches and draw up proposals. Amy Garvey described the parade as "miles long," garnering "the admiration of the crowds, who lined the route." She adds that the "onlookers could not help but catch the spirit of the occasion; they clapped, waved flags and cheered."[28] Tens of thousands of African Americans watched as units of the African Legion and the Black Cross Nurses waved the UNIA's flag—black for Negro skin, green for Negro hopes, and red for Negro blood—and sang the UNIA anthem, "Ethiopia, Thou Land of Our Fathers."[29]

During the parade, Garveyites and ordinary citizens would take to the streets of Harlem. James Weldon Johnson called Harlem a "parade ground," in which parades were almost a constant presence (see figure 10).[30] But, as E. David Cronin asserted, even Harlem, familiar with spectacular parades, found Garvey's parade "an extravaganza not soon to be forgotten." Harlem streets, Cronin noted, "rang with stirring martial airs," with the "splendor and pageantry of a medieval coronation," exhilarating the crowds.[31] Elton Fax observed that the parade was "a rousing New York spectacular" that "got right into the guts of Harlem."[32] Roi Ottley was even more descriptive, telling how Garvey "led the demonstration bedecked in a dazzling uniform of purple, green and black, with gold braid, and a thrilling hat with white plumes." Ottley observed that Garvey, standing in the rear of his "big high-mounted black Packard," would acknowledge "the ovations of the crowds that lined the side walks."[33] Garvey stood in his car and saluted the cheering crowds (see figure 11).

There were several elements that bolstered Garvey's popularity, but two were of particular significance: the marching parade and his theatrical oratory. According to social historian Mary Ryan, the success of marching parades during the late nineteenth and early twentieth centuries issued from three factors of cultural expression: parades provided "a well-rounded documentation of past culture"; in parades "an organized body, usually of men, marched into the public streets to spell out a common social identity"; and parades offered "a very high level of generality."[34] Garvey was aware that parades, festivals, and spectacles encapsulated a culture and displayed it publicly. In 1920, the parade had become for Garvey the locus of physicality as well. Marching, gesturing, and spectacle established reflexes and habits that were reinforced and consolidated in the repetition and uniformity.

Garvey's parade provided a site for those who lacked identification with common social identity and national pride. The UNIA parade became a place and time where African Americans made public their racial identity and group solidarity. It also served as a focal point for a generalized black consciousness, in which ideological formations could capture the imagination of individuals without outlining specifics that might otherwise attract some while alienating others. Garvey could generalize about politics, avoiding the details of his agenda while at the same time stimulating optimistic expectations. Garvey used pageantry and marching processions to reinforce his ideas, but during the march his ideas could remain generalized. What mattered most was the parade: its uniformity, music, marching steps, and costumes. The visceral experience would supersede substance. The ceremony and enthusiastic display of black solidarity bolstered African Americans who felt alienated from the mainstream, yet it offered little in the way of specifics.

Still, the parade was clearly not without purpose. The ideas underlying the parade stemmed from black folk populism and its confrontational position toward white racism. Garvey combined nineteenth-century idealism and populism with twentieth-century nationalism in forming a community of African Americans isolated from mainstream society yet longing for group identification. Black populism would influence the collectivity of black consciousness through the theatricality and ritual of his parade. Garvey's movement, as economist Robert

Allen points out, had "a certain theatrical quality and flamboyance" that made it "appealing to the black masses." Theatricality, such as colorful uniforms and marching songs, were "distinctive traits of the UNIA."[35] Its inclusive celebration combined music, movement, drama, and an enormous cast into a unified and compelling aesthetic experience. The emphasis on visual symbolism attracted attention and meant that everyone could watch as well as participate.

The stirring uniformity, marching beat, and spectacle created a theatrical scene that was antithetical to the drab and ordinary existence of overcrowded and mechanized urban life. The costumes and uniformity resulted in a blurring of identity; a boundary loss that assisted individuals, feeling isolated, into group initiation. Among participants in parades, individuality would be replaced by the feelings, created by rhythmic marching, that the marchers participated in a collective way of looking at the world. This blurring of self-consciousness and heightening of mutual feeling was available to all who joined in the ceremony. The parade incorporated the significant meaning of solidarity and group affiliation. Like Du Bois's *The Star of Ethiopia*, the parade's ultimate goal was Black Nationalism. Although Garvey's nationalism was more extreme in its emphasis on separatism than that of Du Bois, they shared an understanding of the importance of public display as a means of galvanizing the masses toward collective consciousness and nationalistic pride. Nationalism is best understood as a collective consciousness that underscores the uniqueness of a group of people, emphasizing shared attitudes, memories, and a feeling of belonging to a common mission. Garvey used the parade to inspire self-respect, share cultural missions, and inculcate historical memories. This was of particular importance to a group of disparate and fragmented peoples, new to the urban scene, and living amidst hostility and isolation.

Many in Harlem at the time were migrants from the South whose familial ties had been severely and abruptly severed. Approximately 25 percent of Harlemites over the age of 15 were either foreign born or recently arrived from the South.[36] Not only did moving from rural to urban life mean loosening one's link to home, family, and relationships, but urban life also demanded new ways of coping as well. Despite the promises of abundant employment and excitement, the urban environment left many disappointed; jobs were scarce, housing was cramped, disease was commonplace, and racism surfaced everywhere. The reality clashed with the dream of a better life, leaving many not only unemployed, but also extremely disillusioned. Given the alienation of the black working class, Garvey offered an immediate alternative. His pageantry succeeded in bringing together a collective display of black pride, with a prospective future linked to black social and political initiatives. A. F. Elmes aptly observed in 1925 that in the parade all "the gorgeous periphery in dress, court, display, fantastic titles were very relevant to [Garvey's] aim—the capture of the heart (if not the head) and the imagination of his people, and it worked."[37] The emotions felt while experiencing the marching rhythms and steps of the parade were summed up by historian William H. Mc-Neill, who claims in his book, *Keeping Together in Time*, that marching is "something visceral," something "far older than language and critically important in human history, because the emotion it arouses constitutes an infinitely expandable basis for social cohesion among any and every group that keeps together in time."[38] For many living in Harlem, the parade was a moment that transcended the daily grind; it was a departure from the monotony, from the routine of labor and searching for labor, and from the realization of dreams deferred.

The parade ended at Madison Square Garden, where Garvey's rhetoric did not disappoint. His self-confident, forceful voice and fully bedecked costume appealed to the black working class, who were suffering from self-effacement and despair. He was, by all standards of fashion at the time, unattractive. Short, stocky, and dark, Garvey presented a figure frequently ridiculed in the press, advertisements, and rhetoric of the age. During a time when beauty meant lean, tall, and white, Garvey's appearance flew in the face of such pretensions. He was unaffected by the media's idea of beauty, creating instead his own self-image and projecting it proudly. He appeared devoid of self-doubt; his voice echoed with self-confidence; and his gait and stride presented an aura of self-worth. Poised in a finely tailored uniform, wearing a huge, feathered hat, and speaking without hesitation, Garvey symbolized the dreams of many in the audience. He defied the trends of beauty and attacked racism unapologetically. He was adamantly opposed to gradual advancements for African Americans and the poor; instead, he demanded immediate results. His speeches went directly to the point: economic improvement of the black working class everywhere. He would accept nothing less than a complete overhaul of current conditions. His extremism appealed to those impatient with incrementalism; the immediacy of his tone struck a chord with the masses. He was a self-made individual and a fiery rhetorician, representing to the masses the idea that they, too, could emulate his defiant posture and make their lives worthwhile.

The success of Garvey's pageantry was tied to the promotion of other important objectives: "racial uplift," which had already gained currency in the black community; a nationalism transcending borders; making the country aware—via the military display—of black participation in World War I; and lending voice to those who would no longer tolerate lynching. In Garvey's view, if other nations and nation-states promoted their agendas of nationalism and self-promotion through militaristic exhibitions and displays of national and racial superiority, blacks, too, could join together to occupy and build a fraternity based on racial solidarity and self-protection. Garvey cautioned in the *Negro World*, "mobs of white men all over the world will continue to lynch and burn Negroes so long as we remain divided among ourselves." In light of this, Garvey maintained that the "very moment all the Negroes of this and other countries start to stand together, that very time will see the white man standing in fear of the Negro race."[39] Lynching and racism were very real facts in daily life; the parade provided a place where black people might voice their objections in unity.

Garvey announced to the crowds gathering in Madison Square Garden: "We are here this morning as a free people, claiming equal right with the rest of mankind. We are here because this is an age when all peoples are striking out for freedom, for liberty, for democracy."[40] Twenty years later, Claude McKay would write about it as a dramatic occasion that "went over with theatrical éclat." McKay remarked that this "most gorgeous show was organized by Garvey," and that delegates arrived to join forces with Garvey from "Africa, Brazil, Colombia, Panama and other Central American countries, and from the islands of the West Indies."[41] Significantly, the parade would provide the starting point for Garvey's economic plan.

THE ECONOMIC AGENDA

> *We, too, have been mobilizing the sentiments of our people to return to our Fatherland, where a great African Empire will be founded. We hail with delight the activities of the company of the Black Star Line, which we assure you will be a giant success. And we can vouch that Negroes far and near, and from the remotest ends of the earth, will send across all available funds in order that the Black Star Line may, in the very near future, begin to plough the seas.* —Marcus Garvey (1919)[42]

Garvey's economic plan centered on trade and industry based on the infrastructure of blacks cooperating on a worldwide basis. At the convention the delegates drew up a "Declaration of Negro Rights" in 55 articles, calling for economic separatism and an end to discrimination.[43] The parade was motivated in part as a means to collectivize African Americans, who would then stand behind his movement through financial and political support. Garvey realized that parades alone would not sustain the interest of the average black citizen. In 1919, he announced to the UNIA membership: "We cannot live on sentiment. We have to live on the material production of the world."[44] The aim of Garvey's movement was to unify blacks through economic boosterism and worldwide financial cooperation. In delivering his report in 1919 to UNIA members, Garvey unveiled his plan and underscored his commitment to its implementation: "I am here representing the Black Star Line Steamship Corporation of the world." The purpose of the corporation, Garvey declared, was "to float a line of steamships to run between America, Canada, the Westindies, South and Central America and Africa, carrying freight and passengers." This unification would, he maintained, link the economic power "of the four hundred million Negroes of the world."[45]

Garvey's agenda appealed to those disillusioned with black leaders detached from ordinary folk. He reached out to the proletariat, seeking to develop black capitalism based on Booker T. Washington's idea of a skilled labor pool.[46] However, Garvey, while an admirer of Washington, moved beyond Washington's themes. Rather than developing small businesses as Washington had intended, he envisioned a large corporate organization based on racial solidarity. Washington failed to understand that American capitalism had by the early twentieth century left behind free competition and entered into monopolies and conglomerates; bank loans and credits replaced the skilled artisan. Garvey understood this transition, picking up where Washington had left off, seeking to make full use of twentieth century technology and economics.[47]

Garvey's goal was to establish a black presence in world capitalism. Despite the fact that African Americans had been cut off from banking capital and the UNIA lacked the twin pillars of industry and commerce, Garvey attempted to establish the grounds on which black industry and commerce might flourish. He constructed his economic theories on the idea that if black people, segregated by Jim Crow laws and prejudice, could not enjoy the fruits of American freedom, they could at least enjoy its economic prosperity. In an American system of apartheid, he believed that for two different cultures inhabiting radically different societies within a common geography, any attempt at reconciliation would prove futile. He rejected violent opposition to the white majority, since such a posture invited catastrophic retribution. Instead, Garvey advocated economic separatism. E. David Cronin confirms this, noting that Garvey's corporation successfully developed "a chain of co-operative grocery stores, a restaurant, a steam laundry, a tailor and dressmaking shop, a millinery store, and a publishing house." These efforts, says Cronin, were created "to seek out good business opportunities and to interest Negroes in developing them."[48] In the Garvey movement, emphasis was placed on African American business activities and economic advancement. As Garvey himself insisted in 1919, if black people are to become a significant national force, they must develop business enterprises of their own. Central to Garvey's plan was the development of a worldwide network of banking, trade, industry, and consumer power.

Garvey's "back-to-Africa" movement was a significant yet ambiguous part of his agenda. Afrocentrist Molefi Kete Asante points out that "back-to-Africa" was never "a central part" of Garvey's program.[49] Rather, Garvey used back-to-Africanism as a symbol of ethnic nationalism similar to Zionism, which would spur economic consolidation. According to Garveyite Arnold Crawford, Garvey "told people about their homeland in Africa and that he wanted to bring Black people's minds back to Africa, to make them Africa conscious." But the back-to-Africa movement itself, says Crawford, "was nonsense." Rather than returning to Africa, Garvey wanted instead "to wake up the consciousness of Black people, to make them know from whence they came, the home of their ancestors."[50] Africa became a symbolic state of mind and an idealized image that Garvey hoped might galvanize black creativity and inspire ordinary African American citizens to support his endeavors.

Although he intended to base his operations in the United States, Garvey often spoke of a movement to form an African state. In a 1924 letter to Darwin J. Messerole, Garvey wrote that the members of the UNIA movement

> are endeavoring to so create sentiment among the fifteen million Negroes of America and other parts of the world, as to lead them to see that the only and best solution for the race problem, is for us to have a nation of our own in Africa, whereby we would not be regarded in countries like America, as competitors of the white race for the common position in politics, industry and society, but that we would be regarded as a people striving in our own country to present to the world a civilization and culture of our own.[51]

This need for a transatlantic connection between the United States and Africa was part of Garvey's vision of collective black world unification.

Garvey's position on Africa as a nation-state for African Americans no doubt flip-flopped over the years, but one thing is certain: he demanded to know why African Americans could not profit from economic exchange with Africa as well as the West Indies, since "the white man is now doing it, not with the intention of building for other races, but with the intention of building for himself—for the white race."[52] Garvey scholar Judith Stein argues that Garvey's "Pan-Africanism stemmed from the elite tradition of ambition and uplift, not the mass desire for land."[53] Garvey asserted that African Americans, once united and joined by their racial and national self-interest, might establish a firm position in the world. If racial unity took root within a worldwide network of black capitalism, blacks across the globe might be able to combine investments and eventually develop economic alternatives to isolation and degradation.

Garvey was adamantly opposed to incrementalism. He maintained that the race leaders of his era were moving too slowly and that radical measures were required. An editorial in the *Negro World* criticizing W. E. B. Du Bois illustrates this point: Du Bois, the paper reported, wanted to promote "small, efficient, honest enterprises, quietly and carefully carried on for years, until in fifty years or a century we shall have knit the Negro world together in thrift." This sort of economic leadership, the paper claimed, was "senseless provincialism, an utter failure to understand the revolt of the black proletariat against his fifty-year-or-a-century political economics." The paper concluded its broadside by urging Du Bois to "fall in line and back up the corporate business policies" of Garvey, or remain "fiercely ignorant of modern economic development."[54] Since there was, as Judith Stein points out, a "boom in African commodities in 1919 and 1920," which "encouraged Americans to begin thinking of Africa in terms of raw materials, not big game,"[55] Garvey's shipping industry, the Black Star Line, stood to profit from Africa's natural resources.

Garvey was determined to realize black economic independence. His strategy would be implemented from a platform of three companies: the Negro Factories Corporation, the newspaper *Negro World*, and the Black Star Line.[56] The last, a fleet of steamships operating between the ports of America, the Caribbean, and West Africa, was the most ambitious of these undertakings. What he wanted to do, noted Truman Talley in 1921, was to organize a transoceanic commerce system that would benefit "Africa, West Indies, and America," turning Africa's "oil and rubber, copra and cotton, [and] gold and timber" for profit.[57] He planned on financing such a worldwide super-corporation through contributions from the average working-class African American.

By selling shares of his shipping industry at five dollars a share, Garvey hoped to build a corporate enterprise (see figure 12). The yearly parades became a focal point for donations; Garvey hoped that the audiences attending the parade and the subsequent speeches at Madison Square Garden might be compelled to pay the five dollars in exchange for a theatricalized display of black pride and self-determination. It was felt that the greater the display of pomp and ceremony, the greater likelihood donations might accumulate. By building from small donations, Garvey hoped to secure the financial base from which he could then operate. Small donations might eventually add up to large capital that would then be invested in the UNIA's various industries. This strategy of small investments proved to be both successful yet difficult to track. Accounting for such piecemeal income was difficult if not impossible to record, and the lack of adequate bookkeeping eventually contributed to Garvey's downfall. However, Garvey's goals were in line with the economic thinking at the time.

Garvey understood market change. Economic historian Martin J. Sklar observed that the United States during the early part of the twentieth century was moving from proprietary—small business enterprises—to corporate capitalism. For many Americans, "the corporation became the new frontier opportunity that the western lands had once symbolized." Corporations represented new bourgeois freedoms; according to Sklar, they "'democratized' and nationalized previously segmented and hierarchic layers of the capital class, with new integrative patterns of hierarchy and new avenues of entry, enrichment, authority, and ascent toward the top or at least to greater affluence."[58] Garvey, aware of the ascendancy of private enterprise and corporate consolidation, had a twofold agenda. First, he realized that the importance of corporate manufacturing within the United States provided the resources for a successful attempt to gain economic independence; his goal, said the *Negro World* editorial of 1922, was "to establish a chain of stores, factories, and other money-making industries."[59] Second, he recognized that the transatlantic market-exchange system was founded on the proliferation of a triangular trade: America, Europe, and Africa. Garvey perceptively sought to capitalize on this triadic exchange, but with a reconfiguration composed of the United States (manufactured goods), the West Indies (produce), and Africa (raw materials), each moving goods fluidly from one port to another. William H. Ferris, literary editor of the *Negro World*, said that Garvey was not only a "magnetic speaker but he also possessed business insight." Garvey realized, Ferris wrote in 1920, that African Americans "could not consistently defy the white man one day and beg him for a job the next day." Only when African Americans achieved "commercial strength and economic independence, and built a real republic or empire in Africa," would black people "command the respect and challenge the admiration of a hostile world."[60] Only through self-determination could African Americans attain liberation and justice.

In light of the above, social critic Eric Walrond's observation that in "actual comprehension of the forces governing the world of trade and commerce, [Garvey] is a hopeless nincompoop,"[61] is most assuredly false. Likewise, Raymond Hall is wrong to conclude that Garvey "made an error in attempting to compete in a capitalistic system with little knowledge of the system."[62] Garvey understood corporate capitalism's modi operandi; what he lacked, like so many of his people before him, were resources and a bureaucracy in place to coordinate any large undertaking. He faced five additional obstacles. White competition, particularly Firestone Rubber with its large land investments in Africa, was threatened by Garvey's organization. Inadequate planning and mismanagement of four steamships resulted in several of them running aground. Also, black banking interests were alienated by Garvey's militant rhetoric. Moreover, he faced sabotage from within and without his organization. Lastly, many black leaders opposed Garvey on the grounds that black corporate enterprises could not realistically be competitive.[63] Without capital management, bureaucracy, and the backing of black leaders, Garvey lacked the necessary support for such large-scale plans. Black power historian Theodore G. Vincent observed that although his agenda of "economic independence from whites" has often been "equated" with the programs of Booker T. Washington, Garvey, unlike Washington, "received no support from existing black businessmen." Black entrepreneurs, Vincent claimed, were unable to back his economic and political struggle.[64] Garvey would therefore depend almost entirely on the small, five-dollar donations from ordinary black citizens.

Garvey's actions were intended to eventuate in an economic base from which African Americans could initiate their competitive enterprises against the industrial status quo. According to Garvey, African "minerals, their diamonds, their gold, and their silver and their iron have built up the great English, French, German, Belgian Empires." He then asked: "how long are we going to allow those parasites to suck the blood of our children?"[65] His point was that if, as he put it, the "great mineral and agricultural lands of our fathers are to be exploited by all the nations of the world,"[66] why should blacks from all corners of the globe be denied their share of Africa's commercial wealth? The racist notion in vogue at the time, that blacks were too "primitive" to take advantage of such enterprises, was, in his view, an intolerable injustice that negated and denied black achievement and potential. Garvey exposed the falsehood underlying anti-black propaganda by attempting to prove that black people, if free from oppression and in control of commercial infrastructures, could market and capitalize on Africa's wealth as well as, if not better than, others. Black people, he proved, were capable of independently organizing their own corporations and factories and running them efficiently. A. F. Elmes's reasoning is therefore most likely correct when he argues that Garvey's Black Nationalism was based on economic logic; Garvey, Elmes asserts, claims that "when the colored man needs a suit of clothes, there should be a colored tailor competent to fit him, a colored wholesale store from the which the goods can be procured, colored factory for the preparation of the raw material and ships manned and owned by men of his race to transport the goods." In this way, Garvey might "close the whole economic circle with agents and agencies of his own people."[67] What Garvey lacked was an economic base. Hoping the parade would provide the revenue needed, he sought ways of stimulating interest in the UNIA through public displays of pomp and pageantry.

In an address to the UNIA membership in Philadelphia in 1919, Garvey spoke of the spirit of self-reliance among black people, but he also warned that if blacks worldwide remained passive, black people would be doomed. "We have started an agitation all over the world," he said, and urged black people to support him: "I want you to understand that if you do not get behind this agitation and back it up morally and financially you are only flirting with your own downfall." Warning that the black man will "die in the next one hundred years if he does not start out now to do for himself,"[68] Garvey realized the urgency of improving the conditions of black people and gambled his whole enterprise on a large-scale, massive action. He relied on oratorical skills and charisma to rally the black working class behind him.

CHARISMA

> The hordes of black peasant folk flock to Garvey. They worship him. They feel that he is saying the things which they would utter were they articulate. They swarm to hear his fiery rhetoric. They pour their money into his coffers. They stand by him through thick and thin. They idolize him as if he were a black Demosthenes. —Eric Walrond (1925)[69]

Although Garvey's appeal was based on the promise of freedom and competitive opportunity, his popularity depended on results. To retain his followers, he and his organization had to maintain a hold on the masses and produce evidence of success. Garvey was under considerable pressure to bring about quick economic gain. He therefore pursued what sociologist Ronald Glassman calls a "media-manufactured charisma" using newspapers, magazines, and mass-printed posters to "create an atmosphere in which the political leader seems ever-present and larger than life." Such charisma is most effectively attained, Glassman notes, "when the group feels a personal, trusting, infantilizing bond with the leader, the leader's constant presence—in bright image," and that these images help "manufacture such leader-led relationships."[70] Garvey used newspapers (*Negro World*) and public spectacles (annual UNIA parades) in order to maintain a constant presence. According to Molefi Asante, Garvey "instituted cultural symbols which captured the essence of a nationalistic philosophy" aimed at the media. As a "media manipulator, growing from his years as a journalist and printer, Garvey knew how to communicate with his audience," with his expansive images captivating the journalists who analyzed his movement.[71] But Garvey was after more than the media image; he needed the grassroots support of the average African American. The parade's pomp, regalia, and uniforms were therefore part of Garvey's theatricalized "production," or rather the production of Garvey himself. The parade served to rally African Americans who otherwise might have been reluctant to contribute to the cause. Garvey had to stir nationalist sentiment among the black masses if he and his organization were to succeed and survive. One way to do this was to establish himself as a charismatic leader through media spectacles.

What appeared as excessive theatricality in Garvey's parades was, in fact, a purposeful attempt to attract the masses. Eric Walrond understood the fact that all "the glamour, all the technique of delusion" was employed by Garvey "to satisfy the craving" of a "repressed peasant folk." Walrond condescendingly remarks: "Essentially a movement of the black proletariat, Garveyism owes its strength largely to jangling swords and flaming helmets, titles and congeries of gold braid."[72] Yet the swords and helmets had a larger purpose: to galvanize the working class through theatrical display and thus motivate donations. Garvey's success was indebted to his realization that policies had to be supplemented by what Garvey historian John Runcie called "the colorful pageantry of massive parades, gaudy uniforms, marching bands, banners, ostentatious titles and 'court receptions.'"[73] For a revolutionary leader to succeed he or she must generate charisma by convincing followers that the visions put forth will succeed. Charisma flows from the leader's control of the revolutionary dream, which is constantly visualized and vitalized by theatricalization.

Today charisma has lost its distinction as a symbol of leadership; it merely denotes an attribute, glamour, and attractiveness of persons and objects. Charisma also tends to dissipate during unstable periods. However, at the beginning of the twentieth century, charisma was considered essential to political leadership. Max Weber describes the qualities of charisma as belonging to those who are "considered extraordinary and treated" as such out of recognition of their "supernatural, superhuman, or at least specifically exceptional powers or qualities."[74] Garvey and his organization possessed, to one degree or another, Weberian characteristics of charisma, with one unfortunate exception: the ability to sustain success. Historian Raymond Hall maintains that Garvey's "dynamic personality, his oratorical ability, his crowd-pleasing antics, his superb use of the dramatic moment—all played an important part in maintaining his image."[75] However, without what Weber calls a "routinization of charisma," in which charisma is "exposed to the conditions of everyday life and to the powers dominating it, especially to the economic interests,"[76] a leader's grip on his or her followers would be tenuous at best.

Personal charm and resounding rhetoric will not sustain a leader's hold forever; parades and rituals will only carry an ideology and dream so far. Proven results must back up charisma; otherwise the rhetoric will appear shallow. A leader's charismatic claim breaks down, says Weber, "if his mission is not recognized by those to whom he feels he has been sent. If they recognize him, he is their master—so long as he knows how to maintain recognition through 'proving' himself."[77] Ultimately, Garvey knew that the ecstasy of charisma would fade quickly unless greater production and more efficient economic progress supplemented, or at least complemented, the demagoguery. Weber uses the notion of *de facto* endurance—"routinization of charisma"— through the symbolic and cognitive reordering of the world as the basis for sustained charismatic authority. As Weber explains, the charismatic leader desires "to transform charisma and charismatic blessing from a unique, transitory gift of grace of extraordinary times and persons into a permanent possession of everyday life."[78] To do this, the charismatic leader must therefore reorganize not only institutions—church, government, work, social life—but must also refashion a world view, confidence in the new vision, and implement this vision in everyday life. The annual parades were part of a process of reordering the symbols and routines of supporters. As sociologist Edward Shils points out, Weber's notion of the routinization of charisma is "intimately related to the need for order." Only through order and results, Shils adds, can the "effectiveness of successful exercise of power on a large scale, on a macro-social scale," evoke a legitimate continuity.[79] Garvey realized that the process of legitimizing new ways of thinking, new routines, firm continuity, and underlying confidence in his economic plan would take time. During the interim, he would attempt to instill confidence in his leadership through "invented" traditions that would suffice until the institutions became familiar and commonplace, and the economic gains would trickle down to the ordinary citizen.

The swords, military regalia, plumed hats, and medals became Garvey's version of invented traditions of black culture. According to E. J. Hobsbawm, invented tradition means "a set of practices, normally governed by overtly or tacitly accepted rules of a ritual or symbolic nature, which seek to inculcate certain values and norms of behavior by repetition, which automatically implies continuity with the past." For Hobsbawm, tradition is distinguished from custom in that custom "is what judges do"; tradition "is the wig, robe and other formal paraphernalia and ritualized practices surrounding their substantial action."[80] In the absence of the practices associated with what Hobsbawm calls "customs"—the day-to-day activities of institutions that would bring immediate economic results—Garvey's ceremonial parades attempted to implement "traditions" by establishing the uniformed regalia and marching parades that conveyed a positive image of black America. In lieu of economic success, which he realized would take time, he and his organization developed a form of pageantry that might encourage expansion of UNIA membership. Garvey gambled on the parades as a way of stalling for time; he thought that the implementation of ritualized patterns might temporarily suffice as a way of deflecting economic hardships that black people endured. Racism and time, however, eventually overcame him and Garvey succumbed.

CONCLUSION

Let it be observed that no man can stand in one of those teeming Liberty
Hall audiences, see one of Garvey's ostentatious parades, hear Garvey's
magnetic voice, read his Negro World, *watch the sweep of his ideas,*
and then say there's nothing to it.   —Benjamin Quarles (1969)[81]

Garvey's contemporaries often criticized his practices and behavior as autocratic, irrational, and foolish. His ideology was authoritarian, and his ceremonial attire and showy parades had their detractors. He was a demagogue who, as Wilson Jeremiah Moses points out, openly asserted his goal "of creating a new African aristocracy."[82] Du Bois, for example, described the UNIA pageant in theatrical terms as a "dress rehearsal of a new comic opera."[83] Others were even more critical: an editorial in the *Messenger* referred to Garvey as a "supreme Negro Jackass"; Claude McKay called Garvey's convention "stupendous vaudeville"; and in the *New York Age,* James Weldon Johnson remarked that Garvey's costumes and regalia were "the apotheosis of the ridiculous."[84] The most virulent attack came from George Schuyler and Theophilus Lewis, who noted in the *Messenger* that Garvey, a candidate for the "Nobel Mirth Prize," was (in theatrical terms again) "the little octoroon admiral" who "has outdistanced Falstaff, Don Quixote and Bert Williams in the production of guffaws."[85] Elsewhere Schuyler went so far as to suggest that "Garvey anticipated Hitler."[86] The archly anti-Garvey newspaper, the *New York Age,* reported that the "monster mass-meeting" at Madison Square Garden in 1920 "was the tinsel and gilt which Garvey arranged as he proposed to 'pass the hat' among the colored persons of New York." The paper added (once again using theatricality as the metaphor) that the "great majority of colored persons of New York look upon Garvey as a P. T. Barnum who is putting on a big show to amuse them."[87]

To be sure, Garvey's ritual attire and autocratic policies caused suspicion of his underlying purposes. Walter Benjamin's analysis of spectatorship and ideology as performed in the massive rallies of the Nazis is particularly salient here for its emphasis on the ritual elements enacted in Garvey's mass spectacles. Fascism, using the growing "proletarianization" of modern society and the "increasing formation of masses" into an organized body, "sees its salvation in giving these masses not their right, but instead a chance to express themselves." The consequence of this outlet of expression is "the introduction of aesthetics into political life," what Benjamin calls Fascism's *"Führer* cult."[88] Garvey's mass spectacles played into the notion of heroic cult worship that was similar to many mass rallies at the time. Garvey, by and large, set the standard of militaristic and authoritative ideological trends by pushing forward what Benjamin would later describe as cult aesthetics through mass assemblages of the *Volk.*

Still, Garvey's intent was not without merit and his downfall had as much to do with subversion as it had with corruption. (Garvey was indicted by a grand jury in 1922 for mail fraud.) In addition to poor decision-making, such as acquiring inadequately built steamships and reliance on untrustworthy associates, Garvey faced government surveillance, sabotage, financial mismanagement, and loss of African support, guaranteeing the demise of his ambitious undertaking. Significantly, Garvey's charisma did not extend to bureaucracy, where leadership would have to combine a dynamic personality with the willingness to perform mundane tasks. In Weberian terms, the charismatic passion to follow a leader is inevitably at odds with the world of bureaucracy. Bureaucratic institutions favor greater productivity and efficient economy over political oratory and theatricalization. The mundane but effective process will ultimately trump all spontaneity and vivid emotional ties in favor of technically sophisticated social organization. Garvey's emphasis on personal charisma and emotional spontaneity rather than nuts-and-bolts detail may have ultimately proved to be his undoing.[89]

However, we ought to take a second look at Garvey's performance from the perspective offered by social scientist Ato Sekyi-Otu, who describes attempts by oppressed people to gain control of their conditions as "a critical tension between the 'absurd drama' of the colonized subject and the 'proleptic universals' of human experience."[90] In other words, rather than a self-aggrandizing discourse, Garvey's agenda should be considered in view of the tensions created by his efforts to merge ritual and ceremony with the anticipatory hope of unifying working-class African Americans. The pomp and pageantry, what Sekyi-Otu might call "absurd drama," was in fact a foregrounding of ceremony that draws attention to parades, pageants, and such rituals that bond social groups and offer hope for a brighter future. Garvey scholar Rupert Lewis contends that although "the ceremonial paraphernalia worn by Garvey, by top UNIA dignitaries, and by the mass of groups may appear somewhat ridiculous," in the context of its time, within "the exclusive dominance of colonial/metropolitan examples of solemnity, order, and self-pride, such forms have to be understood more positively than negatively."[91] Oppressed peoples often do not enjoy the luxury of organized bureaucracies and complex infrastructures that could support widespread and expansive enterprises; instead, there is a dependence on rituals, even though these rituals appear to have little if any practical plan. Rituals without practical support seem to be surface phenomena, but they are, in fact, important means by which subaltern peoples begin to build community and lay the groundwork for folk roots and traditions, and eventually infrastructures of bureaucracy.

Garvey was seeking to manufacture symbols that would take hold in the minds and hearts of black people through his oratory power and the theatricality

of parades. His public speaking was performance art; his speeches were powerful not merely because of the words he used, but also for the way that he performed his words in the public sphere, which deeply affected his audiences. Even
his enemies acknowledged the grandeur of his oratory powers. With Garvey on
trial for fraud, the captain of one of Garvey's ships, Adrian Richardson, testified
against him, but added the following: "You are a good orator, a poor businessman, and a highway robber."[92] Garvey's parades established a tradition of positive symbols through grand oratory, which could be used to dismantle "the last
plantation"—the internalized oppression of the mind.[93] Judith Stein claims that
Garvey's charisma "had its limits," and that his popularity was never as great as it
was during the August 1920 parade and convention.[94] Garvey no doubt knew
this and sought ways of sustaining momentum by creating traditions that could
carry him through what would be the difficult years of empire building.

Perhaps the most intricate issue for Garvey was the diverse nature of black
America; by 1920 it became difficult if not impossible to find one unifying theme
or person to galvanize black constituents. According to Paul Gilroy, the "rich
and volatile mixture" of Harlem "yielded no pure, seamless or spontaneous articulation of black America's world-historic, national spirit." Instead, there was
"only an unstable blend for which Garvey's dynamic Ethiopianism would provide a contradictory expression in the political field." As a result, Garvey's music,
pomp, costume, and ritual "represented a sustained attempt to quell, discipline
and perhaps eviscerate a disorderly, black population."[95] Garvey simply lacked
the infrastructure to hold together disparate emotions, ideas, and agendas.

Garvey's symbolic march was designed to instill pride, and if his ultimate goals
failed, his parade, at least for a time, offered the possibility of hope within its theatricality and ceremony. bell hooks claims that Martin Luther King and Malcolm X
were engaged in a "concrete liberation struggle," and that both these leaders were
"concerned with reaching a mass audience, with talking to those most exploited
and/or oppressed." For hooks, King and Malcolm "showed the method in which
performance art could serve a meaningful role in liberation struggle," through the
power of their oratory skills.[96] Garvey, too, had what hooks calls the oratory skills
of performance art that allowed him the opportunity to engage oppressed people
and fill them with hope, at least for a while. That his bold gambit fell short should
not detract from acknowledging his unique vision and frequently well-intentioned
accomplishments.

CHAPTER 9

WHOSE ROLE IS IT, ANYWAY?: CHARLES GILPIN AND THE HARLEM RENAISSANCE

I created the role of the Emperor. That role belongs to me. That Irishman,
he just wrote the play. —Charles Gilpin (n.d.)[1]

CHARLES GILPIN AND *THE EMPEROR JONES*

Cheer up, nigger, de worst is yet to come.
—Eugene O'Neill, *The Emperor Jones* (1920)[2]

In more than 30 cities and in over 200 performances, Charles Gilpin played the leading role of Eugene O'Neill's *The Emperor Jones* during the play's first nationwide tour (see figure 13).[3] During the tour (1921–1922), the *Boston Globe* reported that Gilpin's acting "of all these exacting scenes cannot be too highly praised. Only an actor of genuine power could save some of them from becoming ludicrous." It is a remarkable performance, said the paper, "one not soon to be forgotten."[4] Critic Philip Hale added that Gilpin "is the play" and that with "genuine tragic power" his portrayal of the Emperor is "remarkable."[5] Throughout the tour Gilpin reaped praise after praise for his performance.[6] He had previously performed in the play, which opened November 1920, over two hundred times in Greenwich Village and on Broadway. Heywood Broun of the *New York Tribune* observed that in the opening production Gilpin was "great," and his performance reached "heroic stature."[7] Kenneth MacGowan wrote in the *New York Globe* that Gilpin's rendition of the Emperor was "a sustained and splendid piece of acting."[8] Alexander Woollcott commented in the *New York Times* that Gilpin's acting was "an uncommonly powerful and imaginative performance," adding, "in several respects unsurpassed this season in New York."[9] Gilpin, the first black actor to achieve Broadway stardom in a non-musical drama, portrayed the beleaguered character Brutus Jones, the Emperor of a Caribbean island whose career as a con artist and huckster helped him gain the position of royalty. However, his sham is discovered and his subjects pursue him to his death. According to Gilpin's biographer, John G. Monroe, *The Emperor Jones* "marked, as [Gilpin] had anticipated, the zenith of his career." In addition to the Broadway run of the show, Gilpin followed with a two-season road tour, several revivals, and special engagements. He played the role of Brutus Jones approximately 1,500 times before his death, from pneumonia, in 1930, at the age of 51.[10]

But notwithstanding his continued success as Brutus Jones from 1920 to 1928, and continually favorable reviews, history has not been especially kind to Charles Gilpin, who is most often remembered as an actor who played a single role and who spent the last decade of his life in alcoholic despair. One historian maintains that

> his success in *The Emperor Jones* helped to destroy him, for he realized, even when his popularity was at its height, that the road he had opened for others lay closed to him. He was too broken and too embittered to benefit from the new interest of playwrights such as O'Neill and Torrence in using the Negro and Negro life as pure dramatic material, or attempt Shakespearean roles such as Othello.[11]

On the contrary, Gilpin never wished to play Othello. He remarked to the *St. Louis Star*:

> I have been asked time and again to play Othello, but have always refused. It would be nothing but a stunt to satisfy curiosity, to see whether by any chance a negro could play the part of a Moor better than a white man. There would be no real dramatic value to the experiment, and it would mean nothing to me artistically. What it actually would do is ruin my career. Imagine a negro playing Othello to a white woman's Desdemona in America![12]

Gilpin's relationship to the text of *The Emperor Jones* serves as another example of how critics have assessed the performer. During his long association with the O'Neill play, Gilpin was criticized for changing the dialogue. He balked at what appeared to him to be an excessive and repetitive use of the term "nigger," preferring instead to use in its place the less offensive terms "black-baby,"

"Negro," or "colored man." According to Eugene O'Neill's biographers, Arthur and Barbara Gelb, O'Neill, bristling at the actor's audacity, was alleged to have said to Gilpin: "If I ever catch you rewriting my lines again, you black bastard, I'm going to beat you up." The O'Neill biography by Louis Sheaffer deleted the "black bastard" epithet, claiming that O'Neill merely said: "If you change the lines again, I'll beat the hell out of you!"[13] Gilpin committed what some consider taboo: changing the author's words without the author's consent. In this chapter, I will examine the potential reasons why he altered the text, proffering the view that Gilpin's performance was informed by the actor's social awareness.

Gilpin's own opinion concerning the changing of the dialogue contrasts sharply with the characterization provided by historians and biographers. For instance, he notes in the *Cincinnati Times Star:*

> My performance of 'Brutus Jones' today is vastly different from my interpreta-tion given when the play opened. My understanding of the character has devel-oped as I have worked with it and new meanings are constantly unfolding. Mr. O'Neill has been very kind in this respect, giving me the liberty of changing the lines to suit the characterization.[14]

While it is true that O'Neill's letters reflect impatience with Gilpin,[15] we must make the effort to see beyond the usual antagonisms between writer and actor. Gilpin's views on the matter have been entirely shut out; neither of the O'Neill biographers, nor other biographical portraits of Gilpin, except for Monroe's, supply the actor's own words on textual matters.

In a letter attempting to discredit Gilpin, O'Neill suggested that the star of his play was "all ham and a yard wide," a "regular actor-brain" who was "drunk all of last season."[16] This remark, which labeled Gilpin an egotistical dipsoma-niac, has become, unfortunately, a part of the conventional wisdom. For exam-ple, one biographical portrait suggested that after 1925, Gilpin "was playing far more performances drunk than sober, and the result was often painfully ludi-crous."[17] There exists no evidence that would support the claim that Gilpin played more performances drunk than sober, nor that his performances were ever "painfully ludicrous." He did appear drunk onstage occasionally. Moss Hart, who performed with Gilpin in *The Emperor Jones* during the second revival in 1926, wrote that Gilpin's drunken performances "occurred not too often."[18] Yet Gilpin seems rarely to have lost his remarkable power to electrify audiences, at least during performances when reviewers were present. As an actor, Gilpin appeared hardly to have deteriorated in his ability to convey the animal magnet-ism and visceral embodiment required for the role.[19]

A sampling of the reviews will serve to underscore this point. In the first of two New York revivals of *The Emperor Jones* during the 1926 season, we find the following notice in the *New York Evening Post*:

> Neither the play nor Gilpin has lost any of the dark magic which bewitched and captured a city away back in the dim days of 1920. . . . When Gilpin lolled on the papermache [*sic*] throne last night and cringed beneath the clawing fingers of the jungle trees, one knew that there will never be a rival to approach him in the part.[20]

During the second 1926 revival at the Mayfair Theatre (November through January 1927), which Gilpin directed and which extended its run to seventy performances, a reviewer wrote in *Billboard*:

> Gilpin again uncannily conceives and lives the part; the same sly bully, gloating over his mastery of the ignorant savages and gradually transforming into a cringing coward when his power is overthrown. Perhaps it is as the latter that Gilpin will best be remembered, for it is as such that he rises to the apex of his ability. . . . A deep rich voice has always been Gilpin's chief asset in his portrayal of the terrorizing Brutus Jones. Its unfailing intensity holds and adequately fulfills its purpose.[21]

The *New York Amsterdam News* summed up the response to Gilpin's performance in the first revival:

> [Gilpin] has lost none of the power and dramatic ability which he displayed in 'The Emperor Jones.' . . . The return of 'The Emperor Jones' to New York discloses to those who might have entertained any doubts of the ability of Charles S. Gilpin, the latent dramatic power which we early discovered in this artist, and which we took pride in pointing out to our readers years before his opportunity came to appear before exacting audiences in a sphere far removed from that of 135th Street.[22]

In the following I will challenge the accepted notion of Gilpin as a drunk who "resorted to liquor, not only during his leisure but, at times, before and even during performance," and who, out of egoism, "tampered with his role" and "began taking other liberties with the dialogue."[23] Gilpin tampered with the role, but I maintain that the motives had less to do with egocentrism and more to do with solidarity with the spirit of the Harlem Renaissance. Verifying this must depend on a certain amount of reasonable speculation. The problem facing any biography of Gilpin is the paucity of raw data and the reliance on an actor's thoughts during press interviews, which are questionable sources when taken alone. Regarding the first point, theatre historian James V. Hatch points out that the careers of black professional actors and actresses, "particularly those from 1880 to 1930, remain sparsely documented."[24] In Gilpin's case, we have his words and we have the background of the Harlem Renaissance. Yet, assessing Gilpin as merely egotistical without fully appreciating his situation as an African American actor during the 1920s creates an incomplete picture of the artist.

It is clearly unfair to label Gilpin an irresponsible drunk, while ignoring his interpretative success in the role of Brutus Jones. No doubt Gilpin drank, but there was more to the actor than mere alcoholism. A great deal of obfuscation has been caused by the recurrent tendency of certain scholars to treat Gilpin as either a sad actor turned to drink or a sad actor unable to realize his potential. Gilpin was far from being an actor who played only one role. His career spanned over 30 years, most of which was spent acting in black communities for black audiences.[25] Emphasis merely on his drinking or his inability to play other roles leads scholars to undervalue constantly—and often to ignore entirely—the influence of the Harlem Renaissance on Gilpin's style of acting. Moreover, imposing the image of Gilpin as "sad and embittered" denies Gilpin, and African Americans in general, the historical prerogative of opposing their oppressors through culture, language, and performance. I suggest that to arrive at the meaning of Gilpin's life requires conceptual strategies that must be receptive to a framework of African American culture. Whereas historians assert that Gilpin's alteration of the text was owing to his egoism and drunkenness, it seems more plausible and more consonant with the culture of the Harlem Renaissance at least to consider an alternative hypothesis centering on language, performance, and the opinions of African Americans toward *The Emperor Jones*.

THE ACTOR BEFORE THE EMPEROR

*In "The Emperor Jones" Gilpin dazzled the theatrical world. He made
stage history and had a great deal to do with making the reputation of a
great dramatist.*   —Theophilus Lewis (n.d.)[26]

Prior to his role in *The Emperor Jones*, Charles Sidney Gilpin's career spanned nearly three decades. He was born in Richmond, Virginia in 1878, the youngest of a large family. At an early age he began singing and dancing in local honky-tonks, where, as he said, he "hung on to this ragged edge of show business" until he "gradually got a little firmer grip on it."[27] By 1892 he and his mother had moved to Philadelphia, where he worked for a time in the mechanical department of a white newspaper, *The Philadelphia Standard*. The prejudice of his fellow white workers drove him from the job, and Gilpin returned to singing and dancing. After working odd jobs, he joined various singing groups, touring in parts of Canada and the United States. In 1905 his first break in show business arrived. He was hired as a chorus singer in the Williams and Walker Company production of *Abyssinia*. From there he was gainfully employed, for a time, as the leading actor in Robert Motts's Pekin Theatre in Chicago. It was at the Pekin that Gilpin acquired his reputation as one of the nation's finest character actors. Motts and his co-director, J. Edward Green (1872–1910), gave Gilpin freedom to demonstrate his versatility. His reputation soon spread and he was hired by Anita Bush (1883–1974) to start up Harlem's Lafayette Theatre in December 1915. Gilpin was also known for his high standards and demanding personality. Eventually, he left the Lafayette for lack of sufficient pay and clashes with management. In 1919 he played the Reverend William Custis in John Drinkwater's *Abraham Lincoln* on Broadway. In spite of several difficulties, including a lack of rehearsal time and hostility from fellow cast members, one reviewer noted that in *Abraham Lincoln* the "sincerity with which [Gilpin] played the old slave [Custis] who comes to thank the Great Emancipator was as simple as it was moving."[28] After a brief interim working as a Pullman porter and elevator operator, Gilpin was invited to perform the role of Brutus Jones in Eugene O'Neill's new play. Years later, Moss Hart described working with Gilpin on the 1926 revival of the *Emperor Jones* that was directed by Gilpin:

> He had the inner violence and maniacal power that engulfed the spectator. . . . Charles Gilpin was the greatest actor of his race. He was limited not by his own range as an actor, but by the limitations of the part the Negro could play in the theatre. Had he not been a Negro, there is no doubt that he would have been one of the great actors of his time.[29]

Gilpin's biographer, John G. Monroe, suggests that during an era of unstable relationships between blacks and whites, "Gilpin realized that his course ahead was a tightrope which he must successfully maneuver or else face a plunge to depths from which he had just recently surfaced." Gilpin was a pragmatist who "dealt with the realities of his life and time in a way which, he thought, would assure his professional and economic survival and which would, simultaneously, engender respect and opportunities for others of his race."[30]

One might ask, how concerned was Gilpin about black opinion of the play? While on tour, Gilpin responded to the question of race, saying:

> It is the educated black that criticizes me most harshly. They ask why I should take the role of a thief, murderer, and ignoramus. Of course, Brutus Jones isn't

much of a criminal—that is, his crimes are treated in a friendly way and the audience takes them lightly. . . . But I tell my friends who protest against Brutus Jones that stage characters are mere stage characters. You take them as you find them.

I ask them to consider that the worthy presentation of a character by a negro actor is a credit to our race, even though the character itself is unworthy. The better educated negroes understand this and are extremely sympathetic toward my work.[31]

Despite Gilpin's effort to present a well-reasoned defense of the play and the lead role, feelings among African American intellectuals were generally disapproving of *The Emperor Jones*. For many African Americans, the play's protagonist was, as literary historian John Cooley points out, "more clown than hero, ultimately a laughable pretender to be pitied and dismissed."[32] There was evidence in numerous black publications that African Americans rejected the play. Black critics, Monroe averred, "had never doubted the existence of skillful black actors of serious drama and were not in the least surprised at Gilpin's performance." However, O'Neill's script was considered "an outrage to many Harlem critics."[33] For example, at the start of the play's tour, Caswell Crews of the *Negro World* had the following to say about *The Emperor Jones:* "To be sure it is pronounced a great play by the critics, but they are white, and will pronounce anything good that has white supremacy as its theme." Crews elaborated: "We imagine that if Mr. Gilpin is an intelligent and loyal Negro his heart must ache and rebel within him as he is forced to belie his race."[34] Many spoke openly against Gilpin and the play, offended by its portrayal of Jones as a buffoonish emperor of a Caribbean island. William Bridges, editor of *Challenge,* called *The Emperor Jones* "a travesty of the African race."[35] In 1921, the *Christian Recorder* maintained: "[w]e could however hope that a better type of Negro had been selected for the fine talents of Mr. Charles Sidney Gilpin."[36] During a performance of the play at Howard University, historian Roseann Pope Bell reports that many African Americans criticized the representation of a criminal black man in *The Emperor Jones,* wondering "how the university could stoop . . . to allow a performance of a play in which the leading character was a crap-shooter and escaped convict." Bell adds that others, "so disgusted with the play, suggested that O'Neill had no standing as a playwright."[37]

Primitivism was the play's central conflict and for some the central objection.[38] The protagonist, who rises to emperor of a Caribbean Island, is eventually branded a criminal and dethroned. The play depicts his slow degeneration into a "primitive" state as he is pursued through the jungle. Many black intellectuals were divided on how to respond to the notion of primitivism in *The Emperor Jones.*

For example, during the second tour, Gilpin encountered antagonistic attitudes toward the play in Cleveland. In a 1935 article devoted to the history of Cleveland's Gilpin Players, Harvey M. Williamson wrote that

> Negro Cleveland was hostile to Gilpin, hostile to this man who, it felt, had betrayed his race by taking part in a play about the superstition of a Negro. The Players were hostile to Gilpin also, but they invited him to speak to them. Gilpin accepted but in his speech he made no defense of or apology for the *Emperor Jones* or his part in it. He so impressed the Players, however, with the dignity of the theatre and the understanding that drama is above belittling that the dubious attitude with which the group had regarded the play was replaced by one of appreciation. So much, indeed, were the Players impressed by Gilpin that at their next meeting they voted unanimously to name the group the Gilpin Players.[39]

Not all African Americans opposed the play outright. Some were ambivalent. In 1922, Jessie Fauset wrote in *Crisis* that among African Americans "Gilpin's rendition of *The Emperor Jones* caused a deep sense of irritation. They could not distinguish between the artistic interpretation of a type and the deliberate travestying of a race, and so their appreciation was clouded."[40] Two contradictory views surface in Alain Locke's *The New Negro* (1925). On the one hand, William S. Braithwaite, discussing the popular and atavistic manner of representing African Americans in plays by white authors, wrote that "the preoccupation, almost obsession of otherwise strong and artistic work like O'Neill's *Emperor Jones, All God's Chillun Got Wings*, and Culbertson's *Goat Alley* with this same theme and doubtful formula of hereditary cultural reversion" yield the fact that, "in spite of all good intentions, the true presental of the real tragedy of Negro life is a task still left for Negro writers to perform." On the other hand, Montgomery Gregory, in the same book, maintained that for any further development of African American drama, "*The Emperor Jones*, written by O'Neill, interpreted by Gilpin, and produced by the Provincetown Players, will tower as a beacon-light of inspiration."[41] A similar contradiction surfaces in the case of W. E. B. Du Bois. In a 1921 commentary entitled "Negro Art" for *Crisis*, he defended the play against its detractors, calling *The Emperor Jones* "a splendid tragedy." However, five years later, Du Bois expressed a somewhat different view. In a program note for the Krigwa Players season of 1926 (reproduced in *Crisis*), he wrote that blacks are "still handicapped and put forth with much hesitation, as in the case of 'The Nigger,' 'Lulu Belle,' and 'Emperor Jones.'"[42] Gilpin was aware of many negative criticisms emerging from black publications at the time. As a result, Gilpin took into account the text of *The Emperor Jones*, finding within it the potentiality of performative alterations.

WHAT'S IN A WORD?

"Do you know what white racists call black Ph.D.'s?" He said some-
thing like, "I believe that I happen not to be aware of that"—you know,
one of these ultra-proper-talking Negroes. And I laid the word down on
him, loud: "Nigger!"   —Malcolm X (1965)[43]

There is evidence, albeit circumstantial, that Gilpin frequently changed the words of O'Neill's *The Emperor Jones*. John Cooley writes that Gilpin, "obviously unhappy with certain aspects of his role, made several changes in the script, including a substitution of 'black baby' for O'Neill's 'nigger.'"[44] The term "nigger" appears throughout the play. Gilpin had begun to question the validity of the term's significance within the context of the role and the play.

We know that during the Harlem Renaissance the term had taken on for many a forceful pejorative significance. Eric Walrond, for example, wrote in the *Negro World* in 1922 that "nigger" represented a "stigma of inferiority," which had been used to "label the Negro as a member of an inferior race."[45] Such terms as "coon" and "nigger," wrote Lester A. Walton in the *New York Age*, "have been worked overtime" by white writers and minstrel comedians.[46] According to Sterling A. Brown, Edgar M. Gray's commentary in the *New York News* "expressed the opinions of many Negroes" about *The Emperor Jones;* the play, he notes, "is uninstructive, degrading and does not conform to history nor geography." The word "nigger" itself, Gray reported, "is used about fifty times," as well as "the phrases 'Money Chaser,' 'black trash,' 'Black heathen' and other disgusting and degrading epithets." However, nowhere "is the Negro made to feel that he is capable of respectable behavior or high attainments."[47]

The term "nigger" was considered by some as part of a rejected "Old World" view of blacks. Yet, in *The Emperor Jones*, Brutus Jones repeatedly uses the term "nigger" to refer to himself and African Americans in general. "Nigger" becomes redundant, as the following passage in the play demonstrates, when the character begins conversing with himself:

Dey're gone. Dat shot fix 'em. Dey was only little animals—little wild pigs, I reckon. Dey've maybe rooted out yo' grub an' eat it. Sho', you fool nigger, what you think dey is—ha'nts? (*Excitedly*) Gorry, you give de game away when you fire dat shot. Dem niggers head dat fo' su'tin! Time you beat it in de woods widout no long waits (*He starts for the forest–hesitates before the plunge—then urges himself in with manful resolution*) Git in, nigger! What you skeered at? Ain't nothin' dere but de trees! Git in! (*He plunges boldly into the forest*).[48]

Admittedly it is difficult if not impossible to know exactly where, how often, and in which of the over 1,500 performances Gilpin changed the text. The aim here is not necessarily concerned with the dates of such changes (something we will never know anyway). In all likelihood Gilpin altered the text differently on different occasions. We know he changed the text; what needs to be investigated is why. Examining the underlying meaning behind Gilpin's actions may provide us with clues to the actor's interpretation. Gilpin's alterations of the text can best be understood as a result of three motives: to make Brutus Jones less offensive to African Americans; to change O'Neill's language, which Gilpin perhaps viewed as overly general, repetitive, and at the same time imprecise, given its place in African American dialect; and to affirm, through performance, his own creative and artistic interpretation in a role that he believed he understood better than the author.

The first motive for changing the text is based on the notion that Gilpin was conscious of the role he played on behalf of African American culture. Throughout his long association with the play, he was continually honored not only as an actor, but as a leading African American figure as well. He often lectured at various civic clubs throughout Harlem,[49] and gave benefit performances of *The Emperor Jones* on behalf of Howard University and other African American organizations.[50] He was awarded the Spingarn Medal in 1921, and was honored in the same year as the *Crisis* "Man of the Month."[51] According to the *New York Age*, on 6 May 1921, he headed an all-star cast for "The Benefit to Aid Boys and Girls."[52] He said of himself, "I am really a race man—a negro and proud of being one, proud of the progress the negroes have made in the time and with the opportunity they have had. And I don't want the public to think anything different."[53] In 1921, Gilpin was one of ten to receive the New York Drama League Award for the 1920–21 theatrical season. He was allowed to attend the League's ceremonial dinner only after a bitter controversy in which some members tried to block his invitation.[54] The *New York Age* reported that Gilpin was the guest of honor at an African American banquet tended by the Denver Colored Civic Association.[55] Speaking of his life, he noted: "I'm the happiest man in the world" when "able to run out of the Broadway district to go to Harlem where my real friends are."[56] His personal connection to Harlem, not Broadway, reveals his commitment to the community and the comfort level he achieved there.

In an effort to deflect the racial controversy inherent in *The Emperor Jones*, Gilpin argued that the play represented humanity. For Gilpin, the story of Brutus Jones was not racial, but universal. The *New York Age* quoted Gilpin as saying at the Denver banquet:

No offense should be taken because of the fact that Brutus Jones, the Negro, is a villain. This is not a racial play; it is universal in its application. The fundamental idea of the play is this: a bully is always a coward, and its moral is simply this: the bigger the bully, the bigger the coward. . . . As to the superstition revealed in the character of Brutus Jones, we as a race have been superstitious, just as every other race has been superstitious, and many of us still are. But superstition is merely ignorance; and we are all more or less ignorant. And that doesn't apply to any one race.

    To appreciate Mr. O'Neill's play, you must look into it; not merely at it. It was designed to make you, and all those [who] see it, think. Don't imagine for one moment that I, a Negro, would hold one type of our race up to ridicule.[57]

By defusing the word "nigger," Gilpin can be said to have shifted the emphasis away from race by endowing Brutus Jones with universality. One can no doubt question Gilpin's success: changing "nigger" to "colored man," "black baby," or "Negro" may be too subtle to have any meaningful effect. There is, however, change nonetheless: by dispersing references to the character's race, Gilpin destabilized the signifier. The singularly offensive word "nigger" and all that it signifies is now somewhat mediated, and the plethora of racial references are scattered into a multiple variance of words. The motive for change emerges from the context of Gilpin's career as an African American actor during the Harlem Renaissance. As Gilpin saw it, the play was not racial, and therefore not offensive. In order to support his claim, he needed to undermine the play's racial tendencies. The word "nigger" takes on a one-dimensional reference; fragmenting the singular word into several words is one way of shifting emphasis to a more ubiquitous meaning.

    The view that Gilpin diminished the use of the term "nigger" because he felt it would improve the image of the African American is based on the reasonable conjecture that he was motivated out of a sense of loyalty to his race. If he desired to conform to perceptions advocated by black intellectuals and social critics at that time, he may have believed that altering the text of the play would help to shape the image of African Americans into an acceptable representation. After making the O'Neill play a success, Gilpin found himself in the precarious position of presenting an unfavorable image of blacks to predominantly white audiences. The identity of Brutus Jones as a representative of African Americans might have been at odds with the identity Gilpin wanted to convey, either about blacks in general or himself specifically. This created a tension within the actor between the text as written and the desire to represent his race in a positive fashion. By representing Brutus Jones as complex, Gilpin may be said to have deflected the racial controversy, at least by implication. It is safe to say, moreover, that his drinking was probably related to the tightrope he walked as a "race man" trying to avoid any appearance of betrayal, and a "Negro actor" in a role that indeed stressed pejorative racial characteristics.

The second reason for change may be found in the use of language itself. It can be argued that the rhetorical use of a single word "nigger" in *The Emperor Jones* to define blacks tends toward hegemony and closure. In "Discourse in the Novel," literary critic and philosopher Mikhail Bakhtin maintains that the centripetal element in linguistics "gives expression to forces working toward concrete verbal and ideological unification and centralization"; these forces develop "sociopolitical and cultural centralization," which lead to a control of group identity and the expression of this identity through language. For Bakhtin, the reduction of language to a controlling common denominator (represented in *The Emperor Jones* by "nigger") attempts to supplant, enslave, and incorporate "barbarians and lower social strata into a unitary language of culture and truth, the canonization of ideological systems," and is "directed away from language plurality to a single proto-language." The other force in language, the centrifugal, refuses this unifying principle by operating in what Bakhtin calls "the midst of heteroglossia," or social diversity of speech.[58] It is suggested here that Gilpin's splintering of self-referentiality into a triadic unit of words works in a Bakhtin-like manner to subvert the project of centralizing and unifying identity through language. This is, of course, a speculation, but one that deserves closer analysis.

It is possible to consider Gilpin's liberties with the text as a contest between the actor's agenda and the playwright's language. According to Toni Morrison, the "most valuable point of entry into the question of cultural or racial distinction, the one most fraught, is its language—its unpoliced, seditious, confrontational, manipulative, inventive, disruptive, masked and unmasking language."[59] Language as a site of confrontation between the writer's and the actor's conflicting agencies might provide us with a basis for analysis that heretofore has been unacknowledged. We know that language played a significant role in the emerging consciousness of the New Negro during the Harlem Renaissance. As Henry Louis Gates, Jr., observed, black Americans, denied access to literacy and the tools of citizenry, "published their individual histories in astonishing numbers, in a larger attempt to narrate the collective history of 'the race.'" If black identity "could not exist before the law," Gates observes, "it could, and would, be forged in language."[60] Charles Gilpin was not primarily a writer, despite having written three unsuccessful plays.[61] Instead, he used his pulpit as an actor to convey his message. He forged his political agency through characterization, performance, and language, and one of the most important facets of Gilpin's theatrical skills was the use of his voice within the context of African American oral tradition.

Gilpin had a remarkably resonant voice. Heywood Broun wrote in the *New York Tribune* that Gilpin sustained the intensity of the play "not only because his voice is one of a gorgeous natural quality, but because he knows just what to do with it. All the notes are there."[62] The *St. Louis Post-Dispatch* reported that Gilpin "rose his singularly rich and musical voice, almost like a disembodied sound. . . . The effect was almost that of a recital, in which the organ-like baritone should set itself to run the whole gamut of emotions."[63] *Vogue* added that throughout the play, Gilpin "develops the character of Jones with the surest sort of artistry. His voice is beautiful, so beautiful that it carries the burden of what is practically one long soliloquy as not more than two or three actors in America could do it."[64] Another reviewer claimed that with "his emotional fervor" and the "rich, deeply modulated voice of his race, Gilpin has also the technical equipment to hold spell-bound sophisticated audiences through the light scenes that are practically one long monologue." Gilpin, the reviewer adds, "touches the heart with pity and fear."[65] Dick Meade of the *Toledo Blade* asserted that "with a mellifluous voice of singing melody that carried the characteristic inflection of his race, a voice that resounds with the vibrant baritone of the Congo swamps, the weary plaint of the galley, the sob of the auction block, Gilpin rose to great heights in 'The Emperor Jones' and gave the most interesting performance we have observed in Toledo this winter."[66] According to Gilbert Seldes of the *Boston Evening Transcript*, Gilpin had a

> voice of color, depth, timbre, perfectly in control . . . a sense of character—of the character—and a capacity to project the character; a delicacy, an intelligence at work; a capacity for sustaining illusion and an incredible modesty. I do not know many actors who can reveal so much in one play, nor many attributes of a great actor which this list emits.[67]

By employing alternating words to express his identity, words that resonated off each other throughout the play, Gilpin used his voice to establish a distinctive rhythmic cadence into the role. This variation of self-referentiality (alternative words to mark his character's identity) created a musical contrapuntal orality, what cultural historian Lawrence W. Levine calls the blues emphasis "upon improvisation, its retention of the call and response pattern, its polyrhythmic effects, and its methods of vocal production which included slides, slurs, vocal leaps, and the use of falsetto," which asserts "central elements of communal musical style."[68] By using a triadic framework for individuality ("black baby," "Negro," and "colored man"), the actor created a mosaic of language cognizant of "signifyin(g)," which is, according to Henry Louis Gates's definition, "a mode of formal revision, [which] depends for its effects on troping," is frequently "characterized by pastiche," and, most importantly, is a linguistic game that "turns on repetition of formal structures and their differences."[69] Gilpin created a pastiche of words referring to African Americans and utilized inversion of formal structures ("nigger" with other implications) to diversify meaning and undermine singular, fixed definitions. Having a voice of skill and dexterity, Gilpin may be said to have endowed his performance with elements of oral tradition, reflecting not only the blues and signifyin(g), but also a trope that marked a sense of distinction from the rest of the cast. Using one word, *nigger,* throughout the play would have limited his efforts to produce differing sounds that might add to the complexity of his characterization.

It is worth repeating Gilpin's comment in the *Cincinnati Times Star:* "My understanding of the character has developed as I have worked with it and new meanings are constantly unfolding. Mr. O'Neill has been very kind in this respect, giving me the liberty of changing the lines to suit the characterization."[70] "New meanings" suggest that Gilpin was continually reinventing the role, implementing new interpretations and gestures, as well as new language. As an actor, Gilpin appears to have rejected a fixed performance in favor of a more flexible, improvisatory approach. It would not be extreme to imply that Gilpin's interpretation anticipates a great deal of what passes for contemporary postmodern performance, or what theatre historian Deborah R. Geis calls the postmodern impulse "to fracture, or deconstruct, the 'masterpiece.'" African American oral tradition resides not in predetermined representation but, rather, in its call-and-response patterns, which in turn requires a "fracturing of the masterpiece" in performance. In theatre this means, in postmodern terms, "an emphasis on the performance moment (the moment at which the audience 'receives' the play; its corresponding act of 'readership') over the text."[71] Gilpin, trained in the black theatre, incorporated African American theatrical orality and stylistic musicality into the role, with an emphasis on improvisatory style over fixity. It is therefore reasonable to assume that Gilpin worked within the traditions of slave songs, which were often fluid, improvisatory, and adaptable. The conflict that eventually surfaced between O'Neill and Gilpin may have arisen from their differing outlooks: O'Neill's expressionistic text-based approach with an emphasis on fixed performances was at odds with Gilpin's improvisational performance technique stressing rupture, spontaneity, and discontinuity.

Finally, I submit that Gilpin changed not only the text, but reinterpreted the role through his skills at complex characterization. For a quarter century before *The Emperor Jones,* Gilpin was recognized in black theatre circles as "the well-known character actor."[72] Walton, reviewing Gilpin's 1916 performance in white-face makeup as the slave owner, Jacob McClosky, in Dion Boucicault's melodrama, *The Octoroon*, noted in the *New York Age* that the actor "so cleverly makes up that he resembles the slave owner of days gone by to a remarkable degree. . . . The best compliment to members of the cast for their fine make-up is paid by their friends, who at first are unable to determine who he was."[73] Gilpin was a superb character actor who used the play to demonstrate his talent. No doubt Gilpin's flaunting of his skills was at odds with the purpose of the play. Such behavior can be deemed undisciplined and selfish. But we must keep in mind that Gilpin, realizing that few if any opportunities to play new roles would materialize, had to make the best of his situation. His opportunity to develop a range of acting roles would have to come within the role of Brutus Jones alone, the role he was destined to play for the rest of his life. Some might condemn this display of egoism; but in the context of Gilpin's world, judgment must include the needs of the actor and the limits of his professional career.

Gilpin's remark quoted at the beginning of this chapter, that he "created the role," offers a significant clue to the actor's outlook. His attempt to decode the text according to his ideas of the role may be owing to his belief that he was better suited to interpret the nuances of Brutus Jones than the playwright. Based on his notion that the role "belonged to him," there is reason to believe that throughout the run of *The Emperor Jones*, Gilpin concurred with reviews that claimed that the play was mediocre except for his presence. Walton wrote that had not "Charles S. Gilpin essayed to appear as Brutus Jones in the season's dramatic success, 'The Emperor Jones,' this play would be slumbering in manuscript, remembered by the Provincetown Players and public as a dramatic potentiality with a meteoric career and now respectfully referred to as 'gone but not forgotten.'"[74] Comparing actors, *New York Times* drama critic Alexander Woollcott noted that "Gilpin continues to give his amazing and unforgettable performance. . . . It is superb acting, and the success of the O'Neill play is so dependent on it that it were better to give . . . 'Samson and Delilah' without [Jacob] Ben-Ami than to attempt 'The Emperor Jones' without Mr. Gilpin."[75] Even after he was dismissed in favor of Paul Robeson in 1924, Gilpin continued to reappear as Brutus Jones in numerous revivals to great acclaim. David Carb believed that despite Robeson's talent, his "Emperor is not so striking as Charles Gilpin's was. It is civilized, conscious, not truly barbaric. It was just that barbaric quality in Gilpin's performance which made it memorable."[76] Gilpin, it seems, captured the visceral qualities necessary to sustain the vital imagery of the role, while simultaneously maintaining a complexity to his characterization.

CONCLUSION

All great actors work in two spheres — the actor's work on himself and
the actor's work on the role.　　　　　　— Lee Strasberg (1957)[77]

Gilpin was a remarkable actor who, like all great actors, conveyed several meanings during performance. The complexity and depth of his performance meant
that he created a three-dimensional characterization complete with subtle contradictions and unpredictability. In addition to changing words, he staked his
claim to the role by adding contradictory elements to diversify the portrayal. According to Helen Bishop of *The Boston Transcript,*

> [o]ne of the many deft touches with which [Gilpin] has built up his characteri-
> zation is the moment, near the end of the first scene, when [Brutus Jones]
> swaggers out of his palace. . . . He whistles. In the written version the author in-
> dicates that the Emperor exits, whistling. . . . [Gilpin] selected an old levee song
> which May Irwin used to sing years ago:
>
> When Ah walks that levee round, round, round;
> When Ah walks that levee round;
> When Ah walks that levee round, round, round,
> Ah'm lookin' for a bully and he cain't be found.[78]

By whistling a "Negro levee song," Gilpin appears to have contradicted his admitted desire to interpret Brutus Jones as universal rather than racial. Contradictions, however, when incorporated into characterization, remain one of the critical
tools of contemporary performance. Bertolt Brecht, whose theories of acting represent for many the foundation of postmodern performance art, wrote that the
"bourgeois theatre's performances always aim at smoothing over contradictions, at
creating false harmony, at idealization. Conditions are reported as if they could not
be otherwise. . . . None of this is like reality, so a realistic theatre must give it up."[79]
Gilpin upset conventional notions of what African Americans were supposed to be.
Theatre historian Ronald Wainscott calls attention to Gilpin's contradictions and
aspects of the trickster in his performance. In the midst of all Gilpin's intensity,
"there must have lurked a wry sense of humor, because in several production photographs one can discern Gilpin wearing a belt buckle bearing the initials 'CSA,' a
relic from a military uniform of the Confederate States of America."[80] Gilpin, it
seems, was experimenting with the role, adding aperçus into his interpretation.

　　In addition to his creative powers, Gilpin's techniques at characterization
and body control enabled him to supply the role of Brutus Jones with the neces-

sary physicality. One reviewer noted that "Gilpin is short in stature and is not of such huge proportions invariably suggested to the audience when he appears on the stage. His ability to suggest a powerfully built personage when in reality he is about medium height, of a slim frame but graceful, is a remarkable feat."[81] By utilizing contradictions and physical control, Gilpin's theatrical craft embodied elements of unpredictability and spontaneity onstage. In order to sustain interest in what was essentially a 90-minute monologue, Gilpin portrayed contradicting facets of Brutus Jones, delineating a dynamic and visceral portrayal. No performance would be repeated exactly alike; Gilpin maintained an edge by eliciting an inner immediacy. His sustaining appeal as an actor appears to derive not from nineteenth-century melodramatic techniques that emphasized rigid characterization, but from improvisatory skills combined with subtle artistic choices.

Gilpin maintained, above all, that he was an artist. This emphasis on artistry prompted him to take liberties. Although he insisted on being paid for his work, acting for Gilpin was not merely, as Fannin Saffore Belcher suggests in his important 1945 study on African American theatre, "a way to earn a living."[82] During the Drama League controversy, in which many whites attempted to block his place at the award's dinner reception, Gilpin modestly said in the *New York Age:* "I am honestly striving to present my art rather than myself to the public."[83] In another interview, he added, "It does not make any difference to me if they don't like me, Charley Gilpin, personally." Rather, he said, "I want them to look at my work; if it is art, I want them to applaud it, if it is not, then let them condemn it."[84] Acting for Gilpin was his art form, which he believed entitled him to interpret Brutus Jones as he envisioned the role. His physical, imaginative, verbal, and vocal skills contributed to the continuing complexity and inner power of his performance. "He has the artistry," wrote one reviewer, "to return to the scene after each intermission, and to grasp and hold the emotional values of the part unerringly."[85]

The above speculations contextualize Gilpin's acting and assume, moreover, that he had aesthetic as well as cultural motives underlying his textual alterations. Because of the paucity of raw data, we must fill in the historical gaps. If we limit our view of Gilpin to the opinion of whites who insisted that his drunkenness was the cause of textual changes, the actor's history will remain narrow. The notion that Gilpin changed his performance merely because of drunkenness ignores the complexity of the actor's world and denies the actor the right to be analyzed based on artistry and cultural awareness. As he said in the *New York Age,* "If my work has the merit of making me remembered for having entertained, instructed and stimulated thought to the slightest degree, I am satisfied. That is all I will ask for my efforts."[86] Despite the lack of recognition, Gilpin was one of America's greatest actors.

"WHAT CONSTITUTES A RACE DRAMA AND HOW MAY WE KNOW IT WHEN WE FIND IT?": THE LITTLE THEATRE MOVEMENT AND THE BLACK PUBLIC SPHERE

Whatever the difficulties of art for the white man, the American Negro has his special burden. The Harlem art of the 1920s shows the strains that he lived under. . . . It attempts to speak with two voices, one from the stage of national culture and the other from the soul of ethnic experience.

—Nathan Irvin Huggins (1971)[1]

INTRODUCTION

If the traditional theatre, then, is now in a rut which affords no room for the one-act play, and if vaudeville is an empty cradle for this branch of dramatic art, where shall we turn? —Walter Prichard Eaton (1917)[2]

By the mid-1920s nearly every major urban center had an African American theatre group. African American professionals and amateurs, especially in Harlem, Chicago, Washington, D.C., and Cleveland, formed theatres and presented plays, musicals, and staged readings. Although black theatres were experiencing what Nellie McKay termed "growing pains,"[3] they retained a small but devoted number of patrons. The rise of the Black Little Theatre Movement from 1918 to 1927 emerged from an urban middle class seeking cultural enrichment and from black actors, playwrights, and directors unable to find work in mainstream theatre. The Black Little Theatre Movement derived its inspiration from a number of sources, including Ireland's Abbey Theatre, Ridgely Torrence's *Three Plays for a Negro Theatre* produced on Broadway in April 1917,[4] Charles Gilpin's success in Eugene O'Neill's *The Emperor Jones,* and a burgeoning little theatre movement in general.

The emergence of community-based African American theatres raised complex questions about the meaning of "black drama." The language used in dramatic texts defined other ethnic theatres; for example, the contours of the Yiddish theatre were rooted in language as well as culture. The Irish theatre was differentiated linguistically and by subject matter, as well as by a national stage.[5] African American theatre, however, presented a more complex situation; issues of authorship, acting, dialect, subject matter, audience, and culture raised serious concerns about the nature and meaning of "race drama." This made it unique. The century-long appearance of white actors "acting black" in blackface exacerbated the problem, as did white minstrel actors claiming to portray blacks "authentically." At the turn of the century, black actors, forced to assume the role created by minstrel caricature, often perpetuated common misconceptions.[6] Much of Harlem Renaissance drama sought ways of reversing this problem.

The new "race" drama required clarification; drama critic Theophilus Lewis, for instance, remarked in 1927 that there "must be a clear understanding of what the term Negro drama means."[7] Lewis was unequivocal, describing "Negro drama" as defined by "the body of plays written by Negro authors."[8] Along similar lines, *Current Opinion*'s 1922 editorial, titled "Why Not a Negro Drama for Negroes By Negroes," concluded, "What is needed seems to be strong, virile plays interpreting Negro life, written by those of color and acted by their excellent players and produced on Broadway or elsewhere."[9] Others saw matters differently, believing that the content of the plays and not the author's race defined "race drama." Drama critic Wallace V. Jackson described Eugene O'Neill as a writer of "Negro dramas" and noted that with "the exception of the 'Emperor Jones' the Negro stage has been given no major role in the great plays by American playwrights."[10]

Social activist Anna Julia Cooper's postcard to Alain Locke, circa mid to late 1920s, typifies the era's uncertainty. Inviting him to her home for a lecture before her guests, Cooper requested that Locke *"tell us just what constitutes a race drama and how we may know it when we find it"* (emphasis added).[11] The goal of this chapter will be to examine the issues raised by Cooper's inquiry. If the post–World War I decade (1918 to 1927) failed to produce enduring African American dramas, it nonetheless initiated debates over the meaning of "race drama," which remain relevant to present-day theatre.

The Black Little Theatre Movement was hardly insulated from the Roaring Twenties, Prohibition, the rising popularity of jazz, economic growth, and emerging isolationism. An enthusiasm for things new was combined with post-war exhaustion, the latter prompting economist John Maynard Keynes to remark in 1920 that his generation had moved "beyond endurance, and needs rest."[12] The so-called lost generation, a term popularized by Gertrude Stein, characterized the period's disillusionment. Although new technology was everywhere, the world, as American historian Warren Susman observes, "found itself unable to cope easily with the vast quantities of differing kinds of knowledge with which it was presented."[13] Amidst a surging economy and exuberant nightlife, the arts yoked the beginnings of an avant-garde movement. Fads came and went, tradition gave way to changing fashion, and novelty wore off quickly. According to economics historian Morrell Heald, the 1920s has come into focus not merely as "an era of rampant materialism, reaction and individualism," but also as "a troubled decade in which old and new were inextricably intermingled and confronted."[14] The rise of religious fundamentalism, xenophobia, and the "red scare" of communism (culminating in the 1921 Sacco and Vanzetti trial, appeal, and execution in 1927) added to the anxiety and a sense of impending disorder.[15] Many were elated by rapid changes, but others were restless.

In theatre, large-scale, "Broadway style" productions—on Broadway itself and in the touring companies that they spawned—created what theatre historian Glenn Hughes described as a theatre "dominated by commercialism."[16] However, many were openly opposed to Broadway's crass commercialism and superficial melodramas. Satirist H. L. Mencken was one among them; in 1911 he set the tone with the following observation: "Why waste a whole evening, once or twice a week, in a stuffy and over-red theater, breathing zymotic air, sniffing discordant perfumery, looking at idiotic scenery, listening to the bleeding English of ignorant and preposterous actors?"[17] Such discontent led to the establishment of experimental theatres. Dubbed the "Little Theatre Movement," actors, playwrights, and directors formed an alliance in opposition to influential producers, particularly the Frohman, Klaw and Erlanger, and Shubert organizations.[18] Many believed that these producers suppressed creativity by grinding out formulaic dramas, producing spectacle but little appreciable substance. The founder of the Provincetown Players in Greenwich Village, George Cram "Jig" Cook, made the movement's intentions clear: "We have no ambition to go up-town and become 'a real theater.'" Instead, he said, "we have a theater because we want to do our own thing in our own way" and that "hard work done in the play spirit has a freshness not found in the theater which has become a business."[19] Cook was representative of a movement influenced by European art, Freudian psychology, James Joyce's literary stream of consciousness, and the Irish Abbey and the Moscow Art theatres.[20] Many American theatre groups so inspired created small-scale one-acts. These intimate plays, whose running times were often less than one hour, expressed the potency and depth of the short dramatic form.

Experimentation in costume, lighting, and new acting styles ensured psychology and detailed characterizations. The bohemian atmosphere of New York's Greenwich Village and the new aesthetics (surrealism, futurism, dadaism, and expressionism, for instance) contributed to the era's counter-culture. This new theatrical spirit, observes cultural historian Adele Heller, took hold of "the imagination of young rebels who were dissatisfied with Broadway, anxious to experiment with their own new forms, and eager to present their native stage plays that dealt realistically with social problems, the arts, politics, and sexual mores."[21] Amid the cultural upheaval appeared numerous production companies worthy of attention, including: Provincetown Players, Neighborhood Playhouse, and Washington Square Players in New York, and Maurice Browne's "Temple of Art" in Chicago (also known as the Chicago Little Theatre).[22] The creation of Actors Equity in 1913, the rise of ethnic theatres, and George Pierce Baker's University Theatre program, first at Harvard and then at Yale, added to the era's sense of change. Technological innovations followed, including those of Adolph Appiah, Gordon Craig, and Robert Edmond Jones in lighting and set design, and new staging techniques influenced by Max Reinhardt. New drama critics such as George Jean Nathan, Alexander Woollcott, Stark Young, Brooks Atkinson, and Heywood Broun were beginning to assert themselves. Encouraged by Eugene O'Neill and his experimental dramas, these critics assisted in the creation of a new style of play analysis, incorporating detailed criticisms of playwriting, acting, directing, and scenery. In his 1914 book, *The New Movement in the Theatre*, Sheldon Cheney extolled the virtues of the Little Theatre Movement's manifesto when he wrote that Little Theatre playwrights, actors, and directors were "stripping the theatre production of all sensational incident, of all those details that are interesting but unimportant, and of all the old insincere adjuncts of plot, acting and setting." In place of old melodramas, dramatic narratives appeared draped "with imaginative beauty, making it emotionally appealing, and adding to it a social significance."[23] It was within this ambience of rejuvenation that the Black Little Theatre Movement made its presence felt.

Conveying the reality of the black experience was the principal goal of black theatre and drama. New Negro playwrights and the theatres that produced their plays sought liberation from a stultifying minstrel past.[24] The "old" represented the docile, compliant, banjo-playing "Negro." The "new" represented confidence and self-reliance. This division of old and new gave rise to the portrayal of black people as complex human beings and not just minstrel buffoons. Inspired by the Negro Players's (sometimes called the Hapgood Players) production of Ridgely Torrence's *Three Plays for a Negro Theater* in 1917, W. E. B. Du Bois wrote that in the coming years "the present spiritual production in the souls of black folk is going to give to the American stage a drama that will lift it above silly songs and leg shows."[25] Drama held the potential of a new perspective and an indigenous art form. In his 1925 essay, "Growth of the Negro Theatre," Eric Walrond (1898–1966) identified this potential when he noted that "in Negro dramatic art" there were emerging "young unheralded playwrights, critics, actors and actresses," creating a theatre that is "dazzlingly Negroid."[26] In 1926, Theophilus Lewis (1895–1974), the *Messenger's* principal drama critic from 1923 to 1927 and one of the foremost critics of the mid-1920s, declared that drama, "more than any other art form except the novel embodies the whole spiritual life of a people."[27] Similarly, Montgomery Gregory (1887–1971), cofounder (with Locke) of the Howard Players, urged the development of a "National Negro Theater" where "the Negro playwright, musician, actor, dancer, and artist in concert shall fashion a drama that will merit the respect and admiration of America." The implementation of a "Negro theatre," he declared, "must come from the Negro himself, as he alone can truly express the soul of his people."[28] New theatres included Anita Bush's Lafayette Theatre, the Lincoln Theatre, the Hapgood Players, the Krigwa Little Theatre, the Acme Players, and the Sekondi Players (later changed to the New Negro Art Theatre in 1927), all of Harlem; the Krigwa Theatre and the Howard Players of Washington, D.C.; the Pekin Players and the National Ethiopian Art Theatre of Chicago; the Gilpin Players of Karamu House in Cleveland; the Dunbar Dramatic Club of Plainfield, New Jersey; the Dunbar Players of Philadelphia; the Maud Coney Hare Players of Boston; and the Dixwell Players of New Haven, Connecticut.[29] In his essay, "The Harlem Little Theatre Movement," John G. Monroe surmised that while no "continuously active, long-lived little theatre group" emerged in the 1920s, all the significant groups that did appear "produced plays by black playwrights, focused most of their energies toward the black community, and worked mostly *within* the black community."[30]

Even the most optimistic supporter realized, however, that African American theatre during the time was not entirely successful. Critics were disappointed by a lack of playwrights, unsophisticated audiences, and inadequate actor training. Theophilus Lewis noted that at no time during the 1921–1922 theatre season was there "a single theatre in the United States solely devoted to the production of serious drama by or for Aframericans." Lewis believed the reasons were financial: "there is not enough money in the Negro's craving and genius for the legitimate theatre arts to make it profitable." Without economic backing, playwrights and actors were excessively preoccupied with making a living to devote any time "exclusively" to the "satisfaction and expression" of African American drama.[31] Lewis was a stalwart supporter of black dramatists who believed that drama "is the precious life blood of the theater." However, he could not hide his disappointment, saying, "Negro theater has made only puny and abortive attempts to encourage drama."[32] He insisted that a canon of serious black drama was sorely needed. Critical of Broadway musicals and Harlem nightlife, Lewis wrote in 1925 that African Americans "seize every opportunity to indulge in social dancing" and that African American theatre audiences "seem never to tire of fast hoofing." However, he had hoped that "the Negro's aptitude for the stricter theatre arts, so generally taken for granted, ought to manifest itself in a similar urge for expression."[33]

Disappointingly, a large-scale groundswell of support for African American drama failed to materialize. This failure was due in part to a feeling among many well-intentioned middle-class African Americans that theatre meant minstrelsy and was therefore to be shunned. There seemed, at the time, much to encourage this impression; Broadway musicals were exploiting "Negro primitivism" and Harlem's fast-paced nightclubs were attracting a mix of unsavory characters and whites looking to do some uptown slumming. In 1923, the front page of the *New York Age* referred to Harlem as the "Hooch-Seller's Paradise," where gin and narcotics were sought by whites and blacks looking for speakeasies and "home-brews."[34] Moreover, white patrons and investors hesitated to support experimental productions. There was simply no guarantee that plays, however good, would attract sufficient audiences. This lack of support had an unfortunate result, undercutting opportunities for improvement. In a 1920 essay worth quoting at length, the performer and director Salem Tutt Whitney (1868–1934) clarified the situation in detail:

> We are necessarily breadwinners, we must produce and sell according to demand, and just now there is not sufficient demand or a large enough market for the Negro drama to make its productions a paying proposition. . . . Managers of white theatres could not be induced to play a Negro drama as a regular attraction, and a four or eight weeks' season would not prove alluring to the players. . . . Managers of colored shows are now dependent upon white managers of white theatres for most of their bookings . . . naturally the white companies get the preference and the colored companies must take what is left wherever and whenever they can get it. . . . Now is the time for colored capitalists to act. . . .

Give us the theatres and we will give you the shows. Not only the first-class vaudeville and high-class musical comedy, but the legitimate Negro drama.[35]

Black critics themselves questioned the seriousness of black audiences. In 1925, Romeo Dougherty, drama critic for the *Amsterdam News,* called for "an intensive campaign" by the Lafayette Theatre "to reach the better class of colored people."[36] In an editorial, the *Messenger* asked in 1925, "*Do Negroes Want High Class Anything?*" The editorial was of the opinion that African Americans, as patrons of the arts, "are bored by the opera, while most classical dramas lull them to sleep like chloroform."[37] W. E. B. Du Bois was no less harsh: "We are appreciative people," he wrote in 1916, "but our appreciation need not take the form of loud ejaculations and guffaws of laughter, particularly when the laughter breaks out in the wrong place."[38] Dramatist Eulalie Spence saw matters as being even worse, remarking that African American drama was "from twenty to thirty years behind the novel and short story." She went on to single out black dramatists, saying that they "have failed to reach a larger and more discriminating public."[39]

The acting, too, was criticized. The renowned Paul Robeson (1898–1976)—actor, singer, scholar, athlete, lawyer, and Charles Gilpin's replacement in *The Emperor Jones* in 1924—had gained much attention by the mid-1920s. His portrayal of Brutus Jones won praise, as did his performances in Eugene O'Neill's *All God's Chillin Got Wings* (1924), Ned Bagby Stephens's *Roseanne* (1924),[40] and Frank Dazey and Jim Tully's *Black Boy* (1926). In a 1927 interview, he went so far as to say that his thespian peers lacked "imagination" because they had not "had enough training."[41] Despite several attempts to start training programs,[42] black actors typically and unfortunately learned their craft haphazardly. Criticizing African American theatre, Theophilus Lewis wrote that the "low-comedy stage," with its "most gifted actors" devoted to the portrayal of misfits, might at least "develop" their comedic skills into a "very high degree of excellence." Unfortunately, Lewis found that even the rollicking vaudevilles and musical comedies were devoid of training.[43] Black critics found that plays written by whites also fell short of the mark. Lewis, one of the sternest critics, condemned white dramatists for presenting "bogus" and "hokum" productions that "pretend to be plays of Negro life." Despite the fact that "white playwrights know very little about the way Negroes live and the white public knows even less," plays such as David Belasco's *Lulu Belle* (1926; co-authored by Charles MacArthur and Edward Sheldon), Paul Green's *In Abraham's Bosom* (1926), and Em Jo Basshe's *Earth* (1927) would be acclaimed by critics as "Negro drama." White critics, Lewis concluded, "are going to keep calling them 'Negro' drama until Negro playwrights learn to write Negro plays for Negro actors to act before Negro audiences."[44]

The paucity of African American dramatists was the primary cause for concern. In 1925, Eugene O'Neill wrote an open letter to socialist labor leader and editor of the *Messenger*, A. Philip Randolph, asking: "where are your playwrights?"[45] The *Messenger*'s first drama critic, Lovett Fort-Whiteman, also complained that the "Negro dramatic stage can hardly be said to exist." The reason, he argued, was "due almost wholly to a dearth of Negro playwrights; dramatists who may be able to strike a trenchant truth and give honest and artistic reflection to Negro life and manners."[46] Many of the playwrights, while talented, were not mastering their craft. Practicing playwrights needed actors and theatres; yet without financial support for rehearsals and tryouts, and an audience to test the plays, playwrights were denied the required experience. Consequently, many of the era's dramas yielded soporific melodrama and formulaic plot devices that disappointed spectators and provoked negative criticism. Despite critic Randolph Edmonds's hopeful declaration in 1930 that there was "drama in Negro life,"[47] African American theatre for many would remain far from satisfactory.

RACE DRAMA, NATION BUILDING, AND THE BLACK PUBLIC SPHERE

The idea of a subaltern public sphere highlights the problem of understanding how specific power arrangements shape and reshape the discursive spaces within which social groups interpret their needs, invent their identities and collectively formulate their political commitments.

— Steven Gregory (1995)[48]

No single definition of "race drama" has been more influential than the one offered by W. E. B. Du Bois. Referring to his Krigwa Little Theatre and the burgeoning interest in the "Negro Little Theatre Movement" in general, Du Bois remarked in 1926 that the movement was in need of "guiding lights." According to Du Bois, a few "excellent groups of colored amateurs" existed; however, these groups missed "the real path." "Negro Theatre" must, in his words, follow "four fundamental principles":

1. *About us.* That is, they must have plots which reveal Negro life as it is. 2. *By us.* That is, they must be written by Negro authors who understand from birth and continual association just what it means to be a Negro today. 3. *For us.* That is, the theatre must cater primarily to Negro audiences and be supported by their entertainment and approval. 4. *Near us.* The theatre must be in a Negro neighborhood near the mass of ordinary Negro people.[49]

Curiously, in a program note for the opening of the Krigwa Players' "Little Negro Theatre," Du Bois modified his position, inviting contributions without regard to race. In "High Harlem," he said, "Little Theatre" should serve "primarily Negro actors before Negro audiences [to] interpret Negro life as depicted by Negro artists." However, his "Negro Theatre" would also welcome "all artists of all races and for all sympathetic comers and for all beautiful ideas."[50] Despite this, Du Bois's notion of "about us, by us, for us, and near us" remained his dominant theme. Before analyzing this and other observations by Du Bois, the term "us" is in need of clarification. Du Bois's definition can be understood in terms of the rise of the "black public sphere."

The "black public sphere" refers to the post–World War I urban, primarily (though not exclusively) bourgeois class, which had developed public forums devoted to the timely issues of race, drama, literature, art, and culture. The participants were educated "world citizens" who utilized newspapers, journals, theatres, lectures, libraries, coffee houses, and public meeting places as centers for public debate. Plays served as one of many subject matters for discussions pertaining to "Negro" identity and racial solidarity. Encouraged by the northern migration, urban-educated African Americans had begun to redefine themselves, their culture, and their tastes. Black migrants escaped from the South in the hopes of finding a more tolerant and prosperous environment; when they learned that racial privilege knew no Mason-Dixon line, they sought new ways of achieving their goals. African Americans began to challenge the forces that contributed to perpetuating their predicament. In his 1925 essay, "Color Line," Walter F. White effectively addressed the situation:

> There are here [in New York City] many whites . . . whose minds have indelibly fixed upon them the stereotype of a Negro who is either a buffoon or a degenerate beast or a subservient lackey. From these the Negro knows he is ever in danger of insult or injury. Upon most the acquisition of education and culture, of wealth and sensitiveness causes a figurative and literal withdrawal . . . from all contacts with the outside world where unpleasant situations may arise. This naturally means the development of an intensive Negro culture and a definitely bounded city within a city.[51]

These developments signaled change, reflecting what Jürgen Habermas has since described as the "structural transformation of the public sphere."[52]

Habermas defines the "public sphere" as a forum in which private individuals come together to form "public opinion."[53] The public sphere, he explains, is both "the world of the man of letters" as well as the "*salons* in which 'mixed companies' [engage] in critical discussions."[54] The underlying purpose of public consolidation and reflection is to engage in rational discourse over law, labor, social life, taste, and art. In the black public sphere of the Harlem Renaissance, reaction to the Ku Klux Klan, the persistence of lynchings, the hardening of Jim Crow segregation, and the lack of economic opportunities amid increasing wealth created a black "public opinion" that challenged the status quo. For example, Hubert H. Harrison argued in 1920 that although the nation had returned from a "war to make the world 'safe for democracy,'" the "Negro's contention in the court of public opinion is that until this nation itself is made safe for twelve million of its subjects," African Americans "will refuse to believe the democratic assertions of the country." Black people, Harrison added, "are suspicious of everything that comes from the white people of America," because "every movement for the extension of democracy here has broken down as soon as it reached the color line."[55]

The public sphere is the designated communal space where self-formation and public rhetoric create a network of identity through social action; a site for the production and circulation of competing discussion rather than formal state proclamations; and a place for deliberation and rational communication. Such was the case with the "New Negro" Renaissance. Through newspapers, journals, theatres, salons, and meeting halls, the black public sphere asserted its identity and articulated its opposition to racism. The issues at stake were practical and theoretical, often posed at the level of how to produce an "authentic" Negro drama. The rise of the black urban public sphere coincides with the emergence of black theatre and drama, and understanding one requires an understanding of the other.

When Habermas asserts that in modern society rational discourse and consensus are the keys to solving problems through procedures suitably dealing with civic responsibility, he strikes a chord with the New Negro Renaissance. The 1919 report of the National Association for the Advancement of Colored People (NAACP) maintained that the association was striving "to become so strong in number and so effective in method" that no white institution "will dare commit any indignity against colored people without realizing that the legitimate and constitutional rights of the race will be defended in the press, on the platform, at the ballot box and in the courts."[56] African Americans, denied access to power, engaged in internal activity related to consensus building and legitimization. In a 1923 editorial, the *New York Age* remarked, "The need for a real constructive program in building up racial solidarity is . . . insisted upon as a vital necessity." Prejudice and discrimination, the editorial added, "have driven the members of the race to combine in order to serve their special interests in business and other relations in life."[57] The purpose of consensus building was to locate an effective mode of group solidarity by communication that might facilitate African American unity. The black community offered various forms of communicative acts such as performance (parades, sports, dance, church, music, and theatre) and publications (newspapers, novels, poetry, and drama), which increased significantly during the period.

To Habermas, newspapers were the most important public forums during the Enlightenment. The same can be said of the Harlem Renaissance. James De Jongh notes that the number of black newspapers in New York City alone "had doubled between 1912 and 1921," conveying "black nationalist, communist, and socialist ideologies (as well as more conservative philosophies) across a wide political spectrum to a mass readership."[58] In 1926, Eugene Gordon reported that 87 newspapers across the nation were members of the Associated Negro Press.[59] In addition to the regularly circulating black newspapers such as the *New York Age*, *New York Amsterdam News*, *Indianapolis Freeman*, *Pittsburgh Courier*, *Baltimore Afro-American* (*Afro-American Ledger* prior to 1915), *Chicago Defender*, *Chicago Broad Ax*, *Chicago Whip*, Garvey's *Negro World*, Virginia's *Norfolk Journal and Guide*, and *Washington Bee*, four major magazines were published during the period. W. E. B. Du Bois's *Crisis*, which began in 1910, maintained a circulation of one hundred thousand by 1920. In addition, Carter Woodson's *The Journal of Negro History*, beginning in 1916; A. Philip Randolph and Chandler Owen's socialist journal, the *Messenger*, beginning in 1917; and the Urban League journal, *Opportunity*, beginning in 1923, and edited by Charles S. Johnson, all contributed to the expansion of magazines. In his 1928 essay, "The Rise of the Negro Magazine," Johnson reported that "increasing literacy, economic improvement, and the shifting facets of such general social questions as temperance, religion and morals," had enhanced the popularity of the African American press.[60] Indeed, this was the "golden age" of black newspapers and magazines, inspiring readers to engage in an enlightened exchange of ideas. African Americans at the time were better educated and had greater access to the media, both black and white, than before. Social and political clubs as well as churches flourished along with Harlem's nightlife. Churches, in particular, observes historian and social critic John Hope Franklin, became an "important agency for maintaining group cohesion and rendering self-help."[61] Reading salons, such as Georgia Douglas Johnson's literary group in Washington, D. C., inspired broad discussion. The black community was experiencing an information revolution.

Nevertheless, comparisons between Habermas's view of the European Enlightenment and the New Negro Renaissance of the 1920s, however tempting, must be made with considerable care. Western, European Enlightenment and New Negro Renaissance cultures differed in time and place; moreover, the fact of race, while paramount for New Negroism, was of little significance to events leading up to the Enlightenment. Above all, Jim Crow segregation created what St. Clair Drake and Horace R. Cayton called a "black metropolis." At the time, urban blacks patterned their participation in the culture at large just as did other immigrant groups settling in the United States, with one significant difference: African Americans were not absorbed into the general population. As Drake and Cayton make clear, the African American communities remained "athwart the least desirable residential zones." As the population grew larger and larger, it discovered that it was "unable either to expand freely or to scatter."[62] Black communities had to forge their own infrastructure within the boundaries marked out by segregation.

Habermas's view of the public sphere must be amended in order to realize its application to an urban black community. His critics have sought to expand his monolithic conception of the public sphere to include what Oskar Negt and Alexander Kluge have called the "proletarian public sphere." This public sphere is best understood in terms of "horizons of experience," in which the public sphere serves not only professionals, but is also "something that concerns everyone."[63] The public sphere is manifest in theatres, reading societies, and print, as well as in the more humble ambience of city streets, alleyways, and homeless shelters. The black urban public sphere was, to borrow historian Mary Ryan's words, present in a "variegated, decentered, and democratic array of public spaces."[64] Habermas's notion of the liberal bourgeoisie as the "authentic public" is therefore in need of correction. For African Americans, the notion of a bourgeois public sphere is a contradiction in terms; black people's arrival to the new world was not as bourgeois property owners, but as owned property. Their relationship to the public sphere cannot be accommodated in Habermasian terms without being aware of this irony.

Still, the similarities of the New Negro Renaissance and European Enlightenment in respect of new social formations and group solidarities are noteworthy and worth pursuing.[65] The development of the European Enlightenment and New Negro public spheres reveal numerous common traits: both were primarily, though not exclusively, organized by and around the bourgeoisie; both moved from the private realm of rural life to the public realm of the city; both sought self-determination; both were expressed through newspapers, journals, social clubs, theatres, and public spaces; both experienced and induced a social transformation; and both shared in the belief that reason and common sense would lead to social justice. "Negro life," Alain Locke maintained, "is seizing upon its first chances for group expression and self-determination."[66] Within the horizon of black experience circa 1920, African

American performers and writers engaged in what might be described by Habermas as "communicative action."

According to Habermas, "communicative action" is social discourse distinguishable by a speaker who attempts to reach consensus, coordinate action, and advance socialization through understanding.[67] It occurs when two or more people come together seeking consensus through cooperation. This cooperation, Habermas says, "depends on reason," where "rational expressions have the character of meaningful actions, intelligible in their context, through which the actor [i.e., the individual committed to social action] relates to something in the objective world."[68] Habermas's argument is that, in making an assertion backed by an intention and evaluation, we invite counter-arguments; communicative action is then brought about by a tacit agreement that coalesces in "reciprocal understanding, shared knowledge, mutual trust, and accord with one another."[69]

Alain Locke had a similar view of communicative action when in 1927 he said that an "open society" of interracial and intercultural communications makes possible "free and unbiased contacts between the races on the selective basis of common interests and mutual consent," in contrast to the "dictated relations of inequality based on caste psychology and class exploitation."[70] The agenda of the New Negro was to break down barriers, demystify social problems, and build consensual agreement. In 1923, an editorial in the *New York Age* responded to the question, "What does the Negro want," with the following: "He wants exactly what you or any other human being wants. He wants food, comfort, safety, tolerance, education—and as much money as his ability entitles him to."[71] Within the black public sphere, communication between African Americans to African Americans, and blacks to whites, became increasingly important. Written, oral, or performative communication provided venues for expression, consensus, and explication. There was, to a degree, faith in the efficacy of communicative action. Habermas might be viewed as a commentator on these developments when he asserts that the social individual "stands face to face with that situationally relevant segment of the lifeworld that impinges on him as a problem, a problem he must resolve through his own efforts." In this case the problem was racism and a lack of equality. By confronting the problem, the individual "is carried or supported from behind, as it were, by a lifeworld that not only forms the context for the process of reaching understanding but also furnishes resources for it."[72] Shared lifeworld experiences, clarification of problems, and expressions of frustration through public forums, newspapers, art, and theatre, provided the resources necessary for black communication and survival. For Habermas, the basis on which communicative action takes place is "a result of the certainty which the actor feels thanks to proved solidarities and tested competences."[73] The survival of the black community depended on proven solidarities, tested competences, and shared lifeworld resources of a community under siege.

COMMUNICATIVE ACTION AND THE BLACK DRAMATIC CANON

The spirit of a language is thus also the spirit of a nation's literature.
—Johann Gottfried von Herder (1877)[74]

In order to define African American identity in the black public sphere, a literary canon had to be established. Literature, the popular magazine *Opportunity* reported in 1925, "has always been a great liaison between races," offering "emotions" and "brotherhood," which convey cultural relations "both in likenesses and in differences."[75] Black literature and drama would provide a potent symbol of ethnic pride and a meeting ground for public discourse. Writers attended to the idea of the black "folk," a term that came to represent migrating rural black immigrants who become urbanized. As literary scholar J. Martin Favor astutely remarks, in order to "know black culture, the artist or critic must know the folk; folk experience forms the core of the New Negro identity."[76] Yet, the classification of "folk" was complicated by ideas of the "modern"; the folk was considered pre-industrial and expressive of "roots." The modern age emphasized technology *and* primitivism; modernism was a fluid concept that absorbed progressive ideas, while simultaneously being validated by the supposed "primal authenticity" of cultural productivity.

However much black intellectuals and artists attempted to describe black art, literature, and drama in terms of authenticity, they faced twin challenges: the charges made by whites that black authors and actors were inept, and the fact that black cultural output was frequently under the control of white producers and publishers. Theatre raised a number of additional issues, including the presence of black actors in white-authored plays; the question of whether or not to appeal to crossover audiences; and to what extent a play's content should reflect African American values. Such uncertainties added to the polemical debates proliferating over the following questions:

1. Should black writers search for an indigenous form or copy Western standards of drama?
2. Should black playwrights look to folk (i.e., rural) traditions or introduce new, urban themes removed from a rural past?
3. Should black plays use black "dialect" or treat it as a relic of the past?

4. Should black plays concentrate on black themes or universal themes?[77]
5. Should black writers appeal to the mainstream audiences or the black community (or both)?
6. Should black plays glorify African American achievements or create characters who appear neither "good" nor "bad?"[78]

Proponents of a new, authentic black artform and those who defended Western traditions as accurate descriptions of black aesthetics clashed. Langston Hughes, for example, was adamant that black identity had to cast off "whiteness"; for him there was a "mountain standing in the way of any true Negro art in America," exacerbating "the urge within the race toward whiteness." Jazz, in contrast to whiteness, was symbolic of "one of the inherent expressions of Negro life in America: the eternal tom-tom beating in the Negro soul." Conservative George Schuyler saw matters differently. For him, white aesthetics were the correct paradigms; new beginnings were just "hokum." Black art, he remarked, "is identical in kind with the literature, painting and sculpture of white Americans."[79] We see, then, that within the black public sphere itself, communicative action struggled to form consensus and build solidarity.

These complications extended into the fabric of artistic productivity. In 1928, James Weldon Johnson raised the important problem of the "double audience." Segregation had forced theatres not only to separate audiences, but even to create separate theatres. The rise of race dramas and race films (Oscar Micheaux's movies, for instance), in which audiences were divided along racial lines, was commonplace. Johnson realized that black writers often looked to both audiences for sustenance; but it was a "divided audience, an audience made up of two elements with differing and often opposite and antagonistic points of view." This divide forced hard choices: "To whom shall he [the author] address himself, to his own black group or to white America?"[80]

Johnson also called attention to the matter of dialect. The so-called "Negro dialect" came to refer to the "happy-go-lucky, singing, shuffling, banjo-picking being," who was a "more or less pathetic figure."[81] Concentrating on the idea of black "folk," Johnson and his contemporaries wanted to change the locus of the African American from the "log cabin" to the "Harlem flat." In order to effect this transition, some African American authors looked to Irish writers, who, as Johnson said, discovered "a form that will express the racial spirit by symbols from within rather than by symbols from without." This new form, he added, was able to express "the imagery, the idioms, the peculiar turns of thought, and the distinctive humor and pathos" of "the deepest and highest emotions and aspirations." It would also allow for "the widest range of subjects and the widest scope of treatment."[82] Johnson summarized what most critics wanted: up-to-date literature, and an honest and representative vernacular.

The period (1918–1927) was also concerned with identity and self-expression. Historian Rebecca T. Cureau aptly notes that the Harlem Renaissance brought African Americans from the question "Who am I?" to the question "How shall I express who I am?"[83] The identity issue intensified over the phenomena of race mixing. In 1919 the editor of *Negro World*, W. A. Domingo, confronted the one-sixteenth ("one-drop") rule, saying bluntly:

> The Caucasian has said that if a man has one-sixteenth black blood, such a person is black. While this is an absurdity in logic, still it is a fact in practice, hence such a person has no choice but to accept the name given to the black race, a little of whose blood flows in his veins. To do otherwise would be to proclaim a longing to be included in a race that despises him.[84]

During the first quarter of 1920, the *New York Age* ran a symposium, titled "New Negro—What Is He?" The symposium, in the form of letters that ran intermittently from January through March, gathered opinions from writers, intellectuals, and ordinary citizens. A particularly salient letter carried the observation that "a class has been gradually built up among Negroes" that "has had no personal contact with the white race." This "New Negro" rejected the past, embraced education, and no long considered whites "as the superior human being of creation."[85] Reacting to the *Age*'s symposium, the *Messenger*, in an editorial similarly titled "The New Negro—What Is He?," reported that the "New Negro" must assert "education and physical action in self defense." The editorial went on to counsel African Americans to cast aside the "doctrine of non-resistance" and support "self determination."[86] In 1926, *Crisis* ran its own symposium, titled, "The Negro in Art: How Shall He Be Portrayed?" Questions were sent out to various literary figures. They revealed a great deal about the period and how the editor, W. E. B. Du Bois, sought to define African American identity. Du Bois asked the following questions: Are African American artists obliged to create black characters?; Can they be criticized for showing the best or worst in African Americans?; Can publishers be condemned for refusing to publish works that portray African Americans of distinction?; What should African Americans do in the face of demeaning depictions?; Should educated African Americans be portrayed sympathetically?; Is the ongoing portrayal of African Americans as criminals accurate?; Are young writers tempted to follow popular trends by portraying underworld characters?; And, most fundamentally, how shall African Americans be "authentically" portrayed?[87]

From 1918 to 1927, the term "authentic" meant a new black person in opposition to the Sambo-Coon-Aunt Jemima stereotypes of the past. "Authenticity" was a term intended to convey an effort to cleanse the stain of minstrelsy. Authenticity would challenge minstrelsy's claim to the "real," with black people themselves creating the truly authentic image. Artists and performers were keenly aware of the continuing redefinition of African American identity, with the question of authenticity becoming an internal as well as interracial issue.[88] In his essay, "Towards a Definition of American Modernism," Daniel Joseph Singal remarks that American modernity at the dawn of the twentieth century demanded an authenticity in the form of "a blending of the conscious and unconscious strata of the mind so that the self presented to the world is the 'true' self in every respect."[89] Black culture at the time was no less influenced by the emphasis on authenticity.

For African American critics, authenticity became crucial. Montgomery Gregory said at the time that the "only avenue of genuine achievement in American drama for the Negro lies in the development of the rich veins of folk-traditions of the past and in the portrayal of *the authentic life of the Negro masses of to-day*" (emphasis added).[90] Harlem Renaissance critics promoted art less for its own sake than as an instrument for depicting reality. It must, then, come as little surprise that in a 1925 editorial titled "On Writing About Negroes," *Opportunity Magazine* asserted that "prose fiction nowadays must carry some conviction of reality."[91] Du Bois, as well, reflected this sentiment in his call for black playwrights to enter his "Krigwa literary contest," which was being sponsored by *Crisis:* "We want especially to stress the fact that while we believe in Negro art we do not believe in any art simply for art's sake." Black writers and playwrights perceived reality as something tangible. "We want the earth beautiful," Du Bois notes, "but we are primarily interested in the earth."[92]

TELLING IT LIKE IT IS: DU BOIS, PROPAGANDA, DRAMA, AND HISTORY

The American Negro must remake his past in order to make his future.
—Arthur A. Schomburg (1925)[93]

In his 1926 essay, "Criteria of Negro Art," Du Bois made the claim that "all art is propaganda and ever must be, despite the wailing of the purists." To drive home his point, he added, "I do not care a damn for any art that is not used for propaganda."[94] In his book, *Color and Culture: Black Writers and the Making of the Modern Intellectual*, Ross Posnock asserts that "art is propaganda" is one of Du Bois's "most quoted yet misunderstood statements."[95] Posnock contends that for Du Bois saying "propaganda in art" is an act of "troping" in which he "radically defamiliarizes propaganda" by elevating its artistic function to the restoration of "beauty" in an "impoverished American culture." This troping, Posnock claims, "mime's arts power to confound classifications, to dissolve identity."[96] Du Bois was indeed seeking to elevate propaganda, but his concerns stressed something other than the dissolution of identity. Rather than confound classification and bolster defamiliarization, as Posnock would have it, propaganda for Du Bois meant defining and elucidating racial identity through facts, truth, and history.

According to Du Bois, propaganda in art must be used to redress the imbalance in the presentation of history. Drama in particular gathers the historical facts and presents them in a lucid, truthful, and creative way. One function of drama is to expose lies. "I am one," he said, "who tells the truth and exposes evil and seeks with Beauty and for Beauty to set the world right." To tell the truth— to tell it like it is—means correcting distortions. Du Bois believed that the art of his time needed to present the truth that had been obfuscated by minstrelsy. Truth had to be offered "with beauty," he said, but beauty had to be created not at the expense of facts, but rather by using facts. Art and beauty hover "above Truth and Right" and together they are "unseparated and inseparable." The efficacy of art resides in its ability to bring African Americans face to face "with our own past as a people."[97] Nothing in art should divert attention from the truth.

For Du Bois, blacks as well as whites must be held accountable for their misrepresentations. In his essay, "The Negro and the American Stage," Du Bois identified a growing "self-consciousness" on the part of African Americans that followed upon their having been "maligned and caricatured and lied about." For a century, he remarked, depictions of blacks had been the "occasion for an ugly picture, a dirty illusion, a nasty comment or a pessimistic forecast." He continued: "the Negro today fears any attempt of the artist to paint Negroes." Not satisfied "unless everything [was] perfect," African Americans were reluctant to reveal "human foibles and shortcomings" that had been used for a different kind of propaganda, described in his terms as "hateful propaganda."[98] Blacks had shielded themselves from the truth because, as he said, they "thought nothing would come out of that past which we wanted to remember." However, he said, the desire to remember and to know African American history "is taking form, color and reality, and in a half shamefaced way we are beginning to be proud of it."[99]

"Criteria of Negro Art" was delivered in late June of 1926 during a banquet ceremony for Carter Godwin Woodson at the Chicago Conference of the National Association for the Advancement of Colored People (NAACP). (The speech was subsequently printed in the October edition of *Crisis*.) Woodson, an influential historian (Harvard Ph.D. in history, 1912) and founder of the *Journal of Negro History* in 1916, was to receive *Crisis's* twelfth annual Spingarn Medal for outstanding service. It has frequently been overlooked that Du Bois was ad-

dressing historians, not artists. He began the speech by explaining why he selected the subject of art for such an occasion. Why, Du Bois asked, should an organization of historians and radicals have any interest in art? His answer: art and
history have identical objectives. Du Bois made clear in his pageant, *The Star of
Ethiopia*, that for him the purpose of art must be to bring history to the people.[100]
In 1925, he staged *The Star of Ethiopia* for the last time in Los Angeles. In his
essay advertising the pageant, "A Negro Art Renaissance," he remarked that
during the last decade, "the world and the American negro have rediscovered
Africa and her marvelous history," a history forgotten "because of the propaganda of slavery and the slave trade."[101] Theatre, he said, must challenge the
minstrel image of buffoonery and the propaganda of slavery by means of true
(authentic) historical representation. Thus, Du Bois's "Criteria of Negro Art"
was part of his larger agenda: to connect art and history.

Du Bois believed that black theatre had not yet been utilized for this purpose. The portrayal of African Americans in theatre had been little more than a
gallery of hoofers and clowns. Laughter and mirth had its place, but the theatre,
he believed, should offer what he termed "justifiable propaganda."[102] This justifiable propaganda would counter "hateful propaganda," creating equilibrium. His
1925 letter to Carl Van Vechten clarified his position; the seamy side of "Negro
life," he wrote, "has been overdone and there is almost no corresponding work
on the other side."[103] The Jazz Age had prompted an interest in one side of black
culture, fixated on the sordid and clownish. Du Bois wanted representations of
another sort:

> We can go on the stage; we can be just as funny as white Americans wish us to
> be; we can play all the sordid parts that Americans like to assign to Negroes; but
> for any thing else there is still small place for us.[104]

Du Bois desired balance in stage representations. Always the dialectical
thinker, he sought to nullify negative stage images with positive ones. In his review of Marc Connelly's *Green Pastures* (1930), Du Bois called attention to this
imbalance when he noted that the "difficulty" with African Americans onstage is
that the white audience demands "caricatures," while the black audience and
performer "either cringes to the demand because he needs the pay, or bitterly
condemns every Negro book or show that does not paint colored folk at their
best." Criticism, he observed, "should be aimed at the incompleteness of the art
expression," noting that a lack of balance denied "a full picturing of the Negro
soul."[105] With mere negative depictions saturating the stage, the full stage picture
was incomplete and in need of correction.

Subordinating art to accurate, historical portrayals enabled Du Bois to induce the proper balance. Building on John Keats's notion that beauty is truth
and truth beauty, Du Bois extended this by claiming that art is beauty, beauty is
truth, and truth is *history set right*. "The apostle of Beauty," he says, "becomes the
apostle of Truth and Right not by choice but by inner and outer compulsion."
Justice is the compulsion that obliges the artist to tell it like it is. African Americans were free, he noted, "but freedom is ever bounded by Truth and Justice."
Art fails to achieve its aims when it is "denied the right to tell the Truth or recognize an ideal of Justice."[106] He draws on DuBose Heyward's 1925 novel *Porgy*,
converted into a play by Dorothy and DuBose Heyward and staged on Broadway in 1927, as an example. Heyward, Du Bois notes, writes "beautifully of the
black Charleston underworld." However, Heyward "cannot do a similar thing
for the white people of Charleston," because if he did, whites "would drum him
out of town." The only possibility for Heyward "to tell the truth of pitiful human
degradation [is] to tell it of colored people." Whites, Du Bois claims, demand
from their artists "racial pre-judgment which deliberately distorts Truth and Justice" and they "will pay for no other" artwork.[107] This situation was in need of
correction; whether from a black or white perspective, history had to be told.
Telling the truth for Du Bois implied a willingness to face facts without bias,
shame, or reservation.

According to Du Bois, history was not a functional arrangement of facts, but
a system that provided meaning and significance to cultural identity. In 1935, he
published his monumental study, *Black Reconstruction in America, 1860–1880*. In this
work, Du Bois examined the history of Reconstruction and criticized false representations constructed by white historians. In the concluding chapter, titled "The
Propaganda of History," he surmised that "unfair caricatures of Negroes have
been carefully preserved," while the "serious speeches, successful administration
and upright characters" were "universally ignored and forgotten." Du Bois
wanted artists and historians to reverse the trend; the "most significant drama in
the last thousand years of human history," he maintained, "is the transportation
of ten million human beings out of the dark beauty of their mother continent into
the new-found Eldorado of the West."[108] Du Bois called for history and drama to
share goals: rewrite history according to the "facts." Through the depiction of fic-
tionalized but accurate episodes, dramatized history, like history itself, could
substantiate how individuals contributed to historical currents.

Perhaps more than anyone of the era, Du Bois opposed the enthusiasm of
"primitivist" art that was all the rage. He was, in sociologist Robert E. Washington's words, a "virtual pit bull" in his tenacious criticism of black and white writers who promoted the vogue of Negro primitivism.[109] Rather than celebrating

works such as *Nigger Heaven* (1926), Carl Van Vechten's paean to "Negro subculture," Du Bois believed that the sensationalization of the exotic was wrongheaded and impeded the progress of civil rights. Du Bois took a hard line against any work that exploited the black masses; for him, the lower classes had to be educated, uplifted, and rehabilitated, not celebrated by romanticizing squalor, poverty, and loose morals. Propaganda, handled correctly, would provide the right vehicle for a new drama and literature offering enlightenment and progress.

Du Bois demanded what his biographer David Levering Lewis calls a hardline "masculinist" approach to propaganda, by which art's social purpose must stress its "civic function."[110] His views on drama developed simultaneously as a reaction against Alain Locke's "effete" aestheticism. Locke, he felt, had succumbed to the idea of a "folksy drama" that was only a mere degree better than the primitivist vogue. However, the disparity between Du Bois and Locke was more about form than content. Du Bois, in fact, sought an idiom much like Locke's "folk drama." While Locke was more tolerant of aestheticism, they were at one with the desire to depict black life realistically, with historical accuracy. Du Bois looked to grand historical narratives; Locke drew from beauty found in the more commonplace. Nevertheless, they shared a belief in the importance of stage realism. Even though Du Bois rejected any art that failed to advance social justice, he believed in drama as an aesthetic form subject to historical accuracy.

For all his insistence on propaganda, Du Bois rejected isolationism. Like Locke, he opposed both unwavering assimilation as well as total separation. Racial differences must be preserved, but not at the expense of interracialism. This aim left Du Bois seeking a dual goal: equality with whites was mandatory, as was the development of a unique black culture. He, like Locke, wanted to preserve African American culture and custom, yet insisted on fair and equitable treatment under the same laws. The emphasis on equality and uniqueness was made clear enough in his practical advice. For him, black actors should follow a threefold approach: perform plays by whites for white audiences; perform plays for the black community; and reveal the painful history of the black experience. He saw a legitimate role for black actors in white theatres, but he also believed in the part actors must play in the black community. Du Bois additionally realized that theatres take time to develop; the emergence of black theatre would take place, he said, only when the "black world gains something of that leisure and detachment for artistic works which every artist must have." At the time, African Americans, as a whole, were too impoverished and distracted "by the grimness of mere living" to appreciate art.[111] But once economic justice took hold, theatre and art would flourish.

By the mid-1920s Du Bois had grown impatient with the black bourgeoisie, who he claimed were "ashamed of sex." The black proletarians also came under his criticism, because he felt they accepted religious superstitions uncritically. For both classes, the "worst side" of black people had been "so shamelessly emphasized that we [were] denying we have or ever had a worst side."[112] He encouraged African Americans to accept reality because there was nothing to fear; art and drama would "lend the whole stern human truth about ourselves to the transforming hand and seeing eye of the Artist, white and black."[113] Urging writers and performers neither to abandon their past nor forget their heritage, he described an unacceptable pattern:

> Just as soon as true Art emerges; just as soon as the black artist appears, someone touches the race on the shoulder and says, "He did that because he was an American, not because he was a Negro; he was born here; he was trained here; he is not a Negro—what is a Negro anyway? He is just human; it is the kind of thing you ought to expect."[114]

By emphasizing history, Du Bois set a precedent in African American drama for realism ("historical truths"). The linguist Roman Jakobson contends that realism is an artistic mode that "aims at conveying reality as closely as possible and strives for maximum verisimilitude."[115] If we juxtapose Du Bois's terms "past" and "truth" with Jakobson's "reality" and "verisimilitude," similarities emerge. However, for Du Bois, "maximum verisimilitude" meant balancing the sordid representation with uplifting images. He wanted a new drama accurately representing the black experience, but he was also pragmatic. Rogues and buffoons had dominated the stage; uplifting images would bring true perspectives for the first time. Since the negative had been explored *ad nauseam,* alternatives would provide steps toward an equalization. The rise of black drama and the Little Theatre Movement reflected this philosophy.

BLACK DRAMA AND THE LITTLE THEATER

[Art] is self-expression and therefore it must be the Negro himself who shall depict in dramatic form his emotions and experiences.
—Montgomery Gregory (1921)[116]

By the early 1920s, many African American actors in New York City, with the notable exception of Bert Williams in the Ziegfeld Follies, looked toward Harlem for employment. Cabarets and playhouses flourished uptown, attracting the talented; but most importantly, Harlem theatre began to emerge. James Weldon Johnson described the 1910s "exile" of black performers from Broadway as the principal cause of Harlem's "real Negro Theatre," a theatre "in which Negro performers played to audiences made up almost wholly of people of their own race."[117] During this period, black theatre explored community issues away from white audiences and the demand to please them. By the 1920s, when white audiences enamored with black music and Harlem's "night life," black performers created new forms—jazz, musicals, dance, and cabarets—to accommodate them. But black actors and playwrights maintained for the most part the Du Boisian aims of a "Negro theatre" by, for, about, and near African Americans.

In 1917, white author Ridgely Torrence's *Three Plays for a Negro Theatre* broke the color line for serious drama on Broadway. Produced by three whites— the playwright Torrence, the designer Robert Edmond Jones, and the socialite Emilie Hapgood—the "Hapgood Colored Players," as they were sometimes called, opened on Broadway in April at the Garden Theatre in New York. This opening, according to James Weldon Johnson, marked "the first time anywhere in the United States" that African American actors commanded "the serious attention of the critics and of the general press and public."[118] Torrence's three one-act plays—*The Rider of Dreams*, *Granny Maumee*, and *Simon, the Cyrenian*—ran one month on Broadway. Lester A. Walton drew attention to the importance of this production when he said, "drama, America and the Negro will greatly profit by this daring and unique move."[119]

Following Torrence's lead, many white writers delved into the psychology of African American life. The success of Eugene O'Neill's *The Dreamy Kid* (1919), which was included in Locke's collection, *Plays of Negro Life* in 1927, led almost immediately to his *Emperor Jones* (1920) and later *All God's Chillun Got Wings* (performed by Paul Robeson in 1924). White authors added their voices in support of a rising interest in "Negro drama": Ernest Culbertson's *Rackey* (1919) and *Goat Alley* (1922), both of which appeared in Locke's *Plays of Negro Life*; Belasco's *Lulu Belle* (1926); and Paul Green's *White Dresses* (1920), *The No 'Count Boy* (1924), and *In Abraham's Bosom* (1926). Nevertheless, the breaking of new ground by white writers addressing black life left many black critics dissatisfied. While the white-authored plays prompted drama critic George Jean Nathan to say in 1929 that "Melodrama and the Negro are cut from the same cloth," Sterling Brown responded to the white-authored dramas by saying that, however much the "colorful romantic spectacle" of these plays shows "something of the grimness of Southern life," they are for the most part "only incidentally realistic."[120] Walton added to this sentiment when he noted in 1928 that Harlem and African Americans had "been misrepresented and maligned by plays and novels."[121] It was felt by many that African American theatres, using their own actors performing in their own plays, would best represent the African American experience.

Notwithstanding the importance of the many African American theatres that appeared from 1918 to 1927, the Lafayette in New York and the Ethiopian Art Theatre in Chicago had the most significant effect. Anita Bush (1883–1974), known as "the Little Mother of Negro Drama," and Lester A. Walton (1892–1965) founded the Lafayette in 1915.[122] Supported by the Quality Amusement Corporation,[123] Walton and Bush succeeded in setting a trend by presenting Broadway dramas to audiences with all-black casts. Walton wrote in 1920:

> It is beginning to dawn on the managers and actor folk on Broadway that something worthy of more than passing consideration to those interested in the drama is taking place weekly at the Lafayette Theatre further uptown. No longer are the Lafayette Players when under discussion along the "rialto" referred to in a jocular manner. . . . Nowadays stage celebrities in goodly numbers are wending their way to Seventh Avenue and 131st St. by limousine to look upon the efforts of these colored thespians with serious eye.[124]

Around 1914, Walton convinced banker and real estate owner Meyer Jarmulowsky to turn over his building for the purpose of establishing a black theatre company.[125] In 1912, John Mulonski built the Lafayette Theater, located between 131st and 132nd Streets on Seventh Avenue in Harlem. With Walton as production manager and Bush as artistic director, several actors took up residence at the theatre and began performing. The Lafayette Players, originally called the Anita Bush Stock Company, officially opened on 27 December 1915 with *Across the Footlights*, starring Bush and Charles Gilpin. The Lafayette, along with the Lincoln Theatre on West 135th Street (a storefront theatre with 297 seats that opened in 1908), catered to black audiences. For more than a decade, the Lafayette produced mostly white-authored plays with all-black casts. The objective of the Lafayette Players, wrote Theophilus Lewis in 1927, "was to present Broadway successes to Negro audiences at popular prices."[126] By 1922, Bush had withdrawn from the company; by 1927, the Lafayette was unable to compete with the rising interest in film. Eventually it was forced to move to Los Angeles and the building in New York began to show movies exclusively. However, the company did enjoy a dozen prosperous years: Lafayette Theatre historian Mary Francesca Thompson said that despite its history of exploitation and mismanagement by white managers and "the public's apathy," the Lafayette Players were "responsible for helping to raise the standards of black entertainment."[127]

Unlike the Lafayette, the Ethiopian Art Theatre of Chicago earned its reputation as a mainstream theatre. Its white producer, Raymond O'Neil, incorporated a group of African American actors in Chicago for the purpose of

establishing a national black theatre company that had the ambitious goal of performing for blacks and whites. By 1923, the Ethiopian Art Theatre (sometimes
called the "Colored Folk Theatre" or the "Negro Folk Theatre") had produced
the medieval drama *Everyman*, Molière's *The Follies of Scapin*, the German expressionist drama *George*, Oscar Wilde's *Salomé*, Shakespeare's *The Taming of the Shrew*
and *The Comedy of Errors* (in a "jazz" style), and Willis Richardson's *The Chip
Woman's Fortune*. In the same year, they came to New York with three shows
from their repertoire: *The Chip Woman's Fortune*, *Salomé*, and *The Comedy of Errors*.
Their plays were first presented at the Lafayette. With only modest success, they
opened on Broadway for two weeks and then returned to the Lafayette before
closing their New York engagement and disbanding entirely.

A great deal of controversy surrounded the Ethiopian Art Theatre. Its brief
history, 1922–1923, revealed a rapid appearance matched by a quick collapse.[128]
Its problems stemmed from internal conflicts within the company and external
problems as well. When the show opened in New York on 7 May 1923, it faced enforced segregated seating at Broadway's Frazee Theatre. The African American
press and many in the audience were given seats in the balcony, but they "flatly refused to occupy them."[129] Eventually the management withdrew segregated seating and the performances continued for two weeks before returning to Harlem.[130]

Problems arose during performances. The Ethiopian Art Players had presented Wilde's *Salomé* at the Lafayette; however, according to the *New York Age* reviewer, W. E. Clark, audiences were less than appreciative. Clark complained that
despite the fact that the acting "is among the best that has been seen in New York
City this season," the production was "handicapped by unappreciative audiences."
Many attendees of the opening night's performance had to be forcibly removed
from the theatre, while others interrupted with "laughter and loud talk" during the
"the climax of the play."[131] The production also had difficulty deciding what shows
to present. O'Neil, eager to capitalize on the "novelty" of African American actors
in "mainstream" plays, frequently switched shows at the last minute. Audiences,
purchasing tickets with the guarantee for a particular show, were infuriated at discovering that the bill had been switched at curtain time and another show was
being offered. This not only angered the audience, it upset the actors, who only at
the last minute learned what show they would perform.[132] As a consequence, the
acting suffered and the Broadway productions received mixed reviews.[133]

The mercurial rise and fall of the Ethiopian Art Theatre was too abrupt to
have had an enduring impact, but its productions did permit audiences to view
Evelyn Preer (1896–1932). Playing the haggard Chip Woman in Richardson's
play and the elegant, sensual Salomé in Wilde's play in the same evening, audiences were allowed a glimpse of this remarkable character actress. Preer, called a

"pioneer in the cinema world for colored women,"[134] began her film career in 1918, starring in Oscar Micheaux's *The Homesteader,* the first feature-length black film. She would later star in Micheaux's *Within Our Gates* (1920), *The Brute* (1920), *The Gunsaulus Mystery* (1921), *Birthright* (1924), *The Devil's Disciple* (1925), *The Conjure Woman* (1926), and several other films. At the Lafayette she performed onstage in *Madam X, Bought and Paid For, Branded, The Warning,* and other popular melodramas. In 1923 she joined the Ethiopian Art Players, in which she played leading roles. Preer's performances of Salomé and the Chip Woman garnered praise from every corner. Walton dubbed her "the greatest dramatic actress of her Race," and Percy Hammond of the *New York Tribune* wrote, "Miss Preer, who is so complete as the gorgeous and abnormal voluptuary of 'Salome,' plays the sloppy negress in 'The Chip Woman's Fortune' and she plays it perfectly."[135] The *New York Age* reported that her "interpretation" of Salome had been "heralded by the Chicago critics as being artistic to a high degree," and her "Dance of the Seven Veils" in Wilde's *Salomé* had been "marvelous in its beauty."[136] She also appeared on Broadway in leading roles in Belasco's *Lulu Belle* (1926), and Miller and Lyles's *Rang Tang* (1927). In his tribute at her memorial service in 1932, film director Oscar Micheaux called Preer "beautiful, intelligent," and "a born artist." She was, he observed, "more versatile than any [actress] I have ever known" and "could play any role assigned to her."[137]

Preer's performance in *Salomé* was not without controversy. Critical of black actresses playing "white" roles, John Corbin of the *New York Times* wrote that Preer was merely "adequate," although she "rose to every requirement." Corbin said that in the final scene, she performed "quite without distinction" required for "great art." He attributes this lack of distinction not to Preer's acting *per se,* but to the "fact that the play was performed by negroes" and "performed with an ostensibly philanthropic purpose," which "added a peculiarly poignant touch of disgust."[138] Responding to Corbin's remarks, Abram L. Harris wrote the following in the *Messenger:*

> To some of us it does seem ridiculous to see a "Salome" acted by a person of Negro origin. Despite this foolish sentimentality which has nothing to do with art, the mere possession of Negro blood or the fact that one was born in a Negro environment does not inhibit one's effective and accurate delineation of a character such as was Wilde's "Salome."[139]

The controversy over black performers in roles "designed" for whites reflected the era's obsession with race. No less a personage than President Warren Harding maintained in 1921 that there are "fundamental, eternal, and inescapable race differences" that compel enforcement of Jim Crow laws.[140] Harding and others urged African Americans to develop their own culture, because, in the words of Lothrop Stoddard, America was "founded by White men," whose "institutions, ideals, and cultural manifestations" were an "expression of their racial temperament and tendencies" and "must absolutely refuse to countenance the spread" of African Americans "through our stock of racial strains."[141] Despite efforts to integrate the theatre, productions and audiences remained, by and large, segregated.

Several playwrights of the era sought ways of influencing segregation, lynching, and racism. While their works were few, their cumulative effect was significant. The Dunbar High School teacher Mary P. Burrill (1879?–1946) was one of the dramatists who wrote for the purpose of propaganda. Burrill was Angela Weld Grimké's friend and taught Willis Richardson while he was at Dunbar High in Washington, D.C. Her two short plays, *They That Sit in Darkness* and *Aftermath*, are straightforwardly protest dramas. The former, published in the September 1919 issue of *Birth Control Review*, was concerned with birth control in the African American community. The latter, published in the April 1919 edition of the socialist journal *Liberator*, was produced in 1928 by W. E. B. Du Bois's Krigwa Players (in conjunction with the Workers Drama League of Manhattan).[142] It deals with lynching and African American veterans of World War I.

Aftermath reflects Du Boisian ideals of historical drama. Its theme centers on the mistreatment of returning black soldiers. In 1919, more than 350,000 African Americans had returning home from the service. Although admired as heroes in France, they were shunned in the United States; some were lynched in uniform. During the war, manufacturers recruited blacks. Production demands increased and blacks went north to fill vacant jobs. In the summer of 1917, angry white workers in East St. Louis attacked African Americans.[143] According to Oscar Leonard, the superintendent of St. Louis's Jewish Educational and Charitable Association, the attacks were nothing short of a "pogrom." Whites in East St. Louis, wrote Leonard, "fired the homes of black folk and either did not allow them to leave the burning houses or shot them the moment they dared attempt to escape the flames."[144]

Reports of the riot and the treatment of returning black soldiers shook the black community. In a 1919 *Crisis* editorial titled "Returning Soldiers," Du Bois wrote "we are cowards and jackasses if, now that the war is over, we do not marshall every ounce of our brain and brawn to fight a sterner, longer, more unbending battle against the forces of hell in our own land."[145] In the same issue of *Crisis*, Du Bois insisted that the facts about black soldiers be heard. In an essay entitled "History," he wrote that most African Americans "do not realize that the imperative duty of the moment is to fix in history the status of our Negro troops."

Claims were being made to discredit black officers. "The black laborers did well—the black privates can fight," Du Bois said, but many were claiming that the "Negro officer is a failure." While the facts existed to disprove the smear campaign against the officers, the proof, Du Bois insisted, "must be marshalled with historical vision and scientific accuracy."[146]

Burrill was stirred by Du Bois's rallying cry. Her play *Aftermath* takes place in South Carolina, set in a modest cabin of an "average" black family. At the opening, Mam Sue, an elderly woman, and Millie, a young girl of 16, are doing household chores. Amidst sewing, singing, and ironing, the two women reveal the play's exposition: World War I has ended and Millie's brother John is returning home. We learn that Millie has failed to inform her brother of the lynching of his father because she feared that the news would add to his misery in the trenches. She decides to wait till he returns. When he enters in uniform, including medals, the stage directions read: *"His brown face is aglow with life and the joy of homecoming."*[147] No longer believing in the values he once had placed in God and faith, trench warfare had taken its toll. "Prayers ain't no good!," he says, adding that it is the individual who must change the world.

Through a friend, Mrs. Hawkins, John learns of his father's lynching. His father had become involved in an altercation with a white man, resulting in mobs, hounds, and finally the symbolic rope. John asks if there was at least a trial for his father. When he discovers that justice was denied, he turns to revenge. Holding a revolver, John says:

> I'm sick o' these w'ite folks doin's—we're 'fine, trus'worthy feller citizuns' when they're handin' us out guns, an' Liberty Bonds, an' chuckin' us off to die; but we ain't a damn thing when it comes to handin' us the rights we done fought an bled fu'! I'm sick o' this sort o' life—an' I'm goin' to put an end to it![148]

Although Burrill's melodrama is predictable, the play's emotional intensity and immediacy drive home the point. Drama of this sort was typical of the period; its call for action reflected the aggressive politics of "New Negroism."

Garland Anderson's *Appearances* (1925) falls into the same category, being confrontational and blunt. It deals with a hotel bellman falsely accused of attempted rape. The play, originally titled *Judge Not According to Appearances*, was the beneficiary of some luck when Al Jolson read it and helped Anderson, who was a San Francisco bellhop at the time, to produce it. In his memoirs, Anderson, known as the "San Francisco bellhop playwright," described his journey from writing the play to seeing it through to production.[149] Once the three-act play had been written, it was read at the Waldorf Astoria Hotel in New York on 5 April 1925 before six hundred people. After raising fifteen thousand dollars, the play opened on Broadway at the Frolic Theatre on 13 October and ran for 23 performances.

The play's hero is a morally upright bellhop, Carl, falsely accused. Carl and his friend, Rufus, stand trial for the alleged crime of rape. In the climactic trial scene of Act Two, Carl tells the jury that "when a man tells the truth," truth and justice will prevail.[150] The characters are exonerated because the plaintiff is found to be of ill repute. The play received lukewarm reviews from both the black and white press. *Messenger* drama critic J. A. Rogers claimed to have questioned a "dozen Negroes of intelligence," who unanimously agreed that the play was "the worst mess they had ever seen."[151] However, the *New York Times* was less severe, calling the drama a "finely conceived, crudely wrought protest against lynch law," that contains "moments of power and a great many moments of ponderousness and stiffness." The reviewer added, "out of a passionate protest in his own heart the playwright has fashioned an eloquent appeal for reason and justice."[152] Despite its formulaic plot and unconvincing dialogue, the play still received another production in San Francisco and Los Angeles in 1927.[153]

In 1927, Du Bois's Krigwa Players' Little Negro Theatre opened their second season with two plays by Eulalie Spence (1894–1981), entitled *Her* and *Foreign Mail.* Both plays were critically praised by the black press, but William E. Clark of the *New York Age* wrote that they were "more Latin American in theme and treatment than Negro," prompting him to ask "whether it is wise or not for the Little Negro Theatre to stick to Negro plays exclusively?"[154] *Her* is a ghost story, which, although using African American dialect, contains no real social message. Du Bois, respecting Spence's playwriting skills, tried to persuade her to write propaganda. Despite their mutual admiration, Spence rejected Du Bois's ideas of social protest, claiming that plays "should never be for propaganda." She responded to Du Bois by asserting that she had little if any knowledge of lynching; rather, she wrote plays "for fun."[155] In 1928, she noted that propaganda plays are of little use, since "the white man is cold and unresponsive" to scenes of "lynching and rape." A playwright ought instead to portray the "life of his people," with a "little more laughter" and "fewer spirituals."[156] A talented writer of dialogue, Spence wrote several plays, but eventually turned to teaching to earn a living.

Arguably the most gifted writer of the period was Marita O. Bonner (1899–1971). Educated at Radcliffe (A. B. in English, 1922), Bonner (married name Occomy) wrote mostly short stories, but her three plays, *Exit: An Illusion, The Pot Maker,* and *The Purple Flower* (all written in 1927), suggest an imaginative and daring dramatist.[157] Both *Exit: an Illusion* and *The Purple Flower* received first prize for playwriting in the *Crisis* Contest awards of 1927. Fluent in German (she minored in Comparative literature), Bonner had been influenced by the German Expressionist dramas of the early 1920s, especially those of playwrights Ernst Toller and Georg Kaiser. With exaggerated physicality and adolescent angst, German Expressionist dramas attempted to symbolize reality by underscoring shocking social truths and heightened theatricality that shattered conventions and upended bourgeois complacency. Expressionism portrayed fantasy, dreams, and surreal conditions, generating empathy for the protagonist by representing the thoughts and images of the heroes, who were usually young, angry, and rebellious. Though at times strident and puerile, German Expressionist dramas broke new ground with plays that eschewed nuance and subtlety in favor of didacticism and youthful anarchy. This style forced audiences to view the world in a non-objective way.[158] Bonner's plays are surreal and revolutionary, using expressionist devices such as archetypal characters, strange settings, and illusionistic images.

Bonner's *The Purple Flower* is, according to theatre historian Errol Hill, one of the "most unusual plays ever written on the subject of black liberation."[159] Avoiding realism, Bonner draws on allegorical representations rather than realistic characterizations. The characters dance like snakes, glow red like fire, and appear in bright colors. Set "here, there or anywhere—or even nowhere," the play centers on two groups of people, the "Sundry White Devils," who "must be artful little things," and the "Us's," who "can be as white as the White Devils, as brown as earth, [or] as black as the center of a poppy."[160] Each group occupies a different area of the stage, with "the stage divided horizontally into two sections, upper and lower, by a thin board." The short play narrates the conditions of the Us's in the valley, kept apart from the White Devils at the top of a hill that grows "the Purple Flower-of-life-at-its-fullest." When the Us's try to climb the hill to breathe the purple flower, they are thrown back by the White Devils.

The narrative revolves around the character, Old Man, coming to grips with the futility of passive resistance. In an implied reference to Booker T. Washington's concept of manual labor, the Old Man (who represents Washington himself) is said to have believed that hard work alone brings inner fulfillment and harmony with whites. He discovers this is not the case. Nor did books teach the Us's how to live. As the Old Man listens to Finest Blood, a young man willing to sacrifice his life for an unnamed revolution, he comes to the realization that his past has been delusional and that the only way to dismantle oppression is through violence. Calling for a "New Man" to be "born for the New Day," the Old Man exhorts Finest Blood to fight. As the Old Man explains:

[There's] no other way. It cannot pass. They always take blood. They build up half their land on our bones. They ripen crops of cotton, water them with our blood. Finest Blood, this is God's decree: "You take blood—you give blood. Full measure—flooding full—over—over!"[161]

Finest Blood exits, and in the background the sound of his voice cries out:

White Devils! God speaks to you through me!—Hear Him!—Him! You have taken blood; there can be no other way. You will have to give blood! Blood![162]

The drama closes with the stage directions instructing the actors to pause. The final note asks, "Is it time?"[163]

The play's surreal and ambivalent ending was the exception to most African American dramas at the time. In dramatizing the pathos of the disenfranchised, Bonner allowed her audiences to experience passions in the raw. Her plays relied on sound and sight, oral and visual elements that conveyed images of chaotic disorder and catastrophic conditions of existence. Ahead of its time, Bonner's play rarely made it to the stage during her lifetime.

CONCLUSION

[H]istorically the major contributions to African American theatre have come from people whose backs have been spiked to the wall.
—Samuel A. Hay (1994)[164]

Most of the plays of the period (1918–1927) were inspired by Du Bois's notion of propaganda or Locke's insistence on the folk (discussed in chapter 7). Du Bois and Locke held out the possibility of production and publication: their books, journals, and theatres were the principal venues for African American playwrights. Since many writers depended on Du Bois and Locke to exert their influence, they frequently wrote for their approval. As a result, playwrights often turned out material that fit the ideological mold. Du Bois and Locke, peerless guardians of African American artistic and civic virtue, had demanding agendas and their demands at times restricted creative impulses. Still, the dramas of the period were significant in their efforts to convey important messages.

In 1922, James Weldon Johnson summed up the era as one in which black playwrights and actors simply wanted the opportunity to prove their skills. In his editorial, "The Negro Actor," Johnson responded to a commentary by Alexander Woollcott, drama critic of the *New York Times*. According to Johnson, Woollcott had claimed that with the exception of Charles Gilpin in the *Emperor Jones*, "we have never seen a Negro role acceptably played by a Negro." This was because "acting is more than a matter of impersonation." Implying that blacks are only capable of imitation and nothing more, Woollcott believed that performing is "a matter of emotional infectiousness, of humor and understanding, of concert with other players, of tempo."[165] Johnson agreed with Woollcott's judgment of acting, but he asked how Woollcott expected "to see great Negro actors when no Negroes are given a chance to act great parts?"[166] Johnson and others believed that given a chance, African American theatre would establish its place on the American stage. The Black Little Theatre Movement represented the efforts of dozens of playwrights, actors, and directors eager to demonstrate their craft; that many were denied opportunities to showcase their talents should not prevent us from acknowledging their accomplishments.

CHAPTER ELEVEN

SHUFFLE ALONG AND THE QUEST FOR NOSTALGIA: BLACK MUSICALS OF THE 1920S

*De black folks gits off down in de bottom and shouts and sings and prays.
Dey gits in da ring dance. It am jes' a kind of shuffle, den it git faster and
faster and dey gits warmed up and moans and shouts and claps and dances.*
— Rawick, *American Slave*[1]

INTRODUCTION

*Negroes could always make it with the deplorable darky stereotype, but
whites found it difficult to swallow the concept that there was a real Negro
somewhere who could do anything the white man could do.*
— Al Rose (1979)[2]

Shuffle Along was the most popular musical of the Harlem Renaissance. It was a
Broadway hit and enthusiastically received by both black and white audiences. Opening on 23 May 1921 at the 63rd Street Theatre, it ran for 504 performances, providing
considerable profit for its creators and producers. In 1922, it had a successful year-
long tour. Revivals would appear in New York in 1930, and as late as 1952 another
updated adaptation appeared, although neither earned the accolades of the original.
Described in the program as a "musical mélange," *Shuffle Along*, according to theatre
historian Allen Woll, "legitimized the black musical," spawning "a series of imitators"
that turned African American musical theatre into a "Broadway staple."[3] Included
among these musicals were popular productions such as *Put and Take* (1921), *Strut
Miss Lizzie, Plantation Revue, Oh Joy, Liza* (1923), *Runnin' Wild* (1923; it introduced the

Charleston to the stage), *The Chocolate Dandies, Dixie to Broadway* (1924), *Lucky Sambo* (1925), *Blackbirds of 1926* and *1928,* and *Africana* (1927).

This chapter will examine the script of *Shuffle Along* in detail, taking into account why it succeeded and what followed from it. In addition to achieving success for its creators, *Shuffle Along* aimed to accomplish two things: first, to create progressively minded musical characters with integrity and capable of romance; and second, to appeal successfully to white nostalgia for minstrel humor and Dixie. The success of the musical's Dixie aura, complete with plantation memories and the Mammy character, encouraged other black musicals to follow the trend. In addition, I will consider the significance of the era's three major musical theatre stars: Bert Williams (1876–1922), S. H. Dudley (1872–1940) and Florence Mills (1887–1927), as well as the rise of touring circuits. First, a review of the events leading up to *Shuffle Along* will set the stage.

BACKGROUND

Everyone in town is always singing this song,
Shuffle Along—Shuffle Along.   —*Shuffle Along* (1921)[4]

James Hubert "Eubie" Blake (1883–1983) composed the music and Noble Sissle (1889–1975) wrote the lyrics for *Shuffle Along.* They had met in 1915 and began working together in vaudeville. They subsequently joined James Reese Europe's Society Orchestra in 1916. Europe (1879–1919) was its conductor as well as pioneering musician. He had been influential in organizing professional clubs for African Americans. During World War I, he served as a first lieutenant and was director of the 15th Regiment Band of the 369th Infantry. Sissle and Blake were members of this band, which had been one of the most popular of its kind to tour France. Returning to the United States, Europe became orchestral director of the "Hell Fighters Band," which led the victory parade along New York's Fifth Avenue. Following Europe's untimely death in 1919 (he was stabbed by a disgruntled drummer), Sissle and Blake formed the "Dixie Duo." They sang in Keith's vaudeville circuit, a loose confederation of theatres run by vaudeville owner B. F. Keith and Edward F. Albee. Blake played the piano, Sissle sang, and both wore tuxedoes. They played ragtime, sentimental melodies, and up-tempo jazz. During a benefit concert for the annual meeting of the National Association for the Advancement of Colored People (NAACP) in Philadelphia in August 1920, they met up with the vaudeville team of Miller and Lyles.

Flournoy E. Miller (1887–1971) and Aubrey Lyles (1883–1932) wrote the dialogue for *Shuffle Along.* The text was based on their previous show, *The Mayor of Dixie*, which was first performed at Chicago's Pekin Theatre in 1907. Miller and Lyles were blackface comics who met as students at Fisk University (both graduated around 1904). Described by Bernard L. Peterson, Jr., as "the most popular writing, producing, and performing team of the 1920s,"[5] Miller and Lyles originated their routines at the Pekin Theatre (circa 1905–1911) under the leadership of the Pekin's founder and artistic director, Robert Motts. They wrote the show, *The Oyster Man* (1905), which became a vehicle for the popular comedian Ernest Hogan. While enjoying moderate success during the 1910s, *Shuffle Along* marked the highlight of their careers. The production of *Shuffle Along* also initiated the careers of Paul Robeson (1898–1976) and Josephine Baker (1906–1973), as well as Florence Mills.

Despite an abundance of talent in the show, *Shuffle Along* appeared doomed from the outset. There were several reasons for this. First, there was a lack of an established African American star to carry the show. Moreover, no African American musical, with the brief exception of *Darktown Follies* in 1913, had appeared on Broadway since 1910. Williams and Walker's *Bandanna Land* (1907–1909) had been the last successful black Broadway musical, closing while on tour due to the illness of George Walker. Bert Williams had attempted a musical on his own without his partner Walker, *Mr. Load of Koal*, in 1910, but the show quickly closed. He accepted an offer from the Ziegfeld Follies, where from 1910 to 1919 he appeared eight times. After 1919 and until his death in 1922, he appeared only in musical revues.

For at least a decade (1910–1921), white producers refused to consider a black musical on Broadway. Historian Mel Watkins referred to the period as a "virtual washout" of black musical comedy.[6] Watkins is not entirely correct; while Broadway lacked black musicals, the African American vaudeville circuit was successful. The three most popular—the Southern Consolidated Circuit (SCC), the Quality Amusement Corporation (QAC), and Theatre Owners Booking Association (TOBA)—flourished outside of New York (more on these organizations later). The absence of African American Broadway musicals during the 1910s, however, is a reminder of excluded possibilities.

Another obstacle was competition. Although Gerald Bordman makes the claim that post–World War I Broadway was "booming," with new theatres "opening in every direction,"[7] most theatres were booking only white musical comedies, fearing the risks attached to black musicals.[8] Lester A. Walton described the prevailing sentiment: "White amusement seekers would not patronize a colored show as a legitimate theatrical proposition." Whites simply regarded "Negro entertainment merely as a lure for slumming parties." Only a theatre "on the fringe of the theatrical district" would be suitable for a "colored attraction."[9]

The "fringe" meant nightclubs, cabarets, and vaudeville acts—what Walton characterized as "slumming parties"—beyond the legitimized Broadway scene.

In addition, the slumping economy of 1921, which was classified as a depression, gave little encouragement to take risks. Except for 1921, from the end of World War I to 1929, the economy grew. However, during 1921, wartime profits were swallowed up, unemployment increased from 1,305,000 in 1920 to 4,225,000 (averaging almost 12 percent of the workforce), and retail purchasing dropped by a whopping 7.6 billion dollars. With stocks falling as well, few believed that an African American musical, however benign, could succeed during this economic slump.[10]

Added to this was the race riots of 1919, which caused audiences to avoid race-related musicals and plays altogether. In his book, *White Violence and Black Response*, Herbert Shapiro noted that while racial violence in industrial cities had occurred prior to that year, in 1919 "something new" took place: "within a span of weeks racial violence spread from one city to another, and every city feared its turn was next."[11] The "Red Summer of 1919," as James Weldon Johnson described it, saw violence in 22 cities. Furthermore, 74 African Americans were lynched during the year.[12] Johnson comments on one of the underlying reasons for the hostility: black soldiers, having felt that their contributions to the war efforts would result in improved conditions back home, found instead "the reverse to be true." Hostilities escalated, and in one instance, Johnson maintained, a "return[ing] Negro soldier was lynched *because of the fact* that he wore the uniform of a United States soldier" (emphasis in the original). Johnson elaborated:

> Reports from overseas had come back giving warning that the returning Negro soldiers would be a dangerous element and a menace; that these black men had been engaged in killing white men, and, so, had lost the sense of the inviolability of a white man's life; that they had frequently been given treatment accorded only to white men in America, and, above all, that many of them had been favorably regarded by white women.[13]

One week after the opening of *Shuffle Along*, Tulsa, Oklahoma exploded in one of the most violent race riots in American history. On the morning of 30 May 1921, an argument broke out between a black male shoeshine employee and a white female elevator operator at the Drexel office building on Main Street. A charge of rape was lodged against Dick Rowland, the shoeshiner, but the court planned to release him when the elevator operator withdrew her accusation. However, the incident and Rowland's impending release were reported in the morning edition of the *Tulsa Daily Tribune*. The next evening, 31 May, an armed white mob marched to the courthouse with the intent of lynching Rowland; a crowd met them, including black World War I veterans, ready to defend him. Guns were fired and several people lay wounded or dying. Outnumbered by both groups, the police deputized dozens of whites. For the following two days, the police and their deputies proceeded across the railroad tracks that divided the city's population. Greenwood, the name of the thriving black community known as "Little Africa," consisted of over fifteen thousand people and nearly two hundred businesses. At the time Greenwood enjoyed relative prosperity, being the residence of some of the most successful African American business-men in America. The region became the target of the mob, where violence raged for two days. At first African Americans resisted, but they were far outnumbered and eventually overwhelmed. According to the reports from the Tulsa Race Riot Commission, whites set fire to buildings and homes, burning more than a thousand structures. Many blacks were shot as they tried to escape the flames. Forty deaths were officially reported at the time, but according to the Tulsa Commission's historian, Scott Ellsworth, the actual death toll, black and white, was closer to three hundred.[14] In his article for *The Nation*, Walter F. White described the situation a month after the riot. The "reign of terror" that brought about the destruction of Tulsa's black community, he said, "stands as a grim reminder of the grip mob violence has on the throat of America, and the ever-present possibility of devastating race conflicts where least expected."[15]

Within this atmosphere of hostility, racial humor and black musicals were deemed inappropriate. Producers were not only hesitant to finance a black musical comedy on Broadway; they feared for the safety of the touring company. It was difficult to determine which city was "open" to blacks and which had strictly enforced Jim Crow laws. Because of the widespread violence, many towns and cities imposed curfews on African Americans, which meant that shows lasting past the curfew hour could no longer perform without first obtaining a town pass. Rather than face the complexities of race baiting and bureaucratic obstacles, white musicals were preferred on Broadway and elsewhere.

In addition, jazz and its connection to black music fell under criticism. Many sought to curtail music's "black" influence, while others predicted the outright demise of jazz. In a 1918 essay titled "Why Jazz Sends Us Back to the Jungle," *Current Opinion* warned, "one touch of 'jazz' makes savages of us all." *Living Age Magazine* cautioned in 1920 that jazz "inspires a circle of cannibal forms." The following year, critic Clive Bell of the *New Republic* pronounced jazz "dead," adding that it was time to write its "obituary." The reason behind all this, according to Bell, was that jazz lacked "beauty" and "intellect." Black music was not art but adrenaline: "Niggers can be admired artists without any gift more singular than high spirits," he said, "so why drag in the intellect?"[16] In a letter to fellow members of the

musicians union, the union president of Pittsburgh called for the "death of Jazz."
Describing it as a "musical immorality," he claimed that performers act "like a
bunch of intoxicated clowns" whose movements "took me back to 1893 when at
the Chicago's World's Fair I saw in the Dahomeyan village on the 'Midway' a
dance by about 40 African females clad mostly in a piece of coffee bagging." He
implored musicians to refrain from the "Jazz-craze," using race-coded terms such
as "Willie-boys" and "social uplift" to describe African Americans.[17]

Besides such invectives, there were other problems. *Shuffle Along* toured several weeks before opening on Broadway, with prospects for success dimming by
the hour. While the show was successful at African American theatres—in particular the Howard Theatre in Washington, D.C., and the Dunbar Theatre in
Philadelphia—the company was still operating in the red. In order to cut costs,
scenery was stripped to the bare minimum and performers were often unpaid.
One newspaper reported that *Shuffle Along* survived its tour by having "no more
scenery than you could pack in a taxicab."[18] The production was frequently "flat
broke" and unable to pay for carfare.[19] When Henry L. Cort, a white producer
and theatre owner, came to Philadelphia to see the show, he anticipated that
while the show might succeed before African American audiences, this enthusiasm might not transfer to whites. Before risking a New York production, he
arranged for a "graveyard tour," a series of one-night performances in rural
Pennsylvania. The show was well received by predominantly white audiences.
Based on this, Cort proceeded to lease the 63rd Street Music Hall from his father, John Cort, in preparation for a Broadway opening.

In Flournoy E. Miller's unpublished autobiography, he recalls that there remained "many obstacles to overcome," among them being that this was "the first
Negro show to hit New York in many years." The "race problem," he observed,
was still a factor. According to Miller, "a newspaperman told Mr. Cort that the
public would not stand for Negroes" exhibiting romance onstage, suggesting instead that the "love theme" be removed.[20] Furthermore, the 63rd Street Music
Hall was technically not Broadway; as Eubie Blake explained years later, the
theatre "was really Off-Broadway but we caused it to be Broadway." The ticket
(five to seven dollars), Blake recalled, "cost the same as any Broadway show,"
which "made it Broadway."[21] The dilapidated Music Hall was hardly suitable for
a musical or much else. "It violated every city ordnance in the book," noted
Blake.[22] Often used for lectures and meetings rather than plays and musicals, the
space lacked the required depth for a large cast, elaborate choreography, and
large-scale orchestra. The floors and walls needed repair. Adjustments were
made, with the first three rows of seats being removed in order to make room for
dancing and the orchestra. Even so, the stage was shallow, limiting the choreog-

raphy for the large choral numbers. Most problematic was that the production was already in debt for over $17,000 at the time it opened. Producers and creators hoped at least for a break-even return. Surprisingly, *Shuffle Along* proved to be one of the most profitable shows of the decade. In his unpublished autobiography, Noble Sissle surmised that

> very few people of the Broadway theatrical managerial staffs believed us and there were few among our own group who felt we had a chance. However, we felt we had a message—we felt that the gloom and depression as an aftermath of the war had left the country hungry for laughter . . . that was so expressed in our music and rhythms.[23]

Praise for *Shuffle Along* came slowly. The *New York Times* reported that the show, "written, composed and played entirely by negroes, is a swinging and infectious score by one Eubie Blake." However, the *Times* added that "except in a burlesque boxing bout" with Miller and Lyles, the leads "have no marked comic talents."[24] The *New York Herald* was lukewarm, reporting that the plot "prov[ed] to be only fitfully amusing." But, when the singing and dancing appeared, "the world [seemed] a brighter place to live in."[25] The *New York Evening Post* was encouraged by what it saw but hardly enthusiastic, saying the show "was a good deal better than a number of the musical plays offered this season on Broadway." Some, however, recognized the show's potential. According to the *New York World*, *Shuffle Along* was a musical comedy "of the highest order."[26] *Theatre Magazine* declared that it "deserves a place among the best shows of its kind seen along Broadway."[27]

Alan Dale's review in the *New York American* supplied the show with its most enthusiastic praise. Dale called it a "darky musical" full of "pep and real melody." "How they enjoyed themselves," Dale remarked, adding, "How they jiggled and pranced and cavorted, and wriggled, and laughed." The show's energy, he concluded, made it "impossible to resist a jollity that the company itself appeared to experience down to the very marrow."[28] Eubie Blake claimed that Dale's review "really made people want to see the show." Blake calls attention to the backstage anxieties just prior to the show's opening:

> We were afraid people would think it was a freak show and it wouldn't appeal to white people. Others thought that if it was a colored show it might be dirty. One man bought a front row seat for himself every night for a week. I'd notice him—down in the pit you notice things in the audience—and finally, after the whole week was past, he came and told me that now he could bring his wife and children because there was no foul language and not one double-entendre.[29]

The show's lack of offensiveness made an impression on Lester A. Walton. He called *Shuffle Along* the "cleanest and most ambitious colored musical attraction to command the respectful attention of New York theatergoers in recent years."[30] The show's racy humor and sexual innuendoes apparently stayed well within the bounds of decorum.

By mid-June, *Shuffle Along* was the hit of the season. The street in front of the theatre was jammed with people trying to get in, which added to the aura of excitement. Eubie Blake's biographer, Al Rose, describes how the crowds "became so thick that the city had to make Sixty-Third Street one way."[31] The show's popularity resulted in a Wednesday midnight performance to accommodate eager audiences. Six months into the show's run, Walton observed that *Shuffle Along* was like a "steam-roller," owing to the perception that it was "knocking over barriers that have stood in the path of the colored show's progress." Not only had "precedents been set," but the production also showcased Florence Mills as Broadway's rising star (more on Mills later).[32] Langston Hughes believed *Shuffle Along* to be the signifying moment in African American theatre, providing "a scintillating send-off to that Negro vogue in Manhattan." It was, in Hughes's words, a "honey of a show." Audiences returned "innumerable times," creating a production that was "always packed."[33] "Singlehandedly," noted Gerald Bordman, *Shuffle Along* "made black shows voguish."[34] Eubie Blake recalled that opening night was the proudest day of his life, adding that at intermission "all those white people kept saying: 'I would like to touch him, the man who wrote the music.' Well you got to feel that. It made me feel like, well, at last, I'm a human being."[35]

The show's success depended on its appeal to whites. On this matter Lester A. Walton displayed his usual insights. He had seen the production at Philadelphia's Dunbar Theater with an African American audience. There he reported that the show broke "all previous records" of attendance. He believed *Shuffle Along* was noteworthy and deserved recognition for its Broadway potential. Nevertheless, he was skeptical that it could be a "white folks show." For a black show to "win favor" with whites, he maintained, certain "stage types" were mandatory, such as "the old mammy and Uncle Joe variety and blackfaced comedians." The "dandy-darky" was instrumental, Walton believed, provided that "his grin and strut are perpetual." While *Shuffle Along* presented archetypical characters such as "Uncle Joe" and had, to quote Walton, "more than the usual number of comedians under the [blackface] cork," the show portrayed praiseworthy characters. It even had romance, with its keynote song, "Love Will Find a Way," becoming a popular hit. For Walton, a show that represented African Americans as "nice-looking young men and women, well dressed and using plain United States language" was bound to fail. He reminded his readers that only when a show presents the "exotic" can it work: "Eight out of ten managers, especially if you have a vaudeville turn," would insist on the "plantation stuff" if a show was to succeed. Walton went so far as to suggest that if the romantic tune, "Love Will Find a Way," was "featured in a white production it would be proclaimed one of the season's hits."[36] On this last point Walton had underestimated the success of *Shuffle Along;* indeed, virtually every song became a hit. More than a quarter century after the production opened, Harry Truman used Sissle and Blake's song from *Shuffle Along,* "I'm Just Wild about Harry," as the theme for his 1948 Presidential campaign. Simply put, *Shuffle Along* became the most successful African American production of its time. Not everyone, however, was pleased.

After its initial success, *Shuffle Along* and other black musicals of the 1920s were condemned for reinforcing old stereotypes. Leaders of the "New Negro Movement" such as James Weldon Johnson, Alain Locke, and W. E. B. Du Bois "did not enthuse" over blackface musical comedy; they considered it antithetical to the aims of the movement.[37] Nathan Irvin Huggins's critique of *Shuffle Along* epitomized the sentiments of many African Americans then and now. He conceded that the "world needed cheering up in 1921, and it appeared that *Shuffle Along* was just the right tonic" for a nation suffering from "postwar hangover." He admitted that *Shuffle Along* "encouraged a generation of Americans to lose themselves in cabarets, rhythms, dances, and exotica" provided by this "lively Negro musical." Still, he condemned *Shuffle Along* and other musicals for failing "to refine black theatrical arts." These shows, he lamented, "continued to exploit a corrupt tradition."[38] The "corrupt tradition" was the minstrel stereotype.

The comic routines of Miller and Lyles, which represented the bulk of the production, pandered to racial humor. Miller and Lyles's comic dialogue and expert timing had been sharpened by over a decade of vaudeville experience. Their relationship as the characters of Steve Jenkins and Sam Peck in *Shuffle Along* anticipated the routines, the comic characterizations, and relationships of *Amos n' Andy,* which flourished for the next three decades on radio and television. (Miller was, in fact, one of the principal scriptwriters for the early radio versions of *Amos n' Andy* during the 1930s, and in the 1950s he wrote several TV scripts for the show.) Performing the leading roles in *Shuffle Along,* Miller and Lyles wore heavy blackface makeup, spoke in fractured dialect, and performed stereotypes associated with African Americans. The dialogue and storyline of *Shuffle Along* satirized black southern life. Depictions of African Americans as shiftless, dishonest, and pretentious had been popularized during the nineteenth and early twentieth centuries; Miller and Lyles's script did little to reverse this unfortunate state of affairs. Because black performers suffered from what cultural historian Susan Gubar calls a "sense of always looking at themselves through the eyes of whites," efforts by

African American performers to gain a foothold in mainstream theatres could "plummet black actors into the paradox of recycling a highly commodified primitivism" that catered to "prurient stereotypes."[39] Not only this, but the show also exploited light-skinned black women as chorus dancers. Theophilus Lewis forcefully condemned producers, black or white, who "will permit chorus girls to take off more clothes than the law allows because it means increased patronage of the pool-room rats and sex starved stevedores who cannot afford to visit the buffet flats as often as they wish."[40] *Shuffle Along* used blackface denigration and scantily clad chorus dancers, added modern performance style and jazz dancing, to create a potpourri of slapstick comedy, romance, singing, dancing, and lively but sometimes regressive entertainment.

Despite stereotypes, the musical contained progressive elements that countered some of the minstrel traditions. This was made evident by a sentimental love story, which had been taboo in black musicals prior to *Shuffle Along*. The show also helped integrate a number of theatres. Many *Shuffle Along* touring companies insisted on an end to segregated seating; they threatened withdrawal unless some or all of the orchestra seats were offered to African Americans. However, the blackfaced comedy, combined with scantily clad light-skinned female dancers offered up for male pleasure, did little to challenge prevailing fashion. To achieve success, black performers had to provide the usual clichés.

The white press capitalized on the musical's stereotypes, emphasizing that African Americans themselves offered images of inferiority and laziness. These images "verified" the stereotypes. It was assumed that the clichés were only slight exaggerations intended for comedic purposes. The *Boston Transcript,* for example, praised the 1922 tour of the *Shuffle Along,* making it a point to underscore the show's "authenticity":

> No one can burlesque a negro as can a negro himself. He knows the attributes of the Southern darky and he can exaggerate and accentuate them in action and speech with a humorous relish that cannot be duplicated by a white man and in such a wholesome, whole-hearted way that none can take offence. The picture of the shuffling, shiftless negro, suspicious of everybody, deceitful even to his own partner, illiterate to the nth degree, and yet imbued with an egotism and desire for display that knows no bounds, is one of the unlimited possibilities of fun-making.[41]

Nevertheless, the musical was a complex portrayal of African Americans that at times did resist convention. Although its "thin plot," as Bernard L. Peterson, Jr., put it, "served only as a framework for the elaborately staged and beautifully costumed musical numbers, the spectacular singing and dancing, the hilarious comedy routines, and the beautiful chorus girls,"[42] the script was in-deed innovative. The combination of old conventions and new ideas created an artistic contrast that enabled progress while carrying on the minstrel tradition. Examining the text will reveal these paradoxes.

SHUFFLE ALONG

Why sometimes a smile will right every wrong
Keep smiling and Shuffle Along.   —*Shuffle Along* (1921)

The play opens in "Jimtown," a mythic African American city in the South. An election is about to be held for mayor (The original title of the musical was *The Mayor of Jimtown*). Three mayoral candidates compete for the vote: Steve Jenkins (played by Miller), Sam Peck (Lyles), and Harry Walton (Roger Matthews). Jenkins and Peck are partners and proprietors of the local grocery store. Both are known to be unscrupulous, even to each other. Walton is in love with Jessie Williams (Lottie Gee) and hopes to marry her. One thing stands in their way: Jessie's father, Jim Williams (Paul Ford). He will block the marriage unless Walton wins the election, an election in which he is the underdog.

The rousing opening chorus number, "Election Day," brings on three groups, each of which defends their candidate by singing, dancing, and extolling his virtues. The supporters of Steve Jenkins endorse him because he calls for a repeal of Prohibition: "We'll bring back the whiskey, beer and gin / We know that Steve Jenkins will win."[43] A new crowd arrives, led by Sam Peck and his wife, Mrs. Peck (Mattie Wilkes). His supporters make it clear: if they vote for Peck, they will actually "enjoy" both he and his wife in office. Peck is the "hen-pecked" character, subject to his wife's fancy. This theme has long been and con-tinues to be a comic staple in black and white musicals, plays, and film. A third group arrives, singing the praises of Harry Walton.

> Honor is our motto, bright and grand,
> Justice is the platform on which we stand,
> And since we are in it, we are going to win it,
> Harry Walton is the man.[44]

From the outset his potential father-in-law, Jim Williams, describes Walton as a man of "honesty, integrity, and efficiency." He is, therefore, "the right man for the job" of mayor.[45] Walton's citizenship and decency supply little humor. His pur-pose is to represent the moral nexus: the decent man amidst corruption. Walton, juxtaposed against clownish characters, represents a side of African American life that had rarely been seen in mainstream theatres up to this point. His desire to wipe clean the town's corruption, restore integrity, and win the hand of Jessie signified an improvement in the depiction of African Americans. Despite his integrity, Jim Williams remains firm; while he admires Walton, he will not permit his daughter to marry him unless he wins.

Following the rousing opening number, Jessie exuberantly tells her "chum," Ruth Little (originally played by Gertrude Saunders and later replaced by Florence Mills), about her soon-to-be marriage with Walton. Ruth, dismissing marriage as old-fashioned, offers an alternative approach to life. For her, "Jazz" is her main concern and fun is her prerogative. Ruth and the chorus break into one of the show's many upbeat tunes, titled "Simply Full of Jazz." Ruth represents the "new woman" of the 1920s: independent, self-sufficient, and pleasure-seeking. While Gertrude Saunders received praise for her performance, it was Florence Mills who, in fact, turned the role into a star vehicle.

Following the song, Onions (no actor mentioned) approaches Walton, offering to vote for him if he pays him five dollars. Walton refuses (we later discover that it is hardly beneath Peck and Jenkins to "buy" votes). Walton would rather lose the election than win it dishonestly. Jim Williams admires Walton for his principles, but repeats his restrictions, telling Walton that unless he wins, he will "never consent to you becoming my son-in-law."[46] This reveals the depth of Walton's personal values: despite the possibility of losing lover and election, he will never compromise principles.

"Uncle Tom" (Charles Davis), whose name evokes the famous character from Harriet Beecher Stowe's nineteenth-century novel and play, *Uncle Tom's Cabin*, supports Jenkins. He attempts to persuade Mrs. Peck to convince her husband to withdraw from the race, clearing the way for Jenkins. He argues that having Peck and Jenkins run simultaneously will split the vote between them, allowing Walton a clear victory. Tom offers to bribe Uncle Ned (Arthur Porter) to vote for Jenkins. At first Ned takes the money, but then reconsiders and returns it. Ned remembers the "good old bandana days when honesty was the best policy."[47] Ned and Tom sing "Bandana Days," a rendition reminiscing on the old South and calling to mind the Williams and Walker musical of the same name, *Bandanna Land* (1907–1909):

Why the dearest days of my life, were Bandana Days,
Bandana Days though filled with turmoil, trouble and Strife,
Dearest mem'ries will live always.
In those dear old Bandana Days,

Candy and cotton ne're forgotten, Bandana Days,
And in those quaint old Bandana Days.[48]

The song is unthreatening and nostalgic. At a time of racial tensions, the song provided a sanguine tune sung by two elderly, harmless men. It was intended to assuage the fear of white audiences by appealing to their sentimentality.

After Peck and Jenkins offer their campaign speeches to the crowd, everyone except Uncle Tom and Old Black Joe exits. In "Jimtown Electioneers," a duet reminiscent of "plantation revues" popular at the time, the two pay homage to voting:

We are electioneers, Jimtown electioneers,
And since '61, Old Black Joe and Uncle Tom,
At election time, whether rain or shine,
We're down at the polls when they call the roll.[49]

While the message appears benign, the song is a potent statement that African Americans are aware of their participation in democracy.

Voting was sacrosanct. The Thirteenth Amendment to the Constitution abolished slavery (1865); the Fourteenth granted the right to citizenship to African Americans (1868); and the Fifteenth secured the right to vote for African American men (1870). Yet by the 1870s, the South had initiated a judicial process of preventing black voting rights. Several legal methods ensuring voter disenfranchisement were instituted; when legal processes failed, barriers and loopholes in the law were implemented. For example, the advent of the "understanding clause" throughout the South meant that voters had to prove literacy. The "grandfather clause" granted the right to vote only to those whose grandfathers had been citizens (usually determined by property ownership). The "good citizen clause" required proof of tax payments (poll tax) for upwards of 20 years. Falling short of these requirements cancelled one's right to vote, not to mention right to due process. Moreover, "white primaries," in which only white candidates were allowed to run for their party's nomination, kept black candidates from running for office. The effectiveness of these measures is evidenced by the statistics. In Louisiana, for instance, there were 130,334 African Americans registered to vote in 1896; by 1904, the number had declined to 1,342. Within these same years the literacy, property, and poll tax restrictions had been legislated.[50] The song, "Jimtown Electioneers," was, in fact, a significant commentary on the wider struggle for voter rights.

The story quickly turns to racial humor. Tom, Steve Jenkins's campaign manager, admonishes Jenkins for neglecting his campaign duties. Jenkins is accused of spending more time eating "fried chicken" than campaigning. Further, Tom warns Jenkins that his partner, Sam Peck, has been stealing from the cash register in order to finance his campaign. They agree that a detective is needed to investigate Peck. The next scene opens with Peck and his wife. Peck, it seems, has been spending too much time with females, much to Mrs. Peck's chagrin. She informs her husband that Jenkins has been stealing from their business and giving the money to *his* wife. Mrs. Peck has sent for the "great colored detective," Keeneye, to investigate matters. The comic situation is established. Hiring the detective will prove to be the undoing of both characters.

The final scene of Act One takes place in Jenkins and Peck's Grocery Store. It is the longest scene, encompassing nearly 25 percent of the text. The comic dialogue between Jenkins, Peck, and their employee, Onions, sets the stage for slapstick and humor. Onions personifies the allegedly shiftless, lazy African American looking to do the least amount of work for the most amount of money. Customers come and go in this farcical episode. In addition to the racial humor, the scene also makes use of standard comic situations: the overly fussy customer, the bumbling assistant, and the confusion in costumers' orders. The difference from white musical comedies resided in the dialect and the racial content. This influenced other black shows for decades, with similar scenarios widely repeated in plays, movies, radio, and television.

Toward the end of the scene Mr. Penrose (actually Keeneye the detective) arrives disguised, attempting to ensnare both Jenkins and Peck. Keeneye pretends to be a Chicago businessman searching for a retailer to sell his cashmere clothes. At different moments Peck and Jenkins pay Keeneye from the cash register, without their partner noticing. Keeneye leaves, assuring both, separately, that he will catch the other in the act of thievery. At the conclusion of the scene, Sam and Steve confide in each other. They agree that Harry Walton "ain't got a chance" of winning the election, given his honesty.[51] Jenkins assures Peck that if he wins, he will honor Peck by offering him the post of Chief of Police. They shake hands. Soon, a crowd enters the store, announcing that Jenkins has won the election. Jenkins and Peck exit in celebration, leaving Harry and Ruth alone. Ruth's father, Mr. Williams, sadly declares that he must keep his word and prevent the marriage. For the finale of Act One, Ruth, Harry, Williams, and the Chorus sing the melodic love song, "Love Will Find a Way."

The duet between Ruth and Harry represents the first major love theme in African American musical comedy. Theatre archivist Helen Armstead-Johnson has pointed out that *Shuffle Along* was "the first sophisticated Afro-American love story."[52] While there were other romantic plotlines in previous black musicals,[53] the first-act finale containing the song, "Love Will Find a Way," is evidence of a new type of romantic comedy in black musicals. Lester A. Walton's description of the situation at the time is worth quoting at length:

> White audiences for some reason do not want colored people to indulge in too much lovemaking. They will applaud if a colored man serenades his girl at the window, but if while telling of his great love in song he becomes somewhat demonstrative and emulates a Romeo—then exceptions are taken. It may be the general impression prevails that Negroes are only slightly acquainted with Dan Cupid; or maybe it is thought they have no business being ardent lovers.[54]

With few exceptions, there were little to no attempts at creating romance in African American theatre prior to *Shuffle Along*. Noble Sissle relates an anecdote about the song and the cast's anxiety:

> On opening night in New York this song ["Love Will find a Way"] had us more worried than anything else in the show. We were afraid that when Lottie Gee [playing Ruth] and Roger Matthews [Harry Walton] sang it, we'd be run out of town. Miller, Lyles, and I were standing near the exit door with one foot inside the theater and the other pointed north toward Harlem. We thought [Eubie] Blake stuck out there in front, leading the orchestra—his baldhead would get the brunt of the tomatoes and rotten eggs. Imagine our amazement when the song was not only beautifully received, but encored.[55]

"Love Will Find a Way" offsets the blackface humor, representing a breakthrough. It juxtaposes a decent, mature relationship against the backdrop of clownish mayhem. The romance did not replace caricature, but it shared the stage with it, creating an alternative view of African American life that reveals some depth.

Act Two begins with a scene on the "Calico Corner." The Traffic Officer is directing pedestrians through the busy street. He is met with chitchat. Uncle Ned passes by and jokingly says: "Good morning, officer. When did you get out of jail?"[56] The officer responds, "Shuffle Along," which segues into the show's theme song. The Traffic Officer sings:

> Everyone in town is always singing this song,
> Shuffle Along—Shuffle Along,
> Doctors, bakers, undertakers, do the step,
> That's full of pep and syncopation.

The Chorus responds:

> Shuffle Along, Oh, Shuffle Along,

Why, life's but a chance and when times come to choose,

If you lose, don't start asinging the blues,

But just you Shuffle Along, and whistle a song,

Why sometimes a smile, will right every wrong,

Keep smiling and Shuffle Along.[57]

The song's benign advice is a significant moment in the show. The meaning of the song and its accompanying dancing is subject to several levels of interpretation: as a way of dealing with racism, as a form of African retention (the passing down of artifacts, memory, and history from the Middle Passage, through slavery, and to the present), and as a resistance to racism that, without careful analysis, might go undetected.

First, the song suggests, by way of stoic resolve, how African Americans might come to terms with their living circumstances. Surviving day to day brings with it alienation fostered by indignities. Rather than resist these indignities, the song suggests that the best approach is acceptance and simply "shuffling along." Shuffling is a form of masking; one disguises feelings while projecting smiling acceptance. Shuffling emerged as one form of defiance. During slavery, shuffling and the appearance of laziness concealed resistance. It appeared to the slave owner as nothing more than indolence, but shuffling signified solidarity in the absence of any possibility of overt resistance. Shuffling, in effect, was a form of worker's "slowdown." By no means was this activity characteristic of African Americans; such assertions are blatantly false, as well as missing the point. The slave, a privately owned commodity denied access and control over labor, the products of labor, and reproduction, lacks incentives invested in the means and outcome of production. Karl Marx's description of the condition of the slave as a "merely artificial, vegetative existence" is apt.[58] "Shuffling" epitomizes a reaction to slavery's ontological state, providing an outlet, albeit indirect, for frustration and rage. Shuffling was a form of "hidden transcript" that, according to James C. Scott, exists "beyond direct observation by powerholders."[59] The mask of the docile slave carried over into the Jim Crow era, where passivity was advised over overt, active resistance. In his 1895 poem, "We Wear the Mask," Paul Laurence Dunbar poetically called it "the mask that grins and lies / It hides our cheeks and shades our eyes."[60] During an era when many black people were forced into low-wage jobs with little or no incentive, ambition was continually thwarted. The mask of docility kept hostility at bay by its non-threatening presence, while undermining the dominant society's ability to control African Americans, particularly those who saw little hope of economic advancement no matter how hard they tried.

Second, shuffling took root in the African American song and dance called the "ring shout." The "ring shout" is an African-based religious chant and song involving group movements in a circular choreography. In 1867, the *Nation* described the ring shout and referred to shuffling movements as part of the dance:

> . . . the true "shout" takes place on Sundays or on "praise"-nights through the week, and either in the praise house or in some cabin in which a regular religious meeting has been held. Very likely more than half the population of the plantation is gathered together. . . . But the benches are pushed back to the walls when the formal meeting is over, and old and young men and women . . . boys [and] young girls barefooted, all stand up in the middle of the floor, and when the "sperichil" is struck, begin first walking by-and-by shuffling round, one after the other, in the ring. . . . Sometimes they dance silently, sometimes as they shuffle they sing the chorus of the spiritual, and sometimes the song itself is also sung by the dancers.[61]

Through a process of call-and-response, individuals express their contributions to the singing and dancing within the ring. The group rhythmically chants along while soloists come forward, each participant taking turns singing and gesturing. Samuel A. Floyd, Jr., described the ring shout in the following way: the participants "stood in a ring and began to walk around in a shuffle." With feet close to the floor, the shoulders produced a "hitching" motion. The movements and songs were "usually accompanied by a spiritual, sung by lead singers," with hand-clapping or knee-slapping that created a rhythmic and repeated "thud."[62]

Varying facets of African cultures and religious expressions are combined in the ring shout, producing a conglomeration of spiritual singing and dancing that retains original as well as evolving forms. The ring shout made its presence felt during the Middle Passage and the early years of slavery; it then melded together with Protestant revivalist traditions. The circling motion was, in fact, very common to fundamentalist white churches. The ultimate version in the United States evolved by osmosis, blending black and white traditions, creating a hybrid of self-expression. This sort of cultural interface was common in the South, where slaves and masters, as well as black and white laborers, interacted. The inculcation of Christianity into Africanist religious ceremonies developed a hybridized and unique "ring shout." Religion historian Harold Courlander offers the view that the ring shout provided a "scheme" in which the singing and dancing of African religion could be made acceptable to Euro-American Christian fundamentalist traditions, which deemed singing and dancing sinful. "The circular movement, shuffling steps, and stamping conform to the African tradition of supplication," writes Courlander, "while by definition this activity is not recognized as a 'dance.'" Since it lacked definition as a "dance," it was made acceptable to Christian whites insistent on bringing Christianity to the slaves.[63] Yet, however influential white Christianity was in imposing its cultural insignias on black singing and dancing, the ring shout's core Africanist features remained: circular movements combined with song, with a principal singer who exchanges melody with choral refrains (which eventually assisted in developing "call-and-response").

In the movements, gestures, and rhythmic chants of the dance, the enthusiasm increases as the "shout" progresses. Following the quotation that serves as the epigraph of this chapter, the speaker describes the ring shout as a dance where "De black folks gits off down in de bottom and shouts and sings and prays." The "bottom" might imply the slave galleys, where transported Africans would "get up and off" from horrific imprisonment and enjoy fresh air on the ship's deck as long as they sang and danced for the amusement of white sailors. A ring space is created where the dancing occurs, with the dancing itself being "a kind of shuffle" that increases speed. Once "warmed up," the dancer "moans and shouts and claps and dances."[64] To "get off down in the bottom" represents both the steerage where slaves traveled as well as the inner circle of the ring where a synergy of spiritual communication is enacted.

The "ring shout" had several interchangeable objectives: a ceremony in honor of the harvest; a religious celebration commemorating Christian and African religions; a funeral ceremony; and emotional sustenance to a people enslaved. Sterling Stuckey, who has studied the ring shout, observes that the counterclockwise movement of the dance was meant to evoke the presence of "ancestors and gods," with the "tempo and revolution of the circle quickening during the course of movement" to accommodate the rising enthusiasm linked to communal embrace of spiritual connections. For the slave, the retention of formal African rituals and ceremonies through dance provided a means by which the new world and its conditions "could be interpreted" and spiritual longings could be "at least partly met." The ring shout was frequently considered as sacred to African Americans. As Christianity was imbedded into slavery, the "force of the [ring shout] ceremony," notes Stuckey, breathed "new life" into the merger of two religious traditions, Christian and African. The "incantations" of singing and dancing "were heard everywhere" but "especially at dusk," when "the air was full of song and clapping of hands."[65] The ring shout takes on the meaning of "continuum" (the important role of preserving continuity and black people's spirituality in the face of slavery), enacting the spiritual bonding with traditions repressed at every turn. In *Shuffle Along,* the ring shout's ceremonial movements resurface subtly but quite significantly. The notion of shuffling references the ring shout poignantly, albeit indirectly. The infusion of jazz dancing into the rhythms of "Shuffle Along" modernizes the gestures, but the connection to African-based traditions is nonetheless present in the dance's routine.

During the show's run, one young female dancer at the end of the chorus line began to dominate the dance accompaniment of "Shuffle Along." Sixteen-year-old Josephine Baker began performing "some crazy things," according to Eubie Blake. He explained that it was not so much a "routine" as it was "just mugging, crossing her eyes, tripping, getting out of step and catching up, doing all the steps the rest were doing, but funnier."[66] Baker began to steal the show, becoming one of the most popular and well-paid performers in the company. She was a gifted dancer and comedian, combining supple movement with quirky facial expressions. She danced beautifully in sync with the intended choreography, yet her face parodied the movement's seriousness. When she "botched" her dance, she capitalized on the error by mugging, crossing her eyes, and making faces at the audience. Her mistakes became comedy, undermining the image of the sensual and "oversexed" black woman. Her performances were at once graceful and uncoordinated, elegant and clumsy, passionate as well as comedic. Her dual objectives, evocative and satirical, combined humor with a more sensual side. On her first European tour in the mid-1920s, she found her style of sex and satire greatly appreciated. She remained in Paris for the bulk of her career.

Following the song "Shuffle Along" and Baker's scene-stealing performance, the story returns to the election. Jenkins is now burdened with mayoral responsibility. He tries to work his way through a crowd of people attempting to make good on his numerous campaign promises. The crowd wants "kickbacks"—official positions such as tax collector and street cleaner—in return for their support. Sam Peck demands that he live up to his agreement to cast him as police chief. Jenkins sarcastically replies: "If you ain't got no better sense den to pay any attention to dem election promises you ain't got sense enough to be no Chief of Police."[67] The argument between them leads into the show's most popular routine: the boxing match with Peck and Jenkins. The music plays "Jimtown Fisticuffs" while Miller and Lyles, closing out the first scene of Act Two, perform their trademark vaudeville "prizefight." Miller described the fight as lasting "about twenty minutes." They would often ad lib through the routine. One acrobatic trick involved Lyles, who was significantly shorter than Miller, jumping on his partner's back (see figure 14).[68]

Act Two, Scene Two, has Harry Walton singing "Sing Me To Sleep, Dear Mammy, With a Hush-a-Bye Pickaninny Tune." Harry, disappointed that he has lost the election—and worse, that he cannot marry Jessie out of respect for her father's wishes—sings a mournful tune expressing his sadness. Jessie joins him in the duet (they sing to each over the telephone). This song counterpoints the comedy preceding and following it. After the comic prizefight, the audience is ready for a shift from slapstick to sentimentality, only to return to comedy again. The lyrics place an importance on the relation of Harry to his mother (never seen onstage):

> Mammy, I'm feeling tired and weary,
> My heart is heavy laden, too,
> Mammy, there's only one who can cheer me,
> And that only one is you.
> (Chorus)
> So won't you sing me to sleep, dear Mammy,
> With a "Hush-a-bye, of pickaninny tune"
> Just like you did in Alabamy
> Mammy let me hear you croon.[69]

At the song's conclusion, Harry tells Jessie he will try to gather the courage needed to carry on. Sadness overcomes him, however, as he appeals to "Mammy" for guidance.

The "Mammy" stage figure has had a long history. She was generally characterized as a large, buxom, jolly, bandanna-wearing kitchen maid, known for her cooking, nursing, and sagacious advice to white children she was charged to rear. She was housemaid, nursemaid, chief cook, and something more: a repository of "simple, earthy wisdom." Her popularity surfaced in the early nineteenth century, and carried through the minstrel show era of the late nineteenth and early twentieth centuries. By the turn of the century the "Mammy" was ubiquitous, her image appearing on advertisements and billboards. Shortly thereafter she appeared in films. The bearer of many children (the "Mammy" was considered a veritable birthing machine), she dispensed "primitive" insights uncomplicated by modernity's complexities. Joseph Wood Krutch described this in his 1929 book *The Modern Temper*. The modern world, he claimed, became increasing convoluted and in need of explaining. There were explanations of two sorts: the simple and the complex. "Primitive races" possessed knowledge of the former by dint of their living in a simple world. The primitive, he remarked, neither asks "what he gets out of life, nor why he should sacrifice himself to the laborious business of continuing it." Rather, the "lair or the nest is prepared, and the young are born." The young were subsequently "nourished, defended, [and] given such education as they need."[70] "Mammy," above all, nourished the young with uncomplicated wisdom.

The "Mammy" provided a counterpoint to modern life's overindulgences. By the late 1910s and early 1920s, she was seen as a panacea for an overwrought and anxiety-ridden world. Symbolic of the antebellum past, she was evoked in *Shuffle Along* and other venues (musicals, plays, novels, and films) to stimulate feelings of nostalgia. Young people coming of age during the 1920s were enthralled by life's possibilities. Mass consumption of radio, automobiles, gramophones, movies, flight, telephones, and technology, combined with flappers, speakeasies, and a revolution in morals created a sense that the world's mobility had reached a speed never before achieved. The booming stock market conveyed the impression that getting rich took mere savvy and a little nerve. Mass production contributed to the idea that everyone could possess things that before were reserved for the select few. Cars, for example, were no longer luxury items; the assembly line made big-ticket items affordable.

The nation was in a demographic transition as well. By 1920, more United States citizens resided in the cities than in rural regions. On both coasts immigrants poured into the urban scene. Victory in World War I and the rising influence of American culture throughout the world added to a growing perception that the United States, and especially New York City, was now the center of fashion and industry. Americans became caught up in euphoria. America was, for the first time, exporting culture and not just importing it. The feeling was increasingly common in the Jazz Age that the past, with its emphasis on self-sacrifice, family, and the bucolic life, had run its course. The present was a passageway to more technological innovations, influence, and individual wealth. Yet, such a headlong rush into the mechanized future left many alienated and in despair.

Those coming of age at the time needed something to cling to. In his book, *The Metaphysical Club: A Story of Ideas in America,* Louis Menand claims that the Civil War "tore a hole" in the lives of Americans, discrediting the beliefs of the past. It took, he said, half a century for the nation "to develop a culture to replace it, to find a new set of ideas, and a way of thinking that would help people cope with the conditions of modern life."[71] By the 1910s and 1920s, new ideas and ways of thinking had begun to surface. Pragmatism would replace sentimentalism, materialism would supersede spiritualism, and realism would trump idealism. In coping with what Menand terms the "conditions of modern life," Americans had technology and wealth; consumerism promoted the materialistic lifestyle; and hedonism dominated. These ideas, however, were largely disconnected from the past. The desire for wealth and pleasure, and the emphasis on the "new," stripped Americans of their roots. What was lacking, and what *Shuffle Along* supplied, was "nostalgia."

Songs and melodies about "Dixieland" offered a glimpse of "tradition." The mythic Dixie took hold of the imagination because it represented a time when the hurly-burly of urban life was far removed. The evocation of Dixie in *Shuffle Along* encouraged other black musicals to exploit plantation life, creating a past that, however unrealistic, provided Americans with something to cling to. Theatre historian Laurence G. Avery has observed that the presence of Dixie in *Shuffle Along* was a "self-serving" view in the North "that the proper place for African Americans was in the rural South" because blacks migrating North would be "filled with nostalgia for the old folks at home."[72] But this is only half the story. The songs evoked nostalgia for whites as well, helping to remind them of a more bucolic life free from stress. Flournoy Miller's insightful remark that for whites "all colored entertainers were from 'Dixie'" makes clear that the conflation of the South and African Americans bolstered the falsification of black nostalgia for plantation life, but it also helped whites fixate on an idyllic and fictional past. Black performers sustained this view, as they "always advertised as being from Dixie," whether it was true or not.[73] Dixie had taken on the aura of myth and memory, touching an audience looking for a momentary way to connect with a past that was out of step with the new world, yet comforting by way of its pastoral setting. Black performers exploited the notion, using the Dixie myth as entry into mainstream theatres; "Mammy" arose as the principal symbol of a peaceful presence, one freed from the daily grind.

Although "Mammy" is never seen in the play, her "existence" represents an image that had become part of the common lexicon. One characterization on a sheet music cover shows "Mammy" with a white child on her lap (see figure 15). This 1916 song, "They Made It Twice as Nice as Paradise and They Called It Dixieland," captures the relationship of a white child and Mammy surrounded by the illusion of paradise. The Mammy figure projects a warm smile. She gently raises her right index finger, pointing toward the dutiful child, and appears to impart deeply personal knowledge. "And They Called it Dixieland" is sung from the point of view of a white man recollecting his childhood memory:

Principal Singer
I used to have a dear old Mammy
In the days of Old Black Joe.
She used to cuddle me upon her knee
And tell me tales of long ago.
She said the angels built old Dixie
And I know that's not a fib,
For to me it looks like heaven
And I'll tell you what the angels did.

Chorus
They built a little garden for the rose
And they called it Dixieland.
They built a summer breeze to keep the snows
Far away from Dixieland.
Principal Singer
My dear old Mammy never told me
Where she learn'd this mystery.
And if I seemed surpris'd
She'd look so wise
And say "Ma Chile, that's his-to-ry!"
But she liv'd so long in Dixie
She was old enough to know,
And I think she might have been there
When the land was built, so long ago.[74]

"Sing Me to Sleep, Dear Mammy," and "And They Called It Dixieland"
are linked by the same idea: the notion of the Mammy as wise and maternal,
but only on a basic level. We never see Mammy in *Shuffle Along* and we do not
have to. Her recognizable and uncomplicated ways are closed and unavailable
to the ambiguities and contradictions associated with real-world existence. Her
presence, evoked by the singer, inspires the imagination already alert to the
image and its residual meaning. Mammy reassured the audience by way of her
non-temporal, non-spatial presence; impervious to change, she will not be
eroded. In a period where change was the norm, the consistency of Mammy re-
stored confidence that an enduring, idealized past was readily available, if only
by way of imagination.

Following the sentimental and woozy homage to Mammy, the musical's
comic pace returns. Act Two, Scene Three, opens in the Mayor's office. After a
comic exchange between the Office Boy and the Doorman, Mr. Williams
(Jessie's father) enters. He complains to Mr. Penrose, a clerk (but actually Detective Keeneye in disguise), about the town's conditions, the extravagances of
stenographers, and the foolish expenditures of the mayor's office. Penrose says:
"But you must admit, Mr. Williams, that the mayor has some very beautiful stenographers." Beautiful, replies Williams, "and minus ability."[75] The "beautiful"
chorus dancers in the show were hired for their light skin.

Light-skinned chorus dancers became the staple of African American musicals, with *Shuffle Along* essentially beginning this trend. The song, "If You've
Never Been Vamped By a Brown Skin, You've Never Been Vamped at All,"
brings the musical to a close. The song concerns a deacon who has been brought

up on charges of non-support of his wife. His defense is that he had been "vamped" by a "brown skin":

> A high brown gal will make you break out of jail,
> A choc'late brown will make a tadpole smack a whale,
> But a pretty seal-skin brown, I mean one long and tall,
> Would make the silent sphinx out in the desert bawl,
> If you've never been vamped by a brown skin,
> You've never been vamped at all.[76]

The song capitalized on the preference for light-skinned African American women by many males at the time. Skin tones were a major indicator of sexuality. The "brown woman" symbolized the atavistic concept of promiscuity mixed with "civilizing" whiteness. Danger supposedly lurked in the black woman. The "brown" represented cannibalistic, voodoo Africa, yet subdued somewhat by "mixed blood." The brown skin was white enough to obviate racial taboos, but dark enough to attract potential white audiences seeking exoticism.

"Brown skin," moreover, took on the aura of sophistication. The potentially dangerous sexuality was softened with the veneer of high-class style. In 1923, exactly two years after it opened, *Shuffle Along* performed at the Forrest Theatre in Philadelphia. In his review, titled "'Shuffle Along' a Jolly, Jazzy Ethiopian Entertainment," Linton Martin remarked that everybody in *Shuffle Along*, "from the darkest principals to the creamiest-tinted chorus cutup, seems to be having a hugely enjoyable time." He went on to describe the dancing of the chorus as the "Congo capers and jungle jiggles" of the "creamy creoles."[77] The expression "creamy creole" appealed to the requisite sensuality, yet was "civilized" enough to offset the alleged savagery. Representations of blackness were too threatening for white Broadway audiences. Men would not accompany spouses, dates, or escorts to the theatre if the show proved excessively risqué or exceedingly "dark." In order to succeed a balance had to be struck. Ashton Stevens of the *Chicago Herald and Examiner* offered the following evidence in his review. *Shuffle Along*, he said, is "a real colored thing," and while the show had a "perfect pulse," he described it as "clean as a hound's dentistry," and "never so primitive as to offend the intelligence even to the infant in the house."[78] The show succinctly moved along the fine line of enticement and acceptability. The song's reference to "brown skin" was seductive yet within the limits of bourgeois respectability. Even when the dancers, as reported by the *New York Herald*, were said to "wiggle and shimmy in a fashion to outdo a congress of eels," and to "fling their limbs about without stopping to make sure that they are securely fastened on,"[79] the implied danger was tamed by the presence of "fun-loving" chorus dancers whose lightness assuaged suggestions of the "cannibalesque." The "jungle-rhythms" of the dancing and the titillating costumes met the requirements of sexuality, but the "cream-colored mulatto" dancers defanged out-of-control "jungle passions." This balance between the forbidden and the civilized satisfied Broadway's social criteria while it simultaneously offered the best of both worlds. By the standards of the 1920s, the show was risqué, yet inoffensively so.

During the show's conclusion, Penrose tells all: Steve Jenkins robbed Sam Peck, Peck robbed Steve Jenkins, and Onions robbed them both. At this point Walton is justly pronounced mayor and the show ends with several rousing musical numbers that demonstrate the dancing skills of the company.

Shuffle Along was a product of its times. Racial hostility was at a peak and conditions for black performers were constricting. Not only were their roles simplistic; their living conditions were often intolerable. According to Noble Sissle, while he and Eubie Blake toured, "most towns they played to would not allow them to eat or sleep in the hotels or restaurants." Sometimes they would "have to travel 25 or 30 miles to find a place." This situation existed, he said, "in all the white hotels of the country during the 1920s."[80] Sissle and Blake dressed in tuxedos during their careers as the "Dixie Duo," creating an appearance of refinement in order to diminish the perception of jazz as unsuitable for the white middle-class audience. For a black musical to succeed on Broadway and elsewhere, where the majority of audiences were white, African American performers had either to don the mask of refinement or embrace the mask of blackface.

Yet, despite old stereotypes, the modern dancing and music in *Shuffle Along* offered whites an opportunity to reap the benefits of all things modern. During the 1920s black musicals were considered essential to the full experience of the "modern age"; a visit to a black musical was therefore *de rigueur* for anyone wishing to be *au courant*. John McMullin's review of *The Plantation Review* (1922) captured this relationship of modernism and black musicals. In his essay for *Vanity Fair*, "The Fashion and Pleasures of New York," McMullin wrote:

> If by chance you have not seen Florence Mills and her coloured troupe do their fantastic dances and serenades, you are not "in it." All the modernists and musicians, you know, are mad about this new phase of the development of coloured talent.[81]

If, as some historians have observed, race enters modernism "in the form of the primitive,"[82] then singing the tunes and dancing the "primitive" steps from *Shuffle Along* and other musicals certified one's "modern tastes." Together, modernism and primitivism characterized black musical theatre and Harlem cabarets. One became modern by rejecting Victorianism, embracing primitivism (but only temporarily), and enthusing over an "exciting" race of people who would release the desired impulses. Black artists and performers capitalized on these urges; as David Levering Lewis asserts, black artists, writers, and performers "ascended to the Park Avenue penthouse, one after another, to be received as votive primitives" by liberal whites.[83] Whites, in turn, participated eagerly in the idealization of black art. By participating in some uptown slumming, George Tichenor claimed in 1930, whites could "learn" that the African American is "unmoral, Rabelaisian, without the complicated ethics of another race."[84] The rising interest in drugs and the demand for alcohol during Prohibition added to the image of Harlem as a source of inebriation and "fun." Harlem was considered a locale where social propriety was temporarily suspended. In the words of Langston Hughes, "thousands of whites came to Harlem night after night, thinking the Negroes loved to have them there, and firmly believing that all Harlemites left their houses at sundown to sing and dance in cabarets, because most of the whites saw nothing but the cabarets, not the houses."[85]

Shuffle Along was one of the first shows to provide the right mixture of primitivism and satire, enticement and respectability, blackface humor and romance, to satisfy its customers. Many critics praised *Shuffle Along* as an advance in musical theatre and a critical turn away from the minstrel tradition. Yet, *Shuffle Along* complicated minstrelsy. Its blackfaced comedians, fractured dialect, malapropisms, and post-ragtime jazz music were refashioned minstrel theatre, and, according to Ann Douglas, "minstrel fans had thought nothing funnier than the Negro's thoughts and antics when faced with those activities half-forbidden to him, voting and running for office." Douglas adds this salient point: "Anything, but anything, from the latest and hottest Negro dances to the oldest of white blackface routines, was grist to the *Shuffle Along* mill."[86] This mixture of blackface denigration and progressive change, mockery and pride, pandering and resistance created a paradox of competing urges.

Blackface was something progressive African Americans found most difficult to accept. It was one thing to sing and dance; musicals were accepted begrudgingly as a theatrical form. But the reinstitution of the blackface image left a disagreeable aftertaste. African American actors wearing the blackface mask were enacting what Nathan Irvin Huggins has termed the "great charade." This was a sort of game that blacks and whites both agreed to play. The mask, whether onstage or off, "defined the Afro-American as white Americans chose to see him." If the mask was removed, "the black man was either invisible or threatening." African Americans, Huggins lamented, "accepted the pretense" because it enabled them "to move in and out of the white world with safety and profit."[87]

Notwithstanding the performer's talents, the mask became the device guaranteeing success. Flournoy Miller explains this use of the mask for specific theatricalization. "Blackface," he said, "was the bait to draw them in. Once on the inside they would enjoy our fine artists." He made clear that "Broadway was the goal," adding, "we knew that the American public would support a Negro play—once we got there."[88] Blackface, they believed, was the only way to achieve their objective, but there was a price to be paid.

THE CHANGE OF CHANGES

> *It is hardly reasonable to expect, when we take a people as inferiors, as the butt of our jokes, that we should allow representatives of the same people to stand where they can be the recipients of our serious admiration and applause. . . . The fact that Negroes are barred from our best hotels will naturally bar them from the best places on the stage also.*
>   —Hubert H. Harrison (1917)[89]

Many African Americans rejected theatre entirely, considering it inextricably joined to minstrel traditions and therefore degrading no matter what was produced. However, *Shuffle Along*'s popularity among African Americans was undeniable. Intellectuals may have shunned its improprieties, but many welcomed it. It enjoyed success at Harlem's Lafayette Theatre; other productions of the musical in the black communities also proved popular. In 1923, the New York *Amsterdam News* reported that the "third company" of *Shuffle Along* (the first being the 1921 original, the second the 1922 touring company) had opened at Harlem's Lafayette Theatre "to one of the biggest starts made around here." This company, featuring veteran performers Salem Tutt Whitney and Homer Tutt in the leading roles, enjoyed standing-room-only crowds that were "almost six deep."[90] The third company continued the show's success.

In 1917, Hubert H. Harrison astutely observed one of several reasons for the popularity of blackface among African Americans (other reasons will be examined later in this chapter). Although he described the period's vibrant activity of blacks in show business as the "change of changes," he realized that depictions of "the intelligent and cultured Negro on the stage" would fail to "evoke generous applause."[91] When black actors appeared before black audiences they either catered "to that conception of life and its stage-presentation which they have derived from white people," or they "play[ed] to their higher ideals." The latter, Harrison said, generally failed to attract interest.[92] According to him, the reason for the success of the former owed largely to "the fact that color is the great social obsession among our Negroes." Harrison examined the color issue with unusual frankness, noting, for example, that among African Americans, references were made to "good color and good hair"—good in the sense that it represented "similarity to white people's." In social relations, such as "love, marriage, courtship, and society," he said, "lightness of color is perhaps the greatest desideratum." The term "black society," Harrison bluntly asserted, really meant "mulatto society."[93] Only light-skinned blacks seemed to qualify for the social elite.

Color, Harrison alleged, was all-consuming in black culture. He condemned the "silent ostracism" of darker African Americans that not only took place, but also was hypocritically "hidden with especial care from the white outsider." Social separatism based on color, Harrison maintained, found "its most striking organized form in the churches." He saved his strongest condemnation for preachers fostering a "mulatto church," but he also criticized advertisements in African American newspapers promoting "'anti-kinks,' skin-bleaches, blond face powders and other devices for straightening the hair and lightening the complexion of Negroes who, it seems, are no longer pleased with the visible marks of their racial ancestry."[94] With blackface musicals, the light-skinned audiences attending the shows enjoyed blackfaced actors and their foolishness without the threat of self-malignment. If lighter skin meant refinement, darker skin meant barbarism, something to be ridiculed. African Americans accepting this view could participate in *Shuffle Along*'s "fun" without the risk of close association.

Other reasons contributed to the popularity of blackface among African Americans. Mocking the pretenses and affectations of one's own group frees both actors and audiences, temporarily, from perceived social proprieties. Comedy alleviates tension by permitting audiences the enjoyment of human fallibility. It vicariously allows audiences to vent their fears of failing social expectations. At the time, many middle-class African Americans faced considerable pressure to conform to "New Negro" standards and high expectations. The leaders of the New Negro Renaissance prescribed rules of behavior, decorum, and social propriety that demanded disciplined, unwavering adherence. The "racial uplift" movement set out to achieve an enforced civility through specifically normalized public behavior.[95] The effect left many exhausted. The indignity of racism combined with the pressure to conform to "New Negro norms" only added to the burden of daily life. *Shuffle Along* provided an opportunity through laughter to let off steam, even if that laughter was directed at one's own group. Many therefore accepted the musical, even though they disliked blackface and its implications.

For others, increased prosperity in the black community caused many to view *Shuffle Along* as part of the "old South," something disconnected from their actual lives. While the growing number of middle-class African Americans was relatively small, they succeeded in replacing the old notions of the "black aristocracy."[96] Moreover, American acquisitiveness had its effect on the black middle class as well. Material wealth was a defense against humiliation. People could enjoy *Shuffle Along* by associating stereotypes such as the "poor old southern darky" with a bygone era. The old values had been replaced; *Shuffle Along* was considered a mere representation of what was no longer a reality. People would take pleasure in comedies that represented circumstances they had escaped.

Finally, there was the reality of show business. African American audiences realized that a certain degree of bowing and scraping was necessary for the success of the performer. They therefore accepted the "blacking-up" of performers. Once successful, actors were appreciated when they returned something to the community, and were admired somewhat like conquering heroes. Many actors showed their appreciation by supporting the community's development. This was true of the *Shuffle Along* cast and creators. Miller, Lyles, Blake, and Sissle frequently played benefit performances. All four donated to charities, financed businesses, and raised funds. They also attempted to create an indigenous African American theatre, even producing realistic shows that were not popular. For example, Harlem's Lafayette Theatre opened with *The Flat Below* in May of 1922, a drama written by Miller and Lyles.[97] According to the review by Romeo Dougherty, Miller and Lyles made an "exposition of their race that is applicable to the present time and existing conditions right here in our large American cities. They have done this by putting real human beings on the stage who expose their souls."[98] In his review of the show for the *Negro World*, Duse Mohamed Ali called it a "good drama" that "deals with a phase of Negro life which is not particularly Negro, but which is common to all humanity dwelling in the Western Hemisphere."[99] The story centers on a young woman born out of wedlock to a church deacon. Her mother tries to raise her by herself, but dies from shame and exhaustion. Church members raise the daughter, but her past is revealed. She is forced to live in the "flat below," an apartment run by disreputable characters. Eventually the young woman is rewarded for maintaining her virtue.

In 1926, Miller and Lyles stated that they would attempt to create "a theatre devoted to the Negro." This theatre's purpose, they said, was to be serious rather than merely to "amuse." The plan was to appeal "to the cosmopolitan audience" in order to have "artistic productions presenting us as we are." They believed that the "needs of our race and a better understanding of us would be broadcast through such a theatre."[100] Although no such theatre as they envisioned materialized, their effort to create such an establishment had a twofold effect: it gained the respect of the community and it excused, for the most part, their pandering to the mainstream.

BERT WILLIAMS: MISFORTUNE AND CARICATURE

Got one mind for white folks to see,
Another for what I know is me.

—African American Proverb

Bert Williams and his partner, George Walker, created the Williams and Walker Company, the most popular African American theatrical group of the first decade of the twentieth century. There were three main shows, *In Dahomey* (1902–1905), *Abyssinia* (1905–1907), and *Bandanna Land* (1907–1909), all featuring Williams, Walker, and Walker's wife, Aida Overton Walker. Following George Walker's forced retirement owing to illness, the company disbanded in 1909. Williams would spend the next nine years (with one year's absence) with the Ziegfeld Follies. One of his many successful routines in the Follies was the "Poker Game," where he pantomimed a poker player who thinks he has a winning hand only to discover he does not. In 1920 he starred in *Broadway Brevities*. His last production was *Under the Bamboo Tree* in 1922.

During most of his career Williams appeared in blackface (see figure 16). Yet his personal life hardly resembled the character he portrayed. Well-educated and a voracious reader (he owned an enormous library in his Harlem home), black audiences appreciated his success and his personal dignity. Williams was of mixed ancestry (his father was Dutch and his mother Spanish and African American). Yet throughout his 25 years in show business, his roles projected the downtrodden African American; comic misfortune was essential to his craft. In interviews and writings he never appeared bitter about having to play the same character. His well-known view of race was summed up in a brief comment: "I have never been able to discover that there was anything disgraceful in being a colored man. But I have often found it inconvenient—in America."[101]

Notwithstanding stereotypes, two principles of comedy are relevant to blackface and to Williams in particular: misfortune and caricature. Williams personified both. He observed that one of the "funniest sights in the world is a man whose hat has been knocked in or ruined by being blown off—provided, of course, it be the other fellow's hat!"[102] In his essay, "The Comic Side of Trouble," Williams stressed that misfortune motivates laughter, provided that "trouble" happens to someone else. Misfortune allows an audience to enjoy its own comparative safety. Disaster can happen to anyone; seeing it happen to someone else affords a critical distance that sets the stage for laughter.[103]

Williams developed his "sad-sack" characterization because, as he said, "Troubles are funny only when you pin them to one particular individual."[104] The specificity of his characterization helped to establish the recognizable condition for this "one particular individual." For instance, he frequently wore a tuxedo and top hat along with blackface, giving him an appearance of sophistication that contrasted with his lugubrious speech patterns and shuffling gait. His most popular song, "Nobody" (a song he first introduced in 1905, and which became his trademark), accentuated the insignificant loser. His persona was naïve and childlike, clownish characteristics that had become part of black identity in white culture. Since whites had little acquaintance with blacks beyond minstrelsy, he set out to create a stage character easily recognizable, based as it was on the pervasive myths and stereotypes. Many whites believed that blacks actually behaved just as Williams portrayed them. The blackface mask just made matters worse. Williams's blackface (and others who blackened up) signaled to the audience that the presentation would be humorous and light on the one hand, and racially identifiable on the other. If he could make it clear through the blackface mask that his objective was fun, he could achieve the comic response—at the expense of social commentary. And if audiences came to his shows with fixed expectations, he did not disappoint. His downtrodden routine paved the way for many white comedians as well (W. C. Fields, for example, who worked with—and admired—Williams in the Ziegfeld Follies).

Caricature is the basis of blackface comedy. Caricature, Sigmund Freud explained, "brings about degradation" by emphasizing "a single trait which [was] comic in itself but was bound to be overlooked so long as it was only perceivable in the general picture." Isolating a single trait firmly sets public perception by foregrounding mannerisms, speech patterns, or identifiable characteristics of someone from the general picture of their life to the specific focus of their behavior. For the comic actor, exaggerating the trait provides the foundation and immediate recognition appropriate for satire. Freud referred to this comic process as "unmasking," whereby the pretenses of everyday life, generally overlooked, are exposed and evaluated through comic mistakes and fallibility. Unmasking certain prototypical figures, caricature undermines "people and objects which lay claim to authority and respect."[105] In blackface, the alleged pretenses of African Americans were exposed. Through the malapropian, deceitful, and pompous caricatures personified by Miller and Lyles, and the fatalistic, naïve, and set-upon caricature of Williams, the "unmasking" of their alleged superficialities manifested the supposed true image and revealed the so-called real traits of African Americans. Caricature thus assisted in "exposing" pretenses for amusement.

For this, Bert Williams received both praise and condemnation. Booker T. Washington noted that Williams "is a tremendous asset of the negro race." He lauded the fact that Williams "aids" African Americans "many times more than he could have helped the race by merely contenting to whine about racial difficulties."[106] Like Miller and Lyles, Williams was appreciated for his community support, even though his performances were retrogressive. In 1914, the *Chicago Defender* called Williams "one of the greatest comedians America has ever bred and taught." The paper reported that Williams was a performer possessing "dignity of purpose," and would, "if in the skin of a white man, turn the laughing world topsy turvy with delighted amazement."[107] Others, however, saw matters differently. While lamenting his death in 1922, the *Messenger* held that he "rendered a disservice to black people" by playing "in theatres that either barred or Jim-Crowed Negroes."[108] In his 1922 essay titled "The Bert Williams Case," William H. Ferris made the following observation: "When the average Negro sees a Negro comedian with blackened face, red lips and grotesque garb, shuffling and shambling and galloping and cavorting on the stage," they understand that this is "the artistic interpretation of a type." However, this style of performing portrays a "low type" who is a "deliberate travestying of a race." For Ferris, the "average" African American "feels that when a Negro artist portrays a Negro in his grotesque and hideous aspects, to get the applause of the gallery gods, that he is catering to a race prejudice."[109] During his lifetime Williams was caught in the paradox of race politics. But so, too, were most African American performers who rose above the commonplace. Although he achieved the greatest acclaim as well as notoriety of his time, his circumstances were not uncommon. Other blackfaced comedians before and after Williams encountered similar conundrums and made the best of their situations.

S. H. DUDLEY: MORE GEORGIA THAN BOSTON

Colored entertainers always give full measure. —S. H. Dudley (1912)[110]

One of the least recognized major figures of the New Negro Renaissance theatre was Sherman "S. H." Dudley. From 1910 to 1925 he was the most successful African American producer, owning over a dozen theatres. He wrote, performed, and produced several musicals, none of which appeared on Broadway, but they enjoyed considerable success outside New York, especially in the South and Midwest. He negotiated with white producers, leading to the creation of several organizations that coordinated the tours of vaudeville circuits. Bernard L. Peterson wrote that Dudley "worked tirelessly to improve conditions for Black performers in show business by helping them to control their own theatres, circuits, and other aspects of theatrical enterprise."[111] He also achieved notoriety as the actor who actually brought his mule onstage. The routine, "Dudley and His

Mule," was part of his shows (the first mule was named Rastus, and after Rastus died the second mule was Patrick). Dudley was an expert horseman, owning stables and racehorses later in life. His capabilities with horses and mules enabled him to control the animal onstage, creating the desired comic effect. As Ted Vincent put it, "a live mule dressed in pants" would be "trotted on to the stage each night to drive Dudley to distraction while the audience roared with laughter."[112]

Dudley had begun his career in minstrel theatre. In 1905, he organized his own company, "The Smart Set," modeled after the white theatrical company of the same name. He wrote, produced, and performed in several musicals, the most popular being *The Black Politician* (1905–1908, in which he introduced his famous mule), *His Honor, The Barber* (1909–1911), and *Dr. Beans from Boston* (1912–1915). Dudley realized that African American performers were at the mercy of white booking agents. Theatres across the country depended on them to arrange for playhouses and tours. By controlling these bookings and their routes, managers essentially dictated which shows would perform and in what locales. In addition, black actors and shows had to contend with two problems: a difficult time with Jim Crow segregation and the burden of dealing with corrupt and bigoted agents who often refused to pay or pay adequately. Actors were frequently warned in the black newspapers that particular towns along the booking routes had few accommodations for them. One 1924 report cautioned that "colored acts" had "better take camping outfits along with them" because "sleeping accommodations" were nil. The actors requested sleeping arrangements in the theatre, but were "curtly refused" by the management.[113] In other instances actors were confronted by overt hostility and even Ku Klux Klan demonstrations. The Klan's presence at one theatre, reported a newspaper, "practically killed business," leaving black actors stranded and without pay.[114] The complexities of running a show in various parts of the nation caught up with both the desire for vaudeville theatre and segregation, creating difficulties beyond the usual ones of scheduling, lodging, salaries, and transportation.

Dudley addressed the matter by buying up theatres across the country. He accumulated considerable wealth during his early years as an actor and producer by controlling much of his show's profits. He was a shrewd and versatile businessman, able to work with performers and producers, black and white. White agents attempted to control black playhouses, but they had little if any knowledge of the black community's tastes in entertainment. Many white producers and booking agents found Dudley easy to work with; he supplied the needed information, but at a price. The *Pittsburgh Post* reported that by 1913 Dudley had a chain of 12 theatres (he owned 4 outright, and was part of a conglomerate that owned the others). They were used for both movies and live performances. They were predominately located in the South, but Dudley also owned or controlled theatres in Philadelphia, Indianapolis, Cleveland, St. Louis, and Kansas City as well.[115] From 1911 to 1916, he continued to purchase and lease theatres, eventually consolidating his ownership to form the Dudley Theatrical Enterprise. With offices in Washington, D.C., Dudley controlled or owned several theatres in Washington and Philadelphia, as well as others in Virginia and Georgia. The black communities in the South and Midwest clamored for entertainment, and Dudley's company supplied much of it. Sometimes called the "Dudley, Klein, and Reevin's Circuit" (the names of the three most influential producers), Dudley's theatres were recognized as a very real challenge to white booking agencies and producers.[116] By 1916, he had met with several white producers and agents to organize booking arrangements and secure payments for actors.

African American performers participating in touring shows were frequently unpaid, encountered double bookings, and were misinformed about schedules. In 1921, for example, actor and vaudevillian Garnett Warbington criticized managers who abused black performers. Claiming that one producer named "Mr. Cummings" cut salaries "under all kinds of pretenses and excuses," Warbington warned that Cummings was a "typical Southerner" who "hates a Negro like poison."[117] Many shows arrived in towns only to discover that the theatres were "double" booked. Agents and theatre owners would typically overbook for their own protection. Unfortunately, some situations encouraged overbooking, since trains did not always arrive on schedule and some companies disbanded overnight, thus failing to arrive at the appointed theatres. When a show failed to arrive, for whatever reason, it was often too late to find an alternative. Tickets had to be refunded and revenue lost. If two shows were booked on the same night and one failed to arrive, at least the other show went on and profits were kept up. Yet for the actors, double bookings meant a potential loss of revenue. They might arrive at a town with plans to assemble their sets and prepare to perform, only to discover that another show had already begun its preparations. Problems were exacerbated on both ends: the shows were not always dependable, since actors sometimes quit hastily for a better "gig" elsewhere. In response, producers and booking agents would hedge their bets by double-booking. Furthermore, in an unregulated market, widespread corruption was commonplace. Knowing that the shows were likely to leave the next morning for another appearance elsewhere, managers and theatre owners might "disappear" late at night or the next morning when it came time to pay up. Actors had to board the next available train to arrive on time for their following performance with nothing to show for their previous work.

Chaos and corruption moved Dudley and others to form the Southern Consolidated Circuit (SCC). At the time he was the only African American producer and theatre owner with enough authority to make a difference. Corrupt managers and theatre owners were notified that if payment obligations went unfulfilled, shows would no longer be booked there. Actors were fined for irresponsible behavior. As an actor and producer well respected by both blacks and whites, Dudley had earned the right to make such commanding decisions. SCC operated from offices in Chicago, Washington, D.C., and Pensacola. The conglomerate managed 28 theatres altogether. Most were in the South, but the SCC also acquired theatres in Chicago, Detroit, Pittsburgh, Indianapolis, and Cleveland.[118] Dudley was responsible mainly for the southeast, but his influence (except in New York City) extended throughout most of the eastern portion of the nation, North and South.

The 1919 theatrical season saw the launching of a new organization, the Quality Amusement Corporation (QAC). QAC laid a wider net than the SCC, in order to accommodate the growing number of theatres. It provided separate routes for Midwest cities such as Chicago, Cincinnati, Cleveland, and Indianapolis. Romeo Dougherty, drama critic for the *Chicago Defender*, threw his support behind the QAC. In 1920, he wrote that nothing "within the past decade has loomed up so large in the amusement world as it concerns colored people as the big theatrical combine with headquarters in New York and known as the Quality Amusement Corporation."[119] Briefly, Robert Levi (sometimes spelled Levy), a white producer, organized the QAC. E. C. Brown, a black banker and owner of Philadelphia's Dunbar and Brooklyn's Putnam theatres, and Lester A. Walton, eventually gained a controlling interest in the organization. But even the QAC, understaffed and underfinanced, proved inadequate, given the increasing needs of theatre companies.

By 1920, the emergence of hundreds of additional theatres throughout the country made matters even more complicated. The advent of movies created an additional burden on playhouses. Many towns had only one playhouse to accommodate movies, operas, musicals, vaudeville, plays, and other acts. Scheduling efforts tried to avert massive confusion, but problems grew as new theatres surfaced virtually overnight. Charles H. Turpin, owner of the Booker T. Washington Theatre in St. Louis, was appointed temporary chairman of QAC, and Dudley was vice-chairman. Early on Dudley was a significant influence, but later the organization came under the control of the Theatre Owners Booking Association, dubbed the "TOBA" or "Toby" circuit (the original "TOBA" had been formed in 1909, but soon disbanded). Among the well-known TOBA theatres were H. B. Miller's Grand (which housed impresario Billy King and his company) and

Monogram, as well as the Koppin theatres, in Chicago; Turpin's Booker T. Washington Theatre in St. Louis; the Cass and the Koppin (owned by H. S. Koppin) in Detroit; the Regent in Baltimore; the Standard and the Gibson in Philadelphia; the Howard in Washington, D.C. (not to be confused with the Howard University Players); and the 81 in Atlanta. Many others proliferated in small towns across the South and Midwest, providing melodrama, amusement, and musical entertainment for African American audiences. On 26 and 27 May 1920, several theatre managers, black and white, met in Chicago to form what was then called the "National Managers Protective Association." According to one report made by the *Chicago Defender*, two days of meetings with producers were spent discussing "practical methods" that would "best meet the needs of an organization that will be impartial to all theatres catering to Colored patrons." The members agreed that the musicals, plays, operas, vaudeville, and films shown in these theatres "must be encouraged in every way to intersperse their acts with clean, worthwhile offerings in songs and new material." Perhaps most important was the fact that the organization insisted that working arrangements must include "contracts," eliminate "lay-offs," and maintain salaries as agreed upon, with a committee formed to "take up all complaints of managers, actors, or agents."[120]

According to a 1924 report by Kennard Williams in the *Baltimore Afro-American*, TOBA had by then "a monopoly in the placing of colored acts." It controlled "the destinies of several thousand members of acts" rotating across the South, responsible for booking entertainment "to those patrons in the southern section of the country who are segregated in their own playhouses by custom or law."[121] TOBA originally involved 31 black and white theatre owners, but grew incrementally as theatres surfaced across the nation. The Southern Consolidated Circuit and the Managers' and Performers' Circuit (subsidiary organizations) also worked in conjunction with TOBA. Dudley was included; however, by the mid 1920s, the size of TOBA and its subsidiaries had rendered Dudley less important. He was simply one of several producers, some trying to protect black performers from unscrupulous agents and managers, others seeking only self-interest and profit. He was still a force working for the best interests of black artists, but his power had been diminished by the onslaught of new agents and the multifarious needs of the entertainment industry. During the 1920s, TOBA began booking, in addition to plays, vaudeville, musicals, and movies, a conglomeration of circuses, singing groups, and magic acts. In cities and towns across the country, playhouses were being built to accommodate demand. The enormity of TOBA made it impossible for any individual to protect the rights of all artists working in this fast-paced environment. Dudley, and the African American journalist J. A. Jackson, tried to stabilize the industry by having the acts present their shows to a committee for classification. These "try-out" performances would adjudicate each show's talent and set a fixed fee that had to be met. It was hoped this would guarantee salaries. However, TOBA failed to take action on behalf of black performers, and Dudley's plan went unrealized.[122]

Still, Dudley did his best. By 1925, he had controlling interest in the vaudeville booking agency, the Southern Consolidated Circuit. The ubiquitous control of booking arrangements by TOBA producers prompted Dudley to report in 1925 that the "day has gone when an act or show can book independently and make money."[123] When he and his white partner, E. L. Cummings, parted, Dudley formed the Colored United Vaudeville Circuit, which was a subsidiary of TOBA. By this time (circa mid-1920s), Dudley had accumulated considerable property and wealth. He owned a chain of theatres in Washington, D.C., and had 200 to 400 actors, dancers, and singers on payroll, playing to black audiences. He was also the general manager and treasurer of the Colored Actors Union (1921–1924). Dudley created the Union so that African American performers "might have an opportunity of getting together, conversing, noting deficiencies and classifying acts."[124] During the same time, he produced several shows that toured on the TOBA circuit. Among them were *Go Get It* (1922), *Bamville Follies* (1926), and *Ebony Follies* (1928). His operations, as well as Billy King's Company in Chicago, were forerunners of the "Chitlin Circuit," a term for African American touring shows that play primarily to black audiences even to this day.[125]

Throughout his career Dudley was cognizant of the deplorable conditions for black entertainers. He was also well aware of the need for white audiences, since black audiences, representing a smaller audience pool, were limited. White audiences were required if ambitious productions were to succeed. Musical shows demanded enormous resources to produce; with large casts and musicians to be paid, and lavish scenery to be furnished, shows underwent financial strain. In order to regain investments, a typical show needed to appeal to both black and white audiences, and needed to run for at least a year to recoup expenses. Dudley often granted interviews to the white press for promotional reasons. In one interview with the *Columbus Dispatch* in 1913, he predicted that the alleged "clash" between whites and blacks in America "shall never come." He needed to placate whites, and in so doing offered boilerplate notions of race. He urged whites "with race feelings" to consider "that we are only three centuries from savagery and less than half a century from a condition of absolute dependence." It was not uncommon for black performers and producers to provide such reassuring but banal assessments. Theatres had to be filled, even if that meant catering to racist presumptions. After the interview was completed, the *Dispatch* added this codicil:

> In spite of his belief that the negro of the future will compare favorably with the white man in culture and education, Mr. Dudley knows Americans want depicted on the stage the good-natured negro with all of his weaknesses, and consequently in "Dr. Beans from Boston" he is a razor-carrying, watermelon loving "coon," who likes rest and chicken and gawdy colors.[126]

The *Dispatch*, however, did not accurately depict Dudley's *Dr. Beans from Boston*. Dudley was not a "razor-carrying, watermelon loving coon" in the show. He was a con artist who plays a trick on the upper class.

Dr. Beans from Boston is a three-act show with singing and dancing. As a satire of sorts, it involves a scam by two characters: Gymnasium Butts, an "ex-minstrel actor" (played by Dudley), and his partner, Bill Simmons, a "hustler." Simmons discovers that a local drug store located in Buckroe Beach, Virginia, is about to be sold to "Dr. Beans" from Boston. The drug store itself is situated in an affluent neighborhood. Simmons convinces Butts to disguise himself as "Dr. Beans" and gain access to the drug store's wonder drug, a "love potion." The store and the potion will prove to be the ingredient that makes them rich. The action takes place at the Buckroe Beach hotel, which is, as one character explains, "the great resort for rich colored folks."[127]

Once the scam is set in motion, the proprietor of the hotel, Waterbury Lee, invites "Dr. Beans" into the hotel. He throws a party in the Doctor's honor. It is an affair which one character describes as the "grand gathering" of "real Ethiopian aristocracy."[128] Butts meets Lee's daughter, Susie, and immediately falls in love with her. But he runs into trouble when the local opera singer, Sahara Heartburn, seems to think she remembers the real Dr. Beans and cannot reconcile the differences in appearance. The situation allows for a number of comic routines. Butts, however, finally convinces her that he is the real Dr. Beans. While he is continuing to court Susie, the real Dr. Beans arrives, but by way of slapstick, the real Dr. Beans is hit on the head and forgets who and where he is. The play ends with the scam a total success.

The point of this lighthearted farce is its send-up of black middle- and upper-class pretensions. White audiences appreciated poking fun at wealthy African Americans and southern black audiences equally enjoyed satirizing the "upper crusts." Class divisions provided the material from which Dudley drew. In 1913, during the show's run, Dudley reported that:

> All the members of our company are colored. And they ought to be familiar with the various characteristics of the race. I think we have brought them out quite clearly and the public has been very kind to us. Our present play [*Dr. Beans from*

Boston] has for its locale a place which really exists. It is a watering resort, frequented only by colored folks, and we have tried to produce bits of character that actually existed.[129]

Dudley's emphasis on "authenticity" was a promotional effort to convince audiences that his play presented the reality of black life, as opposed to white actors in blackface, who could only be "pretending." *Dr. Beans from Boston* ran for over three years, enjoying successful tours across the South and Midwest.

Dudley's successes were due in large part to his appeal to black audiences as well as whites. While it may appear somewhat odd to report that black audiences enjoyed his blackface comedies, considerable reflection reveals that his appeal, and the appeal of blackface in general, was not wholly surprising. There were several reasons for this, not the least being the quality of the actors. The blackfaced comedians of Dudley's company and others were gifted performers, capable of singing, dancing, slapstick, and impeccable comic timing. Dudley himself was a veteran performer who entertained thousands over several decades.

Adding to his popularity was the fact that Dudley's shows maintained "clean" humor. To southern working- and middle-class African Americans, this factor contributed to his success. He and his conglomerate of theatrical organizations insisted that shows "must be encouraged in every way to intersperse their acts with clean, worthwhile offerings in songs and new material."[130] Southern African Americans caught up in racial uplift stressed bourgeois moral codes of appropriate behavior, even if they were not bourgeois in wealth. Southern "gentility" became one way for black southerners to appeal to moderate and sympathetic whites. But uplift ideology also operated as a tradition of reform and "evangelical progress."[131] For instance, Fannie Barrier Williams wrote in 1906 that black social respectability had compelled "the decent element of the colored people" to remain "socially clean and respectable."[132] Dudley upheld the emphasis on "clean" entertainment and for this the black communities swept up by moral religiosity and bourgeois codes of behavior appreciated him.

Perhaps the most important ingredient to the success of blackface shows to black audiences was the belief that blackface comedy, however self-mocking, was part of a cultural heritage. By the 1910s and 1920s, blackface minstrelsy was several generations old. For better or worse, it had become part of the cultural lexicon. For many African Americans, minstrel shows were their chief entertainment, sometimes the only entertainment for the local community. Actor and vaudeville comedian Tom Fletcher (1873–1954) put it succinctly when he said that as a child, "minstrel shows were my chief delight."[133] Although many, particularly northerners, shunned blackface as reactionary, black southerners accepted its conventions and welcomed its "guilty" pleasures when the touring companies arrived.

Many black intellectuals of the urban North emulated European tastes, while at the same time regarding southern, rural African Americans with disdain and embarrassment. Rural southern blacks were ridiculed for their slowness of speech, religious piety, and superstitions. According to one urban study, the typical migrant traveling north was characterized as a "rural, uneducated farmhand."[134] Black and white Jazz Age urbanites considered their hedonistic, venturesome, exotic, and secular lifestyle superior to the puritanical, mostly Baptist country ways of southern, rural African Americans, epitomizing them as "backward." Black intellectuals frequently demonstrated "uppity" attitudes toward southern blacks, casting aspersions of inferiority on any displays of "rural" attire, prudish behavior, or unsophisticated outlook. Others, especially the southern elite, objected to black minstrel shows on ethical grounds. In a two-part editorial, the *Baltimore Afro-American* reported in 1915 that "low Negro minstrelsy" might abound in "catchy songs," but these shows will eventually "pass from view." Current black minstrelsy "may stand for the simple, childish and blundering Negro in this new civilization," but the "position of the race" must ultimately reject this form of entertainment in favor of "developing another side and getting that side before the people of the country."[135] Despite this and other attempts to limit the appeal of minstrel shows among African Americans, the popularity of the form remained firm during the time.

The reasons for the minstrel show's popularity were as many as they were complex. Dudley's show, *Dr. Beans from Boston,* provided southern and midwestern African Americans an opportunity to release their oppositional feelings toward northern, primarily Harlemite, arrogance and superiority. Thus, instead of rejecting blackface humor and its comic shenanigans, they embraced it, so long as it offered "clean" fun. Popular culture historian William Barlow has argued that blackface shows were under the control of white men who regulated the business end of the touring enterprises. Black performers had to "accommodate the wishes of their white employers"; as a consequence, "fragments of the antebellum blackface minstrel tradition," especially the burnt-cork performance, "survived in black minstrelsy."[136] While it was no doubt true that black touring and tent shows were primarily under the control of white producers, the fact remains that black audiences patronized the theatres on their own. Black performers frequently played before all-black audiences in the South; no white producers followed every show in every town and city. If blackface proved to be unpopular it simply would not have survived, no matter what white producers tried to impose. Blackface survived and flourished in many southern and midwestern African American communities during the 1910s and 1920s because black audiences appeared to have accepted it without being strong-armed into it. Suffice to say, blackface appealed to black audiences at least to some degree. Like the black churches, which permitted the display of uninhibited emotions through singing, dancing, and shouting, the blackface comedies playing to black audiences provided an outlet for vocal and physical expression. Blackface did not disappear from the rollicking humor of vaudeville routines, especially when in these shows the upper classes—the "colored aristocrats"—received their comeuppance. Instead, it provided "down home" humor to audiences eager to unload their daily burdens and laugh without fear.

Moreover, blackface troupes represented an "authentic" tradition of entertainment that many believed was rooted in the South. Jean Toomer's description of black southern life in his unpublished essay (ca. 1924), "The Negro Emergent," makes the case that northern influences undermined African American "roots within the soil." For this reason white southerners, Toomer claimed, were "often closer" to blacks psychologically than northern African Americans. As Toomer explained,

> ever since emancipation, well intentioned white men, aided by Negroes, have been trying to plaster a white image on a black reality—to superimpose Boston on Georgia. This has led to an over-valuing of academic study; a prejudice against hand-training. It became a matter of shame that the men whose muscle had built the South could not read Caesar in the original.[137]

Toomer's assessment lamentably mirrors similar racist complaints made by white southerners, i. e., that carpetbaggers had ruined the complacent "Negro" by stirring up education and trouble. However, if we take Toomer's notion of southern African Americans as having a distinctive lifestyle and culture, we can apply it to the acceptance of blackface comedy as an indigenous form of popular entertainment. To a certain degree, Dudley and his audiences represented people refusing to "superimpose Boston on Georgia." Rather than denigration, the blackface mask evoked an "authentic" folk style that was firmly grounded in southern traditions and roots. However much the blackface habit seems peculiar, its cultural context was undeniable. Dudley had tapped into a rich layer of theatrical history; many black southerners and midwesterners considered his work as part of their folklore and local pride. Blackface, although derogatory, was still a "tradition." For a culture robbed of its roots, even acts mocking in-group behavior provided some semblance of communal recognition and a nexus for fun. Dudley

surfaced from a grassroots tradition of gifted blackface comedians, first-genera-
tion African American comics Billy McClain (1866–1950), Billy Kersands
(1842–1915), Ernest Hogan (1865–1909), and Sam Lucas (1840–1916), who
were less well-known than Williams and Walker or Cole and Johnson, but no
less talented. These artists established a genealogy of uproarious routines and
communal identity firmly grounded in local "folk" flavor.[138] Dudley shared
recognition onstage with many second-generation blackface performers and producers: Chicago's William "Billy" King (1875–?), Salem Tutt Whitney
(1868–1934), and Butterbeans (1895–1967) & Susie (1896?–1963) in particular.
These actors continued a custom of blackface "folk" musicals and vaudeville
shows on the TOBA circuit.[139]

Dudley's entrepreneurship guaranteed his success. However, because his
shows played mostly in the South, Dudley has received little attention. Yet he
was one of the most influential African American producers of his era. His willingness to compromise and work with white producers established his reputation
as a savvy and knowledgeable entrepreneur. More than anyone, he helped create
the TOBA circuit, which established a venue for black performers who otherwise would not have found work. The stage comedies that flourished on the
TOBA circuit went unnoticed by Broadway as well as the black bourgeoisie. Yet
TOBA, "with its all-black audiences and often shabby, ill-kept theatres," Mel
Watkins posits, "was the perfect incubator for a new form of black stage comedy."[140] This new folk style, even in blackface, would form the basis of African
American comedy into the present, and it is S. H. Dudley who deserves much of
the credit for its inception.

FLORENCE MILLS

*The Negroes of New York mourned her, for she was more their idol than
any other artist of the race.*   —James Weldon Johnson (1930)[141]

Except for Josephine Baker, Florence Mills was the most successful African
American female performer of the 1920s. Known as "Little Baby Flo," "Little
Twinks," and "Little Blackbird" because of her delicate and pixyish style, she became popular with black and white audiences in numerous musical comedies. At
the peak of her career (from 1921 to 1927), she appeared in *Shuffle Along* (replacing Gertrude Saunders), Lew Leslie's *Plantation Review* (1922), and *Dover to Dixie*
(in London in 1923), which was renamed *Dixie to Broadway* when it came to New
York (1924–1925). In 1926, she performed in Paris in *Le Revue Nègre,* the same
cabaret act that catapulted Josephine Baker to stardom. Returning to the United

States, she joined Lew Leslie once more for her final show, *Blackbirds of 1926*, which opened not on Broadway but in Harlem's Alhambra Theatre (Seventh Avenue and 126th Street) for six weeks before touring London and Paris. Her hit song, "I'm a Little Black Bird Looking for a Blue Bird," became a bestseller. She died of appendicitis in November 1927.

Beginning her career in vaudeville at the age of six, she was billed "Baby Florence Mills." Mills joined the Williams and Walker Company in their production of *Sons of Ham* (1900).[142] She was a protégée of Aida Overton Walker, who became her mentor and role model. One of the many lessons Mills learned from Walker was her hit song, "Miss Hannah from Savannah," which Mills sang following Walker's death in 1914.[143] Mills learned the cakewalk and buck dance from Walker, winning prizes for her skill. Additionally, she was an accomplished pantomimist and singer, possessing a peculiar "bird-like" voice that was a crowd pleaser. Following the break-up of the Williams and Walker Company in 1909, she joined her two sisters, Olivia and Maude, in forming a musical group called "The Mills Sisters," which toured the vaudeville circuit. Later Mills joined the Bonita Company and the Panama Trio as one of the singing and dancing "pickaninnies" (more on this term "pickaninny" shortly). Around the mid-1910s, she teamed up with Ulysses S. ("Slow Kid") Thompson, an accomplished choreographer and dancer. Together they formed a new touring group called the "Tennessee Ten," making the rounds of the Keith Circuit. She eventually married Thompson.

In 1922, Mills initiated a plantation cabaret act with her husband. After performing in *Shuffle Along*, she would join Thompson during the evening to present their act at the Plantation Club, a nightspot over New York's Winter Garden Theatre. This late-night club, Richard Newman has remarked, drew the "fashionable white clientele and helped create an accepting atmosphere for things Negro."[144] Working with theatrical entrepreneur Lew Leslie, Mills and Thompson transformed the show into the *Plantation Revue*, which went on to achieve considerable success on Broadway.

Although *Plantation Revue* was Mill's first success following *Shuffle Along*, it was her performance in *Dixie to Broadway* in 1924 that secured her international reputation. *Dixie to Broadway* emerged from Mills's show, *Dover to Dixie* (sometimes titled *Dover Street to Dixie*), produced by Leslie and opening in London. Plantation elements remained, but the setting changed from Dover Street to New York. In both shows, Mills was the main attraction. E. W. Osborn described her as a "slender streak of genius, about five feet tall, born a shade or two south of the color line," who "sang and danced and played with all the emotions." Osborn continued to praise Mills, saying that she "held at will a big audience of the mixed and different kind."[145] Writing in the *New York Telegram and Evening Mail*, Gilbert W. Gabriel noted that the "not so dark particular star of this jamboree," Florence Mills, is a "sensational little personality." He referred to her as "slim, jaunty, strung on fine and tremulous wires," adding that she "continues to tease the public's sense of [the] beautiful and odd." He further described Mills as having

> an impudent fragility about her, a grace of grotesqueness, a humor of writhes, ankles, pitching hips and perky shoulders that are not to be resisted. Her voice continues to be sometimes sweet and sometimes further from the pitch than Dixie is from Broadway. She is an exotic done in brass.[146]

These reviews and others reveal a dual emphasis: her beauty and peculiarity. Mills would appear one way, then another. Her voice was sweet, yet at times ribald. There are no extant recordings of her singing, nor are there films of her dancing. However, one can surmise from the accolades that she was a quirky performer who straddled the line between grace and sensuality on the one hand, and pixie boyishness on the other. She was enormously popular among white critics. For many whites, she was no different than any other performer, except for her great talent. For instance, Heywood Broun of the *New York World* noted that the entire cast of the *Dixie to Broadway* company were, "according to the American definition, Negroes," but he added, "there are only a few dark skins among the men and none at all among the women." He continued, "Nor would I say that there is nothing in 'Dixie to Broadway' wholly characteristic of the race from which it draws its performers." For Broun, the show was "black" only in so far as there was "passionate fidelity to the eternal verities of tempo not in the inheritance of Nordics." However, Mills was not to be confused with Broun's "eternal verities." As Broun himself noted:

> The method of Florence Mills is like no one else. She does not precisely sing but she makes strange high noises which seem to fit in somehow with a rapidfire sort of sculpture. Sometimes the intent is the creation of the grotesque and then it fades into lines of amazing beauty. Now I have seen grace.[147]

Mills maneuvered on the fine line between the exotic and the respectable. One reviewer noted that Mills's voice was an "echo of something backwoods and civilization," one yielding a "strange amalgamation" that could render a love song both sentimental and quirky.[148] According to many white critics the show was a "black" revue but hardly different from white Broadway. One reviewer singled out Mills, saying the show's song, "Jungle Nights in Dixieland" might have been "discomforting" had it not been for the "droll, fantastic touch" of Florence Mills, who turned this potentially lascivious song into something "highly laughable and arresting."[149] To the contrary, Percy Hammond dismissed *Dixie to Broadway* as little more than "black performers in a white play." He went on to say, however, that it was Florence Mills "who dominated the sable revels." Alexander Woollcott described her as "flashing and beautiful," a performer who "lights up like a Christmas tree when she dances."[150] White critics struggled to locate the show's "blackness." But in praising Mills, they were united.

Mills's performance techniques mirrored much of the style of the times. High-pitched, reedy voices and Jazz Age Charleston dancing were in vogue for both blacks and whites, and Mills fashioned her career based on these popular trends. Yet Mills faced what white performers did not: she remained in segregated hotels and train cars while on tour, was cast in black shows, and was always considered the "colored" performer. Her acting and musical talents may have been modeled on the styles required by Broadway at the time, but her race was never far from the consciousness of her audience. She bore the burden of representing African Americans, even when her acting, singing, and dancing reflected the general spirit of the age.

The black press extolled Mills and her show *Dixie to Broadway*. Lester A. Walton remarked on the "impressive success" of Florence Mills, saying that the show's company had "shattered some deep-rooted theories" about a truly successful black show. When the company returned from London in 1924, the Shubert organization offered an "indefinite run" at the Broadhurst Theatre. Walton called this "startling and unheard of news."[151] *Dixie to Broadway* ran for 77 performances on Broadway, the sixth-longest running African American musical during the 1920s.[152] The New York *Amsterdam News* praised Mills's appearance at the Lafayette Theatre in Harlem in 1924, describing her as an "artist" who "rises to her heights gradually, just like George Walker and Bert Williams did in the old days."[153] The black press lauded Mills's talent as well as her modesty. This was confirmed by the *Chicago Defender*, which described her as a "modest, refined young woman." The *Defender* went on to report that Mills was a "credit to vaudeville in general, besides being a splendid exemplar of her people in their intensely modern and popular style of musical entertainment."[154] Even Theophilus Lewis, who thought *Dixie to Broadway* was "extremely shoddy, garish, and vulgar," had high praise for the gifted performer. Using such superlatives as "incomparable," he went on to say that Mills was the most "consummate artist I have ever seen on the musical show stage," and that she possessed "perfect control of both the technique of restraint and the technique of abandon."[155]

The black press focused on Mills's efforts to improve the conditions of her race. This was not mere flattery. In 1926 she refused to play the lead in the upcoming Broadway play *Lulu Belle* because, as she put it, "it degraded her race."[156] She was often praised for remembering her roots. In 1923, she brought her *Plantation Review* to Harlem's Lafayette Theatre for two weeks. The *Amsterdam News* reported that she "fully appreciates the support given to her" by the black community, and said that "Florence Mills returned to her own and stopped the show."[157] Following a European tour, Mills returned to New York and was offered a chance to perform in "Greenwich Villages Follies." When several white performers in the show refused to work with her, the black press came to her defense:

> Miss [Daphne] Pollard and her supporters, like those who tried to get bad when Bert Williams first became a member of the Ziegfeld Follies, felt their popularity waning when Florence hit the stage . . . and resorted to the old cracker trick of trying to embarrass the little lady who has carried her honors with so much modesty.[158]

Although Mills frequently spoke of the struggle for equality, she sometimes resorted to clichés. In her essay, "The Soul of the Negro," she compared blacks and whites, saying "Negro instincts" are "white to the core."[159] However, in an interview with Beverley Nichols in 1927, Mills waxed eloquent on behalf of her heritage.

> In the old days . . . my mother would sing negro spirituals. She sang them during times of storm and thunder and lightning. . . . She sang these songs, not because she thought that she was frightening away evil spirits, or anything like that, but simply because they seemed the right thing to sing when the whole world was in the grip of the storm. Then, later on, when I went down south in a show, I remembered those old songs. I was doing a number with another girl, and I began to croon, in just the way my mother used to do.[160]

Turning to the subject of prejudice, she asked the interviewer "Do you know what all this does for us?" She responded to her own question: "*It makes us fight—fight all the harder—till we come out on top*" (emphasis in the original). When the interviewer replied that race relations appear to have improved, Mills replied: "Down South it's still terrible. There isn't slavery any more—not real slavery—but there's something very like it."[161] In another London interview, she continued the theme: "I want to help the coloured people," she said, adding, "The stage is the quickest way to get to the people. My own success makes people think better of other coloured folk."[162]

Mill's final show was *Blackbirds of 1926*, which opened at Harlem's Alhambra Theatre. By opening in Harlem and not on Broadway, Mills demonstrated her support for the community. One review described it as a "homecoming":

It is old home week for Harlem. Harlem loves Florence Mills. She represents success, fame, happiness—all that may be hoped for by a sanguine race. She is the melodious, impish spirit of the Afro-American embodied piquantly. She can charm you with all that is bird-like or squirrel-like in her. Or she can move you to instant laughter with the comical spirit that is always ready to break out of its so-small container. Or she can move something deep down in you with her genius for grotesquerie.[163]

Mills combined dignity with enticement. While touring the vaudeville circuits where honky-tonks were the norm, she portrayed herself as refined and elegant, but not without eccentricity. James Weldon Johnson described her as "pixy, elf, radiant, exotic, Peter Pan, wood-nymph, wistful, piquant, magnetism, witchery, madness, flame." Sometimes she was "whimsical," other times she could become "almost grotesque." But, Johnson added, she "had the good taste that never allowed her to be coarse." Although she could be, in Johnson's words, "risqué and seductive," it was, he noted, "impossible for her to be vulgar, for she possessed a naïveté that was alchemic."[164] Unlike her counterpart in Europe, Josephine Baker, Mills remained steadfastly within the bounds of decorum.

Baker's approach was different that Mills. She challenged the blackface minstrel mask through self-mockery. Baker would exaggerate her sexuality, overacting the racy antics of the so-called primitive, and skillfully mocked the stereotype. Baker represented the "jezebel"; however, she subverted this image by often stumbling and mugging. Mills was the "pickaninny," a hapless imp whose eyes bugged wide and hair stood straight when frightened. The "pick" caricature was smiling, good-natured, mischievous, but ultimately terrified. Mills challenged this prevailing cliché in two ways: with sophisticated charm and grotesquery. While pixyish, she was also grotesquely humorous, exaggerating her gestures and wearing "jungle" outfits. She managed a sense of decorum that contrasted with the childlike "pick" image expected of her.

Both Baker and Mills distanced themselves from the respective sexually frenetic and impish modes by using performance techniques that undermined the very caricatures they were supposed to play. Baker overreached, often performing nude in jungle ambience (see figure 17). Unlike Baker, Mills would appear tomboyish (see figure 18). She wore vagabond clothes, yet her dignity and poise supplied a counterintuitive element that cut against the grain of the caricature. If the seductive, sexually loose image was used to ridicule African American women, Josephine Baker's burlesque overacted the sexuality. And if the impish Mills was supposed to be frightened and stupid, she countered the image by grotesquery, outlandish behavior, or sophisticated charm (see figure 19). Both undermined the stereotype by first inhabiting it and then overplaying it. Florence Mills's gestures and singing developed an appearance of grace and charm (a style she learned from Aida Overton Walker), mixed with quirky humor.

Mills received praise from her fans for embodying the sentiments of her race. A fan letter added to the description of Mills as refined: "Florence Mills is a Broadcasting VOICE for her race."[165] Another wrote: "Even in numbers where the music is given to the wildest abandon of jazz rhythm you maintain a refined interpretation that lends a world of color beautiful to all that you do." The writer added:

> I wonder if you know over the months that have passed since your show [*Dixie to Broadway*] began what a wonderfully golden thread you have woven in the warp and woof of a great evolvement for the race? I wonder if in your busy life you find time to remember how well you are playing the part destiny has assigned you?[166]

Her plaudits came from outside the United States as well. A London fan described Mills as the "Daughter of the Motherland."[167] While Baker was appreciated in Europe as a great dancer and comedienne, Mills was recognized as a standard-bearer for her race.

Upon her death, the African American community let the world know how they felt about Florence Mills. Grief filled the streets of Harlem, where over 150,000 people attended her memorial service. The front page of the *Amsterdam News* headlined "World Weeps as Florence Goes to Rest." The *New York Age* added, "Thousands Mourn Passing of Florence Mills."[168] The *Amsterdam News* compared Mills to Aida Overton Walker, noting:

> Florence Mills did more than give pleasure to millions; she made the world a better place for the Negro to live in. [S]he taught the world that the Negro has something rich to give it. She served her country as well as her race, and in a way that is not generally realized.[169]

Her untimely death at 32 was reported in virtually every New York and London newspaper.

CONCLUSION: LAUGHING APART

It's getting very dark on Old Broadway
You see the change in ev'ry cabaret;
Just like an eclipse on the moon,
Ev'ry café now has the dancing coon.   —*Ziegfield Follies of 1922*[170]

It was a contradictory time for black musical entertainers. The world was filled with teeming inconsistencies. Musicals were increasingly popular, but Jim Crow segregation limited progress. Circumstances were depressingly absurd. For example, in his unpublished autobiography, Flournoy Miller related the following story, revealing the extent to which racist practices existed in southern theatres:

> Clarence Powell, a famous comedian, would tell about the town in Georgia where he would tell one of his hilarious stories. The whites on the main floor of the theater would laugh, then a bell would ring, and the Negroes in the balcony could laugh. In that particular Georgian town, whites and Negroes couldn't even laugh together.[171]

Black musicals could be both a blessing and a curse. They broke barriers and yet perpetuated stereotypes. While many of the shows sought, in a limited way even then, to reverse stereotypes, others, such as *Lucky Sambo* (1925), added strength to the "old ways." Miller and Lyles produced *Runnin' Wild* in 1923, which, according to Gerald Bordman, was "the closest any black musical comedy of the era came to repeating *Shuffle Along*'s success."[172] Sissle and Blake managed to achieve some success with their next show, *The Chocolate Dandies* (1924), though it, too, never equaled *Shuffle Along*.

This was a period fraught with contradictions. It was hard for performers to resist the temptation of catering to the white public. Yet it was also discomforting, being an instrument of one's own repression. The "painful entanglement," notes literary historian Eric J. Sundquist, "between self-determination and racist domination" of the era was never so evident than on the musical stage.[173] With his usual acumen, Theophilus Lewis's description of the situation is well worth absorbing:

> Assembling a show for the diversion of white audiences is in itself innocuous enough, but, indirectly, it exerts an unwholesome influence on the Negro theater. [The white producer] pays higher salaries than the colored actor can earn playing before Negro audiences, and if the show enjoys a moderately successful run the members of the cast subsequently find it easier to get bookings in the white vaudeville stage as well as from the manager catering to colored audiences.[174]

While African American actors were "dissatisfied" with the conditions of black theatre, Lewis believed that the majority "willingly submit[ted] to that degrading condition" because if they could obtain enough return engagements at theatres "they will be able to impress the booking offices of the white vaudeville circuit."

Consequently, actors and writers subscribed to the "distorted standards of white vaudeville because becoming popular with its audiences [was] the surest way to catch the eye of white producers of musical comedies and reviews."[175] Self-determination and the need to please a white audience would combine to define the nature of the struggle that black performers would continue to face.

CHAPTER TWELVE

CONCLUSION:
THE END OF "BUTTER SIDE UP"

In the 1920s a revised form of romantic racialism became something of a national fad, resulting in part, curiously enough, from patronizing white encouragement of the New Negro movement and the Harlem Renaissance.
—George M. Fredrickson (1987)[1]

By 1927, several events had left their indelible mark on African American theatre and performance. Florence Mills had died, Charles Gilpin was no longer active, Marcus Garvey had been deported, and Alain Locke and W. E. B. Du Bois were showing diminishing interest in theatre and drama. In the late 1920s, Locke and Du Bois added little to what they had already said about folk art and the role of propaganda. During 1927, "talkies" were invented and rapidly became popular, attracting a great deal of talent from the theatre. A new crop of actors and performers came on the scene, among them Paul Robeson, Bill "Bo Jangles" Robinson, and Rose Mc-Clendon. S. H. Dudley had, for the most part, withdrawn to his horse farm in Maryland. Playwrights Willis Richardson, Georgia Douglas Johnson, and Angelina Weld Grimké would become less productive after 1927, and only Zora Neale Hurston continued, extending her prolific career into the 1930s and 1940s. New writers, however, soon emerged. Langston Hughes and Wallace Thurman brought with them a different agenda and a new set of objectives.

Such transitions established new trends. A turn from coveting white approval to outright rejection of it was increasingly evident. According to Wallace Thurman, African American artists were tired of appearing "butter side up" once they gained the "ears of the public." African Americans, he said in 1927, had been "misinterpreted and caricatured so long by insincere artists" that once they received attention, they felt obliged to expend a great deal of "spiritual energy feeding the public honeyed manna on a silver spoon."[2] Thurman called for alternative aesthetic and artistic objectives. Instead of catering to the interest in minstrelsy or the usual middle-class standards, artists ought to express their "natural" feelings regardless of race or class.

The black middle class had dominated the literary establishment and many thought that this had led creativity astray. A growing current of rebellion against both the white establishment and the black bourgeoisie began to make its presence felt. In a two-part essay in the *Pittsburgh Courier*, Langston Hughes claimed in 1927 that the "best Negroes, including newspaper critics, still think white people are better than colored people." The "best Negroes," he added sarcastically, are convinced that "what white people think about Negroes is more important than what Negroes think about themselves." Hughes criticized the "nouveau riche class" who could only portray themselves and each other. He called for an art that willingly took risks and showed not only the "excellencies" of the black middle class, but also their "slavish devotion to Nordic standards" and "their detachment from the Negro masses."[3] Hughes then exposed what his agenda entailed: whites would gain a bad impression of blacks from his poems; his poems would be "indelicate," including topics such as "harlots and gin-bibers"; he would reveal indignities heaped on black women in the South; and he would reject earlier black writers and not just white ones. Hughes admitted to "prostituting" his talent. He confined his subject matter to the "low life," and rejected both the "blues" and the notion of artists as official representatives of causes and callings. "My poems," he said, "are my own personal comments on life and represent me alone."[4] Hughes's prescriptive conditions for a new aesthetic would become a manifesto of sorts for the years ahead.

The year 1927 witnessed both an acceptance of sorts for "primitivism" and weariness with it as well. The *Amsterdam News* reported that Ethel Waters's new musical, *Africana*, opened amid "a literal riot of barbaric and primitive splendor."[5] Only rarely before would a black newspaper have referred to these terms as anything other than derogatory. Yet in 1927, the terms "primitive" and "barbaric" had less of a negative connotation, becoming mere convention. By 1927, the terms "primitive" and "barbaric" had also become predictable. Their damning attributes had been exhausted by overexposure. The *New York Times* reported that *Africana*, a "black and tan frolic" that opened in July, 1927, contained "the usual romantic songs about the hypothetical Dixie paradise" as well as the "customary minstrel interludes."[6] This "usual" and "customary" predictability was also evident in *Rang Tang*, a musical comedy by Miller and Lyles that opened the night following *Africana*. The *Times* review observed: "Harlem continues its invasion of the Broadway stage." But while the *Times* considered the dancing in *Rang Tang* as "speedy and expert," the show as a whole was characterized as "sluggish and tedious" and it lacked "spontaneity."[7] Primitivism appeared to have become *de rigueur* in black musicals, but it had also worn out its excitement.

The fatigue with primitivism could be observed in the general view of Harlem itself. The community grew weary of white "tourism." Edgar M. Gray wrote at the time that Harlem had become "an easy prey for depraved joy-seeking whites." As a result, he observed, the community was nothing more "than the devil's playground," with "the toys of the devil's joy" being "the colored residents of Harlem."[8] The "Negro vogue" had become an old and exhausted formula for entertainment. The Depression was two years away, but for many black performers and artists a sense of ennui was already settling in. There were few opportunities to deviate from convention. The only living option was a clean break. New themes arose, especially socialism. The demand for social and political change, personified by Paul Robeson, would shape a new generation. While many continued to pander to the mainstream, others were far less satisfied.

Yet, the period that has been examined here, 1910 to 1927, proved to be copious in its integrity and aesthetic originality. It was not quite the age of black and white interracialism or mongrelized culture as some scholars have argued,[9] but rather a period of advances and retreats in the struggle for justice. Most significantly, it was a time of paradoxes, with efforts demonstrating varying and sometimes startling successes. The situation pulled in several directions at once, forcing many to compromise. Because of these ambiguities, scholars have generally treated the performing arts of the era dismissively. We have already seen a need for correcting this opinion. Historian W. D. Wright makes the point that the creative output of the Harlem Renaissance was "the production of a people just up from slavery," who felt the need "to produce their art in an extreme racist context that disjointed and deprecated their effort." Given these impediments, Wright concludes, the "achievements of the Harlem Renaissance are not to be sneered at and do not have to be viewed as a distraction from later Black artistic achievements."[10]

Many African American performers and playwrights at the time resisted the forces of oppression and yet worked within the status quo. Some idealized the notion of the "New Negro," overcompensating for situations that provided little in the way of encouragement. Pearl Bowser and Louise Spence have noted that the early silent films of Oscar Micheaux, particularly *Within Our Gates* (1920) and *Body and Soul* (1925, starring Paul Robeson), were influenced by "a highly racialized and race-conscious society" that forced Micheaux to be responsible for "a special burden on representation."[11] Performers and playwrights shared Micheaux's paradoxical condition: to create for aesthetic reasons alone, or to create for social causes, with an eye toward representing the race. Within the early Harlem Renaissance a new style of performance and playwriting came about that was informed by social conditions as well as individual creativity. Efforts by artists, performers, and playwrights to change the world were not always successful. Still, the fact that the performers, dramatists, dancers, athletes, orators, and critics we have examined failed to accomplish all that they sought detracts little from the courage, talent, and beautiful pageant they displayed in seeking the initiative.

NOTES

ABBREVIATIONS

The following abbreviations are used throughout the notes:

AG   Alexander Gumby Collection, Columbia University, New York

BR   Billy Rose Theatre Collection, New York Public Library at Lincoln Center, Astor, Lenox, and Tilden Foundation

FLP   Theatre Collection, Free Library of Philadelphia

GM   George Mason University's Special Collection and Archives, VA

HB   Hatch-Billops Collection, New York

HTC   Harvard Theatre Collection, Cambridge, MA

LOC   Library of Congress, Washington, D.C.

MC   Theatre Collection, The Museum of the City of New York

MS   Moorland-Spingarn Research Center, Howard University, Washington, D.C.

SC   Schomburg Center for Research in Black Culture, New York Public Library, Astor, Lenox, and Tilden Foundation

UM   Special Collection and Archives, University of Massachusetts Archives, Amherst, MA

CHAPTER ONE

1. Benjamin Brawley, *The Negro in Literature and Art in the United States* (New York: Duffield & Co., 1918) 4.

2. Alain Locke, ed., *The New Negro* (1925; reprint, New York: Atheneum, 1992), 6.

3. The Harlem Renaissance–New Negro era was a period of the greatest single shift in consciousness of black life and thought prior to the Civil Rights Movement, and the Civil Rights Movement itself was deeply influenced by the Harlem Renaissance's theories and practices. The term "New Negro" dates as early as 1895, but it is primarily known by the title of the book, *The New Negro*, edited by Alain Locke in 1925 and emanating from the essays collected in *Survey Graphic* 6.6 (March 1925) that composed of articles defining a new African American agenda. For a survey of the term "New Negro," see Cary D. Wintz, *Black Culture and the Harlem Renaissance* (Houston: Rice University Press, 1988), 30–47. For other studies on the Harlem Renaissance–New Negro Movement, see, among other works, Jervis Anderson, *This Was Harlem* (New York: Noonday, 1981); Arna Bontemps, ed., *The Harlem Renaissance Remembered* (New York: Dodd, Mead, & Co., 1972); James De Jongh, *Vicious Modernism: Black Harlem and the Literary Imagination* (Cambridge: Cambridge University Press, 1990); Nathan Irvin Huggins, *Harlem Renaissance* (New York: Oxford University Press, 1971);

David Levering Lewis, *When Harlem Was in Vogue* (New York: Penguin, 1981, 1997); Victor Kramer, ed., *The Harlem Renaissance Re-examined* (New York: AMS Press, 1987); Amritjit Singh et al., ed., *The Harlem Renaissance: Reevaluations* (New York: Garland, 1989); Cheryl A. Wall, *Women of the Harlem Renaissance* (Bloomington: Indiana University Press, 1995); and Steven Watson, *The Harlem Renaissance: Hub of African-American Culture, 1920–1930* (New York: Pantheon, 1995).

4. For important collections of plays, see James V. Hatch and Leo Hamalian, eds., *Lost Plays of the Harlem Renaissance* (Detroit: Wayne State University Press, 1996); Hamalian & Hatch, eds., *The Roots of African American Drama* (Detroit: Wayne State University Press, 1991); and Kathy A. Perkins and Judith L. Stephens, eds., *Strange Fruit: Plays on Lynching by American Women* (Bloomington: Indiana University Press, 1998). For an overview of plays by African American women, see Judith L. Stephens, "The Harlem Renaissance and the New Negro Movement," in *American Women Playwrights*, Brenda Murphy, ed. (Cambridge: Cambridge University Press, 1999), 98–117; and Christine R. Gray, "Discovering and Recovering African American Women Playwrights Writing Before 1930," in the same collection, 244–53.

5. For a study on the musicals of the era, see Thomas L. Riis, *Just Before Jazz: Black Musical Theatre in New York, 1890–1915* (Washington, D.C.: Smithsonian Institute Press, 1989); Allen Woll, *Black Musical Theatre: From Coontown to Dreamgirls* (Baton Rouge: Louisiana State University Press, 1989); Bernard L. Peterson, *A Century of Musicals in Black and White* (Westport, CT: Greenwood Press, 1993); Wayne D. Shirley, "The House of Melody: A List of Publications of the Gotham-Attucks Music Company at the Library of Congress," *The Black Perspective in Music* 15.1 (Spring 1987), 79–112; and John Graziano, "Sentimental Songs, Rags, and Transformations: The emergence of the Black Musical, 1895–1910," in *Musical Theatre in America*, ed. Glenn Loney (London: Greenwood Press, 1984), 211–232.

6. Michael North puts it this way: the Harlem Renaissance, he says, "touches on the perpetual rivalries between art and propaganda and between high art and popular culture." As a movement, it was concerned with the "ultimate question about art and politics," which was: "is art the highest expression of an achieved civilization, or is it what a people has instead of political power?" North, "The Harlem Renaissance," in *The Cambridge History of Literary Criticism, Vol. 7: Modernism and the New Criticism*, ed. A. Walton Litz, Louis Menand, and Lawrence Rainey (Cambridge: Cambridge University Press, 2000), 167.

7. Locke, "The Negro and the American Stage," *Theatre Arts Monthly* 10.2 (February 1926), 116.

8. Locke, "The Legacy of the Ancestral Arts," in *The New Negro*, 256.

9. Gregory Holmes Singleton, "Birth, Rebirth, and the 'New Negro' of the 1920s," *Phylon* 43.1 (March 1982), 31.

10. Bernard W. Bell, *The Afro-American Novel and Its Tradition* (Amherst: University of Massachusetts Press, 1987), 114.

11. In this analysis of "paradox" I build on Howard A. Slaatte, *The Pertinence of the Paradox* (New York: Humanities Press, 1968), and Nicholas Rescher, *Paradoxes: Their Roots, Range, and Resolution* (Chicago: Open Court, 2001).

12. Samuel A. Floyd, Jr., *The Power of Black Music: Interpreting its History from Africa to the United States* (New York: Oxford University Press, 1995), 88.

13. This view is more or less in agreement with Daylanne K. English, "Selecting the Harlem Renaissance," *Critical Inquiry* 25.4 (Summer 1999), 807–21. English ar-

gues that by "turning down the volume" on the optimistic voices of Du Bois and Locke and emphasizing the movements "less 'optimistic' tropes and texts," we can "develop alternative constructions of the Harlem Renaissance" (814), which reveal competing and conflictual aims and purposes. William Jordan, in "'The Damnable Dilemma': African-American Accommodation and Protest during World War I," *Journal of American History* 81.4 (March 1995), 1562–1590, also argues that Du Bois was often torn between loyalty to the American cause in the war and a desire to resist supporting the war because of the rampant racism and lynching at the time.

14. W. E. B. Du Bois, *The Souls of Black Folk* (1903), in *Three Negro Classics*, ed. John Hope Franklin (New York: Avon, 1965), 215.

15. Thomas C. Holt, "The Political Use of Alienation: W. E. B. Du Bois on Politics, Race, and Culture, 1903–1940," *American Quarterly* 42.2 (June 1990), 305.

16. Lewis R. Gordon, *Bad Faith and Antiblack Racism* (Atlantic Highlands, NJ: Humanities Press, 1995), 51.

17. David Levering Lewis, "Just Take the A Train," *New York Times Book Review*, 22 April 2001, 9.

18. Eunice Roberta Hunton, "Breaking Through," 684, and Kelly Miller, "The Harvest of Race Prejudice," 682, in *Survey Graphic*, ed. Alain Locke 6.6 (March 1925).

19. Lucius Outlaw, "Toward a Critical Theory of 'Race,'" in *Anatomy of Racism*, ed. David Theo Goldberg (Minneapolis: University of Minnesota Press, 1990), 77.

20. Virginia Woolf, "Mr. Bennett and Mrs. Brown," *Collected Essays*, Vol. 1 (1924; London: The Hogarth Press, 1966), 319–337.

21. Despite its significance, many scholars have criticized the period. Nathan Irvin Huggins, for example, concludes that its greatest lessons were in its "failures" (*Harlem Renaissance*, 9, 308). Cornel West considers the Harlem Renaissance as "not so much a genuine renaissance, but rather a yearning for a renaissance aborted by its major artists owing to a conscious distance from the very cultural creativity they desired" (West, *Keeping Faith: Philosophy and Race in America* [New York: Routledge, 1993], 62). Ralph Ellison adds to this view, noting that because black writers of the era had wanted to curry the favor of whites, this insured the "failure of the 'New Negro' movement" (James Thompson, et al., "A Very Stern Discipline: An Interview with Ralph Ellison," *Harper's* [March 1967], 79). Harold Cruse dismisses the Harlem Renaissance out of hand, calling it a period of "guilty, idealistic, or egotistical interventions of cultural paternalism," while David Levering Lewis is even less sympathetic, claiming that "the more things changed, the more they worsened" (Cruse, *The Crisis of the Negro Intellectual* [New York: Quill, 1984], 38; and Lewis, *When Harlem*, 306). Gerald Early focuses on economics. He reports that the Harlem Renaissance was a failure because blacks "did not control nearly any economic aspect of the community they wished to create" (Early, "Three Notes Toward a Cultural Definition of the Harlem Renaissance," *Callaloo* 14.1 [1991], 138). Henry Louis Gates, Jr., believes that African Americans of the Harlem Renaissance "sought to erase their image by conforming to the conventions of the Western tradition," but that by following Western patterns "they erased or ignored much of the best of their cultural uniqueness." Noting that African Americans created a literary canon "that even the most optimistic historians now find sadly academic when compared to the blues and jazz compositions" sums up his disappointment. Only the creators of blues and jazz, says Gates, "helped shape a new definition of blackness suited to the quickening pace of a new

era" (Gates, "The Fact and Voice of Blackness," in *Modern Art and Society*, ed. Maurice Berger [New York: HarperCollins, 1984], 71, 72).

22. Others have identified the New Negro Renaissance at different periods. Gerald Early dates the New Negro Movement "from exactly 1908," when Jack Johnson won the heavyweight title, "to 1938" (Early, "Introduction," in *My Soul's High Song: The Collected Writings of Countee Cullen* [New York: Anchor, 1991], 24–5). Wilson J. Moses writes persuasively that the New Negro Movement began outside of Harlem, thriving as an intellectually rich activist group of writers and philosophers from 1895 to 1919 (Moses, "The Lost World of the New Negro, 1895–1919: Black Literary and Intellectual Life before the 'Renaissance,'" *Black American Literary Forum* 21.1–2 [Spring–Summer 1987], 61–84). Arthur P. Davis and Saunders Redding, in *Cavalcade: Negro American Writing* (New York: Houghton, 1971), maintain that the New Negro Renaissance took place from 1910 to 1940; Sterling Brown argues for the extension of the Harlem Renaissance well into the 1930s (interview by Charles Rowell, "Let Me Be With Ole Jazzbo," *Callaloo* 14.4 [1991], 795–815). Earnest Allen ("The New Negro," *1915, the Cultural Moment*, eds. Adele Heller and Lois Rudnick [New Brunswick, NJ: Rutgers University Press, 1991]), 48–68, identifies the New Negro Movement from 1910 to 1922. Henry Louis Gates, Jr., defines the boundaries of New Negro Renaissance from 1895 to 1925 (Gates, "The Trope of the New Negro and the Reconstruction of the Image of the Black," *Representations* 24 [Fall 1998], 129–55). Arthur P. Davis and Michael W. Peplow, *The New Negro Renaissance: An Anthology* (New York: Holt, Rinehart, and Winston, 1975), date the New Negro period from 1910 to 1940. Samuel A. Floyd, Jr., identifies the "flowering of the New Negro Renaissance in Harlem" from 1917 to 1935 and the "Chicago Renaissance" from 1935 to 1950 [Floyd, *The Power of Black Music*, 100). See also John Michael Spencer, *The New Negroes and Their Music* (Knoxville: University of Tennessee Press, 1997).

23. For a history of African American participation in World War I, see Herbert Aptheker, *Afro-American History: The Modern Era* (New York: Citadel, 1992), 159–72.

24. For important studies on migration, see Alferdteen Harrison, ed., *Black Exodus: The Great Migration from the American South* (Jackson: University of Mississippi Press, 1991); Daniel M. Johnson and Rex R. Campbell, *Black Migration in America: A Social Demographic History* (Durham: Duke University Press, 1981); and Joe William Trotter, Jr., ed., *The Great Migration in Historical Perspective* (Bloomington: Indiana University Press, 1991).

25. Kerry Candaele, *Bound for Glory, 1910–1930* (Philadelphia: Chelsea House, 1997), 7.

26. Johnson and Campbell, *Black Migration*, 74.

27. Locke, "Harlem," *Survey Graphic* 6.6 (March 1925), 629.

28. Still one of the best discussions of migration is Charles S. Johnson, "The Negro Migration: An Economic Interpretation," *Modern Quarterly* 2 (1924–25), 314–26.

29. Gilbert Osofsky, *Harlem: The Making of a Ghetto* (New York: Harper, 1971), 135.

30. See Lewis, *When Harlem*, 306.

31. For statistics, see Osofsky, *Harlem*, and Allan H. Spear, *Black Chicago: The Making of a Negro Ghetto* (Chicago: University of Chicago Press, 1967).

32. For an excellent essay on black women traveling alone, see Darlene Clark Hine, "Rape and the Inner Lives of Black Women in the Middle West: Preliminary Thoughts on the Culture of Dissemblance," in *Unequal Sisters: A Multicultural Reader*

in U.S. Women's History, ed. Vicki L. Ruiz and Ellen Carol DuBois (New York: Routledge, 1994, 2nd. ed.), 342–47.

33. Langston Hughes, *The Big Sea* (1940; reprint, New York: Hill & Wang, 1997), 228.

34. Sterling Brown, *Negro Poetry and Drama* (1937; reprint, New York: Atheneum, 1969), 138, 139.

35. James Weldon Johnson, "The Dilemma of the Negro Author," in *American Mercury* 15.60 (December 1928), 477.

36. Benjamin Brawley, "The Negro Literary Renaissance," *The Southern Workman* 56.4 (April 1927), 177.

37. De Jongh, *Vicious Modernism*, 15.

38. For an illuminating study on the rise of Harlem's Caribbean community, see Irma Watkins-Owens, *Blood Relations: Caribbean Immigrants and the Harlem Community, 1900–1930* (Bloomington: Indiana University Press, 1996). For a general study of early Harlem, see Osofsky, *Harlem*.

39. Lester Walton, *New York World*, 1 April 1923, sec. 2, pg. 4.

40. Gottfried Benn, ed., *Lyrik des expressionistischen Jahrhundert* (*Lyrics of the Expressionistic Century*, 1955), quoted in Thomas Harrison, *1910: The Emancipation of Dissonance* (Berkeley: University of California Press, 1996), 1.

41. See, for instance, *Up South: Stories, Studies, and Letters of This Century's Black Migrations*, ed. Malaika Adero (New York: New Press, 1993).

42. Early, "Introduction," in *The Collected Writings of Countee Cullen*, 38.

43. Richard Schechner defines performance as "the formal relations among play, games, sports, theatre, and ritual." Play, for Schechner, "is 'free activity' where one makes one's own rules." Ritual, he adds, "is strictly programmed, expressing the individual's submission to forces 'larger' or at least 'other' than oneself" (*Performance Theory* [New York: Routledge, 1977], 13, 14).

44. Michael A. Gomez, *Exchanging Our Country Marks: The Transformation of African Identities in the Colonial and Antebellum South* (Chapel Hill: University of North Carolina Press, 1998), 14.

45. Alain Locke, "Introduction," *Plays of Negro Life*, eds. Locke and Montgomery Gregory (New York: Harper, 1927), n.p.

46. See, for instance, Anthony Giddens, *Modernity and Self-Identity: Self and Society in the Late Modern Age* (Stanford: Stanford University Press, 1991), in which he notes that individuals in the modern age "tend to develop multiple selves in which there is no inner core of self-identity" (100), and that the self "in modern society is frail, brittle, fractured, [and] fragmented" (169).

47. Manthia Diawara, "Cultural Studies/Black Studies," in *Borders, Boundaries, and Frames: Cultural Criticism and Cultural Studies*, ed. Mae Henderson (New York: Routledge, 1995), 209.

48. Editorial, "The New Negro—What Is He?," *The Messenger* 2.4–5 (August 1920), 74.

49. James C. Scott, *Seeing Like a State: How Certain Schemes to Improve the Human Condition Have Failed* (New Haven: Yale University Press, 1998), 4, 90.

50. Ibid., 6.

51. Yvonne Ochillo, "The Race-Consciousness of Alain Locke," *Phylon* 47.3 (Fall 1986), 174.

52. W. E. B. Du Bois, "The Talented Tenth (1903)," in *Writings* (New York: Library Classics, 1986), 842–861.

53. Astradur Eysteinsson, *The Concept of Modernism* (Ithaca: Cornell University Press, 1990), 9.

54. James Weldon Johnson, "Preface to the First Edition," *The Book of American Negro Poetry* (New York: Harcourt Brace, 1922), 9.

PART I

1. Alain Locke, "Harlem," *Survey Graphic* 6.6 (March 1925), 629.

2. Richard Powell, "Re/Birth of a Nation," in *Rhapsodies in Black: Art of the Harlem Renaissance*, ed. Powell et al. (Berkeley: University of California Press, 1997), 16.

3. Hubert H. Harrison, *When Africa Awakes: The Inside Story of the Stirrings and Strivings of the New Negro in the Western World* (New York: Porro Press, 1920), 6.

4. Jacqui Malone, *Steppin' on the Blues: The Visible Rhythms of African American Dance* (Urbana: Illinois University Press, 1996), 73.

5. Harold Cruse, *The Crisis of the Negro Intellectual* (New York: Quill, 1984), 71.

CHAPTER TWO

1. William H. Wiggins, Jr., "Jack Johnson as Bad Nigger: The Folklore of His Life," in *Contemporary Black Thought*, ed. Robert Chrisman and Nathan Hare (Indianapolis: Bobbs-Merrill Co., 1973), 67.

2. Richard Barry, "The Prize Ring," *Pearson's Magazine* 24. 1 (July 1910), 10.

3. See, among many reports, the *New York Times*, 5 July 1910, 2, which contains photos of the thousands who gathered outside the Times building to hear reports of the fight. Thousands waited outside the newspaper offices in other cities as well; see, for instance, the *Chicago Tribune*, 5 July 1910, 1.

4. *New York Times*, 5 July 1910, 1; *Chicago Tribune*, 5 July 1910, 1.

5. "Is Prize Fighting Knocked Out?," *Literary Digest*, 16 July 1910, 85.

6. See Arthur Ruhl, "The Fight in the Desert," *Collier's* XLV (23 July 1910), 12–13, 22; Harris Merton Lyon, "In Reno Riotous," *Hampton Magazine* 25 (September 1910), 386–96; Denzil Batchelor, *Jack Johnson and His Times* (London: Phoenix Sports Books, 1956), 82; Al-Tony Gilmore, *Bad Nigger! The National Impact of Jack Johnson* (Port Washington, N. Y.: Kennikat Press, 1975), 42; and Randy Roberts, *Papa Jack: Jack Johnson and the Era of White Hopes* (New York: Free Press, 1983), 103. The song was based on Ernest Hogan's musical review of the same name in 1895.

7. Roi Ottley, *Black Odyssey: The Story of the Negro in America* (New York: Charles Scribner's Sons, 1948), 206.

8. Herbert Croly, *The Promise of American Life* (1909, Boston: Northeastern University Press, 1989), 81.

9. Sal Fradella, *Jack Johnson* (Boston: Branden, 1990), 3.

10. Jeffries, quoted in *The Literary Digest* 41.3 (16 July 1909), 85.

11. Jarvis Anderson, for example, reports that Johnson "sometimes taunted his opponents, left his chin or his chest wide open and invited them to throw their best punches; and did not take as much pleasure in knocking out opponents as he did in outboxing them, embarrassing them, prolonging their suffering" (Anderson, "Black Heavies," *American Scholar* 47 [Summer 1978], 390). Lawrence W. Levine adds that it was "not Johnson's physical prowess alone that infuriated whites; it was his entire life style: his fast cars, fancy clothes, ready tongue, white wife (the

first of three white women he married), and white mistresses" (Levine, *Black Culture and Black Consciousness: Afro-American Folk Thought from Slavery to Freedom* [New York: Oxford University Press, 1977], 432).

12. Ruhl, "The Fight in the Desert," 22.

13. Bob Fitzsimmons, "What the Wise Ones Think of the Jeff–Jack Fight," *Omaha Daily News*, 2 July 1910, 1.

14. For the most thorough description of the history of the Johnson-Burns fight, see Jeffrey Wells, *Boxing Day: The Fight That Changed the World* (Sidney, Australia: Harper Sports, 1998).

15. Quoted in Wells, *Boxing Day*, 165.

16. The final round can be seen in the film, *Jeffries/Johnson, 1910* (original footage put together on video tape in 1971, black and white, 21 minutes), directed by William Kimberlin.

17. Roberts, *Papa Jack*, 84.

18. Jack Johnson, *In the Ring and Out: The Autobiography of Jack Johnson* (1927; New York: Citadel, 1992), 185.

19. Johnson, *In the Ring and Out*, 63, 184.

20. *Jack Johnson versus Jim Jeffries* (1910), complete fight, obtained from ESPN's "Big Fights," tape no. BFE000001201. My thanks to Mike Cocchi, ESPN Enterprises, for his assistance in obtaining the tape. For an interesting study of boxing on film, see Dan Streible, "A History of Boxing Films, 1894–1915," *Film History* 3.3 (1989), 235–257.

21. John L. Sullivan, "Johnson Wins in 15 Rounds; Jeffries Weak," *New York Times*, 5 July 1910, 2.

22. Rex Beach, "Johnson and Age Defeat Jeffries," *Chicago Tribune*, 5 July 1910, 1.

23. Harry C. Carr, "Butchery at Reno," *Los Angeles Times*, 5 July 1910, 1.

24. Drawing, unknown artist, *Los Angeles Times*, 6 July 1910, 7.

25. Finis Farr, *Black Champion* (Greenwich, CT: Fawcett, 1964), 113.

26. *Omaha Bee*, 5 July 1910, 6.

27. Roberts, *Papa Jack*, 105. Fradella, in *Jack Johnson*, reports that Johnson also prolonged the fight to punish Burns, maintaining that Johnson said: "I figured that Burns had something coming to him" (35).

28. Jackson J. Stovall, "Jack Johnson and Jim Jeffries," *Chicago Defender*, 2 July 1910, 1. Randy Roberts, in *Papa Jack*, agrees, noting that Johnson's style "was ascribed to economics: a good aggressive black could not get lucrative fights with white boxers. It actually paid a black boxer never to look too strong or too good against a white opponent" (25). In *The Culture of Bruising: Essays on Prizefighting, Literature, and Modern American Culture* (Hopewell N. J.: Ecco Press, 1994), Gerald Early raises the interesting point that "this style went by the boards when blacks fought each other." Early contends that there is a "vital connection between oral culture, masculine aggression, and prizefighting," and that African American oral culture is less a defensive response to racism and more of a violent ritual in which there is a possibility that "blacks fought each other as a real release of the aggression that they would have preferred directing toward whites but which, after a point, they began to enjoy directing at each other" (27).

29. Quoted in Farr, *Black Champion*, 119.

30. *New York Morning Telegraph*, reprinted in the *New York Age*, 18 February 1909, 6.

31. *Illustrated Sporting*, 3 December 1908; quoted in Richard Broome, "The Australian Reaction to Jack Johnson, Black Pugilist, 1907–1909," in *Sport in History: The*

Making of Modern Sporting History, ed. Richard Cashman and Michael McKernan (St. Lucia, Queensland: University of Queensland Press, 1979), 351.

32. Jack London, *New York Herald*, 27 December 1908, sec. 2, pg. 1; see also, London, *San Francisco Call*, 27 December 1908, 33.

33. Quoted in Robert H. deCoy, *Jack Johnson: The Big Black Fire* (Los Angeles: Holloway House, 1969, 1991), 114; and Howard Bingham and Max Wallace, *Muhammad Ali's Greatest Fights: Cassius Clay vs. the United States of America* (New York: M. Evans and Co., 2000), 33.

34. W. E. B. Du Bois, *The Souls of Black Folk, Three Negro Classics*, John Hope Franklin, ed. (1903; reprint, New York: Avon, 1965), 221.

35. See, for instance, Henry van Dyke, *The Spirit of America* (New York: MacMillan, 1910), in which he says "the spirit of fair play" (71) and Roosevelt's "square deal for everyone" (85) are symbolic of Americanism. These ideas of "fair play" and "square deal" would force public opinion to favor a fight with Johnson, provided that a white hope could be found to defeat him.

36. Quoted in Gilmore, *Bad Nigger*, 35.

37. James Weldon Johnson, *Black Manhattan* (1930; New York: Da Capo Press, 1991), 66.

38. Max Balthazar, "Jeff is Fit to Fight Battle of Century," *Omaha Daily News*, 3 July 1910, Sporting section, pg. 1.

39. John Hoberman, *Darwin's Athletes: How Sports Has Damaged Black America and Preserved the Myth of Race* (Boston: Houghton Mifflin Co., 1997), 164.

40. Alfred Henry Lewis, *San Francisco Examiner*, 1 July 1910, 13. Lewis went on to compare the fight metaphorically as one "between a grizzly and a gorilla," with the prediction that the "bear" would come out ahead (14).

41. *Fairplay Magazine*, 7 January 1908; quoted in Broome, "The Australian Reaction to Jack Johnson," 357.

42. Frederick L. Hoffman, *Race Traits and Tendencies of the American Negro* (Ithaca: Andrus & Church, 1896); Charles Carroll, *The Negro as Beast* (St. Louis: American Books and Bible House, 1900); Thomas Nelson Page, *The Negro: The Southern's Problem* (New York: Charles Schribner's Sons, 1904); Thomas Dixon, *The Clansman* (New York: Gosset Dunlap, 1905), Robert Shufeldt, *The Negro: A Menace to American Civilization* (Boston: R. G. Badger, 1907); Alfred P. Schultz, *Race or Mongrel* (Boston: L. C. Page & Co., 1908); and William P. Pickett, *The Negro Problem* (New York: G. P. Putnam's Sons, 1909).

43. Richard Hofstadter, *Social Darwinism in American Thought* (Boston: Beacon Press, 1944, reprint, 1992), 172.

44. Henry van Dyke, for instance, asked in 1910 how African Americans could possibly secure in "their civil rights without admitting them to a racial mixture." Black people, he concludes, "were better off under slavery because they were like children, needing control and protection" (*The Spirit of America*, 102, 103).

45. John W. Burgess, *Reconstruction and the Constitution, 1866–1876* (New York: Charles Schribner's Sons, 1902), 133.

46. George W. Stocking, Jr., "The Turn-of-the-Century Concept of Race," *Modernism/Modernity* 1.1 (January 1994), 6.

47. See, for instance, C. Vann Woodward, *The Strange Career of Jim Crow* (New York: Oxford University Press, 1955, 1974), 74. See also Nancy Leys Stepah and Sander L. Gilman, "Appropriating the Idioms of Science: The Rejection of Scien-

tific Racism," in *The Bounds of Race: Perspectives on Hegemony and Resistance*, ed. Do-
minick LaCapra (Cornell: Cornell University Press, 1991), 72–103.

48. Waldemar Young, *San Francisco Chronicle*, 2 July 1910, 13.

49. According Randy Roberts, for many whites, the black race as an "incipient
species" and that "physically blacks and white were different" (Roberts, *Papa Jack*,
62).

50. According to Finis Farr, Jeffries "had the myth-making quality of a real folk hero;
people believed, for example, that he had cured himself of pneumonia by drinking
a case of whiskey in two days" (Farr, *Black Champion*, 69).

51. For a discussion on the ways in which the working class employs fantasy as a vi-
carious means of compensating for their experience within the alienating labor
process, see Oskar Negt and Alexander Kluge, *Public Sphere and Experience: Toward
an Analysis of the Bourgeois and Proletarian Public Sphere*, tr. Peter Labanyi et al.
(Minneapolis: University of Minnesota Press, 1993; German edition, 1972),
32–38.

52. Dorothy Forrester, "Jim-a-da-Jeff," quoted in Lester S. Levy, *Give Me Yesterday:
American History in Song, 1890–1920* (Norman: University of Oklahoma Press,
1975), 214.

53. Alexander Walters and Monroe Trotter, "National Negro Political League Issues
Call," 22 June 1910, reprinted in the *Richmond Daily Planet*, 16 July 1910, 1.

54. Rex Beach, "Red-Blooded Men Throng to Reno," *Chicago Tribune*, 3 July 1910, 6.

55. W. E. B. Du Bois, "The Relation of the Negro to the Whites in the South," *The Annals of the American Academy of Political and Social Sciences* 18 (July 1901), 123.

56. Benedict Anderson, *Imagined Communities: Reflections on the Origins and Spread of Nationalism* (London: Verso, 1983).

57. Susan Hegeman, borrowing the term "superorganic" from anthropologist Alfred
Louis Kroeber, defines culture as "the realm of behavior that was not biologically
inherited, but learned and transmitted through contact with other persons: skills
techniques, styles, belief systems, languages, [and] refinements of talent" (Hegeman, *Patterns for America: Modernism and the Concept of Culture* [Princeton: Princeton
University Press, 1999], 82); see, A. L. Kroeber, "The Superorganic," *American Anthropologist* 19.2 (April–June 1917), 163–213.

58. Van Dyke, *The Spirit of America*, 102.

59. Leon F. Litwack, *Trouble in Mind: Black Southerns in the Age of Jim Crow* (New York:
Vintage, 1998), 327.

60. See Fradella, *Jack Johnson*, 33.

61. *Indianapolis Freeman*, 16 July 1910, 1.

62. *Richmond Planet*, 9 January 1909; quoted in Gilmore, *Bad Nigger*, 32.

63. Post-fight review of the Johnson-Burns bout in Australia, 1908, quoted in Jeff
Wells, *Boxing Day*, 198.

64. Terry Eagleton, *The Ideology of Aesthetics* (London: Blackwell, 1990), 13.

65. For a discussion of prizefighting and the prohibition against it, see Jeffrey T. Sammons, *Beyond the Ring: The Role of Boxing in American Sport* (Urbana: University of
Illinois Press, 1990), chapter 1, "Crime or Sport," 3–29.

66. Pierre Bourdieu, "How Can One Be a Sports Fan?," in *The Cultural Studies Reader*,
ed. Simon During (London: Routledge, 1993), 431.

67. Theodore Roosevelt, *The Strenuous Life* (1905; reprint, Bedford, MA: Applewood
Books, 1991), 10, 29, 30.

68. Edmund Morris, *The Rise of Theodore Roosevelt* (New York: Ballantine Books, 1979), 112–13.

69. Michael Kimmel, *Manhood in America: A Cultural History* (New York: The Free Press, 1996), 139.

70. Richard Barry, "The Prize Ring," *Person's Magazine* 24.1 (July 1910), 4.

71. Duffield Osborn, "A Defense of Pugilism," *North American Review* 46 (April 1888), 430–35.

72. E. D. Cope, "The Effeminisation of Man," *Open Court* 7.43 (26 October 1893), 3847.

73. Elliot J. Gorn, *The Manly Art: Bare-Knuckle Prize Fighting in America* (Ithaca: Cornell University Press, 1986), 141, 247.

74. John Boyle O'Reilly, *Ethics of Boxing and Manly Sport* (Boston: Ticknor & Co., 1888), 85, 83, 84.

75. Gail Bederman, *Manliness and Civilization: A Cultural History of Gender and Race in the United States, 1880–1917* (Chicago, University of Chicago Press, 1995), 8.

76. Gilmore, *Bad Nigger*, 14.

77. *Chicago Tribune*, 4 April 1909, sec. 3, p. 4.

78. Jeffries, quoted in "Jeffries Will Not Permit Johnson to Carry Off Title," *San Francisco Call*, 24 December 1908, 9.

79. Anderson, "Black Heavies," 388.

80. John Callan O'Laughlin, "Johnson Victory Bad for Negroes," *Chicago Tribune*, 4 July 1910, 4.

81. James L. Corbett, "All Who Want to Know Who Will Win Go," *Chicago Tribune*, 29 June 1910, 13.

82. Jack London, "Both Fighters Will Rely on Cumulative Effect of Blows," *San Francisco Chronicle*, 1 July 1910, Sports sec., pg. 1.

83. Bob Fitzsimmons, "Fitz and Burns Pick Jeffries to Win Fight," *Washington D.C. Evening Star*, 29 June 1910, 12.

84. Jim Jeffries, quoted in the *New York Times*, 3 July 1910, 8.

85. Charles F. Woodruff, "The Failure of Americans as Athletes," *North American Review* 633.183 (October 1907), 202.

86. *New York Times*, 3 July 1910, 8.

87. Tip Wright, "Johnson is Putting in Some Hard Work," *Omaha Daily News* 28 June 1910, 6.

88. Mike Murphy, quoted in Ruhl, "The Fight in the Desert," 13.

89. Tom Shevlin, quoted in Ruhl, "The Fight in the Desert," 13.

90. Max Balthazar wrote: "No one has arisen to dispute the cleverness of Johnson, and Jeffries, least of all, has not blinded himself to the cleverness of the man whom he expects to conquer; but if he winces at the thought of having his face lacerated and bruised in spite of the pickling solution he has been using on it for several weeks, he gave no outward indication of his thoughts." In Balthazar, "Jeffries Sleeps Well and is Ready for Fray," *Omaha Daily News*, 4 July 1910, 6.

91. Pat Kenrick, quoted in the *New Orleans Daily Picayune*, 3 July 1910, 9.

92. Mike Murphy, *New York Herald*, 4 July 1910. Murphy, however, predicted Johnson's victory, maintaining that no one can return to boxing after a six-year layoff.

93. James Corbett, "Tradition Factor in the Big Fight," *Chicago Tribune*, 1 July 1910, 13.

94. James Corbett, *Chicago Tribune*, 2 July 1910, 11.

95. Ruhl, "The Fight in the Desert," 22.

96. Jack London, *New York Herald*, 5 July 1910, 2.

97. Corbett, "Tradition Factor in the Big Fight," 13.

98. Broome, "The Australian Reaction to Jack Johnson," 352, 353.

99. *Australian Star*, 20 November 1908; quoted in Broome, "The Australian Reaction to Jack Johnson," 352.

100. Randolph Bedford, Melbourne *Herald*, 26 December 1908; quoted in Broome, "The Australian Reaction to Jack Johnson," 357.

101. *New York Times*, 3 July 1910, 14.

102. Wiggins, "Jack Johnson as Bad Nigger," 68.

103. Frantz Fanon, *Black Skin, White Mask*, tr. Charles Lam Markmann (New York: Grove Press, 1967), 116.

104. *Current Literature*, 49.1 (July 1910), 57–8.

105. *Cleveland Leader*, quoted in *Current Literature* 49.2 (August 1910), 130.

106. "Intellectuality of the New Pugilism," *Current Opinion* 54.2 (February 1913), B1.

107. "Jeffries and Johnson Offered Purse of $50,000," *San Francisco Call*, 28 December 1908, 6.

108. Jack London, "Report from Reno, NV," 29 June 1910, quoted in *Jack London Reports*, ed. King Hendricks and Irving Shepard (Garden City, N. Y.: Doubleday, 1970), 280–81.

109. London, *Jack London Reports*, 281.

110. René Descartes, *Principles of Philosophy* (1644 in Latin, 1647 in French), in *The Philosophical Writings of Descartes*, Vol. 1, ed. John Cottingham, tr. Robert Stoothoff and Dugald Murdoch (Cambridge: Cambridge University Press, 1985), 208.

111. René Descartes, *Discourse on Method*, Part 4 (1637), in *Discourse on Method and Meditations on First Philosophy*, tr. Donald A. Cress (Indianapolis: Hackett Pub. Co., 1998), 19.

112. Rex Beach, "Picks Jeffries to Win," *San Francisco Chronicle*, 4 July 1910, 12.

113. Stanley Ketchel, quoted in Barry, "The Prize Ring," 9, and reprinted in *Current Literature* 49.2 (August 1910), 129. Johnson agreed to fight Ketchel, a middleweight, in 1909, owing to the lack of adequate (white) opponents in the heavyweight division. The plan was for Johnson to "carry" Ketchel through the fight without hurting him. But in the twelfth round Ketchel knocked Johnson down. Johnson arose and hit Ketchel so hard that his front teeth were found lodged in Johnson's gloves. The fight was filmed and despite the primitive quality of the film, one can see Johnson hit Ketchel so hard that Johnson himself falls over him from the momentum of the blow. See *Johnson/Jeffries 1910* (1971), William Kimberlin, director (21-minute documentary).

114. Frederic Cople Jaher, "White America Views Jack Johnson, Joe Louis, and Muhammad Ali," *Sport in America: New Historical Perspectives*, Donald Spivey, ed. (Westport, CT: Greenwood Press, 1985), 150. Al-Tony Gilmore wrote: "Johnson's triumph caught many white on the horns of a dilemma." Before the fight, the match was perceived as vindication of Anglo-Saxon supremacy; after the fight, many found it "necessary to subvert the racial implications of the match" (*Bad Nigger*, 43).

115. *Chicago Tribune*, 5 July 1910, 10.

116. Theodore Roosevelt, "The Recent Prize Fight," *Outlook* 95.11 (16 July 1910), 550, 551.

117. "Editorial," *Washington Evening Star*, 5 July 1910, 6.

118. "Editorial," *New York Times*, 5 July 1910, 12.

119. "Editorial," *Los Angeles Times*, 6 July 1910, 4.

120. *New York Herald*, 5 July 1910, 1.

121. *New York Times*, 5 July 1910, 1.

122. Sammons, *Beyond the Ring*, 42.

123. *Richmond Daily Planet*, 9 January 1909, 1.

124. Lester A. Walton, "In the World of Sport," *New York Age*, 30 June 1910, 6.

125. Reverend Reverdy C. Ransom, quoted in Lester A. Walton, "In the World of Sport," *New York Age*, 30 December 1909, 6.

126. Walton, "Johnson is now Undisputed Champion," *New York Age*, 7 July 1910, 6.

127. E. L. Blackshear, quoted in *Current Literature* 48.6 (June 1910), 606.

128. *Current Literature* 49.2 (August 1910), 130. See also, *Independent* (NY) 59.3214 (7 July 1910), 3; and *Outlook* (USA) 95.11, 541.

129. George L. Knox, "Timely Advice Concerning Johnson–Jeffries Fight," *Indianapolis Freeman* 9 July 1910, 4.

130. Knox, "Jack Johnson Warned," *Indianapolis Freeman*, 5 February 1910, 4.

131. Knox, "Advice to Jack Johnson," *Indianapolis Freeman*, 14 July 1910, 4.

132. Booker T. Washington, quoted in John W. Blassingame's introduction to Gilmore, *Bad Nigger*, 4. Gerald Early, in *Culture of Bruising*, writes that the black middle class's "censure of Johnson" as a "poor role model" was based on the "black philistine's cry for standards and achievements that whites would be bound to respect because the black philistine never wanted freedom for blacks, only the right and access to be absorbed by massive white philistinism" (41).

133. "Advice to Jack Johnson," *New York Age*, July 14, 1910, 4.

134. *Chicago Broad Ax*, 9 July 1910, 1.

135. *Chicago Defender*, 2 July 1910, 1.

136. John Hope Franklin, *From Slavery to Freedom: A History of American Negroes* (New York: Alfred A. Knopf, 1947), 389.

137. Walton, "Theatrical Comment," *New York Age*, 7 July 1910, 6.

138. Quoted in the *New York Age*, 7 July 1910, 1.

139. Litwack, *Trouble in Mind*, 443.

140. Roger D. Abrahams, "Some Varieties of Heroes in America," *Journal of Folklore Institute* 3.3 (December 1966), 341, 344, 343.

141. Lewis R. Gordon, *Existentia Africana: Understanding Africana Existential Thought* (New York: Routledge, 2000), 87.

142. Gilmore, *Bad Nigger*, 12. See also Wiggins, "Jack Johnson as Bad Nigger," 54, and Levine, *Black Culture and Black Consciousness*, 429. For an interesting discussion on "bad" and its relationship to play in African American life, see the "Introduction" in *After Africa*, Roger D. Abrahams and John F. Szwed, ed. (New Haven: Yale University Press, 1983), 1–48.

143. Fanon, *Black Skin, White Mask*, 109.

144. Ibid., 110.

145. Lewis R. Gordon, *Fanon and the Crisis of European Man* (New York: Routledge, 1995), 29.

146. Fanon, *Black Skin, White Mask*, 110–111.

147. See, for instance, Jeffries's discussion of his "plans" in an interview by John L. Sullivan, "Confident Air Pervades Camp," *Chicago Tribune*, 4 July 1910, 10.

148. Ralph Ellison, *Shadow and Act* (New York: Vintage, 1953, reprint, 1995), 190.

149. Gena Dagel Caponi, *Signifyin(g), Sanctifyin', and Slam Dunking: A Reader in African American Expressive Culture* (Amherst: University of Massachusetts Press, 1999), 3.

150. Johnson's defensive skills were allegedly developed under the tutelage of Joe Choynski, a fighter who knocked out Johnson in three rounds early in Johnson's career in Galveston, Johnson's birthplace, in 1901. After the fight both were arrested for participating in an illegal prizefight. While incarcerated together, they fought for the amusement of the local warden. Choynski provided Johnson with boxing lessons and was reported to have said "a man who can move like you should never have to take a punch. Don't try to block, man, you're fast enough to move clear out of the way. Forget blocking." Quoted in Farr, *Black Champion*, 21; and deCoy, *Jack Johnson*, 42.

151. Zora Neale Hurston, "Characteristics of Negro Expression," in *Negro: An Anthology*, ed. Nancy Cunard (New York: Negro University Press, 1934, reprint, 1969).

152. Kimberly W. Benston, *Performing Blackness: Enactments of African-American Modernism* (London: Routledge, 2000), 30.

153. Houston A. Baker, Jr., *Blues, Ideology, and Afro-American Literature: A Vernacular Theory* (Chicago: University of Chicago Press, 1984), 5.

154. Tad Dargan, quoted in *The Autobiography of Jack Johnson: In and Out of the Ring* (New York: Citadel Press, 1992), 13.

155. Jack London, *New York Herald*, 5 July 1910, 1.

156. Rex Beach, "Instincts Primeval," *Los Angeles Times* 2 July 1910, 8.

157. Ellison, *Shadow and Act*, 55; "Change the Joke and Slip the Yoke," 45–59.

158. Jane Duran and Earl L. Stewart, "Alain Locke, Essentialism, and the Notion of a Black Aesthetic," in *The Critical Pragmatism of Alain Locke*, ed. Leonard Harris (Lanham: Rowman and Littlefield, 1999), 121.

159. deCoy, *Jack Johnson*, 119.

160. *New York Times*, 5 July 1910, 2. deCoy writes that Johnson said: "Oh, Mr. Jeff, stop loving me so" (*Jack Johnson*, 118).

161. *New York Herald*, 5 July 1910, 2.

162. *Chicago Tribune*, 5 July 1910, 25; *New York Times*, 5 July 1910, 2 (John L. Sullivan reporting); *Los Angeles Times*, 5 July 1910, 19; *New York Herald*, 5 July 1910, 2 (Jack London reporting).

163. Exchange reported by Sullivan in his round-by-round commentary of the fight, *New York Times*, 5 July 1910, 2.

164. Wiggins, "Jack Johnson as Bad Nigger," 66.

165. Quoted in Nat Fleischer, "Johnson, Craftiest Boxer," *The Ring* (August 1946), 76. From the Johnson file, no. 1925–74, 002, 556, SC.

166. Robert Motts, quoted in the *Chicago Tribune*, 7 July 1910, 3.

167. Ibid.

168. "Cheering Throng Greets Johnson," *Chicago Defender*, 8 July 1910, 13.

169. A. S. (Doc) Young, "Was Jack Johnson Boxing's Greatest Champ?," *Ebony* 17.3 (January 1963), 68.

170. "Editorial," *New York Times*, 5 July 1910, 12.

171. From a report by the *Indianapolis Freeman*, 2 July 1910, 1. Estimates of the earnings from the fight vary, as records were informally kept.

172. Lucille B. Watkins, *Richmond Daily Planet*, 16 July 1910, 1.

173. Quoted in J. Manson Brewer, *Worse Days and Better Times: Folklore of the North Carolina Negro* (Chicago: Quadrangle Books, 1965), 178.

174. *Chicago Broad Ax*, 30 July 1910, 1.

175. John Lardner, "The Jack Johnson Era of Boxing," *Negro Digest* 8.1 (November 1949), 25.

176. Everett H. Akam, "Community and Cultural Crisis: The Transfiguring Imagination of Alain Locke," *American Literary History* 3.2 (1991), 270.

CHAPTER THREE

1. bell hooks, "Selling Hot Pussy: Representations of Black Female Sexuality in the Cultural Marketplace," in *Black Looks: Race and Representation* (Boston: South End Press, 1992), 62.
2. Katrina Hazzard-Gordon, "Dancing Under the Lash: Sociocultural Disruption, Continuity, and Synthesis," in *African Dance: An Artistic, Historical and Philosophical Inquiry*, ed. Kariamu Weish Asante (Trenton, NJ: Africa World Press, 1996), 101.
3. See, for instance, Roger Copeland, "Founding Mothers," *Dance Theatre Journal* 8.3 (1990), 6–9, 27–29, who identified Isadora Duncan, Loïe Fuller, Ruth St. Denis, Doris Humphrey, and Martha Graham as "founding mothers" of modern dance. Helen Thomas, in *Dance, Modernity and Culture: Explorations in the Sociology of Dance* (London: Routledge, 1995), adds Maud Allen to the pantheon of "major forerunners of American modern dance" (24), and Elizabeth Dempster, in "Women Writing the Body: Let's Watch a Little How She Dances," in *Bodies of the Text: Dance as Theory, Literature as Dance*, ed. Ellen W. Goellner and Jacqueline Shea Murphy (New Brunswick: Rutgers University Press, 1995), identifies Duncan, Fuller, St. Denis, and Allen as choreographers who developed "a decisive and liberating break with the principles and forms of the European ballet" (27–8). According to Jane C. Desmond, in "Dancing Out the Difference: Cultural Imperialism and Ruth St. Denis's 'Radha' of 1906," *Signs: Journal of Women in Culture and Society* 17.1 (Autumn 1991), St. Denis, Fuller, and Duncan are "always cited" as "the three 'mothers' of modern dance" (30), while in Mark Franko, in *Dancing Modernism/Performing Politics* (Bloomington: Indiana University Press, 1995), affirms the popular idea that Duncan was the "founding mother" of modern dance, responsible for the "organic society" that challenged the "Victorian experience of female culture" (2).
4. Thomas DeFrantz, "Simmering Passivity: The Black Male Body in Concert Dance," in *Moving Words: Re-Writing Dance*, ed. Gay Morris (London: Routledge), observes that for black dancers, racial divisions, cultural fragmentation, and "the absence of critical theory devoted to Afro-performance have contributed to the historical displacement of dance created by African-American[s]" (107).
5. For a history of the *Salome* dance and its popularity, see Elizabeth Kendall, *Where She Danced* (New York: Alfred A, Knopf, 1979), 73–90, and Elaine Showalter, *Sexual Anarchy: Gender and Culture at the Fin de Siècle* (New York: Penguin Books, 1990), 144–68. Although informative, neither book discusses Aida Overton Walker and her version of *Salome*.
6. Ann Douglas, *Terrible Honesty: Mongrel Manhattan in the 1920s* (New York: Noonday, 1995), 335. Sandra R. Lieb, in *Mother of the Blues: A Study of Ma Rainey* (Amherst: University of Massachusetts Press, 1981), claims that Ethel Waters sang with precision, with a tone quality "quite pure, lacking any blue notes: only in the lower register does she show she is capable of real blues singing" (70). In contrast, Bessie Smith's version of "Oh Daddy," a song made popular by Waters, "is more relaxed and bluesy than Ethel's." Smith's tone, "while not quite as pure as Ethel's, is quite sweet and open, almost yawny" (70–1).
7. For a study of Dora Dean, see Jo A. Tanner, *Dusky Maidens: The Odyssey of the Early Black Dramatic Actress* (Westport, CT: Greenwood Press, 1992), 53–6; of Florence

Mills, see Richard Newman, *Words Like Freedom: Essays on African-American Culture and History* (West Cornwall, CT: Locust Hill Press, 1996), 77–87; and of Josephine Baker, see Phyllis Rose, *Jazz Cleopatra: Josephine Baker in Her Time* (New York: Doubleday, 1989).

8. Trinh T. Minh-ha, *Woman Native Other* (Bloomington: Indiana University Press, 1989), 6.

9. Ann Wagner, *Adversaries of Dance: From the Puritans to the Present* (Urbana: University of Illinois Press, 1997), 255. See also Lewis A. Erenberg, *Steppin' Out: New York Nightlife and the Transformation of American Culture, 1890–1930* (Westport: Greenwood Press, 1981), 150, and Michael Kammen, *American Culture, American Taste: Social Change in the 20th Century* (New York: Alfred A. Knopf, 1999), in which he writes that "around 1910, just as saloon culture was starting to decline in respectability, larger American cities began to show a rapid increase in the number of dance halls" (79).

10. Mark A. Reid, *PostNegritude Visual and Literary Culture* (Albany: State University of New York Press, 1997), 13.

11. Houston A. Baker, Jr., *Modernism and the Harlem Renaissance* (Chicago: University of Chicago Press, 1987) 33, 37.

12. Elie Johnson McDougald, "The Task of Negro Womanhood," in *The New Negro*, ed. Alain Locke (1925; New York: Atheneum, 1992), 369–70. For a study on the stereotypes, see K. Sue Jewell, *From Mammy to Miss America and Beyond: Cultural Images & the Shaping of US Social Policy* (London: Routledge, 1993).

13. Richard J. Powell, *Black Art and Culture in the 20th Century* (London: Thames and Hudson, 1997), 24.

14. Albert C. Barnes, "Negro Art and America," *Survey Graphic* 6.6 (March 1925), 668.

15. Colin Rhodes, *Primitivism and Modern Art* (London: Thames and Hudson, 1994), 16.

16. Winthrop Jordan, in *White Over Black: American Attitudes Toward the Negro, 1550–1812* (Chapel Hill: University of North Carolina Press, 1968), raises a significant point that black people were never as closely associated to the concept of the "noble savage" as Native Americans. As Jordan explains, "even in the eighteenth century, when the savages of the world were being promoted to 'nobility' by Europeans as an aid to self-scrutiny and reform at home, the Negro was not customarily thought of as embodying all the qualities of the noble savage. Certainly he never attained the status of the Indian's primitive nobility" (27).

17. Marianna Torgovnick, *Gone Primitive: Savage Intellects, Modern Lives* (Chicago: University of Chicago Press, 1990).

18. Hayden White, "The Noble Savage Theme as Fetish," *Tropics of Discourse: Essays in Cultural Criticism* (Baltimore: John Hopkins University Press, 1978), 187–8.

19. Harold Isaacs, *The New World of Negro Americans* (New York: John Day, 1963), 233.

20. Sander L. Gilman, "Black Bodies, White Bodies: Toward an Iconography of Female Sexuality in Late Nineteenth-Century Art, Medicine, and Literature," in *"Race," Writing, and Difference*, ed. Henry Louis Gates, Jr. (Chicago: University of Chicago Press, 1986), 248.

21. Carl G. Jung, "Your Negroid and Indian Behavior," *Forum* 83.4 (April 1930), 196.

22. Much of this popularity had its roots in minstrelsy, where whites would attend ribald performances that were seemingly about black culture. But suggested here is the idea that with the rising interest in dance, the attraction grew beyond the bounds of minstrel theatre and into the realm of cabarets, dance halls, nightclubs, and the ever-expanding social scene.

23. Evelyn Brooks Higginbotham, "African-American Women's History and the Meta-language of Race," *Signs: Journal of Women on Culture and Society* 17.2 (Winter 1992), 271. See also Kevin K. Gaines, *Uplifting the Race: Black Leadership, Politics, and Culture in the Twentieth Century* (Chapel Hill: University of North Carolina Press, 1996).

24. Fannie Barrier Williams, "The Club Movement Among the Colored Women," *The Voice of the Negro* 1.3 (March 1904), 102.

25. Hazel Carby, "Exactly What Is It About Josephine Baker?," *New York Times*, March 10, 1991, sec. 2, pg. 31, 33.

26. Paul Gilroy, "To Be Real: The Dissident Forms of Black Expressive Culture," in *Let's Get It On: The Politics of Black Performances*, ed. Catherine Ugwu (Seattle: Bay Press, 1995), 21.

27. For a history of Aida Overton Walker, see Richard Newman, "'The Brightest Star': Aida Overton Walker in the Age of Ragtime and Cakewalk," *Prospects: An Annual of American Cultural Studies* 18 (New York: Cambridge University Press, 1993), 464–481; and David Krasner, "Rewriting the Body: Aida Overton Walker and the Social Formation of Cakewalking," *Theatre Survey* 37.2 (Nov. 1996), 66–92. For her *Salome* dance, see Susan A. Glenn, *Female Spectacle: The Theatrical Roots of Modern Feminism* (Cambridge: Harvard University Press, 2000), 112–118.

28. Aida Overton Walker, "Colored Men and Women on the Stage," *Colored American Magazine* (October 1905), 571, 573.

29. Ibid., 573, 574.

30. Percival Pollard, "The Regnant Wave of the Sensational Dance," *New York Times*, 23 August 1908, 5–7. See also, "The Call of Salome: Rumors that Salome Will Have a Free Hand This Season," *New York Times Magazine*, 16 August 1908, 4.

31. "The Vulgarization of Salome," *Current Literature* 45.4 (October 1908), 437. For information on the *Salome* dance, see Ann Daly, "Isadora Duncan and the Male Gaze," in *Gender and Performance*, ed. Laurence Senelick (Hanover: University Press of New England, 1992), 248; Elizabeth Kendall, *Where She Danced*, 74–90; and Showalter, *Sexual Anarchy*, 144–68.

32. Bram Dijkstra, *Idols of Perversity: Fantasies of Feminine Evil in Fin-de-Siècle Culture* (New York: Oxford University Press, 1986), 385.

33. Ewa Kuryluk, *Salome and Judas in the Cave of Sex* (Evanston: Northwestern University Press, 1987), 189.

34. Françoise Metzler, *Salome and the Dance of Writing: Portraits of Mimesis in Literature* (Chicago: The University of Chicago Press, 1987), 18; Megan Becker-Leckrone, "Salome: The Fetishization of a Textual Corpus," *New Literary History* 26.2 (Spring 1995), 242.

35. Lester Walton, *The New York Age*, 27 August 1908, 6.

36. Unidentified clipping, dated 6 September 1908, "Salome Dance Seen in *Bandanna Land*"; *Bandanna Land* file, HTC.

37. Undated clipping, titled, "Boston to Have Dance of Salome," BR.

38. *Boston Globe*, n.d., HTC.

39. Unidentified clipping, quoted in "Chicago," Jan. 1909, BR.

40. Daly, "Isadora Duncan and the Male Gaze," 247.

41. Ibid., 249.

42. Ibid., 254.

43. Isadora Duncan, *My Life* (New York: Boni and Liveright, 1927), 341, 342.

44. Isadora Duncan, "Dancing in Relation to Religion and Love," *Theatre Arts Monthly* 11.8 (August 1927), 590–1.

45. Robert Speare, "Victoria's Show Pleases Crowds, *New York Telegraph*, 6 August 1912; clipping, BR.

46. "A Salome of Color," *Stage Pictorial*, 1912, BR.

47. Vanity Fair, 3 August 1912, BR.

48. For a discussion of Orientalism and modern dance, see Desmond, "Dancing Out the Difference," 39, 42.

49. "Ragtime Dance for New Salome," *New York Herald*, 6 August 1912, 10.

50. R. G. Doggett, "The Late Aida Overton Walker: The Artist," *Colored American Review* (January 1916), 17.

51. Howe Alexander, "How Dancing Studs the Pages of History," *Half-Century Magazine* 7.2 (August 1919), 16.

52. Salem Tutt Whitney, "How to Join a Show," in *Competitor* 1 (1920), 71.

53. Hazel Carby, "Policing the Black Women's Body in an Urban Context," in *Identities*, ed. Kwame A. Appiah and Henry Louis Gates, Jr. (Chicago: University of Chicago Press, 1995), 130.

54. For a history of Ethel Waters, see Glenda Gill, *No Surrender! No Retreat!: African American Pioneer Performers of Twentieth-Century American Theater* (New York: St. Martin's Press, 2000), 58–73; and Randall Cherry, "Ethel Waters: The Voice of an Era," in *Temples for Tomorrow: Looking Back at the Harlem Renaissance*, ed. Geneviève Fabre and Michael Feith (Bloomington: Indiana University Press, 2001), 99–124.

55. *New York Herald Tribune*, 16 November 1949, 25.

56. Ethel Waters (with Charles Samuels), *His Eye is on the Sparrow* (1951; reprint, New York: Da Capo Press, 1992), 91.

57. *Chicago Defender*, 22 October 1910; quoted in Daphne Duval Harrison, *Black Pearls: Blues Queens of the 1920s* (New Brunswick, NJ: Rutgers University Press, 1988), 253, n. 13.

58. Langston Hughes and Milton Meltzer, *Black Magic: A Pictorial History of the African-American in the Performing Arts* (New York: Da Capo, 1967), 64. For more details on "TOBA," see chapter 11.

59. Henderson, *Black Pearls*, 24.

60. Waters, *Sparrow*, 75.

61. *Current Biography*, April 1941; clipping file, Ethel Waters, BR.

62. Waters, *Sparrow*, 124.

63. Ibid.

64. Ibid., 125.

65. Ibid., 126.

66. Rudolph Fisher, "The Caucasian Storms Harlem," *American Mercury* 11 (August 1927); quoted in *Voices from the Harlem Renaissance*, ed. Nathan Irving Huggins (New York: Oxford University Press, 1995), 76.

67. Zora Neale Hurston, *Dust Tracks on a Road* (1942; New York: Harper, 1995), 199.

68. Ethel Waters file; November 16, 1949, clipping, BR.

69. Irene Castle, quoted in *Dancing Times* (ca. 1919), the Castle Scrapbook, Robinson Locke Collection, BR.

70. Kathy Peiss, *Cheap Amusements: Working Women and Leisure in Turn-of-the-Century New York* (Philadelphia: Temple University Press, 1986), 102.

71. James Weldon Johnson, *Black Manhattan* (1930; New York: Arno Press, 1968), 210.

72. C. Vann Woodward, *The Strange Career of Jim Crow* (New York: Oxford, 1974), 115.

73. Herbert Shapiro, *White Violence and Black Response: From Reconstruction to Montgomery* (Amherst: University of Massachusetts Press, 1988), 146.

74. For a history of the Chicago riot, see William M. Tuttle, Jr., *Race Riot: Chicago in the Red Summer of 1919* (New York: Atheneum, 1970).

75. See James R. Grossman, *Land of Hope: Chicago, Black Southerners, and the Great Migration* (Chicago: University of Chicago Press, 1989), 19–20.

76. "Georgia's Laws Make Peonage a Possibility," *New York Age*, 23 April 1921, 1, excerpted from Rowland Thomas, "The Laws of Georgia Made Peonage a Lawful Condition," *New York World*, n.d.

77. Statistics quoted from Charles S. Johnson, *The Negro in American Civilization* (New York: Henry Holt and Co., 1930), 17.

78. Robin D. G. Kelly, *Race Rebels: Culture, Politics, and the Black Working Class* (New York: Free Press, 1994), 44, 45.

79. "Taylorism," a theory based on the ideas of Frederick W. Taylor, was developed in the early twentieth century to help the efficiency of the work force. Henry Ford utilized Taylorism in 1913 when he modified the workplace in favor of the machine over the individual, creating factories of mass production. See Martha Banta, *Taylored Lives: Narrative Productions in the Age of Taylor, Veblen, and Ford* (Chicago: University of Chicago Press, 1993), for an interesting discussion of Taylorism's influence on literature.

80. Tera W. Hunter, "The Blues Aesthetic and Black Vernacular Dance," *To Joy My Freedom: Southern Black Women's Lives and Labors After the Civil War* (Cambridge: Harvard University Press, 1997); quoted in *Major Problems in African American History*, Vol. II, ed. Thomas C. Holt and Elsa Barkley Brown (Boston: Houghton Mifflin Co., 2000), 208.

81. Harrison, *Black Pearls*, 6.

82. William Gardner Smith, "Phylon Profile, 21: Ethel Waters," *Phylon* 11.2 (1950), 115, 116.

83. See David Levering Lewis, *When Harlem was in Vogue* (New York: Penguin, 1979, 1997), 174.

84. Elaine Feinstein, *Bessie Smith* (New Viking, 1985), 24.

85. Waters, *Sparrow*, 175.

86. Langston Hughes, *The Big Sea* (1940; reprinted, New York: Hill and Wang, 1993), 225.

87. Darlene Clark Hine, *Speak Truth to Power* (Brooklyn, NY: Carlson, 1996), 56.

88. Allan H. Spear, *Black Chicago: The Making of a Negro Ghetto* (Chicago: University of Chicago Press, 1967), 151.

89. Angela Y. Davis, *Blues Legacies and Black Feminism* (New York: Pantheon, 1998), xi.

CHAPTER FOUR

1. Frantz Fanon, *The Wretched of the Earth*, tr. Constance Farrington (New York: Grove, 1968), 210.

2. Martin Delany, *The Condition, Elevation, Emigration and Destiny of the Colored People of the United States, Politically Considered* (Philadelphia: Harper, 1852), 210.

3. See, for example, "Negro Exposition Opens," *New York Times*, Thursday, 23 October 1913, 5, and W. E. B. Du Bois, "The Star of Ethiopia: A Pageant," *Pamphlets and Leaflets by W. E. B. Du Bois*, ed. Herbert Aptheker (White Plains, N.Y.: Kraus-Thomson, 1983), 161. Productions were performed at the New York Emancipa-

tion Exposition, 22–31 October 1913; Washington, D.C. American League Baseball Park, 11, 13, and 15 October 1915; Philadelphia's Convention Hall for the General Conference of African Methodist Episcopal Church, 16, 18, and 20 May 1916; and Los Angeles's Hollywood Bowl, 15 and 18 June 1925.

4. W. E. B. Du Bois, "The Clansman," *Crisis* 10.1 (May 1915), 33.

5. David Levering Lewis, *W. E. B. Du Bois: A Biography of a Race* (New York: Henry Holt, 1993), 461.

6. Arnold Rampersad, *The Art and Imagination of W. E. B. Du Bois* (New York: Schocken, 1976), 230.

7. My use of the term nationalism avoids the categories of Black Nationalism that have been coined in our time—Cultural Nationalism, Revolutionary Nationalism, Afrocentrism, or other ideologies that gained currency during the Garveyite period and reached an apex during the 1960s. Du Bois's nationalism grew out of Alexander Crummell's conservative values, which were more authoritative than egalitarian. Wilson Moses writes that although Du Bois "was an agitator for racial equality, he believed that the assimilation of the black race would have been a great tragedy. He was a cultural nationalist, then, and his roots were in the nineteenth-century black nationalist tradition" (Moses, "The Evolution of Black Nationalist-Socialist Thought: A Study of W. E. B. Du Bois," in *Topics in Afro-American Studies*, ed. Henry J. Edwards [Buffalo: Black Academic Press, 1971], 81). For a study on the origins of Pan-Africanism, see John J. Bracy et al., ed., *Black Nationalism in America* (Indianapolis: Bobbs-Merrill, 1970); P. Olisanwuche Esedebe, *Pan-Africanism: The Idea and Movement, 1776–1963* (Washington, D. C.: Howard University Press, 1982); Edward S. Redkey, *Black Exodus: Black Nationalist and Black-to-Africa Movements, 1890–1910* (New Haven: Yale University Press, 1969); Sterling Stuckey, ed., *The Ideological Origins of Black Nationalism* (Boston: Beacon, 1972); and Dean E. Robinson, *Black Nationalism in American Politics and Thought* (Cambridge: Cambridge University Press), 2001.

8. George M. Parker, "The Negroid Line in History," *A. M. E. Church Review* 25 (October 1908), 28.

9. Du Bois, *Black Reconstruction in America, 1860–1880* (1935; reprint, New York: Atheneum, 1992), 727.

10. Du Bois, "The Drama Among Black Folk," *Crisis* 12.4 (August 1916), 171.

11. "The Star of Ethiopia," *Washington Bee*, 23 October 1915, 1.

12. Fredric J. Haskins, "The Gift of Ethiopia," *Crisis* 11.2 (December 1915), 75. Walter C. Daniels, "W. E. B. Du Bois' First Efforts at Playwriting," *CLA Journal* 33.4 (June 1990), wrote that Du Bois attempted to establish a "black national theatre that was written by blacks about blacks and acted by blacks" (418).

13. Du Bois, *Dusk of Dawn* (1940; New Brunswick: Transaction, 1983), 272.

14. Du Bois, "The Drama Among Black Folk," 173.

15. Du Bois, "Criteria of Negro Art," *Crisis* 32.6 (October 1926), 296.

16. Burroughs, a drama student at Wilberforce and the Boston School of Expression, directed all four productions. See Samuel A. Hay, *African American Theatre: An Historical and Critical Analysis* (Cambridge: Cambridge University Press, 1994), 247; and Lewis, *W. E. B. Du Bois*, 462.

17. *The Star of Ethiopia*, Materials in Du Bois Papers, Reel 87, UM. Future references to the script will be listed as UM.

18. See Hay, *African American Theatre*, 195.

19. Du Bois, "The Star of Ethiopia: A Pageant," 162.

20. UM.

21. *Washington Bee*, 23 October 1915, 1.

22. Robert "Bob" Cole and J. Rosamond Johnson (brother to the author James Weldon Johnson) were, along with Bert Williams and George Walker, the most popular black performers in musical theatre during the first decade of the twentieth century. From 1897 to 1901, Bob Cole performed in his production, *A Trip to Coontown*. Cole wrote, produced, and directed the musical farce with his partner, Billy Johnson (no relation to Rosamond Johnson), establishing himself as the first independent black producer of black musical comedy. By 1901 Cole had teamed with J. Rosamond Johnson, both becoming highly successful songwriters. In 1907, Cole and Johnson produced *The Shoo Fly Regiment*, and in 1909, *The Red Moon*. The two songs in *The Star of Ethiopia* were borrowed from *The Red Moon*. For a biography of Bob Cole, see David Krasner, "Bob Cole," *American National Biography* (Oxford: Oxford University Press, 1999), Volume 5, 203–4; and Krasner, chapter 2, *Resistance, Parody, and Double Consciousness in African American Theatre, 1895–1910* (New York: St. Martin's Press, 1997). Cole died in 1911.

23. Du Bois lamented: "But the money. The way the funds rained through my fingers was quite unbelievable. . . . Everything seemed to be costing twice as much as it should" (Du Bois, "The Star of Ethiopia," *Crisis* 11.2 [December 1915], 93).

24. For the Philadelphia production, Du Bois wrote, "The tickets were late. The costumes were later and the properties latest of all" (Du Bois, "The Star of Ethiopia," 93).

25. Ibid.

26. David W. Blight, "W. E. B. Du Bois and the Struggle for American National Memory," in *History and Memory in African American Culture*, ed. Geneviève Fabre and Robert O'Meally (New York: Oxford University Press, 1994), 46.

27. Anthony Appiah, "The Uncompleted Argument: Du Bois and the Illusion of Race," *Critical Inquiry* 12 (Autumn 1985), 25.

28. Du Bois, "Can the Negro Serve the Drama?" *Theatre Magazine* 38 (July 1923), 68.

29. *Washington Bee*, 23 October 1915, 1.

30. Du Bois, "The African Roots of War," *Atlantic Monthly* (May 1915), 707.

31. William Chauncy Langdon, "The Pageant-Grounds and Their Technical Requirements," *Bulletin of the American Pageantry Association* 11 (1 December 1914), 1.

32. Steve Golin, "The Paterson Pageant: Success or Failure," *Socialist Review* 13 (1983), 56. My thanks to my friend and cousin Stanley Comet, who alerted me to this essay.

33. Du Bois, "Letter to Ellis P. Oberholtzer," June 20, 1913; found in the Historical Society of Philadelphia. My thanks to Linda Stanley, Manuscripts and Archives, for sending a copy of the letter.

34. Haskins, "The Gift of Ethiopia," 75.

35. Du Bois, "The Conservation of Races: Speech to the American Negro Academy, 1897," *African American Social and Political Thought, 1850–1920*, ed. Howard Brotz (New Brunswick: Transaction, 1993), 487–88.

36. Freda L. Scott, "The Star of Ethiopia," unpublished manuscript, 1, HB.

37. Linda Nochlin, "The Paterson Strike Pageant of 1913," *Art in America* 52 (May–June 1974), 67.

38. Du Bois was not, however, a back-to-Africa emigrationist as was Bishop Turner and Edward W. Blyden. During the time of the pageant, Du Bois was essentially

optimistic about prospects for black advancement, despite the chorus of racist propaganda, Jim Crowism, and lynching. From 1913 to 1916, Du Bois enjoyed a period of unchallenged leadership. Booker T. Washington's influence was declining (he died in 1915) and Marcus Garvey had yet to make his appearance on the political scene.

39. Du Bois, *Dusk of Dawn*, 199.
40. Liah Greenfield, *Nationalism: Five Roads to Modernity* (Cambridge: Harvard University Press, 1992), 3, 487.
41. Wilson Jeremiah Moses, *The Golden Age of Black Nationalism, 1850–1925* (New York: Oxford University Press, 1978), 133.
42. Joel Williamson, "W. E. B. Du Bois as a Hegelian," in *What Was Freedom's Price?*, ed. David G. Sansing (Jackson, MI: University of Mississippi Press, 1978), 34.
43. David Levering Lewis writes that Du Bois discovered in the Hegelian World-Spirit a "profoundly appealing concept" (*W. E. B. Du Bois*, 139–40). For a discussion of Hegelian influences on Du Bois, see Williamson, *The Crucible of Race: Black-White Relations in the American South Since Emancipation* (New York: Oxford University Press, 1984), 402–13; for German influences in general, see Francis L. Broderick, "German Influences on the Scholarship of W. E. B. Du Bois," *Phylon Quarterly* 19 (Winter 1958), 367–71.
44. Johann Gottfried von Herder, *Outline of a Philosophy of the History of Man* (1784–1791), quoted in Elie Kedourie, *Nationalism* (Oxford: Blackwell, 1993), 48.
45. Bernard W. Bell, *The Folk Roots of Contemporary Afro-American Poetry* (Detroit: Broadside, 1974), 21.
46. Du Bois, *The Negro* (1915; London: Oxford University Press, 1970), 9.
47. Rampersad, *Art and Imagination*, 143.
48. See, for example, Frederick B. Bridgeman, "The Ethiopian Movement in South Africa," *Missionary Review of the World* (June 1904), 434–45, and Wilson J. Moses, "The Poetics of Ethiopianism: W. E. B. Du Bois and Literary Black Nationalism," *American Literature* 47.3 (November 1975), 411–26.
49. J. Mutero Chirenje, *Ethiopianism and Afro-Americans in Southern Africa, 1883–1916* (Baton Rouge: Louisiana State University Press, 1987), 1.
50. F. Nnabuenyi Ugonna, "Introduction," *Ethiopia Unbound: Studies in Race Emancipation*, ed. J. E. Casely Hayford (London: F. Case, 1969), xxiv.
51. B. F. Lee, "Selection, Environment and the Negro's Future," *A. M. E. Church Review* 20 (1904), 389.
52. Edmund J. Keller, *Revolutionary Ethiopia: From Empire to People's Republic* (Bloomington: Indiana University Press, 1991), 34.
53. See, for instance, Clarence G. Contee, "The Emergence of Du Bois as an African Nationalist," *Journal of Negro History* 54 (1969), 48–63.
54. Henry Highland Garnet, "The Past and the Present Condition, and the Destiny of the Colored Race," 14 February 1848; quoted in Bracey, *Black Nationalism in America*, 119.
55. Martin Delany, *Principia of Ethnology: The Origins of Race and Color* (Philadelphia: Harper, 1879), 72.
56. Richard Powell, *Black Art and Culture in the Twentieth Century* (London: Thames and Hudson, 1997), 36.
57. Charles Alexander, *Indianapolis Freeman*, 2 April 1898, 1.
58. Daniels, "Du Bois' First Efforts as a Playwright," 425.

59. UM.

60. Du Bois, "The Star of Ethiopia," 91.

61. Du Bois, *Dusk of Dawn*, 272–73.

62. See Hay, *African American Theatre*, 262.

63. UM.

64. Du Bois, "The Drama Among Black Folk," 169.

65. Du Bois, "The Star of Ethiopia: A Pageant," 206.

66. Du Bois, "The National Emancipation Exposition," *Crisis* 6.9 (November 1913), 339.

67. For a discussion on Du Bois's theories based on Franz Boas's lectures in 1906 on the origins of iron smelting, see Sterling Stuckey, *Going Through the Storm: The Influence of African American Art in History* (New York: Oxford University Press, 1994), 130.

68. UM.

69. Du Bois, "The Star of Ethiopia: A Pageant," 206.

70. UM.

71. Du Bois, "The Star of Ethiopia: A Pageant," 206.

72. UM.

73. Ibid.

74. Ibid.

75. See, Du Bois, *Dusk of Dawn*, 274.

76. Du Bois, "The Conservation of Races: Speech to the American Negro Academy (1897)," quoted in *African-American Social and Political Thought, 1850–1920*, ed. Howard Brotz (New Brunswick: Transaction, 1993), 491.

77. Sterling Stuckey, *Slave Culture: Nationalist Theory and the Foundations of Black America* (New York: Oxford University Press, 1987), 276.

78. Stuckey, *Going Through the Storm*, 134.

79. Quoted in Julio Finn, *Voices of Négritude* (London: Quartet, 1988], 58. Négritude emerged as a protest against French rule in Africa. It retained a respect for French and European poetry and philosophy, but emphasized the importance of African heritage exemplified by Africa's "closeness to nature." Western culture, it maintained, was out of step with the rhythms of human existence.

80. Frantz Fanon, *The Wretched of the Earth*, tr. Constance Farrington (New York: Grove Press, 1968), 213.

81. Wole Soyinka, *Myth, Literature and the African World* (Cambridge: Cambridge University Press, 1976), 129, 127.

82. Rampersad, *Art and Imagination*, 62.

83. Edward W. Said, *Culture and Imperialism* (New York: Alfred A. Knopf, 1994), 226.

84. Du Bois, "A Negro Art Renaissance," *Los Angeles Times*, 14 June 1925, 27.

85. Du Bois, "The Drama Among Black Folk," 169.

86. Du Bois, "Editorial: A Pageant," *Crisis* 10.5 (September 1915), 230.

87. Blight, "W. E. B. Du Bois," 50.

PART II

1. Charles S. Gilpin, allegedly spoken to the actors of the Karamu House circa 1923 after a performance of *The Emperor Jones;* quoted in Ruben Silver, "A History of the Karamu Theatre of Karamu House, 1915–1960" Ohio State University, Ph.D. Dissertation, 1961, 110–111.

2. Freda Scott Giles, "Willis Richardson and Eulalie Spence: Dramatic Voices of the Harlem Renaissance," *American Drama* 5.2 (Spring 1996), 4.

3. Larry Neal, "The Black Arts Movement," in *The Black Aesthetic,* ed. Addison Gayle (Garden City, NY: Doubleday, 1971), 273.

4. Henry Louis Gates, Jr. and Nellie Larson, ed., *Norton Anthology of African American Literature* (New York: Norton, 1997), 935.

5. See, Kathy A. Perkins and Judith L. Stephens, *Strange Fruit: Plays on Lynching by African American Women* (Bloomington: Indiana University Press, 1998).

CHAPTER FIVE

1. Hilton Als, "GWTW," *Without Sanctuary,* ed. James Allen et al. (New York: Twin Palms, 2000), 41. "GWTW" stands for *Gone with the Wind.*

2. Thomas F. Gossett, *Race: The History of an Idea in America* (New York: Oxford University Press, 1963, 1977), 270.

3. See Sandra L. Richards, "Foreword," in *Strange Fruit: Plays on Lynching by American Women,* ed. Kathy A. Perkins and Judith L. Stephens (Bloomington: Indiana University Press, 1998), x.

4. *Rachel* was written in 1916 and submitted to the Drama Committee of the National Association for the Advancement of Colored People (NAACP). It was originally produced in Washington, D.C., at the Mrytill Miner School, and at New York's Neighborhood Playhouse in 1917.

5. Patricia R. Schroeder, *The Feminist Possibilities of Dramatic Realism* (Madison: Fairleigh Dickson University Press, 1996), 112.

6. Judith L. Stephens, "Anti-Lynching Plays by African American Women: Race, Gender, and Social Protest in American Drama," *African American Review* 26.2 (Summer 1992), 332. Elsewhere, Stephens characterizes lynching plays as "ground for interracial feminist dialogue" (Stephens, "The Anti-Lynch Play: Toward an Interracial-Feminist Dialogue on Theatre," *Journal of American Drama and Theatre* 2.3 [Fall 1990], 60).

7. Will Harris, "Early Black Women Playwrights and the Dual Liberation Motif," *African American Review* 28.2 (Summer 1994), 205.

8. Tisch Jones, in commenting on Grimké's *Rachel,* suggests that her play was "the first attempt by a Black woman to use the stage for race propaganda" (Jones, "Introduction to *Rachel,*" in *Black Theatre USA,* ed. James V. Hatch and Ted Shine [New York: Free Press, 1996], 134). Gloria Hull offers the reasoned conjecture that *Rachel* intended to achieve increased social awareness "by showing how American racial prejudice blighted the lives of a good, upstanding, attractive black family" (Hull, *Color, Sex and Poetry: Three Women Writers of the Harlem Renaissance* [Bloomington: Indiana University Press, 1987], 117). Jeanne-Marie A. Miller observes that Grimké wrote *Rachel* as a reaction to the negative stereotype and "used characters from a struggling black genteel class to protest vigorously the ill treatment of blacks by white America" (Miller, "Angelina Weld Grimké: Playwright and Poet," *CLA Journal* 21.4 [June 1978], 514–15).

9. Judith L. Stephens, "Lynching, American Theatre, and the Preservation of a Tradition," *Journal of American Drama and Theatre* 9.1 (Winter, 1997), 65.

10. For a history of the play's reception, see Robert J. Fehrenbach, "An Early Twentieth-Century Problem Play of Life in Black America: Angelina Weld Grimké's *Rachel* (1916)," in *Wild Women in the Whirlwind: Afra-American Culture and the Contemporary Literary Renaissance,* ed. Joanne M. Braxton and Andrée Nicola McLaughlin (New Brunswick: Rutgers University Press, 1990), 89–106; and Hull, 117–124.

11. Grimké, *Rachel,* quoted from *Black Theatre, USA,* 136.

12. Ibid., 139.
13. Angelina Weld Grimké, "'Rachel': The Play of the Month: The Reason and Synopsis by the Author," *Competitor* 1.1 (January 1920), 52.
14. Grimké, *Rachel*, 152, 157.
15. Grimké, "'Rachel': The Play of the Month," 52.
16. Hull, *Color, Sex and Poetry*, 123. Jeanne Miller adds to this view, stating: "Though the work is distracting in several ways—some of its contrivances being too obvious, such as the circumstances leading to Rachel's adoption of the little neighbor boy [Jimmy] and the entrance of the woman [Mrs. Lane] and the child ravaged by racism; the language in the long speeches being too artificial to be convincing as real speech; and Rachel's hypersensitivity seeming almost incredulous by today's standards—this sentimental work does achieve its purpose in stressing some of America's unjust treatment of the black race" (Miller, "Angelina Weld Grimké: Playwright and Poet," 516).
17. Lyrics to "Strange Fruit," by Abe Meeropol, 1937; originally an anti-lynching poem published in the *New York Teacher* and later made famous by the singer Billie Holliday. See David Margolick, *Strange Fruit: The Biography of a Song* (New York: Ecco Press, 2001).
18. Walter Benjamin, *The Origin of German Tragic Drama*, tr. John Osborne (1925; reprint, London: Verso, 1977), 119.
19. Mary Church Terrell, "Prominent Club Woman Reviews Lynching Causes," *The Atlantic Monthly*, 1905, reprinted in the *Chicago Defender*, 20 December 1924: part 8, pg. 6. For pamphlets describing the horrors of lynching, see also Ida B. Wells, *Southern Horrors and Other Writings: The Anti-Lynching Campaign of Ida B. Wells, 1892–1900*, ed. Jacqueline Jones Royster (Boston: Bedford Books, 1997).
20. Leon F. Litwack, "Hellhounds," *Beyond Sanctuary*, 14.
21. Walter Benjamin, *Gesammelte Schriften I & II*, ed. R. Tiedemann and H. Schweppenhäuser (Frankfurt/am: Suhrkamp, 1977), II, 137. All translations are my own, unless otherwise indicated. I will refer to the volume of Benjamin's work (either I or II) as *GS* followed by the page. For a full translation of *Die Bedeutung der Sprache in Trauerspiel und Tragödie* (written by Benjamin in 1916 and unpublished in his lifetime), see *Walter Benjamin: Selected Writings* Vol. 1, 1913–1926, eds. Marcus Bullock and Michael W. Jennings, tr. Rodney Livingston (Cambridge, MA: Harvard University Press, 1996), 59–61.
22. Benjamin, *GS* II, 138.
23. Ibid.
24. Ibid., 139.
25. Ibid., 140.
26. Nellie McKay, "'What Were They Saying?': Black Women Playwrights of the Harlem Renaissance," in *Harlem Renaissance Re-examined*, ed. Victor A. Kramer and Robert A. Russ (Troy, NY: Whitston Publishers, 1997), 154.
27. Margaret Cohen, *Profane Illumination: Walter Benjamin and the Paris of Surrealist Revolution* (Berkeley: University of California Press, 1993), 1–2.
28. See, for instance, Rainer Nägele, *Theatre, Theory, Speculation: Walter Benjamin and the Scenes of Modernity* (Baltimore: John Hopkins University Press, 1991), 113–14 for an interesting comparison between Benjamin's and Nietzsche's theories of tragedy.
29. Benjamin, *Origin*, 187.
30. George Steiner, "Introduction" to *Origin of German Tragic Drama*, 17.
31. Grimké, *Rachel*, 157.

32. Benjamin, *Origin*, 210.

33. Ferenc Feher, "Lukács and Benjamin: Parallels and Contrasts," *New German Critique* 34 (Winter 1985), 126.

34. Sigmund Freud, "Mourning and Melancholia," *The Freud Reader*, ed. Peter Gay (New York: Norton, 1989), 687.

35. Fredric Jameson, *Marxism and Form* (Princeton: Princeton University Press, 1971), 68.

36. Grimké, *Rachel*, 145.

37. Angelina Weld Grimké Papers, Box 38–13, MS.

38. From a book proposal/manuscript, edited by Perkins and Stephens *Plays on Lynching by American Women* (p. 13), HB. This book eventually became a collection of anti-lynching plays published by Indiana University Press.

39. Jacqueline Goldsby, "The High and Low Tech of It: The Meaning of Lynching and the Death of Emmett Till," *Yale Journal of Criticism* 9.2 (1996), 274.

40. Benjamin, *Origin*, 166.

41. Ibid., 178.

42. Hans-Georg Gadamer, *Truth and Method*, tr. Joel Weinsheimer and Donna G. Marshall (New York: Crossroad, 1992), 80.

43. For discussions on the devaluation of allegory, see Paul de Man, *Blindness and Insight: Essays on the Rhetoric of Contemporary Criticism* (Minneapolis: University of Minnesota Press, 1983), 187–228; and E. D. Hirsch, Jr., "Transhistorical Intentions and the Persistence of Allegory," *New Literary History* 25.3 (Summer 1994), 549–67. For a discussion of allegory's relationship to Weimar Neoclassicism, see Albrecht Schöne, *Emblematik und Drama im Zeitalter des Barock* (München: C. H. Beck, 1964), 30–34.

44. Benjamin, *Origin*, 160.

45. For a record of lynching postcards and photographs, see *Without Sanctuary*.

46. For an interesting study of lynching as a ritualize act, see Kirk W. Fuoss, "Lynching Performances, Theatres of Violence," *Text and Performance Quarterly* 19.1 (January 1999), 1–37.

47. Robyn Wiegman, "Whiteness Studies and the Paradox of Particularity," *Boundary 2* 26.3 (Fall 1999), 119.

48. Trudier Harris, "Before the Strength, the Pain: Portraits of Elderly Black Women in Early Twentieth-Century Anti-Lynching Plays," in *Black Women Playwrights*, ed. Carol P. Marsh-Lockett (New York: Garland), 32.

49. Bainard Cowan, "Walter Benjamin's Theory of Allegory," *New German Critique* 22 (Winter 1981), 116.

50. Rochester, New York, *Post Express*, 14 September 1920; book review clipping, Grimké Papers, MS.

51. Benjamin, *Origin*, 166.

52. Grimké, *Rachel*, 168.

53. Max Pensky, *Melancholy Dialectics: Walter Benjamin and the Plays of Mourning* (Amherst: University of Massachusetts Press, 1993), 34.

54. Benjamin, *Origin*, 162.

55. See, for instance, Miller, "Angelina Weld Grimké," in which she calls Rachel's sentimentality and contrivances "distracting," and the long speeches "too artificial to be convincing as real speech" (516).

56. Terry Eagleton, *Walter Benjamin* (London: Verso, 1981), 23.

57. Marita O. Bonner, "On Being Young—A Woman—and Colored, *Crisis* 31.2 (December 1925), 64.

58. Grimké, "Rachel," *Competitor*, 52.

CHAPTER SIX

1. Martin Heidegger, "Building Dwelling Thinking," (1954) in *Poetry, Language, Thought*, tr. Albert Hofstadter (New York: Harper Row, 1971), 154.

2. Donna Kate Rushin, "The Bridge Poem," *This Bridge Called My Back: Writings by Radical Women of Color*, ed. Cherríe Moraga and Gloria Anzaldúa (New York: Kitchen Table, 1981, 1983), xxii.

3. For studies on the Great Migration see, for instance, Daniel M. Johnson and Rex R. Campbell, *Black Migration in America* (Durham: Duke University Press, 1981); Alferdteen Harrison, ed., *Black Exodus: The Great Migration from the American South* (Jackson: University of Mississippi Press, 1991); and Joe William Trotter, Jr., ed., *The Great Migration in Historical Perspective* (Bloomington: Indiana University Press, 1991).

4. See, James R. Grossman, "A Chance to Make Good, 1900–1929," *To Make Our World Anew: A History of African Americans*, ed. Robin D. G. Kelley and Earl Lewis (New York: Oxford University Press, 2000), 386.

5. Alain Locke, "Harlem," *Survey Graphic* 6.6 (March 1925), 629.

6. Hazel Carby, "The Politics of Fiction, Anthropology, and the Folk: Zora Neale Hurston," in *New Essays on Their Eyes Were Watching God*, ed. Michael Awkward (Cambridge: Cambridge University Press, 1990), 75.

7. Zora Neal Hurston's play *Color Struck* was completed in 1925, and printed in 1926. It was first published in the inaugural (and only) edition of *Fire!* (1926), a journal "Devoted to Younger Negro Artists," 7–14, edited by Wallace Thurman. In this essay I will quote from the version in the journal *Fire!* For brief discussions and history of the play, see Bernard L. Peterson, Jr., *Early Black American Playwrights and Dramatic Writers* (New York: Greenwood Press, 1990), 115; Judith L. Stephens, "The Harlem Renaissance and the New Negro Movement," in *The Cambridge Companion to American Women Playwrights*, ed. Brenda Murphy (Cambridge: Cambridge University Press, 1999), 111; Christine R. Gray, "Recovering African American Women Playwrights," in *The Cambridge Companion to American Women Playwrights*, 248; and Leslie Catherine Sanders, *The Development of Black Theater in America* (Baton Rouge: Louisiana State University Press, 1988), 85.

8. Crispin Sartwell, *Act Like You Know: African-American Autobiography and White Identity* (Chicago: University of Chicago Press, 1998).

9. Carby, "The Politics of Fiction, Anthropology, and the Folk," 77.

10. Barbara Johnson, "Metaphor, Metonymy, and Voice in *Their Eyes Were Watching God*," in *A World of Difference* (Baltimore: John Hopkins University Press, 1987), 159.

11. See, for instance, Deborah A. Gordon, "The Politics of Ethnographic Authority: Race and Writing in the Ethnography of Margaret Mead and Zora Neale Hurston," in *Modernist Anthropology: From Fieldwork to Text*, ed. Marc Manganaro (Princeton: Princeton University Press, 1990), 146–62; Graciela Hernández, "Multiple Subjectivities and Strategic Positionality: Zora Neale Hurston's Experimental Ethnographies," in *Women Writing Culture*, ed. Ruth Behar and Deborah A. Gordon (Berkeley: University of California Press, 1996), 148–165; and Gwen-

dolyn Mikell, "The Anthropological Imagination of Zora Neale Hurston," *Western Journal of Black Studies* 7.1 (1983), 27–35.

12. Franz Boas, "The Limitations of the Comparative Method of Anthropology," *Science* 4 (1896), 905; reprinted in Boas, *Race, Language, and Culture* (Chicago: University of Chicago Press, 1940, reprint, 1982), 270–280.

13. See Boas, "What is Anthropology?," in Boas, *Anthropology and Modern Life* (1928; reprint, New York: Dover, 1986), 11–17.

14. These two developments epitomized what George W. Stocking, Jr., termed the 1920s "classical period" of modern anthropology. See Stocking, "The Ethnographic Sensibility of the 1920s and the Dualism of the Anthropological Tradition," in *Romantic Motives: Essays on Anthropological Sensibility,* ed. Stocking (Madison: University of Wisconsin Press, 1989), 212.

15. Boasian influence encouraged anthropologists to turn their backs on the Darwinian-Spenserian view that had dominated the field in the late nineteenth and early twentieth century. Among his many disciples were Ella Deloria, Ruth Benedict, Melville Herskovits, Ruth Landes, Robert Lowie, Alfred Louis Kroeber, Margaret Mead, Paul Radin, Edward Sapir, and Hurston. For an interesting reading of Boas and his influence, see Susan Hegeman, *Patterns for America: Modernism and the Concept of Culture* (Princeton: Princeton University Press, 1999), 32–65.

16. Boas, "Anthropology," Lecture Delivered at Columbia University, 18 December 1907, quoted in *A Franz Boas Reader,* ed. George W. Stocking, Jr. (Chicago: University of Chicago Press, 1974), 269.

17. Hurston, *Mules and Men* (1935), quoted in *I Love Myself When I Am Laughing: A Zora Neale Hurston Reader,* ed. Alice Walker (New York: Feminist Press, 1979), 82.

18. Lee D. Baker, *From Savage to Negro: Anthropology and the Construction of Race, 1896–1954* (Berkeley: University of California Press, 1998), 162. For discussions of Hurston's relationship to Boasian anthropology, see also Mary Katherine Wainwright, "The Aesthetics of Community: The Insular Black Community as Theme and Focus in Hurston's *Their Eyes Were Watching God,*" in *The Harlem Renaissance: Reevaluations,* ed. Amritjit et al. (New York: Garland, 1989), 233–43; bell hooks, "Saving Black Folk Culture," in *Yearnings: race, gender, and cultural politics* (Boston: South End Press, 1990), 136; and Alice Gambrell, *Women Intellectuals, Modernism, and Difference: Transatlantic Culture, 1919–1945* (Cambridge: Cambridge University Press, 1997), 115.

19. Robert E. Hemenway, *Zora Neale Hurston: A Literary Biography* (Urbana: University of Illinois Press, 1980), 63.

20. The first draft of *Color Struck* was submitted to *Opportunity Magazine* and was awarded second prize (along with honorable mention for her play, *Spears*) at the *Opportunity* Award Banquet on 1 May 1925. Hurston received a Barnard scholarship during the summer and began to attend classes in the fall of 1925, at least five months after writing the play.

21. Benigno Sánchez-Eppler has suggested a similar observation, noting that during the mid-1920s, "just before her enrollment in Columbia and after her exposure to higher education at Howard University, Hurston had spent a relatively short but productive period in contact with the full roster of artists, intellectuals, and patrons of the Harlem Renaissance." Hurston drew on "her acquaintance with Southern black folklore for writing stories and for storytelling in social gatherings" ("Telling Anthropology: Zora Neale Hurston and Gilberto Freyre Disciplined in Their Field-Home-Work," *American Literary History* 4.3 [Fall 1992], 472).

22. For an interesting discussion of Hurston's work in literature and anthropology, see Sieglinde Lemke, "Blurring Generic Boundaries. Zora Neale Hurston: A Writer of Fiction and Anthropology," *Real: Yearbook of Research in English and American Literature* 12 (1996), 163–77.

23. Pearlie Mae Fisher Peters, *The Assertive Woman in Zora Neal Hurston's Fiction, Folklore, and Drama* (New York: Garland, 1998), 26. For other negative critiques, see Warren J. Carson, "Hurston as Dramatist: The Florida Connection," in *Zora in Florida*, ed. Steve Glassman and Kathryn Lee Seidal (Orlando: University of Central Florida Press, 1991), 123–124, and Hemenway, *Zora Neale Hurston*, 47.

24. See, for instance, H. Lin Classon, "Re-evaluating *Color Struck:* Zora Neale Hurston and the Issue of Colorism," *Theatre Studies* 42 (1997), 5–18; Lynda Marion Hill, *Social Rituals and the Verbal Art of Zora Neale Hurston* (Washington, D. C.: Howard University Press, 1996), 108; and Deborah G. Plant, *Every Tub Must Sit on Its Own Bottom: The Philosophy and Politics of Zora Neale Hurston* (Urbana: University of Chicago Press, 1995), 158.

25. Zora Neale Hurston, *Dust Tracks on a Road* (1942; reprint, New York: Harper, 1995), 184.

26. For a discussion of the relationship between "Mammyism" and the Hottentot Venus in the play, see Jasmin L. Lambert, "Resisting the 'Hottentot' Body: Themes of Sexuality and Femininity in Select Plays by Female Playwrights from the Harlem Renaissance," Ph.D. dissertation, Bowling Green State University, 1998, 148–72.

27. Sandra L. Richards, "Writing the Absent Potential: Drama, Performance, and the Canon of African-American Literature," in *Performativity and Performance*, ed. Andrew Parker and Eve Kosofsky Sedgwick (New York: Routledge, 1995), 77.

28. Ibid., 79.

29. Ibid., 75.

30. Under the influence of white patron Charlotte Osgood Mason, many African American artists, musicians, and writers were encouraged to indulge in what Mason called their "innate primitivism." However, it was not until 1927 that Hurston formally met Mason, at which time she offered to subsidize Hurston's research trip to Eatonville. See Lillie P. Howard, *Zora Neale Hurston* (Boston: Twayne, 1980), 22–25.

31. In their study of African American journals, *Propaganda & Aesthetics: The Literary Politics of African-American Magazines in the Twentieth Century* (Amherst: University of Massachusetts Press, 1979), Abby Arthur Johnson and Ronald Mayberry Johnson contend that the editor of *Fire!*, Wallace Thurman, "was primarily interested in aspects of black life generally considered disreputable by the more proper Afro-Americans" (80).

32. Langston Hughes observed that *Fire!* "would burn up a lot of old, dead, conventional Negro-white ideas of the past, *épater le bourgeoisie* into a realization of the existence of the younger Negro writers and artists" (Hughes, "In the Twenties," *Saturday Review of Literature* 22 [22 June 1940], 13).

33. Alain Locke, "Fire: A Negro Magazine," *The Survey Graphic* 58.10–12 (15 August–15 September 1927), 563.

34. Hurston, "Letter to Annie Nathan Meyer," 10 November 1925, pg. 2, from the American Jewish Archives, Hurston–Meyer Correspondence file. My gratitude to Anthea Kraut for discovering this letter and sending it to me. Barbara Speisman, "From 'Spears' to *The Great Day:* Zora Neale Hurston's Vision of a Real Negro

Theater," *Southern Quarterly* 36.3 (Spring 1998), 34–46, claims that "the Negro Art Theater of Harlem opened with [Hurston's] play, *Color Struck*" (36). However, Speisman fails to supply evidence to support this claim. Other than Hurston's letter, no other evidence exists, to my knowledge, to substantiate that an actual performance, or performances, took place.

35. Anthea Kraut, "Reclaiming the Body: Representations of Black Dance in Three Plays by Zora Neale Hurston," *Theatre Studies* 43 (1998), 30.

36. For a social history of the cakewalk, see David Krasner, "Rewriting the Body: Aida Overton Walker and the Social Formation of Cakewalking," *Theatre Survey* 37.2 (November 1996), 67–92.

37. Michael North, *The Dialect of Modernism: Race, Language and Twentieth-Century Literature* (New York: Oxford University Press, 1994), 176, 177. Along similar lines, Nina Miller, *Making Love Modern: The Intimate Public Worlds of New York's Literary Tradition* (New York: Oxford University Press, 1999), writes that the play's setting "is vintage Hurston: an all-black, Eatonville-like society, within which white racism counts for very little, but the foibles of black folk are on prominent display" (167).

38. Toni Morrison, "Afterword," *The Bluest Eye* (New York: Plum, 1994), 210.

39. Hurston, *Dust Tracks on a Road*, 177.

40. Ibid.

41. Hurston, *Color Struck*, 7.

42. John Lowe raises the point that this presentation of rural blacks in most of Hurston's literary output may have caused critical dismissal of her work up until the 1970s (Lowe, "Hurston, Humor, and the Harlem Renaissance," in *Harlem Renaissance Re-examined*, ed. Victor Kramer [New York: AMS Press, 1987], 305–31).

43. Hurston, *Color Struck*, 7.

44. Hill, *Social Rituals and the Verbal Art of Zora Neale Hurston*, 109.

45. Hurston, *Color Struck*, 8.

46. Ibid.

47. Hurston, *Dust Tracks on a Road*, 146.

48. Carole Boyce Davies, *Black Women, Writing and Identity: Migration of the Subject* (London: Routledge, 1994), 47.

49. For illuminating discussions of women and migration narratives, see Farah Jasmine Griffin, *"Who Set You Flowin'?": The African-American Migration Narrative* (New York: Oxford University Press, 1995), and Sandra Gunning, "Nance Prince and the Politics of Mobility, Home and Diasporic (Mis)Identification," *American Quarterly* 53.1 (March 2001), 32–69.

50. James Clifford, *Routes: Travel and Translation in the Late Twentieth Century* (Cambridge: Harvard University Press, 1997), 32.

51. Houston A. Baker, Jr., *Blues, Ideology, and Afro-American Literature: A Vernacular Theory* (Chicago: University of Chicago Press, 1984), 200, 202.

52. Hazel Carby, "'It Jus Be's Dat Way Sometime': The Sexual Politics of Women's Blues," in *Unequal Sisters: A Multi-Cultural Reader in U.S. Women's History*, ed. Vicki L. Ruiz and Ellen Carol DuBois (New York: Routledge, 1994), 334.

53. Edward Said, "Minds in Winter: Reflections on Life in Exile," *Harper's Magazine* 269 (September 1984), 51.

54. Una Chaudhuri, *Staging Place: The Geography of Modern Drama* (Ann Arbor: University of Michigan Press, 1997), 13.

55. Hurston, *Color Struck*, 9.

56. Ibid., 10.
57. Marita O. Bonner, "On Being Young-A Woman—and Colored," *Crisis* 31.2 (December 1925), 64.
58. Hurston, *Color Struck*, 11.
59. Juliana Schiesari, *The Gendering of Melancholia: Feminism, Psychoanalysis, and the Symbolics of Loss in Renaissance Literature* (Ithaca: Cornell University Press, 1992), 3–4, 13. Schiesari observes that the term melancholia is a Latin transliteration of the Greek word meaning "black bile" or "*atra bilis*," a bodily fluid whose excess is responsible for the condition of melancholia. According to Aristotle, the melancholic temperament affected all "great men" (6).
60. Saidiya V. Hartman, *Scenes of Subjection: Terror, Slavery, and Self-Making in Nineteenth-Century America* (New York: Oxford University Press, 1997), 108.
61. Claudia Tate, *Psychoanalysis and Black Novels: Desire and the Protocols of Race* (New York: Oxford University Press, 1998), 13.
62. Julia Kristeva, *Black Sun: Depression and Melancholia,* tr. Leon S. Roudiez (New York: Columbia University Press, 1989), 128.
63. Hurston, *Color Struck*, 12.
64. Susan Willis, *Specifying: Black Women Writing the American Experience* (Madison: University of Wisconsin Press, 1987), 36.
65. Hurston, *Color Struck*, 12.
66. Ibid., 13.
67. Ibid.
68. Ibid.
69. For a study of African American women's relationship to beauty, hair, and especially the history of Madam C. J. Walker, the entrepreneurial business leader who developed an empire of beauty products (ca. 1905 to 1919), see Noliwe M. Rooks, *Hair Raising: Beauty, Culture, and African American Women* (New Brunswick: Rutgers University Press, 1996).
70. Hurston, *Color Struck*, 14.
71. Ibid.
72. For discussions on silence, see Peter Hitchcock, *Dialogics of the Oppressed* (Minneapolis: University of Minnesota Press, 1993), and Bernard P. Dauenhauer, *Silence: The Phenomenon and Its Ontological Significance* (Bloomington: Indiana University Press, 1980).
73. Sartwell, *Act Like You Know*, 156, 158.
74. Hurston, "How It Feels to Be Colored Me," quoted in *I Love Myself When I Am Laughing: A Zora Neale Hurston Reader,* 155.
75. Hurston, *Color Struck*, 14.
76. Toni Morrison, *Beloved* (New York: Signet, 1991), 336.

CHAPTER SEVEN

1. Montgomery Gregory, unpublished essay titled, "Negro Drama," Gregory Collection, Box 37–3, folder 92, MS.
2. Alain Locke, *Race Contacts and Interracial Relations* (1916), ed. Jeffrey C. Stewart (Washington, D. C., Howard University Press, 1992), 88.
3. Thomas Pearce Bailey, *Race Orthodoxy in the South* (New York: Neale Pub. Co., 1914), 40.
4. Frederick L. Hoffman, *Race Traits and Tendencies of the American Negro* (New York: MacMillan Co., 1896), 95.

5. James Kimble Vardaman, *Greenwood [Mississippi] Commonwealth*, quoted in Albert D. Kirwan, *Revolt of the Rednecks: Mississippi Politics, 1876–1925* (Lexington: University of Kentucky Press, 1951), 146.

6. William Hannibal Thomas, *The American Negro: What He Was, What He Is, and What He May Become* (New York: MacMillan, 1901), 180.

7. Thomas Nelson Page, *The Negro: The Southern's Problem* (New York: Charles Scribner's Sons, 1904), 78.

8. Ellis Paxson Oberholtzer, *The History of the United States Since the Civil War*, Vol. 1 (New York: MacMillan Co, 1917), 73.

9. Lothrop Stoddard, "The Impasse at the Color Line," *The Forum* 78.4 (October 1927), 511–12.

10. Carter G. Woodson, *The Mis-Education of the Negro* (1933; Washington, D. C.: African World Press, 1993), 81.

11. Three other playwrights, Mary P. Burrill (1884–1946), Eulalie Spence (1894–1981), and May Miller (1899–1995), made an impact on African American drama during the 1920s. However, Burrill was chiefly known as a teacher of drama; Spence's important contributions were largely as a critic; and Miller's literary productivity blossomed primarily in the 1930s.

12. For information on Johnson's life, see Gloria T. Hull, *Color, Sex, and Poetry: Three Women Writers of the Harlem Renaissance* (Bloomington: Indiana University Press, 1987), 155–211.

13. See, Claudia Tate's biographical portrait of Johnson in her "Introduction," in *Selected Works of Georgia Douglas Johnson*, ed. Tate (New York: G. K. Hall, 1997), xxix.

14. Hull, *Color, Sex, and Poetry*, 164.

15. Willis Richardson, "Introduction" to his play, *The Broken Banjo*, *Crisis* 31.4 (February 1926), 167.

16. For discussions on race relations and the history of African Americans in Washington, D.C., see, for instance, James Borchert, *Alley Life in Washington: Family, Community, Religion, and Folklife in the City, 1850–1970* (Urbana: University of Illinois Press, 1980); and Constance McLaughlin Green, *The Secret Society: A History of Race Relations in the Nations Capital* (Princeton: Princeton University Press, 1967).

17. "Howard University and Its Lesson," *New York Age*, 4 March 1915, 4.

18. Herbert Aptheker, *Afro-American History: The Modern Era* (New York: Citadel Press, 1971, 1992), 175.

19. Census figures taken from *Major Problems in African-American History*, Vol. II, ed. Thomas C. Holt and Elsa Barkley Brown (Boston: Houghton Mifflin Co., 2000), 128.

20. However, during the 1920s Harlem's population increased at a greater proportion than any other African American community.

21. Paul Laurence Dunbar, "Negro Life in Washington," *Harper's Weekly* 6 (January 1900), 32, and Dunbar, "Negro Society in Washington," *Saturday Evening Post* (14 December 1901), 9.

22. Mary Church Terrell, "Society Among the Colored People of Washington," *The Voice of the Negro* 1.1 (March 1904), 151.

23. Willard B. Gatewood, *Aristocrats of Color: The Black Elite, 1880–1920* (Fayetteville, AR: University of Arkansas Press, 2000), 348.

24. Jeffrey C. Stewart, "A Biography of Alain Locke: Philosopher of the Harlem Renaissance, 1886–1930," Ph.D. dissertation, Yale University, 1979, 212.

25. Gwendolyn B. Bennett, "The Ebony Flute," *Opportunity* 5.7 (July 1927), 212.

26. See Johnson's biographical sketch, Georgia Douglas Johnson Papers, Box 162–1, folder 1, MS.

27. Willis Richardson, "Recorded Interview by Larry Gavin," July 1974, HB. See also Langston Hughes, *The Big Sea* (1940; reprint, New York: Hill & Wang, 1997), 216, for a list of Johnson's regulars.

28. Montgomery Gregory, "The Drama of Negro Life," in *The New Negro*, ed. Locke (1925; New York: Atheneum, 1992), 156.

29. Winona L. Fletcher, "From Genteel Poet to Revolutionary Playwright: Georgia Douglas Johnson," *Theatre Annual* 40 (1985), 41.

30. Quoted in David E. Shi, *Facing Facts: Realism in American Thought and Culture, 1950–1920* (New York: Oxford University Press, 1995), 7.

31. Richardson, Garvin interview (1974); Johnson, quoted in Hull, *Color, Sex, and Poetry*, 173.

32. Langston Hughes, "Our Wonderful Society: Washington," *Opportunity* 5.8 (August 1927), 226, 227.

33. Richardson, "Characters," *Opportunity* 3.30 (June 1925), 183.

34. Richardson, "The Negro Audience," *Opportunity* 3.28 (April 1925), 123. Richardson's biographer, Christine Rauchfuss Gray, contends that Richardson lacked the college education or social connections of Washington's black elite society, which may account for his frequent criticism of upper-class African Americans. Gray, *Willis Richardson: Forgotten Pioneer of African-American Drama* (Westport, CT: Greenwood Press, 1999), 63.

35. Richardson, "Propaganda in the Theatre," *Messenger* 6.11 (November 1924), 354.

36. Richardson, "Characters," 183.

37. Johnson, "The Negro in Art: How Shall He Be Portrayed," *Crisis* 32.4 (August 1926), 193.

38. See, Tate, "Introduction," in *Selected Works of Georgia Douglas Johnson*, lix.

39. The term "race pride" had grown during the New Negro Movement. It represented a new sense of self-awareness, pride in all things black, and a sense of distinctiveness in black culture. Locke wrote in the *New Negro* (1925) that "Nowhere is this more apparent, or more justified than in the increasing tendency to evolve from the racial substance something technically distinctive, something that as an idiom of style may become a contribution to the general resources of art" (51).

40. Leon F. Litwack, "Hellhounds," in *Without Sanctuary*, ed., James Allen et al. (New York: Twin Palms Publishers, 2000), 31.

41. Christine Gray argues that Du Bois influenced Richardson. No doubt Du Bois shaped his ideas, and published his plays *The Deacon's Awakening* and *Broken Banjo* in his journal, *Crisis*, as well as articles and commentaries (Gray, *Willis Richardson*, 60–1). Richardson's pageants were certainly modeled on Du Bois's *The Star of Ethiopia*. However, Richardson first met Du Bois somewhere between 1925 and 1926 (Garvin interview [1974]); his personal contacts with Du Bois were minimal and less than his personal contacts with Locke, at least prior to 1925.

42. For a discussion about the close relationship between Locke and Johnson, see Jeffrey C. Stewart, "Alain Locke and Georgia Douglas Johnson, Washington Patrons of Afro-American Modernism," *George Washington University Washington Studies* 12 (1986), 37–44.

43. For instance, Johnson wrote to Locke (14 March 1919), "I wish some one to go over some manuscripts with me in a critical way. . . . Will you allow me one hour of

your time that I may lay my material before you and have the benefit of your great advantage?" Alain Locke Papers, Box 164–40, folder 35, MS.

44. Locke, "Foreword," *An Autumn Love Cycle,* xix, quoted in *Selected Works of Georgia Douglas Johnson,* 197.

45. Richardson, "Letter to Locke," 9 August 1925, Locke Papers, Box 164–80, folder 19, MS.

46. Alain Locke, "Values and Imperatives," in *American Philosophy: Today and Tomorrow,* ed. Horace M. Kallen and Sidney Hooks (New York: Lee Forman, 1935), 314. Kallen was Locke's teacher and friend at Harvard.

47. He left Howard briefly to receive his Ph.D. at Harvard in 1917.

48. From 1925 to 1928, Locke was dismissed from Howard for supporting pay raises and student demands to end compulsory chapel and ROTC.

49. Locke, "Autobiographical Sketch," *American Philosophy: Today and Tomorrow,* 312.

50. Locke, "Steps Toward the Negro Theatre," *Crisis* 25.2 (December 1922), 68.

51. Locke, "Review of 'Goat Alley,'" *Opportunity* 1.2 (February 1923), 30.

52. Locke, "Introduction," *Plays of Negro Life,* ed. Locke and Montgomery Gregory (New York: Harper & Brothers, 1927), n.p.

53. Locke, "The Drama of Negro Life," *Theatre Arts Monthly* 10.10 (October 1926), 704.

54. Locke, "Art or Propaganda?," *Harlem: A Forum of Negro Life* 1.1 (November 1928), 12.

55. Locke, "New Themes," *Crisis* 27.4 (February 1924), 178.

56. Locke, "The Negro's Contribution to American Art and Literature," *The Annals of the American Academy of Politics and Social Science* 140.229 (November 1928), 240, 241.

57. Henry Louis Gates, Jr., raises the point that black intellectuals of the Harlem Renaissance "seemed to believe that their racist treatment at the hands of whites merely imitated their racist 'treatments' in art. Accordingly, if life did indeed imitate art, if reality imitated the image, then to manipulate the image of the black was, in a sense, to manipulate reality. The Public Negro Self, therefore, was an entity that had to be crafted." (Gates, "The Face and Voice of Blackness," in *Modern Art and Society: An Anthology of Social and Multicultural Readings,* ed. Maurice Berger [New York: HarperCollins, 1994], 65).

58. Locke, "Race or Propaganda?," *Race* 1.2 (Summer 1936), 73.

59. Locke, *Race Contacts and Interracial Relations,* 12. These lectures were first offered in 1915 at Howard and revised in 1916.

60. Locke, Course Outline (syllabus, circa 1916) for "Race Contacts and Interracial Relations," quoted in *The Critical Temper of Alain Locke: A Selection of His Essays on Art and Culture,* ed. Jeffrey C. Stewart (New York: Garland Publishers, 1983), 411.

61. Locke, "The Problem of Race Classification," *Opportunity* 1.9 (Sept. 1923), 261.

62. Locke did not study directly with James as he did with Santayana and Royce, but he was familiar with James and his work.

63. Values for Locke may be sub-categorized into seven criteria: the economic, which can be divided into use value (teleological) or exchange value (payment); the ethical; the aesthetic; those pertaining to pleasure or pain; the religious, which can be subdivided into spirituality and faith; the biological (survival value); and the logical, which consists in scientific or normative values. See Locke, "Value," undated, unpublished paper, Locke Papers, MS; also quoted in *The Philosophy of Alain Locke,* 115–16.

64. Locke, "Values and Imperatives," 313.

65. William James, *Pragmatism* (1907), quoted in *Pragmatism and The Meaning of Truth* (Cambridge: Harvard University Press, 1975), 123.

66. Locke, "Values and Imperatives," 314, 315.

67. Ibid., 319.

68. According to Santayana, judgments are made "to establish an ideal," because in finding the good or the beautiful, our standards evoke judgments that are "intrinsic and ultimate." However, at the next moment, our mind moves to "another footing," evoking a "new ideal," one which is "no less absolute than the previous judgement." Thus, the shifting relationship of values and judgments informs our tastes and experiences. Santayana, *The Sense of Beauty: Being the Outline of an Aesthetic Theory* (New York: Charles Schribner's, 1896; New York: Dover, 1955), 9.

69. As Richard Keaveny observes, Locke argued that the "social environment was the main contributor to the ways in which people assessed their emotions." Keaveny, "Aesthetics and the Issue of Identity," in *The Critical Pragmatism of Alain Locke*, ed. Leonard Harris (Lanham: Rowman & Littlefield Publishers, 1999), 129.

70. Locke, "Values and Imperatives," 321. For an interesting comparison of Locke's essay with other early twentieth-century anthropologists, see Mark Helbling, "Feeling Universality and Thinking Particularistically: Alain Locke, Franz Boas, Melville Herskovits, and the Harlem Renaissance," *Prospects: An Annual of American Cultural Studies* 19 (Cambridge: Cambridge University Press, 1994), 289–314.

71. Kallen wrote that cultural pluralism celebrates "variations of racial groups" as well as "spontaneous differences of social heritage, institutional habits, mental health, and emotional tone; upon the continuous, free and fruitful cross-fertilization of these by one another" (Kallen, *Culture and Democracy in the United States* [New York: Boni and Liveright, 1924], 42).

72. Locke, "The Concept of Race as Applied to Social Culture," *Howard Review* 1 (1924), 290–299; quoted in *The Philosophy of Alain Locke*, 195.

73. Locke, "Epilogue," *The Oxford Cosmopolitan* 1.1 (June 1908), 16.

74. Locke, "The Contribution of Race to Culture," *The Student World* 23 (1930), 349–353; quoted in *The Philosophy of Alain Locke*, 202–3, 206.

75. The repressive climate at Howard and throughout the United States after World War I may have contributed to Locke's retreat from radical politics and toward art, literary, and dramatic criticism.

76. Locke, "Introduction," *Four Negro Poets*, ed. Locke (New York: A. L. Burt, Co., 1927), 5.

77. Immanuel Kant, *Kritik der Urteilskraft*, ed. Karl Vorländer (1790; Hamburg: Felix Meiner, 1990), [8.49], 31. Kant builds his aesthetic concepts upon the basis of four principles: quality, quantity, relation, and modality. Quality is detached, or disinterested appreciation; quantity is the art-object's universality; relation is manifest through an appreciation of a purposefulness without purpose; and modality exhibits that which is apodictic but only through example.

78. Ibid., [6.39], 23.

79. Kant says that "purposefulness can thus be without purpose, insofar as we do not stress the causes of this form in volition, but yet can only make the explanation of it . . . by deriving from volition"; *Kritik der Urteilskraft*, [10.33], 59. Thus, for Kant, the purposiveness of an object can be appreciated as beautiful without the aid of reflective concepts, or ideas, creating a union of imagination and understanding free from purely cognitive notions. A sunset, for example, can be appreciated without the aid of cognitive notions of sunsets; we appreciate its aesthetic harmony,

and its purpose, based on our imagination and reason, and untrammeled by the notion of a sunset's utilitarian (purposeful) value, such as creating darkness for the purpose of reinvigorating nature.

80. Locke, "Introduction," *Plays of Negro Life*, n. p.

81. Locke, "The Drama of Negro Life," *Theatre Arts Monthly*, 705, 706.

82. Ibid., 705.

83. Locke, "Propaganda or Poetry?," 73, 87.

84. Locke, "Spiritual Truancy," *The New Challenge* 2.2 (Fall 1937), 83, 84.

85. Locke, "Spiritual Truancy," 85. Locke was influenced by his Harvard mentor Josiah Royce and Royce's book *The Philosophy of Loyalty* (1908; reprint, Nashville: Vanderbilt University Press, 1995). All virtues, Royce maintained, *"in so far as they are indeed defensible and effective, are special forms of loyalty to loyalty,"* because *"all duties which we have learned to recognize as the fundamental duties of the civilized man . . . are to be rightly interpreted as special instances of loyalty to loyalty"* (61, 66). For Royce, loyalty is a virtue by means of its interconnectedness with one human to another. Our commitments to people, groups, and social bonds are termed "loyalty," and when enacted, loyalty becomes virtuous. Locke built on Royce's dictum of loyalty to loyalty, but expands it to include his ideas of relative values. The "Roycean principal of 'loyalty to loyalty,'" he maintained, emphasized less "the tradition of absolutism" and more a "relativism of values and a principle of reciprocity" (Locke, "Values and Imperatives," 332).

86. Locke, "The Drama of Negro Life," *Theatre Arts Monthly*, 706.

87. Locke, "The Negro and the American Stage," *Theatre Arts Monthly* 10.2 (February 1926), 112. Elsewhere, Locke made the claim that the black actors' "temperament still moves natively and spontaneously in the world of make-believe with the primitive power of imaginative abandon and emotional conviction." "Introduction," *Plays of Negro Life*, n.p.

88. Locke, "The Saving Grace of Realism," *Opportunity* 12.1 (January 1934), 8.

89. Samuel A. Hay, *African American Theatre: An Historical and Critical Analysis* (Cambridge: Cambridge University Press, 1994), 3, 5. Hay's defining agenda, the sublation of Locke and Du Bois's theories into the plays of Suzan Lori-Parks and August Wilson, reflects the 1960s Black Arts Movement and its emphasis on black modernity's cohesion and finality. Paul De Man describes this desire for totality as a modernity that "exists in the form of a desire to wipe out whatever came earlier, in the hope of reaching at last a point that could be called a true present, a point of origin that marks a new departure" (De Man, "Literary History and Literary Modernity," *Blindness and Insight* [Minnesota: University of Minnesota Press, 1983], 184). The Black Arts Movement sought a new departure from past representations in order to form a new distinctiveness and a "true present." For Hay, Parks and especially Wilson represent the arrival of a true present via the union of Lockean folk drama and Du Boisian propaganda.

90. Charles Scruggs, *The Sage in Harlem: H. L. Mencken and the Black Writers of the 1920s* (Baltimore: John Hopkins University Press, 1984), 144, 157. Patricia R. Schroeder also asserts that Du Bois and Locke shared the common goals of "stage realism," where the "demeaning legacy of minstrel shows" could be "replaced by representations of human beings" (Schroeder, "Remembering the Disremembered: Feminist Realists of the Harlem Renaissance," in *Realism and the American Dramatic Tradition,* ed. William W. DeMastes [Tuscaloosa: University of Alabama Press, 1996], 92).

91. Locke, "The Certain of Our Philistines," *Opportunity* 3.29 (May 1925), 155. The reliance on facts follows the precepts of William James's Pragmatism, which claimed that the "pragmatist clings to facts and concreteness, observes truth at its work in particular cases, and generalizes." James, *Pragmatism* (1907; reprint, Buffalo, NY: Prometheus Books, 1991), 33.

92. Christine R. Gray, "Recovering African American Women Playwrights," in *The Cambridge Companion to American Women Playwrights*, ed. Brenda Murphy (Cambridge: Cambridge University Press, 1999), 246.

93. Locke, *The New Negro*, 52.

94. Charles Sanders Peirce, "Some Consequences of Four Incapacities," originally published in the *Journal of Speculative Philosophy* (1868), and reprinted in *Philosophical Writings of Peirce*, ed. Justus Buchler (New York: Dover, 1955), 247.

95. Locke, "The Drama of Negro Life," 703.

96. Locke Papers, Box 164–139, folder 29, MS.

97. For a discussion on the relation between Locke and Pragmatism, see George Hutchinson, *Harlem Renaissance in Black and White* (Cambridge: Harvard University Press, 1995), especially, "Pragmatist Aesthetics," 42–50; Nancy Fraser, "Another Pragmatism: Alain Locke, Critical 'Race' Theory, and the Politics of Culture," in *The Revival of Pragmatism: New Essays on Social Thought, Law, and Culture*, ed. Morris Dickstein (Durham: Duke University Press, 1998), 157–175; and Richard Shusterman, "Pragmatist Aesthetics: Roots and Radicalism," in *The Critical Pragmatism of Alain Locke*, 97–110.

98. Locke, "The Ethics of Culture," *Howard University Record* 17 (1923), 178.

99. Locke, "Who and What is 'Negro?," *Opportunity* 20 (1942), 36–41, 83–87; quoted from *The Philosophy of Alain Locke*, 213.

100. Nancy Fraser concurs with this assertion, noting that for Locke, "Negroes should cultivate a self-conscious relation to their distinctive 'social culture,' which is a syncretistic blend of African and Anglo-American elements" (Fraser, "Another Pragmatism," 170).

101. Stewart, "A Biography of Alain Locke," 2. Stewart maintains that Locke remained grounded in genteel impressionism and the inherent beauty of the work of art, building a kind of Kantian universalism into his aesthetic theories.

102. Locke, *Race Contacts*, 97.

103. Locke, "The High Cost of Prejudice," *The Forum* 78.4 (October 1927), 502; Du Bois, "The Talented Tenth," (1903), reprinted in Du Bois, *Writings*, ed. John Hope Franklin (New York: Library of America, 1986), 842

104. Dale E. Peterson, *Up From Bondage: The Literature of Russian and African American Soul* (Durham: Duke University Press, 2000), 154.

105. Locke, *Race Contacts*, 98.

106. Locke Papers, Box 164–139, folders 27 and 29, MS.

107. Locke, *Race Contacts*, 10.

108. Ibid., 79.

109. Locke, "Harlem," *Survey Graphic* 6.6 (March 1925), 630.

110. Johnny Washington accentuates this point when he says that for Locke, human associations and relationships "were determined by certain stressed values" that become "prized by a group, and as a derivative fact, race determined the group's values" (Washington, *A Journey into the Philosophy of Alain Locke* [Westport, CT: Greenwood Press, 1994], 93).

111. Locke, *Race Contacts*, 45. Locke's views anticipate Michael Omi and Howard Winant's definition of race *"as an unstable and 'decentered' complex of social meanings constantly being transformed by political struggle"* (emphasis in original). Omi and Winant, *Racial Formation in the United States: From the 1960s to the 1980s* (New York: Routledge, 1986), 68.

112. Locke, *Race Contacts*, 100.

113. William B. Harvey, "The Philosophical Anthropology of Alain Locke," in *Alain Locke: Reflects on a Modern Renaissance Man*, ed. Russell S. Linnemann (Baton Rouge: Louisiana State University Press, 1982), 20.

114. Locke, "The Drama of Negro Life," *Theatre Arts Monthly*, 704. Kant states that taste "is the faculty of estimating an object or method of representation by means of delight or aversion apart from any interest [*ohne alles Interesse*]." The results of such judgment, he adds, "with its attendant consciousness of detachment from all interest, must contain a claim to validity for all men." Kant, *Kritik der Urteilskraft*, [5.15, 6.18], 48, 49.

115. Locke, "New Themes," 178.

116. Richardson, "Propaganda in the Theatre," 353.

117. Margaret B. Wilkerson, "Introduction," *9 Plays by Black Women* (New York: Mentor, 1986), xvii.

118. Richardson, Garvin interview (1974). Richardson is referring to a letter written to him by the Karamu House of Cleveland. The Karamu Players wrote asking if they could produce his play. In the letter (18 December 1951, Richardson Collection, BR), the producer of the Karamu House, Rowena Woodham Jelliffee, referring to a past production of Richardson's *Compromise*, wrote: "I had then and still have the deepest respect for the dignity and majesty with which you portrayed the likes of simple, humble people."

119. Richardson, "The Hope of Negro Drama," *Crisis* 19.1 (November 1919), 338.

120. Richardson, Garvin interview (1974).

121. Information on Richardson's life can be found in Gray, *Willis Richardson*; Bernard L. Peterson, Jr., "Willis Richardson: Pioneer Playwright," in *The Theatre of Black Americans*, ed. Errol Hill (New York: Applause Books, 1980, 1987), 113–125; and Peterson, *Early Black American Playwrights and Dramatic Writers* (New York: Greenwood Press, 1990), 165–69.

122. Alexander Woollcott, "Shouts and Murmurs," *New York Herald*, 9 May 1923, 12.

123. John Corbin, *New York Times*, 8 May 1923, 22.

124. Corbin, "Jewels in Ethiope's Ear," *New York Times*, 20 May 1923, sec. 7, pg. 1.

125. Richardson, "The Negro and the Stage," *Opportunity* 2.22 (October 1924), 310.

126. Richardson, Garvin interview (1974).

127. Leslie Catherine Sanders, *The Development of Black Theater in America: From Shadows to Selves* (Baton Rouge: Louisiana State University Press, 1988), 30, 33.

128. Richardson, *The Chip Woman's Fortune* (1923), quoted in *The Roots of African American Drama*, ed. Leo Hamilton and James V. Hatch (Detroit: Wayne State University Press, 1991), 164.

129. Christine Gray raises the salient point that the play may have been written for an audience of black people newly arriving north. Migrants would have understood the circumstances of boarders, as in the case of the Chip Woman. See Gray, *Willis Richardson*, 87.

130. Richardson, *Chip Woman's Fortune*, 176.

131. This may reflect Richardson's own inability to attend Howard because he lacked the money for tuition.

132. *Mortgaged*, published in *The New Negro Renaissance: An Anthology*, ed. Arthur P. Davis and Michael W. Peplow (New York: Holt, Rinehart and Winston, 1975), 111.

133. Richardson, *Mortgaged*, 113.

134. Ibid.

135. Ibid.

136. *Compromise*, in Locke's *New Negro*, 195.

137. In a letter to Montgomery Gregory (13 December 1922), Richardson wrote: "You cannot imagine how delighted I am at having met you and Professor Locke and having found you both so interested in Negro Drama. . . . I think we may all be of help to each other in the development of this new art, and I know I shall do all within my power to advance it." Gregory Papers, Box 37–2, folder 52, MS.

138. Locke, "The Drama of Negro Life," 705.

139. Richardson, Garvin interview (1974).

140. Gray, *Willis Richardson*, 21. In the Garvin interview (1974), Richardson describes the falling out with Locke somewhat lightly, implying that Locke's childishness was not to be taken too seriously; whether or not this falling out "damaged" Richardson seems speculative. Richardson's productivity declined after 1930, but it would be difficult to verify this incident as the nodal point of declining creative output.

141. Locke, "Goodbye Messrs. Chips," *Time Magazine* (29 June 1953), 68.

142. The two versions of *A Sunday Morning in the South*, plus four reviews (play reports) of both *A Sunday Morning* and *Blue Eyed Black Boy*, are located in GM. My thanks to Jennifer E. Bradshaw, Archivist, for locating and photocopying the plays and reviews.

143. The second version is reproduced in Kathy A. Perkins, *Black Female Playwrights: An Anthology of Plays before 1950* (Bloomington: Indiana University Press, 1989), 31–37; and in Perkins and Judith L. Stephens, *Strange Fruit: Plays on Lynching by American Women* (Bloomington: Indiana University Press, 1998), 103–09.

144. For a discussion of Johnson's plays and their relationship to "Negro spirituals," see Judith L. Stephens, "Politics and Aesthetics, Race and Gender: Georgia Douglas Johnson's Lynching Dramas as Black Feminist Cultural Performance," *Text and Performance Quarterly* 20.3 (July 2000), 251–267.

145. All quotes are from the Federal Project Play Reports (circa 1935–1939) in GM. For further discussion of Johnson, see Megan Sullivan, "Folk Plays, Home Girls, and Back Talk: Georgia Douglas Johnson and the Women of the Harlem Renaissance," *CLA Journal* 38.4 (June 1995), 404–19; and Jeanne-Marie A. Miller, "Georgia Douglas Johnson and May Miller: Forgotten Playwrights of the New Negro Renaissance," *CLA Journal* 33.4 (June 1990), 349–66.

146. Quoted from reviews of *A Sunday Morning in the South*, the Federal Project, GM.

147. Locke, "The Drama of Negro Life," 703.

148. Locke, "The Negro Contributions to America," *The World Tomorrow* 12.6 (June 1929), 256.

149. Locke, "Value," *The Philosophy of Alain Locke*, 112.

150. Johnson, *Sunday Morning*, GM.

151. In a letter to Locke (11 August 1925), Johnson writes, "I have finished a mighty *good play* called 'Blue Blood.' Would like you to read it?" Locke Papers, Box 164–40, folder 35, MS.

152. Judith L. Stephens, "Racial Violence and Representation: Performance Strategies in Lynching Dramas of the 1920s," *African American Review* 33.4 (Winter 1999), 659.

153. Jurij Striedter, *Literary Structure, Evolution, and Value: Russian Formalism and Czech Structuralism Reconsidered* (Cambridge: Harvard University Press, 1989), 170.

154. Locke, "The Concept of Race as Applied to Social Culture," *The Philosophy of Alain Locke*, 195.

155. Quoted in *Selected Works of Georgia Douglas Johnson*, 323–24.

156. Ibid., 329.

157. Johnson, "Book Chat," *Norfolk Journal and Guide*, 4 October 1930, 12. It is interesting to note that Johnson calls for a drama about the middle class during the beginnings of the Great Depression.

158. Locke, handwritten note (circa 1925), Locke Papers, Box 164–139, folder 25, MS.

159. Charles Scruggs, "Alain Locke and Walter White: Their Struggle for Control of the Harlem Renaissance," *Black American Literature Forum* 14.3 (1980), 97.

160. Locke, "Notes on Drama" (circa 1925–26), Locke Papers, Box 164–139, folder 30, MS.

PART III

1. Leon F. Litwack, "Hellhounds," in *Without Sanctuary*, ed. James Allen et al. (New York: Twin Palms, 2000), 31.

2. Henry Louis Gates, Jr., "The Face and Voice of Blackness," in *Modern Art and Society*, Maurice Berger, ed. (New York: Harper Collins, 1994), 58.

3. James Weldon Johnson, *Black Manhattan* (1930; New York: Da Capo Press, 1991), 93.

4. Nellie McKay, "Black Theatre and Drama in the 1920s: Years of Growing Pains," *Massachusetts Review* 28.4 (Winter 1987), 617.

5. Editorial, "Way to Build a Race," *New York Age*, 17 February 1923, 4.

CHAPTER EIGHT

1. Marcus Garvey, "Black Men All Over the World Should Prepare to Protect Themselves," in *Negro World*, 18 October 1919; found in the *Federal Surveillance of Afro-Americans (1917–1925), The First World War, the Red Scare, and the Garvey Movement*, ed. Theodore Kornweibel (Frederick, MD: University Publications of America, Inc., 1985), Microfilm Reel 4.

2. Frantz Fanon, *Black Skin, White Mask*, tr. Charles Lam Markmann (New York: Grove Weidenfeld, 1967), 35.

3. UNIA Papers, Box 1, SC.

4. John Henrik Clarke, *Marcus Garvey and the Vision of Africa* (New York: Vintage, 1974), 95.

5. August Meier and Elliot Rudwick, *From Plantation to Ghetto* (New York: Hill & Wang, 1976), 248.

6. *Negro World*, 14 January 1922, 4.

7. See, for instance, Hazel Carby, "Policing the Black Woman's Body in an Urban Context," in *Identities*, ed. Kwame Anthony Appiah and Henry Louis Gates, Jr. (Chicago: University of Chicago Press, 1995), 131.

8. Robert H. Brisbane points out that much of Garvey's appeal was based on skin color within the black community. Brisbane notes that "it is hardly an overstatement to say

that much of Garvey's success can be attributed to the existence of the color-caste system not only between the white and the blacks, but that existing within the Negro race itself" there resides a degree of prejudice (Brisbane, *The Black Vanguard: Origins of the Negro Social Revolution, 1900–1960* [Valley Forge: Judson Press, 1970], 85). Fair-skinned African Americans, Brisbane adds, "constituted the backbone of the Negro bourgeoisie" at the time, and notes that within "two generations after emancipation, they had erected a color-caste system within the race somewhat analogous to that prevailing in India" (86). Garvey used his dark skin and Jamaican heritage in at-tacking mulattos, like Du Bois, whom he regarded as race traitors.

9. For an interesting study on class relationships within the black community, see Willard B. Gatewood, *Aristocrats of Color: The Black Elite, 1880–1920* (Bloomington, Indiana University Press, 1990); and Kevin Gaines, "Rethinking Race and Class in Africa-American Struggles for Equality, 1885–1941," *American Historical Review* 102.2 (April 1997), 378–87.

10. For biographies of Marcus Garvey, see E. David Cronin, *Black Moses: The Story of Marcus Garvey and the Universal Negro Improvement Association* (Madison: University of Wisconsin Press, 1969); Elton C. Fax, *Marcus Garvey, The Story of A Pioneer Black Nationalist* (New York: Dodd, Mead, & Co., 1972); Rupert Lewis, *Marcus Garvey: Anti-Colonial Champion* (Trenton, NJ: Africa World Press, 1988); Tony Martin, *Race First: The Ideological and Organizational Struggles of Marcus Garvey and the Univer-sal Negro Improvement Association* (Westport, CT: Greenwood Press, 1976); Judith Stein, *The World of Marcus Garvey: Race and Class in Modern Society* (Baton Rouge: Louisiana State University Press, 1986); and Theodore G. Vincent, *Black Power and the Garvey Movement* (San Francisco: Ramparts Press, 1972). Judith Stein discusses the "debate" between those who identify the Garvey movement as "rooted in des-peration" and the "bankrupt product of deep alienation" (supported by E. David Cronin, E. Franklin Frazier, and Theodore Draper) and those who describe Gar-veyism as an enlightened response to racism and a movement unique to the "black urban experience" (supported by Tony Martin and Theodore Vincent). Stein comes down on the side of Martin's and Vincent's conclusions that Garvey at-tempted to solve the economic, political, and cultural problems of African Ameri-cans. See Stein, *The World of Marcus Garvey*, 3.

11. John T. McCartney, *Black Power Ideologies: An Essay in African-American Political Thought* (Philadelphia: Temple University Press, 1992), 76.

12. E. Franklin Frazier, "The Garvey Movement," *Opportunity* 4 (November 1926), 346.

13. Imanuel Geiss, *The Pan-African Movement: A History of Pan-Africanism in America, Eu-rope and Africa*, tr. Ann Keep (New York: Africana Publishing, Co., 1968), 268. Raymond L. Hall has it that Garvey's message "struck a responsive chord among black people because what they needed at that time most of all was something or someone who could buoy their sense of worthiness" (Hall, *Black Separatism in the United States* [Hanover: University of New England Press, 1978], 60).

14. Hubert H. Harrison, *Negro World*, 8 October 1921, n.p.

15. E. Franklin Frazier, "Garvey: A Mass Leader," in *Marcus Garvey and the Vision of Africa*, ed. John Henrik Clarke and Amy Jacques Garvey (New York: Vintage, 1974), 237.

16. *Negro World*, 1 January 1921; reprinted in the Baltimore *Afro-American*, 7 January 1921; found in Vincent, *Black Power*, 104.

17. Truman Hughes Talley, "Marcus Garvey—Negro Moses?" *World's Work* 41.2 (De-cember 1920), 153.

18. Charles S. Johnson, "The New Frontage on American Life," in *The New Negro*, ed. Alain Locke (1925; New York: Atheneum, 1992), 285.

19. Paul Gilroy, "Modern Tones," in *Rhapsodies in Black: Art of the Harlem Renaissance*, ed. Richard J. Powell et al. (Berkeley: University of California Press, 1997), 105.

20. Robert H. Brisbane, "Some Light on the Garvey Movement," *Journal of Negro History* 36.1 (January 1951), 55.

21. Nationalism in general was a significant force promoting ethnic and nation-state roots during the first half of the twentieth century. Useful studies of nationalism are: Peter Alter, *Nationalism* (London: E. Arnold, 1985), Liah Greenfeld, *Nationalism: Five Roads to Modernity* (Cambridge: Harvard University Press, 1992), and John Hutchinson and Anthony D. Smith, *Nationalism* (Oxford: Oxford University Press, 1994). For studies on Black Nationalism, see Betty Lanier Jenkins and Susan Phillis, ed., *Black Separatism: A Bibliography* (Westport, CT: Greenwood Press, 1976); Agustina and Charles C. Herod, ed., *Afro-American Nationalism: An Annotated Bibliography of Militant Separatist and Nationalist Literature* (New York: Garland Press, 1986); and Dean E. Robinson, *Black Nationalism in American Politics and Thought* (Cambridge: Cambridge University Press, 2001).

22. C. L. R. James, "Marcus Garvey," in *On the Negro Question*, ed. Scott McLemme (1940; reprint, Jackson: University of Mississippi Press, 1996), 115.

23. See for instance, W. A. Domingo, "Gift of the Tropics," *The New Negro*, 341–49, for an interesting discussion on the rise of black migration from the British West Indies during the time and its importance to Garvey's presence in the United States.

24. Lewis, *Marcus Garvey*, 85.

25. Quoted in *The Marcus Garvey and the Universal Negro Improvement Association Papers*, Vol. II, ed. Robert A. Hill (Berkeley: University of California Press, 1983), 480.

26. Letter by Garvey to the NAACP, 14 July 1922, located in NAACP Administrative File, Box C-04, LOC.

27. *Marcus Garvey Papers*, Vol. II, ed. Hill, 480.

28. Amy Jacques Garvey, *Garvey and Garveyism* (Jamaica: United Printers, Ltd., 1963), 46.

29. Meier and Rudwick, *From Plantation to Ghetto*, 246–47.

30. James Weldon Johnson, *Black Manhattan* (1930; New York: De Capo Press, 1991), 168.

31. Cronin, *Marcus Garvey*, 62, 63.

32. Fax, *Garvey*, 1.

33. Roi Ottley, "New World A-Coming," *Inside Black America* (Boston: Houghton Mifflin, 1943), 76.

34. Mary Ryan, "The American Parade: Representations of the Nineteenth-Century Social Order," in *The New Cultural History*, ed. Lynn Hunt (Berkeley: University of California Press, 1989), 133.

35. Robert Allen, *Black Awakening in Capitalist America* (Garden City, NJ: Doubleday, 1969), 85–86.

36. See Herbert G. Gutman, *The Black Family in Slavery and Freedom, 1750–1925* (New York: Vintage, 1976), 453.

37. A. F. Elmes, "Garvey and Garveyism—An Estimate," *Opportunity* 3 (May 1925), 140.

38. William H. McNeill, *Keeping Together in Time: Dance and Drill in Human History* (Cambridge: Harvard University Press, 1995), 2.

39. Found in *Federal Surveillance*, Reel 4.

40. Quoted in Stein, *Marcus Garvey*, 86.

41. Claude McKay, *Harlem: Negro Metropolis* (New York: E. P. Dutton, 1940), 155.

42. Marcus Garvey's speech, 26 September 1919, Pittsburgh, PA; reprinted, 17 October 1919; *Federal Surveillance*, Reel 12.

43. For the full text of the UNIA "Declaration," see William L. Van Deburg, *Modern Black Nationalism: From Marcus Garvey to Louis Farrakhan* (New York: NYU Press, 1997), 24–31; and Marcus Garvey, *Philosophy and Opinions of Marcus Garvey* Vol. II, ed. Amy Jacques Garvey (New York: Atheneum, 1992), 135–143.

44. Marcus Garvey, quoted in Liz Mackie, *The Great Marcus Garvey* (Hertfordshire: Hansib Printing, Ltd., 1987), 116.

45. Ibid.

46. For an interesting discussion of Garvey's relationship to Booker T. Washington, see Harold Cruse, *The Crisis of the Negro Intellectual* (New York: Quill, 1967), 426; and Amy Jacques Garvey, *Garvey and Garveyism*, 26.

47. According to Theodore G. Vincent, in *Black Power and the Garvey Movement*, Garvey and Garveyites "held together an unprecedented black coalition which included cultural nationalists, political nationalists, opponents of organized religion (atheists, separatists, or simply reformers), advocates of armed rebellion, pacifists, women's liberation fighters, participants in Democratic and Republican machine politics, a smattering of left-wingers, many who wanted no contact with whites, and a small but significant number who wanted the UNIA to cooperate with integrated civil rights organizations to end discrimination and segregation" (20).

48. Cronin, *Black Moses*, 60–61. Robert H. Brisbane, in *The Black Vanguard*, adds to the list of products manufactured by Garvey's organization, noting: "'Garveyism' stimulated the first large-scale production and sales of black baby dolls in the country. UNIA executives and officials puffed on *Marcus Garvey* brand cigars; millinery shops owned by Garveyites offered a variety of styles in chic summer hats turned out by expert Negro designers; and steam laundries run by Garvey followers offered to do the family washing" (91).

49. Molefi Kete Asante, *Afrocentricity* (Trenton, NJ: Africa World Press, 1992), 11.

50. Arnold L. Crawford, "Interview," 16–17 July 1975, Brooklyn, NY; in *Footsoldiers of the Universal Negro Improvement Association: Their Own Words*, ed. Jeannette Smith-Irvin (Trenton, NJ: Africa World Press, 1989), 57.

51. Garvey, "Letter to Mr. Darwin J. Messerole," 31 March 1924, NAACP Administrative File, Box C-304, Manuscript Division, LOC.

52. Quoted in Garvey, *Philosophy and Opinions*, Vol. II, 65.

53. Stein, *Marcus Garvey*, 109.

54. "Editorial," *Negro World*, 15 April 1922, 4.

55. Stein, *Marcus Garvey*, 65.

56. Others of his organizations included the Universal African Legion, Universal Black Cross Nurses, Universal African Motor Corps, and the Black Eagle Flying Corps, each with their own uniforms and ceremonies. See the UNIA & African League Papers, Box 1, SC.

57. Truman Hughes Talley, "Garvey's 'Empire of Ethiopia,'" *World's Work* 41.3 (January 1921), 268.

58. Martin J. Sklar, *The Corporate Reconstruction of American Capitalism, 1890–1916* (Cambridge: Cambridge University Press, 1988), 26.

59. "Editorial," *Negro World*, 9 September 1922, 4.

60. William H. Ferris, "Garvey and the Black Star Line," *Favorite Magazine* 4.6 (July 1920), 397.

61. Eric Walrond, "Imperator Africanus, Marcus Garvey: Menace or Promise?," *Independent* 114 (3 January 1925), 10.

62. Hall, *Black Separatism in the United States*, 73.

63. A. Philip Randolph, "Garveyism," *Messenger* 3.4 (September 1921), 248–252, presents a reasoned argument against Garveyism on the grounds that black capitalism was too nascent to compete favorably with the large national interests of the United States, England, France, and Germany, and that private corporations had already gained a foothold in Africa, one that would be too difficult to dislodge even by the collective energies of blacks worldwide.

64. Vincent, *Black Power*, 18.

65. Quoted in Mackie, *The Great Marcus Garvey*, 106.

66. Quoted in *Federal Surveillance*, Reel 12, from a speech by Garvey, 26 September 1919 (recorded in *Federal Surveillance*, 17 October 1919), at the Rodman Street Baptist Church, Pittsburgh.

67. Elmes, "Garvey and Garveyism," 140.

68. Quoted in Cary D. Wintz, ed., *African American Political Thought, 1890–1930* (Armonk, NY: M. E. Sharpe, 1996), 204.

69. Walrond, "Imperator Africanus," 9.

70. Ronald M. Glassman, "Manufactured Charisma and Legitimacy," in *Charisma, History and Social Structure*, ed. Glassman and William H. Swatos (New York: Greenwood Press, 1986), 122.

71. Asante, *Afrocentricity*, 11.

72. Walrond, "Imperator Africanus," 9.

73. John Runcie, "Marcus Garvey and the Harlem Renaissance," in *The Harlem Renaissance: Analysis and Assessment, 1980–1994*, ed. Carl D. Wintz (New York: Garland Press, 1996), 326.

74. Max Weber, *Economy and Society* Vol. I & II, ed. Guenther Roth and Claus Wittich (Berkeley: University of California Press, 1978), Vol. I, 241.

75. Hall, *Black Separatism*, 69.

76. Weber, *Economy and Society*, Vol. II, 1121–22.

77. Weber, "The Sociology of Charismatic Authority," *Economy and Society* Vol. III, chapter 9, quoted in *From Max Weber: Essays in Sociology*, ed. and tr. H. H. Gerth and C. Wright Mills (London: Routledge, 1948), 246.

78. Weber, *Economy and Society*, Vol. II, 1121.

79. Edward Shils, "Charisma, Order, and Status," *American Sociological Review* 30.1 (April 1965), 204.

80. E. J. Hobsbawm, "Introduction: Inventing Traditions," in *The Invention of Tradition*, ed. Hobsbawm and Terrence Ranger (Cambridge: Cambridge University Press, 1983), 2, 3.

81. Benjamin Quarles, *The Negro in the Making of America* (New York Macmillan, 1969), 197.

82. Wilson Jeremiah Moses, *The Golden Age of Black Nationalism 1850–1925* (New York: Oxford University Press, 1978), 264.

83. W. E. B. Du Bois, "Back to Africa," *Century Magazine* 105.4 (February 1923), 539.

84. *The Messenger* 5.1 (January 1923), 561; McKay, *Harlem*, 9; *New York Age*, 19 August 1922, 4.

85. Schuyler and Lewis, "Shafts and Darts," *Messenger* 6 (July 1924), 213.

86. George Schuyler, *Black and Conservative* (New Rochelle: Arlington House, 1966), 120.
87. *New York Age*, 28 August 1920, 2.
88. Walter Benjamin, "The Work of Art in the Age of Mechanical Reproduction," *Illuminations*, tr. Harry Zohn (New York: Shocken, 1968), 241.
89. Cedric J. Robinson, in *Black Marxism: The Making of the Black Radical Tradition* (Chapel Hill: University of North Carolina Press, 1983), suggests that Garvey's organization possessed "a protonational bureaucracy," wherein security forces, women auxiliaries, a national church, an international network of chapters, and the beginning of an economic base consisting of small businesses and services constituted the UNIA's infrastructure (314).
90. Ato Sekyi-Otu, *Fanon's Dialectic of Experience* (Cambridge: Harvard University Press, 1996), 22.
91. Lewis, *Marcus Garvey*, 85–86.
92. Adrian Richardson, court testimony against Garvey, quoted in the *New York Amsterdam News*, 30 May 1923, 6.
93. Itabari Njeri, *The Last Plantation: Color, Conflict, and Identity: Reflections of a New Black World* (Boston: Houghton Mifflin Co., 1997).
94. Judith Stein, "The Ideology and Practice of Garveyism," in *Garvey: His Work and Impact*, ed. Rupert Lewis and Patrick Bryan (Trenton, NJ: African World Press, 1991), 209.
95. Gilroy, "Modern Tones," 107.
96. bell hooks, "Performance Practice as a Site of Opposition," in *Let's Get it On: The Politics of Black Performance*, ed. Catherine Ugwu (Seattle: Bay Press, 1995), 218.

CHAPTER NINE

1. Quoted in Arthur and Barbara Gelb, *O'Neill* (New York: Harper, 1962), 450; Louis Sheaffer, *O'Neill: Son & Artist* (New York: Paragon House, 1973), 37.
2. Eugene O'Neill, *The Emperor Jones* (1920) in *Nine Plays by Eugene O'Neill* (New York: Modern Library, 1941), 18.
3. Information on the tour can be found in the "Provincetown Scrapbook: The Emperor Jones Tour," BR.
4. *Boston Globe*, 28 March 1922, n.p., HTC.
5. Philip Hale, unidentified clipping, HTC.
6. It would be impossible to quote all the reviews here. Suffice it to say, they were all in agreement that Gilpin's performance was superlative. The 30-city tour included most major cities in the east and Midwest, as well as Canada and many smaller cities in New York State. See "Provincetown Scrapbook," BR; Gilpin File, SC; and John G. Monroe, "Charles Sidney Gilpin," M.A. Thesis, Hunter College, 1974.
7. Heywood Broun, *New York Tribune*, 4 November 1920, 8.
8. Kenneth MacGowan, *New York Globe*, 4 November 1920, n.p., HTC.
9. Alexander Woollcott, *New York Times*, 7 November 1920, sec. 2, pg. 1.
10. John G. Monroe, "Charles Gilpin and the Drama League Controversy," *Black American Literary Forum* 16 (1982), 141.
11. Laurilyn J. Harris, "Charles Gilpin: Opening the Way for the American Black Actor," *Theatre History Studies* 2 (1982), 100. Ridgely Torrence's *Three Play for a Negro Theatre* occurred three years prior to *The Emperor Jones*.
12. Quoted in Monroe, "Charles Sidney Gilpin," 87.

13. Gelb, *O'Neill*, 449; Sheaffer, *O'Neill*, 35.

14. *Cincinnati Times Star*, 2 February 1922, n.p., HTC.

15. See, "Letter to Michael Gold," [5/?/23], in, *Selected Letters*, ed. Travis Bogard and Jackson R. Bryer (New Haven: Yale University Press, 1988), 177. Years later, O'Neill changed his opinion of Gilpin, calling him the only actor "who carried out every notion of a character I had in mind." Quoted in M. W. Estrin, ed., *Conversations with Eugene O'Neill* (Jackson: University of Mississippi Press, 1990), 172.

16. O'Neill, *Selected Letters*, 177.

17. Harris, "Charles Gilpin," 99.

18. Moss Hart, *Act One* (New York: Random House, 1959), 104.

19. The only review I have uncovered that suggests anything remotely indicative of Gilpin's potential falling off comes from the *Pittsburgh Courier*, 20 March 1926. The paper's reviewer, H. W., reports that the revival of the play "is typical of its predecessor," in that it works effectively. However "Gilpin, although outstanding as a consummate artist," offers the "impression of a slight loss of enthusiasm in the role" (10).

20. *New York Evening Post*, 7 February 1926, 14.

21. *Billboard* 38.47, 20 November 1926, 90.

22. *New York Amsterdam News*, 24 February 1926, n.p., Gilpin File, SC.

23. Sheaffer, *O'Neill*, 35. Sheaffer's view of Gilpin's behavior during performances of *The Emperor Jones* (which tour? which production?) was based entirely on observations of one source, Pauline H. Turkel, who worked with the Provincetown Group, but hardly knew Gilpin. Sheaffer failed to seek out Gilpin's opinion on the matter, leaving issues entirely one-sided.

24. James V. Hatch, "Here Comes Everybody: Scholarship and Black Theatre History," in *Interpreting the Theatrical Past: Essays in the Historiography of Performance*, ed. Thomas Postlewait and Bruce A. McConachie (Iowa City: University of Iowa Press, 1989), 160.

25. See David Krasner, "Charles S. Gilpin: The Actor Before the Emperor," *Journal of American Drama and Theatre* 4.3 (Fall 1992), 62–75.

26. Theophilus Lewis, Gilpin file, SC.

27. Gilpin, from an interview with Mary B. Mullet, "Where Do I Go From Here?," *American Magazine* 91 (June 1921), 53.

28. W. A. L., "A Negro Genius in Greenwich Village," *Theatre Magazine* 33 (January 1921), 8.

29. Hart, *Act One*, 98.

30. Monroe, "Charles Gilpin and the Drama League Controversy," 141.

31. Quoted in Monroe, "Charles Sidney Gilpin," 86.

32. John Cooley, "In Pursuit of the Primitive: Black Portraits by Eugene O'Neill and Other Village Bohemians," in *The Harlem Renaissance Re-examined*, ed. Victor A. Kramer (AMS Press, 1987), 56.

33. John G. Monroe, "A Record of Black Theatre in New York City, 1920–1929," Ph.D. dissertation, University of Texas, Austin, 1980, 97.

34. Crews, 17 May 1921; quoted in Sterling A. Brown, "The Negro on the Stage," in "The Negro in American Culture," Section D, unpublished research MS, Carnegie-Myrdal Study, 1940, p. 80, SC.

35. William Bridge's review, *Negro World*, 26 March 1921; quoted in Tony Martin, *Literary Garveyism: Garvey, Black Arts, and the Harlem Renaissance* (Dover, MA: Majority Press, 1983), 10.

36. Quoted in Monroe, *Charles Sidney Gilpin*, 63.

37. Roseann Pope Bell, "The Crisis and Opportunity Magazine: Reflections of a Black Culture, 1920 –1930," Ph.D. dissertation, Emory College, 1974, 166–7. The Howard University review, 3 June 25, 123, comes from a performance Gilpin gave as a benefit for the College. For a history of the benefit, see Kenneth MacGowan's article "Negro University Has Dramatic Department on Lines of Harvard's," Gilpin File, SC.

38. Diana N. Lockard wrote "if white audiences were fascinated by the "primitive" Emperor, many African Americans "disliked the play, either because they construed it as sociology, a study of the superstition and bestiality of their group, or because they resented the portrayal of a Negro criminal" (Lockard, "The Negro on the Stage of the Nineteen Twenties," Ph.D. dissertation, Columbia University, 1960, 30–31).

39. Harvey M. Williamson, "The Gilpin Players," *Crisis* (1935), in Gilpin file, SC.

40. Jessie Fauset, "The Symbolism of Bert Williams," *Crisis* 24.1 (May 1922), 12.

41. William Stanley Braithwaite, "The Negro in American Literature," 35; Montgomery Gregory, "The Drama of Negro Life," 157; both in *The New Negro*, ed. Alain Locke (1925; reprint, New York: Atheneum, 1992).

42. W. E. B. Du Bois, "Negro Art," *Crisis* 22.2 (June 1921), 56; "Krigwa Players," *Crisis* 32.3 (July 1926), 134. African Americans have generally expressed continuing dissatisfaction with the play. According to Cooley, *The Emperor Jones* "is an example of the way in which old racial clichés and myths were perpetuated, even in highly regarded literature" (Cooley, "In Pursuit of the Primitive," 53). Kathy A. Perkins writes that, while many "sympathized with the efforts of white writers" such as O'Neill, Marc Connelly, and Paul Green in their efforts to portray blacks dramatically, African Americans "felt that these plays lacked the 'true spirit and soul' of the Negro." Despite the claims of so-called authenticity, Perkins remarks "white-authored plays did not change substantially the prevailing view on blacks" (Perkins, ed., *Black Female Playwrights: An Anthology of Plays Before 1950* [Bloomington: Indiana University Press, 1990], 4). Along similar lines, Leslie Catherine Sanders notes that *The Emperor Jones* "established a pattern for white use of Negro material. The dramatic attraction of Negro figures lies in their primitiveness, which is imagined either as exotic or as innocent" (Sanders, *The Development of Black Theater in American* [Baton Rouge: Louisiana State University Press, 1988], 9). Houston A. Baker, Jr., suggests that "if only O'Neill had bracketed the psycho-surreal final trappings of his Emperor's world and given us the stunning account of colonialism," then the play might contain some "intimacy and reverence" (Baker, *Modernism and the Harlem Renaissance* [Chicago: University of Chicago Press, 1987], 7). Nathan Irvin Huggins condemns the play unequivocally, observing that despite black objections to the play, no white critic "complained about *The Emperor Jones* for its reduction of the Negro to primitivism." Huggins's final comments about the play are quite severe: O'Neill's general statements about African Americans, he says, are "a testimony to the deep and unshakable tradition of Negro stereotype in the theatre" (Huggins, *Harlem Renaissance* [London: Oxford University Press, 1971], 297, 297–98).

43. Malcolm X, quoted in Alex Haley, *The Autobiography of Malcolm X* (New York: Grove, 1965), 284.

44. Cooley, "In Pursuit of the Primitive," 54.

45. Eric Walrond, "The Word Nigger," *Negro World*, 4 February 1922, 4, also quoted in *African Fundamentalism*, ed. Tony Martin (Dover, MA: Majority Press, 1983), 100–101.

46. Lester A. Walton, *New York Age*, 9 January 1924, 6.
47. Edgar M. Gray, 17 February 1921, quoted in Brown, "The Negro on the Stage," 79, SC.
48. O'Neill, *The Emperor Jones*, 20.
49. See Fannin Saffore Belcher, Jr., "The Place of the Negro in the Evolution of the American Theatre, 1767 to 1940," Ph.D. dissertation, Yale University, 1945, 364.
50. See Gilpin file, SC.
51. "Man of the Month," *Crisis* 21.4 (February 1921), 171–72.
52. *New York Age*, 30 April 1921, 6.
53. Quoted in Monroe, "Gilpin and the Drama League," 141. See also, James Weldon Johnson, "The Gilpin Incident," *New York Age*, 26 February 1921, 4.
54. See Monroe, "Gilpin and the Drama League," for a detailed discussion of the controversy. See also an editorial in the *Messenger* 3.3 (March 1921), 203–204, which challenged Gilpin to react more militantly.
55. *New York Age*, 25 November 1922, 6.
56. Clipping, Gilpin file, HB. This quote ought to cast doubt on anything Gilpin may have been quoted as saying to white members of *The Emperor Jones*'s cast.
57. *New York Age*, 25 November 1922, 6.
58. Mikhail Bakhtin, "Discourse in the Novel," in *The Dialogic Imagination*, ed. Michael Holquist, tr. Caryl Emerson and Holquist (Austin: University of Texas Press, 1981), 271.
59. Toni Morrison, "Unspeakable Things Unspoken: The Afro-American Presence in American Literature," *Michigan Quarterly Review* 28.4 (1987), 11.
60. Henry Louis Gates, Jr., ed., *Bearing Witness: Selections from African-American Autobiography in the Twentieth Century* (New York: Pantheon, 1991), 4.
61. On Gilpin's stationery, the following appears in the letterhead: "Chas. S. Gilpin: Character Comedian. Author of 'Her Other Husband,' 'Matrimony and Insurance,' and others," Gilpin file, HTC. The *NY Amsterdam News* obituary (14 May 1930, n.p., Gilpin file, SC) adds another play, "Listen, Dearie."
62. Haywood Broun, *New York Tribune*, 4 November 1920, 8.
63. *St. Louis Post-Dispatch*, 31 November 1921, 8.
64. *Vogue*, 1 January 1921, BR.
65. Clipping, Gilpin file, HB.
66. Dick Meade, *Toledo Blade*, 9 January 1922, 15–16.
67. Gilbert Seldes, *Boston Evening Transcript*, 8 November 1920, 15–16.
68. Lawrence W. Levine, *Black Culture and Black Consciousness: Afro-American Folk Thought from Slavery to Freedom* (Oxford: Oxford University Press, 1977), 223–24.
69. Henry Louis Gates, Jr., *The Signifying Monkey* (New York: Oxford University Press, 1988), 52.
70. *Cincinnati Times Star*, 2 February 1922, HTC.
71. Deborah R. Geis, *Postmodern Theatric(k)s: Monologue in Contemporary American Drama* (Ann Arbor: University of Michigan Press, 1993), 33, 34.
72. Henry T. Sampson, *The Ghost Walks: A Chronological History of Blacks in Show Business, 1965–1910* (Metuchen: Scarecrow, 1988), 526.
73. Lester A. Walton, *New York Age*, 6 January 1916, 6.
74. Walton, *New York Age*, 30 April 1921, 6.
75. Alexander Woollcott, *New York Times*, 28 December 1920, 9.
76. David Carb, "To See Or Not To See," *Bookman* 59 (July 1924), 582. See also the *Pittsburgh Courier*, 17 May 1924, which reported that while "it is next to impossible

to mention, or even think of this play without speaking or thinking of Charles Gilpin," Robeson's interpretation of the role "left nothing to be desired" (8).

77. Lee Strasberg, "Introduction," *The Paradox of Acting & Masks or Faces?* (New York: Hill & Wang, 1957), xiii.

78. "Gilpin Wants to Play Comedy," *Boston Transcript*, 1922, n.p., HTC. The song is from May Irwin's "Bully Song," words and music by Charles E. Trevathan (White-Smith Music Publishers, Inc., Boston, 1896).

79. Bertolt Brecht, *Brecht on Theatre*, tr. & ed. John Willett (New York: Hill and Wang, 1964), 277.

80. Ronald Wainscott, *Staging O'Neill: The Experimental Years, 1920–1934* (New Haven: Yale University Press, 1988), 57.

81. Clipping, HB.

82. Belcher, *Place of the Negro*, 375.

83. "Drama League Dinner Causes Discussion of the Color Line," *New York Age*, 26 February 1921, 6.

84. Clipping, Gilpin file, HB.

85. Ibid.

86. *New York Age*, 25 November 1922, 6.

CHAPTER TEN

1. Nathan Irvin Huggins, *Harlem Renaissance* (London: Oxford University Press, 1971), 194.

2. Walter Prichard Eaton, "Introduction," *Washington Square Plays* (Garden City: Doubleday, Page, and Co., 1917), xi.

3. Nellie McKay, "Black Theater and Drama in the 1920s: Years of Growing Pains," *Massachusetts Review* 28.4 (Winter 1987), 615–26.

4. Ridgely Torrence's three one-act plays opened on Broadway in 1917, running for one month. See Susan Curtis, *The First Black Actors on the Great White Way* (Columbia: University of Missouri Press, 1998).

5. For a discussion about the rise of national stages, see Loren Kruger, *The National Stage: Theatre and Cultural Legitimation in England, France, and America* (Chicago: University of Chicago Press, 1992).

6. For a discussion about black actors at the turn of the century, see David Krasner, *Resistance, Parody, and Double Consciousness in African American Theatre, 1895–1910* (New York: St. Martin's Press, 1997). For another interesting observation of black performers, see Barbara L. Webb, "The Black Dandyism of George Walker: A Case Study in Genealogical Method," *TDR* 45.4 (Winter 2001), 7–24.

7. Theophilus Lewis, "Main Problems of the Negro Theatre," *Messenger* 9.7 (July 1927), 229.

8. Ibid.

9. "Why Not a Negro Drama for Negroes By Negroes," *Current Opinion* 72.5 (May 1922), 640.

10. Wallace V. Jackson, "The Negro Stage," *Messenger* 5.6 (June 1923), 746.

11. Postcard from Anna Julia Cooper to Alain Locke (12 May ?), Alain Locke Papers, Box 164–21, folder 53, MS.

12. John Maynard Keynes, *The Economic Consequences of the Peace* (New York: Brace and Howe, 1920), 297.

13. Warren Susman, *Culture as History: The Transformation of American Society in the Twentieth Century* (New York: Pantheon Books, 1984), 106.

14. Morrell Heald, "Business Thought in the Twenties: Social Responsibility," *American Quarterly* 13.2 (Summer 1961), 126.

15. See, for instance, the documents in *The Culture of the Twenties*, ed. Loren Baritz (Indianapolis: Bobbs-Merrill, Co., 1970).

16. Glenn Hughes, *A History of American Theatre, 1700–1950* (New York: Samuel French, 1951), 355.

17. H. L. Mencken, "Getting Rid of the Actors," *Smart Set* (1911), in *H. L. Mencken's Smart Set Criticism*, ed. William H. Nolte (Ithaca: Cornell University Press, 1968), 54.

18. See, for instance, Arthur Frank Wertheim, "The Little Theatre Movement," in Wertheim, *The New York Little Renaissance: Iconoclasm, Modernism, and Nationalism in American Culture, 1908–1917* (New York: New York University Press, 1976), 149–163.

19. George Cram "Jig" Cook, quoted in Susan Glaspell, *The Road to the Temple* (New York: Frederick A. Stokes, Co., 1927), 263.

20. The Abbey Theatre toured the United States during the 1911–1912 season. Stanislavsky's Moscow Art Theatre appeared in 1923 and 1924.

21. Adele Heller, "The New Theatre," in *1915: The Cultural Moment*, ed. Heller and Lois Rudnick (New Brunswick: Rutgers University Press, 1991), 221.

22. For an interesting study on the rise and fall of the Chicago Little Theatre, see Dale Kramer, *Chicago Renaissance: The Literary Life in the Midwest, 1900–1930* (New York: Appleton–Century, 1966), 192–96, 310–12.

23. Sheldon Cheney, *The New Movement in the Theatre* (1914; reprint, Westport, CT: Greenwood Press, 1971), 14, 93. See, also, Cheney, *The Art Theatre* (New York: Alfred A. Knopf, 1917, 1925), and Constance D'Arcy Mackay, *The Little Theatre in the United States* (New York: Henry Holt, and Co., 1917), for an overview of the period's Little Theatre Movement.

24. See, for instance, Gregory Holmes Singleton, "Birth, Rebirth, and the 'New Negro' of the 1920s," *Phylon* 43.1 (March 1982), 29–45, for an interesting discussion on the concept of "rebirth" and the "new" during the Harlem Renaissance.

25. W. E. B. Du Bois, "The New Negro Theater," *New York Call*, 22 April 1917, 6.

26. Eric Walrond, "Growth of the Negro Theatre," *Theatre Magazine* 41 (October 1925), 20.

27. Theophilus Lewis, "Survey of the Negro Theatre—III," *Messenger* 7.10 (October 1926), 302.

28. Montgomery Gregory, "The Drama of Negro Life," in *The New Negro*, ed. Alain Locke (1925; New York: Atheneum, 1992), 159.

29. For a study of the Lafayette Theatre, see Sister Mary Francesca Thompson, "The Lafayette Players 1915–1932," Ph.D. dissertation, University of Michigan, 1972; for a study of the Krigwa, see Ethel Pitts Walker, "Krigwa, A Theatre By, For, and About Black People," *Theatre Journal* 40.3 (October 1988), 347–56; for a study of the Lincoln Theatre, see Richard Newman, "The Lincoln Theatre: Once a Carnival of Merrymaking," in Newman, *Words Like Freedom: Essays on African-American Culture and History* (West Cornwall, CT: Locust Hill Press, 1996), 93–97; for a history of African American theatre in New York, see John Gilbert Monroe, "A Record of the Black Theatre in New York City," Ph.D. dissertation, University of Texas at Austin, 1980; and for a study of the Karamu House Theatre, see Rueben

Silver, "A History of the Karamu Theatre of the Karamu House, 1915–1960," Ph.D. dissertation, Ohio State University, 1961.

30. John G. Monroe, "The Harlem Little Theatre Movement, 1920–1929," *Journal of American Culture* 6.4 (Winter 1983), 69.

31. Theophilus Lewis, "Same Old Blues," *Messenger* 7.1 (January 1925), 14.

32. Lewis, "The Theater: The Souls of Black Folk," *The Messenger* 8.10 (October 1926), 302. For an illuminating review of Lewis and African American theatre, see Theodore Kornweibel, Jr., "Theophilus Lewis and the Theater of the Harlem Renaissance," in *The Harlem Renaissance Remembered*, ed. Arna Bontemps (New York: Dodd, Mead, & Co., 1972), 171–189.

33. Lewis, "Same Old Blues," 14.

34. "Harlem, the Hooch-Seller's Paradise, By the Evidence," *New York Age*, 21 April 1923, 1.

35. Salem Tutt Whitney, "The Colored Thespian," *Competitor* 1.1 (January 1920), 57.

36. Romeo Dougherty, "About Things Theatrical," *Amsterdam News*, 11 March 1925, 5.

37. "Editorial," *Messenger* 7.1 (January 1925), 20.

38. Du Bois, "The Colored Audience," *Crisis* 12.5 (September 1916), 217.

39. Eulalie Spence, "A Criticism of the Negro Drama," *Opportunity* 6 (June 1928), 180.

40. There appears to be some discrepancy as to who starred in *Rosanne*. According to Lester A. Walton, Charles Gilpin appeared in the role (*New York Age*, 15 March 1924, 6). However, subsequent announcements about the play state that Robeson assumed the leading role.

41. Paul Robeson interviewed by Floyd J. Calvin, *Pittsburgh Courier*, 8 January 1927, sec. 2, pg. 2.

42. See, for instance, the rise of the Ethiopian Art Theatre School (no connection to the Ethiopian Art Players), *New York Age*, 22 March and 28 June 1924, 6; and "Dramatic Art School Opens in Chicago," *Baltimore Afro-American*, 4 April 1919, 1.

43. Theophilus Lewis, "Magic Hours in the Theatre," *Pittsburgh Courier*, 26 February 1927: sec. 2, pg. 2.

44. Theophilus Lewis, review of Em Jo Basshe's *Earth*, "They Call This Negro Drama," *Pittsburgh Courier*, 2 April 1927: sec. 2, pg. 2.

45. Eugene O'Neill, "Letter to A. Philip Randolph," *Messenger* 7.1 (January 1925), 17.

46. Lovett Fort-Whiteman, "Drama," *Messenger* 5 (1923), 671.

47. Randolph Edmonds, "Some Reflections on the Negro in American Drama," *Opportunity* 8.10 (October 1930), 303.

48. Steven Gregory, "Race, Identity and Political Activism: The Shifting Contours of the African American Public Sphere," in *The Black Public Sphere* (Chicago: University of Chicago Press, 1995), 157. This book was reprinted from *Public Culture* 7.1 (Fall 1994), 153.

49. Du Bois, "Krigwa Players Little Negro Theatre," *Crisis* 32.3 (July 1926), 134.

50. Program note, Krigwa Players, circa 1926, BR.

51. Walter F. White, "Color Line," *Survey Graphic* 6.6 (March 1925), 681.

52. Jürgen Habermas, *The Structural Transformation of the Public Sphere: An Inquiry into a Category of Bourgeois Society*, tr. Thomas Burger (Cambridge: MIT Press, 1991). See also Michael C. Dawson's excellent description of the "black counterpublic," in *Black Visions: The Roots of Contemporary African-American Political Ideologies* (Chicago: University of Chicago Press, 35–42).

53. Habermas, *Structural Transformation*, 25–26.

54. Ibid., 106.

55. Hubert H. Harrison, *When Africa Awakes: The "Inside Story" of the Stirrings and Strivings of the New Negro in the Western World* (New York: Porro Press, 1920), 14, 41.

56. "Ninth Annual Report for 1918," *The National Association for the Advancement of Colored People*, edited by *Crisis* (New York, January 1919), 22.

57. "Editorial: Way to Build a Race," *New York Age*, 17 February 1923, 4.

58. James de Jongh, *Vicious Modernism: Black Harlem and the Literary Imagination* (Cambridge: Cambridge University Press, 1990), 8.

59. Eugene Gordon, "The Negro Press," *American Mercury*, 8 June 1926, 213.

60. Charles S. Johnson, "The Rise of the Negro Magazine," *Journal of Negro History* 13.1 (January 1928), 7.

61. John Hope Franklin, *From Slavery to Freedom: A History of American Negroes* (New York: Alfred A. Knopf, 1947), 397.

62. St. Clair Drake and Horace R. Cayton, *Black Metropolis: A Study of Negro Life in a Northern City* (Chicago: University of Chicago Press, 1945, 1993), 17.

63. Oskar Negt and Alexander Kluge, *Public Sphere and Experience: Toward an Analysis of the Bourgeois and Proletarian Public Sphere*, tr. Peter Labanyi (Minnesota: University of Minnesota Press, 1993), 2.

64. Mary Ryan, "Gender and Public Access: Women's Politics in Nineteenth-Century America," in *Habermas and the Public Sphere*, ed. Craig Calhoun (Cambridge: MIT Press, 1997), 264. For another critique of Habermas, see *The Phantom Public Sphere*, ed. Bruce Robbins (Minneapolis: University of Minnesota Press, 1993).

65. Thomas C. Holt raises the point that Habermas's notions of the public sphere can "provide a powerful entry into the interrelatedness of matters" that appear "disparate and unconnected" given the complexities and multiplicities of black public life (Holt, "Afterwards: Mapping the Black Public Sphere," in *The Black Public Sphere*, 326).

66. Alain Locke, *The New Negro*, 7.

67. See Habermas, *The Theory of Communicative Action: Lifeworld and System*, Vol. II, tr. Thomas McCarthy (Boston: Beacon Press, 1984), 126.

68. Habermas, *The Theory of Communicative Action: Reason and the Rationalization of Society*, Vol. I, tr. Thomas McCarthy (Boston: Beacon Press, 1984), 13.

69. Habermas, *Communication and the Evolution of Society*, tr. Thomas McCarthy (Boston: Beacon Press, 1976), 3.

70. Alain Locke, "The High Cost of Prejudice," *The Forum* 78.4 (October 1927), 504–505.

71. Editorial, "Northern Employment and Migration," *New York Age*, 6 October 1923, 4.

72. Habermas, *Moral Consciousness and Communicative Action*, tr. Christian Lenhardt and Shierry Weber Nicholsen (Cambridge: MIT Press, 1996), 135.

73. Habermas, "Remarks on the Concept of Communicative Action," in *Social Action*, ed. Gottfried Seebass and Raimo Tuomela (Dordrecht: D. Reidel, 1985), 167.

74. "*[D]er Genius der Sprache ist also auch der Genius von der Literatur einer Nation,*" Johann Gottfried von Herder, *Sämtliche Werke I*, ed. B. Supham (Berlin: Weidmann, 1877), 148.

75. "Editorial: On Writing About Negroes," *Opportunity* 3.32 (August 1925), 227.

76. J. Martin Favor, *Authentic Blackness: The Folk in the New Negro Renaissance* (Durham: Duke University Press, 1999), 12.

77. See, for instance, Brenda Ray Moryck, "A Point of View," *Opportunity* 3.32 (August 1925), 246–249, 251–252. Moryck warns that there is a danger "in confining a

writer to certain limits." Writers, she argues, should write freely about any subject and not confine themselves to single subjects.

78. The final three questions can be found in *The New Negro Renaissance*, ed. Arthur P. Davis and Michael W. Peplow (New York: Holt, Rinehart and Winston, 1975), 464.

79. Langston Hughes, "The Negro Artist and the Racial Mountain," *The Nation* 122.318, 23 June 1926, 692, 694; George S. Schuyler, "The Negro-Art Hokum," *The Nation* 122.319, 16 June 1926, 662.

80. James Weldon Johnson, "The Dilemma of the Negro Author," *American Mercury* 15.60 (December 1928), 477.

81. James Weldon Johnson, "Preface," *The Book of Negro Poetry* (New York: Harcourt, Brace, & Co., 1922), xl.

82. Ibid., xli.

83. Rebecca T. Cureau, "Towards an Aesthetic of Black Folk Expression," in *Alain Locke: Reflections on a Modern Renaissance Man*, ed. Russell J. Linnemann (Baton Rouge: Louisiana State University Press, 1982), 77.

84. W. A. Domingo, "What Are We, Negroes or Colored People," *Messenger* 2.6 (May–June 1919), 24.

85. William E. Ready, "Letter to the *Age*, 14 February 1920," *New York Age*, 28 February 1920, 1, 2.

86. "Editorial," *Messenger* 2.7 (August 1920), 74.

87. Symposium, "The Negro in Art: How Shall He Be Portrayed?'" *Crisis* 31.5 (March 1926), 219. The symposium ran from April to November (excluding July). Contributors included Carl van Vechten, Sinclair Lewis, Sherwood Anderson, Langston Hughes, Georgia Douglas Johnson, Alfred Knopf, H. L. Mencken, DuBose Heyward, Mary W. Ovington, J. E. Spingarn, Countee Cullen, and Walter White, among others.

88. For a study on the significance of "authenticity" in American life, see Miles Orvell, *The Real Thing: Imitation and Authenticity in American Culture, 1880–1940* (Chapel Hill: University of North Carolina Press, 1989).

89. Daniel Joseph Singal, "Towards a Definition of American Modernism," *American Quarterly* 39.1 (Spring 1987), 14.

90. Montgomery Gregory, "The Drama of Negro Life," *The New Negro*, 159.

91. "Editorial: On Writing About Negroes," 228.

92. Du Bois, "Krigwa, 1926," *Crisis* 31.3 (January 1926), 115.

93. Arthur A. Schomburg, "The Negro Digs Up His Past," *Survey Graphic* 6.6 (March 1925), 670.

94. Du Bois, "Criteria of Negro Art," *Crisis* 32.6 (October 1926), 296.

95. Ross Posnock, *Color & Culture: Black Writers and the Making of the Modern Intellectual* (Cambridge: Harvard University Press, 1998), 139.

96. Ibid., 142.

97. Du Bois, "Criteria," 292.

98. Du Bois, "The Negro and the American Stage," *Crisis* 28.3 (July 1924), 56, 57.

99. Du Bois, "Criteria," 292.

100. In 1926, the Governor of Pennsylvania, Gifford Pinchot, was planning a pageant to commemorate for his state the one hundred and fiftieth anniversary of the Declaration of Independence. Having completed his final presentation of *The Star of Ethiopia* in Los Angeles the year before, Du Bois attempted to persuade the governor to add a dramatic presentation of the role of black people in the state's history.

While the Governor rejected Du Bois's plea, it is significant to note that Du Bois had considered another presentation of his pageant *The Star of Ethiopia* at the time he wrote "Criteria for Negro Art." See Du Bois's letter to Governor Pinchot, 8 May 1926, in *The Correspondence of W. E. B. Du Bois: Vol. I*, ed. Herbert Aptheker (Amherst: University of Massachusetts Press, 1973), 336–37.

101.   Du Bois, "A Negro Art Renaissance," *Los Angeles Times*, 14 June 1925, 26.

102.   Du Bois, "Negro Art," *Crisis* 22.2 (June 1921), 55.

103.   "Letter to Van Vechten," 5 November 1925, in *The Correspondence of W. E. B. Du Bois*, *Vol. I*, 325.

104.   Du Bois, "Criteria," 296.

105.   Du Bois, "Review of Marc Connelly's *Green Pastures*," *Crisis* 37.5 (May 1930), 162.

106.   Du Bois, "Criteria," 296. For an interesting discussion on the failure of Du Bois to clarify his concept of beauty, see Darwin T. Turner, "W. E. B. Du Bois and the Theory of a Black Aesthetic," in *Critical Essays on W. E. B. Du Bois*, ed. William L. Andrews (Boston: G. K. Hall, 1985), 73–92.

107.   Du Bois, "Criteria," 297.

108.   Du Bois, *Black Reconstruction in America, 1860–1880* (1935; reprint, New York: Atheneum, 1992), 721, 727.

109.   Robert E. Washington, *The Ideologies of African American Literature: From the Harlem Renaissance to the Black Nationalist Revolt* (Lanham: Rowman & Littlefield, 2001), 41.

110.   David Levering Lewis, *W. E. B. Du Bois: The Fight for Equality and the American Century, 1919–1963* (New York: Henry Holt, and Co., 2000), 162, 175.

111.   Du Bois, "Can the Negro Serve Drama?," *Theatre Magazine* 38 (July 1923), 68.

112.   Du Bois, "Criteria," 297.

113.   Du Bois, "Negro Art," 55.

114.   Du Bois, "Criteria," 297.

115.   Roman Jakobson, "On Realism in Art," *Language in Literature* (Cambridge: Harvard University Press, 1987), 20.

116.   Montgomery Gregory, "For a Negro Theatre," *The New Republic*, 16 November 1921, 350.

117.   James Weldon Johnson, *Black Manhattan* (1930; New York: Da Capo, 1991), 170.

118.   Ibid., 175.

119.   Lester A. Walton, "Negro Actors Make Debut in Drama at Garden Theatre," *New York Age*, 12 April 1917, 1. According to Susan Curtis, in *The First Black Actors*, the short run of the plays was due largely to the racism of the time, and not necessarily because of the war.

120.   George Jean Nathan, "Negro Drama," *American Mercury* 17 (May 1929), 117–18; Sterling Brown, *Negro Poetry and Drama* (Washington, D.C.: Associates in Negro Folk Education, 1937), 118. Brown was specifically referring to *Porgy* (1927); however, his comments could apply to most of the white-authored plays.

121.   Lester A. Walton, "Across the Footlights," *The Southern Workman* 57.11 (November 1928), 437.

122.   Quoted in the *Daily News* "Obituary," February, 1974, 54, Lafayette Theatre file, BR; and in Thompson, *The Lafayette Players*, 147. For a biography of Walton, see Artee Felicita Young, "Lester Walton: Black Theatre Critic," Ph.D. dissertation, University of Michigan, 1980.

123.   For a history of the Quality Amusement Corporation, see Bernard L. Peterson, *The African American Theatre Directory, 1816–1960* (Westport, CT: Greenwood Press, 1997), 171–172.

124.   Lester A. Walton, *New York Age*, 17 January 1920, 6.

125.   See Monroe, *A Record of the Black Theatre*, 14.

126.   Theophilus Lewis, "Magic Hours in the Theatre," *Pittsburgh Courier*, 12 March 1927, sec. 2, pg. 2.

127.   Thompson, *The Lafayette Players*, 270.

128.   See Addell Austin Anderson, "The Ethiopian Art Theatre," *Theatre Survey* 33.2 (November 1992), 132–143; and Jane T. Peterson, "Pride and Prejudice: The Demise of the Ethiopian Art Theatre," *Theatre History Studies* 14 (1994), 141–149. Peterson takes a dimmer view of O'Neil than Anderson, blaming him for a series of compromises and indecisions that eventually led to the disintegration of the company.

129.   W. E. Clark, "Negro Press Refused to Be Segregated at 'Salome,'" *New York Age*, 23 May 1923, 6.

130.   See the *Amsterdam News*, 30 May 1923, 5, and the *New York Age*, 21 April 1923, 6.

131.   W. E. Clark, "Harlem Audiences Spoil Strong Drama Given By Chicago Colored Players," *New York Age*, 28 April 1923, 6.

132.   See Garvin interview of Willis Richardson, 21 July 1974, HB.

133.   According to Willis Richardson, the production opened the first week to good reviews and box office success. However, the producer-director Raymond O'Neil decided to change the bill after the first week, adding Shakespeare's *Comedy of Errors*. This change "almost caused a riot," since paying costumers had not anticipated the alteration. "People demanded their money back," Richardson said, and O'Neil "left the [Ethiopian Art] Players stranded in New York." Richardson, Garvin interview (1974).

134.   Floyd J. Calvin, "Evelyn Preer," *Pittsburgh Courier*, 16 April 1927, sec. 2, pg. 1.

135.   Lester A. Walton, *New York Age*, 21 April 1923, 6; Percy Hammond, "The Theatres," *New York Tribune*, 13 May 1923, sec. 6, pg. 1. For a biographical portrait of Preer, see Francesca Thompson, "Evelyn Preer," in *Notable Women in the American Theatre: A Biographical Dictionary*, ed. Alice M. Robinson et al. (New York: Greenwood Press, 1989), 731–35.

136.   "At the Lafayette," *New York Age*, 21 April 1923, 6.

137.   Oscar Micheaux, *New York Age*, 26 November 1932, 1.

138.   John Corbin, "Jewels in Ethiope's Ear," *New York Times*, 20 May 1923, sec. 7, pg. 1.

139.   Abram L. Harris, "The Ethiopian Art Players and the Nordic Complex," *Messenger* 5.7 (July 1923), 775.

140.   See "President Harding and Social Equality," *The Nation* 113.2941, 16 November 1921), 561.

141.   Lothrop Stoddard, "Impasse at the Color-Line: Should the Negro Be Encouraged to Cultural Equality," *The Forum* 78.4 (October 1927), 513.

142.   The production, under the direction of David Belasco's Sixth Annual Little Theatre tournament at the Frolic Theatre on 7 May, was fraught with problems. Burrill was displeased by the ending, which was added on without her consent. See *Strange Fruit: Plays on Lynching by American Women*, ed. Kathy A. Perkins and Judith Stephens (Bloomington: Indiana University Press, 1998), 79.

143.   See, for instance, "Anti-Negro Riots Due to Labor Causes," *New York Times*, 8 July 1917, 5. For a comprehensive report of the riot, see Elliott M. Rudwick, *Race Riot at East St. Louis* (Carbondale: Southern Illinois University Press, 1964).

144.   Oscar Leonard, "The East St. Louis Pogrom," *Survey* 38 (14 July 1917), 331.

145.   Du Bois, "Returning Soldiers," *Crisis* 18.1 (May 1919), 14. Though written one month after Burrill published *Aftermath*, Burrill was influenced by other similar de-

mands for justice in the black press. See, for instance, Walter F. White, "The Work of a Mob," *Crisis* 16.5 (September 1918), 221–223. Burrill, moreover, knew Du Bois and was aware of his sentiments for some time.

146. Du Bois, "History," *Crisis* 18.1 (May 1919), 11.

147. Mary P. Burrill, *Aftermath,* quoted from *Liberator* 2.4 (April 1919), 12.

148. Ibid., 14.

149. Garland Anderson, *My Experiences in Writing and Having "Appearances" Produced,* (1925?), manuscript located at the Manuscripts, Archives, and Rare Books Collection, SC.

150. Text of the play is located at the New York Public Library at 42nd St., microfilm division. From the marginal cues and notes on the pages, the text appears to be a stage manager's copy.

151. J. A. Rogers, "Garland Anderson Invades the East," *Messenger* 7.6 (June 1925), 233.

152. *New York Times,* 15 October 1925, 27.

153. See, for instance, Emma Lue Sayers's review of the play in the *Pittsburgh Courier,* 23 April 1927, sec. 2, pg. 3.

154. William E. Clark, "Krigwa Players Show Remarkable Progress as 2nd Season Opens," *New York Age,* 29 January 1927, 6.

155. Eulalie Spence, interviewed by Joshua Carter, 22 August 1973, HB.

156. Eulalie Spence, "A Criticism of Negro Drama," 180.

157. *The Pot Maker* was published in the February issue of *Crisis* in 1927, *Purple Flower* in January 1928, and *Exit: An Illusion,* in October 1929.

158. Ronald Wainscott raises the significant point that in the heyday of American expressionism, the term "expressionism" itself was "less descriptive of a movement or specific style than an artistic umbrella for a host of nonrealistic experiments" (Wainscott, *The Emergence of American Theater,* 1914–1929 [New Haven: Yale University Press, 1997], 2).

159. Errol Hill, "The Revolutionary Tradition in Black Drama," *Theatre Journal* 38.4 (December 1986), 419.

160. Marita O. Bonner, *The Purple Flower,* quoted from *Crisis* 35.1 (January 1928), 9.

161. Ibid., 29.

162. Ibid.

163. Ibid.

164. Samuel A. Hay, *African American Theatre: An Historical and Critical Analysis* (Cambridge: Cambridge University Press, 1994), 2.

165. James Weldon Johnson, "The Negro Actor," *New York Age,* 6 May 1922, 4.

166. Ibid.

CHAPTER ELEVEN

1. Rawick, *American Slave,* 4:142, pt. 3; quoted in Michael A. Gomez, *Exchanging Our Country Marks: The Transformation of African Identities in the Colonial and Antebellum South* (Chapel Hill, NC: University of North Carolina Press, 1998), 266.

2. Al Rose, *Eubie Blake* (New York: Schirmer Books, 1979), 72.

3. Allen Woll, *Black Musical Theatre: From Coontown to Dreamgirls* (Baton Rouge: Louisiana State University Press, 1989, reprint, New York: Da Capo Press, 1991), 60.

4. *Shuffle Along,* copyright 1921, p. 43, music by Blake, lyrics by Sissle, libretto by Miller and Lyles. Original copy found in the Music Division, LOC.

5.　Bernard L. Peterson, Jr., *Profiles of African American Stage Performers and Theatre People, 1816–1960* (Westport, CT: Greenwood Press, 2001), 184.

6.　Mel Watkins, *On the Real Side: Laughing, Lying, and Signifying* (New York: Simon & Schuster, 1994), 161.

7.　Gerald Bordman, *American Musical Theatre: A Chronicle* (Oxford: Oxford University Press, 1992), 350.

8.　Al Rose, in *Eubie Blake,* reported that it "took a considerable amount of courage to offer any kind of a show on Broadway considering the caliber of the competition that year" (72–73).

9.　Lester A. Walton, "Negroes' Dream Realized as Race Plays on Broadway," *New York World,* 23 November 1924, 9.

10.　For details, see Wesley C. Mitchell's "Review" in *Recent Economic Changes in the United States* (New York: McGraw-Hill, 1929); quoted in *The Responsibilities of Power, 1900–1929,* ed. George Harmon Knoles (New York: Free Press, 1967), 272–317, especially pg. 286.

11.　Herbert Shapiro, *White Violence and Black Response: From Reconstruction to Montgomery* (Amherst: University of Massachusetts Press, 1988), 149.

12.　See also William M. Tuttle, Jr., "Views of a Negro During 'The Red Summer' of 1919," *Journal of Negro History* 51.3 (July 1966), 209.

13.　James Weldon Johnson, *Along This Way* (1933; reprint, New York: Penguin, 1990), 341.

14.　Scott Ellsworth, quoted in "Panel Recommends Reparations in Long-Ignored Tulsa Race Riot," *New York Times,* 5 February 2000, A1, A12. See also Ellsworth, *Death in a Promised Land: The Tulsa Race Riot of 1921* (Baton Rouge: Louisiana State University Press, 1982); Tim Madigan, *The Burning: Massacre, Destruction, and the Tulsa Race Riot of 1921* (New York: St. Martin's Press, 2001); and James S. Hirsch, *Riot and Remembrance: The Tulsa Race War and Its Legacy* (Boston: Houghton Mifflin, 2002).

15.　Walter F. White, "The Eruption of Tulsa," *The Nation* 112.2921 (29 June 1921), 909.

16.　Why Jazz Sends Us Back to the Jungle," *Current Opinion* 65.3 (September 1918), 165; "Jazz," *Living Age Magazine* 306.21 July 1920, 280–281; and Clive Bell, "Plus De Jazz," *New Republic,* 21 September 1921, 93.

17.　William L. Mayer, President of the Pittsburgh Musicians Union, quoted in "'Death to Jazz,' Cries Union Musician Head in Pittsburgh," *Variety,* 25 November 1921, 6.

18.　Clipping, dated 18 September 1921, *Shuffle Along* file, HTC.

19.　Robert Kimball and William Bolcom, *Reminiscing with Sissle and Blake* (New York: Viking Press, 1973), 88.

20.　Flournoy E. Miller, unpublished autobiography, Flournoy Miller Collection, in the Helen Armstead-Johnson Collection, Box I, SC.

21.　Eubie Blake, "Once & Future King of Ragtime," *New York Post,* 3 July 1975, 47.

22.　Interview of Blake, quoted in Marshall and Jean Sterns, *Jazz Dance: The Story of American Vernacular Dance* (New York: Da Capo, 1994), 136.

23.　Noble Sissle, unpublished autobiography, Flournoy Miller Collection, Box II, ms pg. 4–5, SC. Some of the printed text is written over and corrected by hand.

24.　*New York Times,* 23 May 1921, 16.

25.　*New York Herald,* 24 May 1921, 11.

26.　*New York Evening Post,* 24 May 1921, 7; *New York World,* 23 May 1921, 11.

27.　*Theatre Magazine* (August 1921), 98.

28. Alan Dale, "'Shuffle Along' Full of Pep and Real Melody," *New York American*, 25 May 1921, n.p., quoted in *Reminiscing with Sissle and Blake*, 99.

29. Blake, quoted in *Reminiscing with Sissle and Blake*, 94, 95.

30. Lester A. Walton, "*Shuffle Along* Latest Musical Gem to Invade Broadway," *New York Age*, 4 June 1921, 6.

31. Rose, *Eubie Blake*, 79.

32. Lester A. Walton, "'Shuffle Along' is in Its Sixth Month Run," *New York Age*, 15 October 1921, 6.

33. Langston Hughes, *The Big Sea* (1940; reprint, New York: Hill and Wang, 1997), 223, 224.

34. Bordman, *American Musical Theatre*, 360.

35. Eubie Blake file, BR; quoted in Woll, 65.

36. Lester A. Walton, "'Shuffle Along' Latest Musical Gem to Invade Broadway," *New York Age*, 4 June 1921, 6.

37. See David Levering Lewis, *When Harlem was in Vogue* (New York: Penguin, 1979, 1997), 96.

38. Nathan Irvin Huggins, *Harlem Renaissance* (New York: Oxford University Press, 1971), 289, 291.

39. Susan Gubar, *Race Changes: White Skin, Black Face in American Culture* (New York: Oxford University Press, 1997), 118.

40. Theophilus Lewis, "Survey of the Negro [in Theatre]: No. II," *The Messenger* 8.9 (September 1926), 278.

41. *Boston [Evening] Transcript*, 31 July 1922, Sec. 2, pg. 3.

42. Bernard L. Peterson, Jr., *A Century of Musicals in Black and White* (Westport, CT: Greenwood Press, 1993), 312.

43. *Shuffle Along*, 2.

44. Ibid.

45. Ibid., 3.

46. Ibid., 7.

47. Ibid., 10.

48. Ibid., 10–11.

49. Ibid., 16.

50. See C. Vann Woodward, *The Strange Career of Jim Crow* (New York: Oxford, 1974), 85.

51. *Shuffle Along*, 38.

52. Helen Armstead-Johnson, "*Shuffle Along*: Keynote of the Harlem Renaissance," in *The Theatre of Black Americans*, ed. Errol Hill (New York: Applause, 1980, 1987), 133.

53. The Williams and Walker production of *Abyssinia* (1905–1907) contains a romance between Aida Overton Walker and her real-life husband, George Walker that is sophisticated and subtle. For a discussion of the romantic scenes between them, see David Krasner, *Resistance, Parody, and Double Consciousness in African American Theatre, 1895–1910* (New York: St. Martin's Press, 1997), 106–109.

54. Walton, "*Shuffle Along* Latest Musical Gem," 6.

55. Sissle, quoted in *Reminiscing with Sissle and Black*, 93.

56. *Shuffle Along*, 43.

57. Ibid.

58. Karl Marx, *Grundrisse, The Marx-Engels Reader*, ed. Robert C. Tucker (New York: W. W. Norton, 1978), 254.

59. James C. Scott, *Domination and the Arts of Resistance* (New Haven: Yale University Press, 1990), 4.

60. Paul Laurence Dunbar, "We Wear the Mask," (1895), quoted in *African-American Poetry of the Nineteenth Century: An Anthology*, ed. John R. Sherman (Urbana: University of Illinois Press, 1992), 402.

61. *Nation*, 30 May 1867, quoted in *Slave Songs of the United States*, ed. William Frances Allen et al. (1867; reprint, New York: Dover, 1995), xiv. See also Marcel W. F. Allen, *Nation*, 14 December 1865, 744–45, reprinted in Bruce Jackson, *The Negro and Early Folklore in Nineteenth-Century Periodicals* (Austin, TX: University of Texas Press, 1967), 79, which supplies first-hand accounts of the ring shout.

62. Samuel A. Floyd, Jr., "Ring Shout! Literary Studies, Historical Studies, and Black Music Inquiry," in *Signifyin(g), Santifyin', and Slam Dunking: A Reader in African American Expressive Culture*, ed. Gena Dagel Caponi (Amherst: University of Massachusetts Press, 1999), 136. See also, Robert Winslow Gordon, "Negro 'Shouts' from Georgia," in *Mother Wit from the Laughing Barrel*, ed. Alan Dundes (Jackson: University of Mississippi Press, 1990), 445–451.

63. Harold Courlander, *Negro Folk Music U. S. A.* (New York: Columbia University Press, 1963), 195.

64. Rawick, *American Slave*, 4:142, pt. 3; quoted in Gomez, *Exchanging Our Country Marks*, 266.

65. Sterling Stuckey, *Slave Culture: Nationalist Theory & the Foundations of Black America* (New York: Oxford University Press, 1987), 12, 24, 57, 85. Eileen Southern adds that the ring shout was a "means of communication with God" where shouters "reached the highest level of worship when the Holy Spirit entered their bodies and took possession of their souls" (Southern, *The Music of Black Americans: A History* [New York: W. W. Norton, 1997, third ed.] 183.

66. Eubie Blake, interview, quoted in Marshall and Jean Sterns, *Jazz Dance*, 134.

67. *Shuffle Along*, 46.

68. Miller, interview quoted in Marshall and Jean Sterns, *Jazz Dance*, 133.

69. *Shuffle Along*, 48.

70. Joseph Wood Krutch, *The Modern Temper* (1924; San Diego: Harcourt Brace, and Co., 1957), 24.

71. Louis Menand, *The Metaphysical Club: A Story of Ideas in America* (New York: Farrar, Straus, and Giroux, 2001), x.

72. Laurence G. Avery, "Stereotypes and the Development of African American Drama," *Journal of American Drama and Theatre* 12.2 (Spring 2000), 67.

73. Miller, unpublished autobiography, Box II, SC.

74. Lyrics by Raymond Egan, music by Richard A. Whiting (New York: Jerome H. Remick & Co., 1916).

75. *Shuffle Along*, 51.

76. Ibid., 61.

77. Linton Martin, "'Shuffle Along' a Jolly, Jazzy Ethiopian Entertainment," *Philadelphia North American*, 21 May 1923, FLP.

78. Ashton Stevens, "'Shuffle Along' Is the Real Thing in Ethiopia," *Chicago Herald and Examiner*, 17 November 1922, *Shuffle Along* file, MC.

79. *New York Herald*, 24 May 1921, 11.

80. Quoted in an interview of Noble Sissle during James V. Hatch's black drama class at City College of New York, 7 March 1972. From the oral history collection at HB, noted on page 3 of the recorded transcript.

81. John McMullin, "The Fashion and Pleasures of New York," *Vanity Fair*, found in the Florence Mills Papers, Helen-Armstead Johnson Collection, MG 599, Box 2 (Scrapbook), SC.

82. Simon Gikandi, "Race and the Modernist Aesthetic," in *Writing and Race*, ed. Tim Young (London: Longman, 1997), 151. See also Marianna Torgovnick, *Gone Primitive: Savage Intellects, Modern Lives* (Chicago: University of Chicago Press, 1990).

83. David Levering Lewis, *When Harlem Was in Vogue* (New York: Alfred A. Knopf, 1981; reprint, New York: Penguin, 1997), 151.

84. George Tichenor, "Colored Lines," *Theatre Arts Monthly* 14.6 (June 1930), 485, 490.

85. Hughes, *The Big Sea*, 225.

86. Ann Douglas, *Terrible Honesty: Mongrel Manhattan in the 1920s* (New York: Noonday Press, 1995), 378.

87. Huggins, *Harlem Renaissance*, 261.

88. Flournoy E. Miller, notes to his unpublished autobiography, Miller Collection, Box I, SC.

89. Hubert H. Harrison, "Negro Society and the Negro Stage, Preamble," *The Voice* (19 September 1917); quoted in *A Hubert Harrison Reader*, ed. Jeffrey B. Perry (Middletown, CT: Wesleyan University Press, 2001), 373.

90. *Amsterdam News*, 14 March 1923, 5.

91. Harrison, "Negro Society and the Negro Stage, Part 2," *The Voice* (3 October 1917), 5, 8; quoted in *A Hubert Harrison Reader*, 373–74.

92. Ibid., 374.

93. Ibid., 375.

94. Ibid.

95. See E. M. Woods, *The Negro in Etiquette: A Novelty* (St. Louis: Buxton & Skinner, 1899), as an example of books advocating "Negro decorum." For an excellent study of the "uplift movement," see Kevin K. Gaines, *Uplifting the Race: Black Leadership, Politics, and Culture in the Twentieth Century* (Chapel Hill: University of North Carolina Press, 1996).

96. See, for example, Willard B. Gatewood, *Aristocrats of Color: The Black Elite, 1880–1920* (Fayetteville: University of Arkansas Press, 2000), 345.

97. The play is referenced in Flournoy Miller's unpublished autobiography, where he comments that the drama "packed the house," though "the admission [price] was small and only eight shows a week, therefore the financial returns were disappointing." Miller Collection, Box II, SC. A handwritten account, slightly different, can be found in Box I, SC.

98. Romeo Dougherty, *Negro World*, 13 May 1922; quoted in Ted Vincent, *Keep Cool: The Black Activists Who Built the Jazz Age* (London: Pluto Press, 1995), 82.

99. Duse Mohamed Ali, "The Flat Below," *Negro World*, 20 May 1922, 6.

100. Miller and Lyles, quoted in the *Empire State Gazette*, 25 July 1926, and the *New York Tribune*, 16 May 1926, found in Reel 17, AG.

101. Bert Williams, "The Comic Side of Trouble," *American Magazine*, 85.1 (January 1918), 34.

102. Ibid., 33. For a biography of Williams, see Eric Ledell Smith, *Bert Williams: A Biography of the Pioneer Black Comedian* (Jefferson, N. C.: McFarland and Co., 1992).

103. For an interesting discussion on the paradox of performance and its emotional effect on an audience, see Noël Carroll, *The Philosophy of Horror, or Paradoxes of the Heart* (New York: Routledge, 1990).

104. Williams, "The Comic Side," 33.

105. Sigmund Freud, *Jokes and Their Relation to the Unconscious* [*Der Witz und seine Beziehung zum Unbewussten*, 1905], tr. James Strachey (New York: Penguin, 1960) 262, 261.

106. Booker T. Washington, quoted in "Genius Defeated by Race," *Literary Digest* 72.12 (25 March 1922), 29.

107. *Chicago Defender*, 25 July 1914, 4.

108. "Bert Williams," *The Messenger* 4.4 (April 1922), 394.

109. William H. Ferris, "The Bert Williams Case," *Negro World*, 27 May 1922, 6.

110. S. H. Dudley, quoted in the *Toledo Blade*, 11 October 1912; found in the S. H. Dudley Clippings file, Robinson Locke Collection, BR.

111. Bernard L. Peterson, Jr., *Profiles of African American Stage Performers and Theatre People, 1816–1960*, 80.

112. Vincent, *Keep Cool*, 58.

113. "All Actors Warned," *Baltimore Afro-American*, 8 November 1924, 7.

114. "Klan Serenade Casts Shadow on Show," *Baltimore Afro-American*, 8 November 1924, 7.

115. *Pittsburgh Post*, 23 January 1913, from the Dudley file, BR.

116. For a listing of the theatres, see the *Chicago Defender*, 12 June 1910, 7.

117. Garnett Warbington, "Big Protest," *Chicago Defender*, 8 October 1921, 6.

118. For a chart and map of these theatres, see Anthony Hill, *Pages from the Harlem Renaissance: A Chronicle of Performance* (New York: Peter Lang, 1996), 69–71. For a list of TOBA theatres, see Nadine George-Graves, *The Royalty of Negro Vaudeville: The Whitman Sisters and the Negotiation of Race, Gender and Class in African American Theater, 1900–1940* (New York: St. Martin's Press, 2000), 131–32.

119. Romeo Dougherty, "The Great Theatrical Combine," *Competitor* 1.4 (April 1920), 69.

120. "Theatre Managers Form Organization," *Chicago Defender*, 19 June 1920, 6.

121. Kennard Williams, "Southern Amusements Need a Cleaning Up," *Baltimore Afro-American*, 22 November 1924, 8.

122. For a discussion of Jackson and Dudley's attempts at correcting unfair salaries, see Hill, *Pages from the Harlem Renaissance*, 88–98.

123. "Dudley Has This to Say about Independent Acts," *Chicago Defender*, 5 December 1925, 6.

124. "S. H. Dudley," *The Messenger* 7.1 (1925), 50.

125. For an interesting discussion about the "Chitlin Circuit," see Henry Louis Gates, Jr., "The Chitlin Circuit," in *African American Performance and Theatre History: A Critical Reader*, ed. Harry J. Elam, Jr., and David Krasner (New York: Oxford University Press, 2001), 132–148.

126. *Columbus Dispatch*, 5 January 1913, Dudley file, BR.

127. S. H. Dudley, *Dr. Beans from Boston*, unpublished manuscript, c. 1912, Act I, pg. 6. My gratitude to Barbara Webb for providing a copy of this script.

128. Dudley, *Dr. Beans*, Act III, pg. 1.

129. S. H. Dudley, unidentified clipping, 19 January 1913, BR.

130. "Theatre Managers Form Organization," *Chicago Defender*, 19 June 1920, 6.

131. Victoria W. Wolcott, *Remaking Respectability: African American Women in Interwar Detroit* (Chapel Hill: University of North Carolina Press, 2001), 13.

132. Fannie Barrier Williams, "Social Bonds in the 'Black Belt' of Chicago," *Charities* 15 (March 1906), 40.

133. Tom Fletcher, *100 Years of the Negro in Show Business* (1954; reprint, New York: Da Capo Press, 1984), 7.

134. "Citizen's Research Council, *Negro in Detroit*, sec. 2, pg. 16; quoted in Wolcott, *Remaking Respectability*, 14.

135. "Why the Name," two editorials in the *Baltimore Afro-American*, 27 November and 11 December 1915, 4.

136. William Barlow, *Looking Up at Down: The Emergence of Blues Culture* (Philadelphia: Temple University Press, 1989), 120.

137. Jean Toomer, "The Negro Emergent," an unpublished manuscript (ca. 1924), quoted from *A Jean Toomer Reader: Selected Unpublished Writings*, ed. Frederik L. Rusch (New York: Oxford University Press, 1993), 88.

138. I am indebted to conversations with Barbara Webb for this insight.

139. Unfortunately, space constraints make it impossible to do justice to a full analysis of these performers. Suffice to say, they were popular and important performers during the era, enjoying successes with largely African American audiences. For their profiles, see Bernard L. Peterson, Jr., *Profiles of African American Stage Performers and Theatre People, 1816–1960* (Westport, CT: Greenwood, 2001), Billy King pg. 158–59, Whitney and his brother J. Homer Tutt pg. 266–69, and Judie "Butterbeans" Edwards and Susie "Susie" Hawthorne Edwards, pg. 45. For a discussion and an excerpt of the Butterbeans & Susie's vaudeville script, see *The Roots of African American Drama: An Anthology of Early Plays, 1858–1938*, ed. Leo Hamalian and James V. Hatch (Detroit: Wayne State University Press, 1991), 152–58.

140. Mel Watkins, *On the Real Side: Laughing, Lying, and Signifying* (New York: Simon and Schuster, 1994), 369.

141. James Weldon Johnson, *Black Manhattan* (1930; New York: Da Capo Press, 1991), 200.

142. There are various reports of her age when she started in show business. I have selected the age of six as an approximation, taking into account reports that she began at the age of three and other reports as high as eight.

143. In his book, *Words Like Freedom: Essays on African-American Culture and History* (West Cornwall, CT: Locus Hill Press, 1996), Richard Newman writes that Aida Overton Walker "was a beautiful, sophisticated, and highly talented star who took time with a ghetto child, thereby becoming Mill's mentor and role model" (78). See also Fletcher, *100 Years of the Negro in Show Business*, where he reports that Mills considered Walker her "idol," and that she tried to follow in her footsteps (181).

144. Newman, *Words Like Freedom*, 80.

145. E. W. Osborn, "Dixie to Broadway," *New York Evening World*, 30 October 1924, Florence Mills clipping file, Dance Collection, BR.

146. Gilbert W. Gabriel, "Dixie to Broadway," *New York Telegraph and Evening Mail*, 30 October 1924, Reel 13, AG.

147. Heywood Broun, "The New Play," *New York World*, 30 October 1924, Florence Mills clipping file, Dance Collection, BR.

148. J. T. Green, "London Cameos," 9 October 1923; Mills File, HTC.

149. Unidentified Clipping, Florence Mills file, Dance Collection, BR.

150. Percy Hammond, *New York Herald Tribune*, 30 October 1924, 12, Alexander Woollcott, *New York Evening Sun*, 30 October 1924, 22.

151. Lester A. Walton, "Negroes' Dream Realized as Race Plays on Broadway," *New York World*, 23 November 1924, Reel 13, AG.

152. After *Shuffle Along*, the longest running shows during the 1920s were *Hot Chocolates*, with 219 performances (1929), *Runnin' Wild* with 213 (1923), *Liza* with 169 (1922), *Keep Shufflin'* with 104 (1928), *The Chocolate Dandies* with 96 (1924), and *Dixie to Broadway* with 77 (1924). Source from Fannin Saffore Belcher, Jr., "The

Place of the Negro in the Evolution of the American Theatre, 1767 to 1940," Ph.D. dissertation, Yale University, 1945, 133.

153. *Amsterdam News*, 20 February 1924, AG.

154. "'Flo' Mills First of Her Race to Headline at the Palace," Chicago Defender, 27 June 1926, Reel 13, AG.

155. Theophilus Lewis, "Theatre," *Messenger* 7.1 (January 1925), 18, 62.

156. Unidentified clipping, "Play 'Degrades' Her Race, And Star Refuses to Act," *Graphic*, Scrapbook, Mills File, Box 2, SC.

157. *Amsterdam News*, 7 and 14 February 1923, 5.

158. "White Actress Jealous of Success of Florence Mills at 'Village' Follies," *Amsterdam News*, 24 October 1923, 5.

159. Florence Mills, "The Soul of the Negro," the *Sun-Chronicle*, London; reprinted in the *Pittsburgh Courier*, 8 January 1927, sec. 2, pg. 3.

160. Florence Mills, interviewed by Beverley Nichols, 16 February 1927, Mills File, SC.

161. Ibid.

162. Florence Mills, interview by Hannen Swaffer, "Florence Mills on the Race Problem," [London] *Daily Express*, undated clipping, Mills file, SC.

163. Unidentified clipping, "Mills of the Gallery Gods," Mills File, FLP.

164. Johnson, *Black Manhattan*, 199.

165. Handwritten letter from H. W. Ash, 138 North Salford St., West Philadelphia, 22 March 1925, addressed to the "Dixie to Broadway Company," Mills Scrapbook, SC.

166. Typewritten letter, author unidentified, letterhead from the "Department of Public Welfare, City of Philadelphia," 23 January 1925, Mills File, SC.

167. Handwritten letter from Madame Davis, 12 Featherstone Buildings, Holborn England, 12 September 1926, Mills File, SC.

168. *Amsterdam News*, 9 November 1927, 1; *New York Age*, 5 November 1927, 1.

169. *Amsterdam News*, 9 November 1927, 4.

170. "It's Getting Dark on Old Broadway," sung by Gilda Gray in the Ziegfeld Follies of 1922, quoted in Woll, *Black Musicals*, 76.

171. Flournoy F. Miller, Unpublished autobiography, Miller Collection, SC.

172. Bordman, *American Musical Theatre*, 382.

173. Eric Sundquist, *To Wake the Nations: Race in the Making of American Literature* (Cambridge: Harvard University Press, 1993), 449–450.

174. Theophilus Lewis, "Survey of the Negro [in Theatre]," 279.

175. Ibid.

CHAPTER TWELVE

1. George M. Fredrickson, *The Black Image in the White Mind* (Hanover, NH: Wesleyan University Press, 1987), 327.

2. Wallace Thurman, "Negro Artists and the Negro," *New Republic*, 31 August 1927, 38.

3. Langston Hughes, "Young Writer Defines Art," *Pittsburgh Courier*, 9 April 1927, sec. 2, pg. 1.

4. Hughes, "Langston Hughes Declares He Makes More Money as a Bellhop than as a Poet-Writer," *Pittsburgh Courier*, 16 April 1926, sec. 1, pg. 8.

5. "Ethel Waters Opens with 'Africana' at Daly's Amid Riot of Barbaric Splendor," *New York Amsterdam News*, 13 July 1927, 11.

6. "'Africana' a Swift Negro Musical Revue," *New York Times*, 12 July 1927, 29.

7. "'Rang Tang' Opens at Royale Theatre," *New York Times*, 13 July 1927, 20.

8. Edgar M. Gray, "The Devil's Playground," *New York Amsterdam News*, 6 July 1927, "Special Articles" section, n.p.

9. See, for instance, George Hutchinson, *Harlem Renaissance in Black and White* (Cambridge: Harvard University Press, 1995), and Ann Douglas, *Terrible Honesty: Mongrel Manhattan in the 1920s* (New York: Noonday Press, 1995).

10. W. D. Wright, *Black Intellectuals, Black Cognition, And A black Aesthetic* (Westport: Praeger, 1997), 145.

11. Pearl Bowser and Louise Spence, *Writing Himself Into History: Oscar Micheaux, His Silent Films, and His Audiences* (New Brunswick, NJ: Rutgers University Press, 2000), 178.

INDEX